MW00777863

The Petersburg Campaign

Vol I: The Eastern Front Battles,
June – August 1864

Edwin C. Bearss

with Bryce Suderow

SB

Savas Beatie
California

Library of Congress Cataloging-in-Publication Data
Bearss, Edwin C.
The Petersburg Campaign / Edwin C. Bearss, with Bryce Suderow.
p. cm.
Includes bibliographical references and index.
"The Attack on Petersburg, June 9, 1864 — The Second Assault on Petersburg, June 15-18, 1864 — The Battle of the Jerusalem Plank Road, June 21-24, 1864 — The Crater, July 30, 1864 — The Battle of the Weldon Railroad, August 18-21, 1864 —The Second Battle of Ream's Station, August 25, 1864"—Vol. 1, table of contents.
ISBN 978-1-61121-090-3
1. Virginia—History—Civil War, 1861-1865—Campaigns. 2. Petersburg (Va.)—History—Siege, 1864-1865. I. Suderow, Bryce A. II. Title.
E476.59.B43 2012
975.5'03—dc23
2012028512

SB

Published by
Savas Beatie LLC
989 Governor Drive, Suite 102
El Dorado Hills, CA 95762

Phone: 916-941-6896
(E-mail) customerservice@savasbeatie.com

05 04 03 02 01   5 4 3 2 1
First edition, first printing

Unless otherwise indicated, all photographs are from the Library of Congress.

Savas Beatie titles are available at special discounts for bulk purchases in the United States by corporations, institutions, and other organizations. For more details, please contact Special Sales, P.O. Box 4527, El Dorado Hills, CA 95762, or you may e-mail us at sales@savasbeatie.com, or visit our website at www.savasbeatie.com for additional information.

Proudly published, printed, and warehoused in the United States of America.

To Sara Beth Bearss
February 21, 1960 – February 13, 2012

Inside Elliott's Salient, east of Petersburg, Virginia

Library of Congress

Contents

List of Maps

List of Maps (continued)

Photos and illustrations have been placed throughout the book
for the convenience of the reader.

Introduction

Good fortune smiled on my future when I entered on duty with the National Park Service (NPS) on September 28, 1955. It was then I began my forty-year career in the NPS as an historian at Vicksburg National Military Park. It was one of the then 179 significant natural, historical, and recreational areas administered by the NPS, a bureau created by Congress on August 25, 1916.

A short four years before, in December 1951, Conrad L. Wirth had become the service's fifth director. On doing so he found the NPS units and their facilities overwhelmed by its "admiring public." Rising personal incomes, the 40-hour week, and the family car "had fueled a postwar travel boom for families young and old, and the national parks, it seemed, bore the brunt" of the surge. Visits to the parks soared from six million in 1942 to thirty-three million in 1950, and to seventy-two million in 1960. Park facilities and roads were overwhelmed.

Wirth's response was the MISSION-66 initiative, "a 10-year program to upgrade facilities, staffing, and resource management throughout the system by the 50th anniversary of the NPS." President Dwight D. Eisenhower endorsed the program while Congress was likewise enthused, appropriating more than a billion dollars over the next ten years for MISSION-66 improvements.

Coincident with MISSION-66 planning, the NPS was confronted by the approach of the Centennial of the Civil War. Since President Franklin D. Roosevelt's Executive Orders of 1933, the NPS had become responsible for the parks and monuments administered by the War Department. These included thirteen Civil War battlefields, forts, and sites.

Encouraged by the burgeoning visitation during the mid-1950s to its flagship Civil War parks, Director Wirth worked with citizen-action groups that successfully lobbied for passage of a federally funded Civil War Centennial Commission (CWCC). This paid off on September 7, 1957, when President Eisenhower signed such a bill into law. In both the legislation and discussions between the CWCC staff headed by Maj. Gen. U. S. Grant III, President Grant's grandson, and Director Wirth, the NPS was "authorized to undertake as part of its MISSION-66 program" the further preservation and development of such battlefields and sites, at such times and in such manners as will insure that a fitting observation may be held at such battlefields or sites on the centennial of the event commemorated. A linkage between the MISSION-66 planning, implementation, and projects was thus established.

At this time, all the services for Civil War battlefield parks, except Antietam and Gettysburg, were located in the Southeast Region headquartered in Richmond, Virginia. To schedule and implement planning to insure that the SE Region could meet Director Wirth's commitment, a meeting of the Washington and Regional managers, planners, and affected park superintendents and historians was held in Rossville, Georgia, at the headquarters of Chickamauga and Chattanooga National Military Park. The meeting took place in the first week of September 1958. These superintendents brought with them the approved MISSION-66 documents to support approved construction, staffing, goals, etc., at their respective parks and to have them in place by the respective centennial dates. Among the key documents needed to guide planners were missing items in the parks' Master Plans, i.e., Historical Base Maps, Troop Movement Maps, etc. and supporting documented narratives.

It was agreed that I would prepare drafts of Historical Base Maps and Troop Movement Maps in those SE Region parks that did not have them and forward drafts to the Eastern Office of Design and Construction (EODC), then located in Philadelphia, to finalize and include in the subject park's Master Plans. To accomplish this assignment, my supervisors transferred me to the SE Regional Office, but I continued working out of the Vicksburg park.

The reason I was promoted and given this plum assignment was an earlier detail I accomplished for the Washington Office. In early December 1956, I had joined a high-profile park service planning team representing the Washington and SE Regional Offices and EODC in determining the boundaries of Pea Ridge National Military Park. This Arkansas park had been authorized by Congress on July 20, 1956. The act, signed by President Eisenhower, provided that the NPS would study the area and designate the boundaries, and the state would acquire the land. My work on this study team was commended by my associates, most of whom had joined the NPS in the mid-1930s.

As Regional Research Historian (RRH), in 1959, I completed drafts for Fort Donelson, Stones River, Vicksburg, and the units of Richmond National Battlefield Park associated with the Seven Days' Battles. The surveyed TMM and Historical Base Maps, drawn by EODC's cartographers, were approved and incorporated in the subject parks' Master Plans. Documented materials in support of the Master Plan drawings were also prepared. Some of these have been published (Fort Donelson, Vicksburg, and Richmond).

In late June of 1960, my horizons expanded. On April 22 of that year, President Eisenhower signed a bill authorizing the establishment of Wilson's Creek National Battlefield Park. Like the earlier Pea Ridge legislation, it mandated that Missouri must first acquire the necessary lands that would be defined by a boundary set by an NPS study team. The Washington Office assigned me to the team study group, which would be carried out by the NPS's Midwest Region headquartered in Omaha.

I spent a week at the battlefield and returned to Vicksburg to prepare the key planning documents and Historical Base Maps, draft TMM, and a documented history of the battles. With these in hand I met on-site with a park planner from the Omaha office. During the next several days we walked the battlefield, met with local committees and landowners, and came up with a recommended boundary map that was reduced by several hundred acres by Regional Director Howard Baker.

The state moved ahead with land purchases and by the centennial date of the battle, August 10, 1961, before a large audience Wilson's Creek became a unit of the NPS. The decade and a half following the successful implementation of MISSION-66 saw much progress on the development of the new park in southwest Missouri. A tour road and trails were built, the Ray House restored and opened for visitation, and a Visitor Center constructed. To enhance the story of the park's interpretive programs, cooperative and friends' associations were formed.

In 1975, one of these decided to publish a documented narrative history I had prepared for in-house use fifteen years before. Re-titled *The Battle of Wilson's Creek* and edited by Park Ranger David Whitman, it included the six Troop Movement Maps along with period drawings selected by the editor. For the next quarter century until the publication by the University of North Carolina Press of William Garrett Piston's and Richard W. Hatcher's critically acclaimed *Wilson's Creek: The Second Battle of the Civil War and the Men Who Fought It*, my *The Battle of Wilson's Creek* remained a popular title at the Wilson's Creek Visitor's Center.

My connection with Petersburg National Battlefield as Regional Research Historian began in the early 1960s. The park staff at that time, as a centennial project, believed that the Gilliams' (Joe Pete and his wife) might be interested in the preservation by the NPS of their large family farm that had been in the Gilliam family since well before the Revolutionary War. The family farm, house, and outbuildings, known as "Burnt Quarters," were intimately associated with 1781 Revolutionary War actions in and around Petersburg and Dinwiddie County and the Civil War battle of Five Forks, frequently referred to as the Waterloo of the Confederacy.

Senior NPS management in Washington and the Richmond Regional Offices familiar with my intimate involvement with the Pea Ridge and Wilson's Creek boundary study teams once again called on me. I was tasked to prepare a documented narrative history of the Five Forks battle and supporting Troop Movement Maps. Again working under a tight deadline, I prepared the subject documents. Although Congress passed supporting legislation signed by President John F. Kennedy on August 24, 1962, no further actions to include a Five Forks unit in Petersburg National Battlefield came because the Gilliams had a change of heart and decided not to sell Burnt Quarters. The narrative history and the draft Troop Movement Maps went back into the files.

Some two years later in 1964, with MISSION-66 projects being implemented at Petersburg with construction of a Visitor Center and a new tour road on schedule, I returned to the park still wearing my hat as Regional Research Historian. I was directed to prepare a comprehensive series of Troop Movement Maps and supporting documentation for the June 1864 assaults on Petersburg and the major battles associated with the nine and one-half month siege. Draft TMM overlays were completed and keyed to period large-scale maps prepared by Union engineers during the postwar years, and documented narrative reports were prepared for the major Petersburg battles. Unfortunately, salient centennial dates for Petersburg actions passed, and insofar as that park's projects were concerned, they no longer commanded high priority. The draft Troop Movement Map overlays were not forwarded to the EODC to be finalized and were consigned to the park files, where they remain to this day. The narrative histories suffered the fate common to all in-house reports through the mid-1960s: they were typed with one hard copy and five tissue copies, the hard copy being filed at the park and the tissues distributed to appropriate offices. The Five Forks narrative history and Troop Movement Maps, however, enjoyed a better fate.

In 1971, Christopher Calkins, a young and dynamic historian, joined the NPS, first as a volunteer and then seasonally at Appomattox Court House National Historical Park. Six years later he transferred to the Fredericksburg-Spotsylvania National Military Park, where he served a four-year stint under the supervision of Robert K. Krick, who possessed a well-deserved talent as mentor to a number of young historians who have made their mark in the NPS. Chris' next stop was in 1981 at Petersburg National Battlefield, where he began a brilliant and productive 28-year career that saw him rise in the hierarchy to the park's Chief of Interpretation.

Chris had not been at Petersburg long when, in cooperation with Harold E. Howard, he rescued my 1962 Five Forks manuscript from the park's files. After clearing it with me, Chris updated the report, used the draft Troop Movement Maps to prepare supplementary maps, and selected illustrations. The manuscript was made available to a larger audience in 1985 when it was published by H. E. Howard, Inc. as *The Battle of Five Forks*, part of the Virginia Battles and Leaders Series. Both Chris and I were listed as co-authors.

By the late 1980s, Joe Pete Gilliam and his wife had died, and battlefield preservation had become a major public policy issue. Chris Calkins and his wife had become close friends with the Gilliam heirs. In their conversations, in which The Conservation Fund became involved, an agreement was reached for the heirs to convey more than 900 acres of their property to The Conservation Fund, while granting a preservation easement on much of the remainder. In a fitting ceremony held onsite on March 29, 1991, at which representatives from the NPS, Conservation Fund, the heirs, and the Secretary of the Interior participated, the 900-acre tract consisting of most of the historic battlefield was conveyed to the United States as part of Petersburg National Battlefield.

The in-house Petersburg draft overlays of the subject Troop Movement Maps and the hard copies of supporting narratives, meanwhile, remained in the park files from the mid-1960s to the present day. During this four-decade period the park staff used these major reports to support planning and interpretive missions and made them available as a library resource to serious students and researchers.

It was in these park files that my original narrative reports on the major battles of the Petersburg Campaign were discovered by Bryce A. Suderow, Civil War historian, bibliophile, and avid researcher. I met Bryce in the mid-1980s when I spoke to a gathering of Civil War Roundtable members of Montgomery County, Maryland. After the meeting a group of us rendezvoused at the Zullo and Van Sickles bookstore. Because of a common interest in Civil War sites, research, and pertinent National Archives Record Groups, in subsequent years I got to know and respect Bryce's skills with excellent credentials as a Civil War researcher. Therefore I was more than a little surprised some five years later when Bryce contacted me following a recent visit he had made to the Petersburg park and its library. There, he had discovered the hard copies and draft overlays of my aforementioned 1960s Petersburg reports and supporting Troop Movement Maps. Familiar with the Petersburg Campaign, Bryce suggested a cooperative venture. He would update my original histories and get them published to satisfy readers interested in the Civil War, especially with the Civil War Sesquicentennial approaching. I told him that was a good idea, but with my battlefield tours and speaking engagements I had "a full platter." But, I added, if he wanted to undertake the project, which I saw as a major challenge updating and editing the whole into a well organized and cohesive publication, I wished him well. And then there was still the issue of finding a good publisher.

As readers will discover, Suderow met his initial challenge in a masterful, thoughtful, and timely fashion. The second hurdle was more time consuming and difficult, but he finally found a perfect match when he contacted Savas Beatie, a specialty history press whose forte is military history books spanning the nation's wars from the American Revolution through the present-day. More important, Savas Beatie had previously edited and published a pair of NPS in-house reports as full-length books. Both were originally prepared as in-house Historic Resource Studies to support archaeological and interpretive projects being undertaken at two Revolutionary War sites for the Bicentennial. The first, authored by Jerome A. Greene, was *The Guns of Independence: The Siege of Yorktown, 1781*, which rolled off the Savas Beatie press in 2005. The second was by John F. Luzader entitled *Saratoga: A Military History of the Decisive Campaign of the American Revolution*, which hit the market in 2008. Both are handsome hardbacks well-illustrated with excellent maps and illustrations. Better yet, they were widely applauded by reviewers and national book club selections.

My association with Theodore P. "Ted" Savas, managing director of Savas Beatie, dates to the early 1980s with his attendance at Jerry Russell's Annual Congress of Civil Roundtables. Inspired by what he saw and learned at the Congresses, Savas joined David B. Woodbury, a fellow Californian, to found Regimental Studies, Inc., a non-partisan, non-profit corporation with two goals: First, to encourage further research of Civil War unit histories, and second, to raise funds for preservation and the protection of neglected Civil War sites. The first copy of their quarterly journal *Civil War Regiments: A Journal of the American Civil War* came off the press in 1990. Besides authoring the Introductions for both the special Vicksburg issue (Vol. 2, No. 1) and the Red River Campaign issue (Vol. 4, No. 1), I also wrote a 25,000-word definitive study of Jeb Stuart's "Ride Around McClellan" for inclusion in a 1993 book of scholarly essays called *The Peninsula Campaign of 1862: Yorktown to the Seven Days*, part of the Savas Woodbury "Campaign Chronicles" series. The Stuart monograph was an expanded version of an in-house study I had prepared for Richmond NBP decades ago in 1959 as a regional research historian.

When Savas and Woodbury amicably ended their partnership in the mid-1990s, Savas continued expanding the operation as Savas Publishing Company and sold the publishing house in 2001. By this time the publishing bug had bitten Ted hard, and after a couple years off writing his own books and coaching his son's little league baseball teams, he was contacted by Russell H. "Cap" Beatie, a successful New York City trial lawyer and Civil War aficionado, to re-enter the world of independent historical publishing. Together, Savas and Beatie—who had authored *Road to Manassas* (Cooper Square, 1961) and is himself a first-rate scholar and writer—formed Savas Beatie LLC in late 2003. Beatie, who had originally been under contract to produce a multi-volume series on the Army of the Potomac for Savas Publishing before that company was sold, published a wide-ranging study of the army's leaders and their decisions in *The Army of the Potomac: Birth of Command, November 1860 – September 1861, Vol. 1* (DaCapo, 2002), followed by *McClellan Takes Command, September 1861 – February 1862, Vol. 2* (DaCapo, 2004). The third volume appeared in 2007, this time under the Savas Beatie imprint, entitled *McClellan's First Campaign, March – May 1862*. After reading an advance copy of Beatie's work I noted in a blurb that he had researched and authored "a tour-de-force."

I want to take this opportunity to thank research extraordinaire Bryce Suderow and our publisher Savas Beatie for undertaking what I deemed to be an impossible mission: editing, designing, and publishing in a handsome book format the series of NPS reports I had prepared so long ago for internal use by NPS managers and planners to help meet their goals at Petersburg National Battlefield.

In thanking Suderow and Savas Beatie for what they have done, I would be remiss if I failed to cite a number of persons and institutions for their support during the years I served as Southeast Regional Research Historian (1958-66) on projects funded in support of MISSION-66 and the Civil War Centennial. They are: Jean C. Harrington, Chief of Interpretation SE Region NPS; Jim Holland, Chief Historian SE Regional Office NPS; Chester Brooks and Martin Conway, superintendents and Lee Wallace, historian, Petersburg NB; Elmer Parker and Sara Dunlap Jackson, Old Military Records Branch, National Archives; Miss Mary Sherard of the Vicksburg Public Library, for servicing all my requests for books for my own use on interlibrary loan from the Library of Congress; and Miss Charlotte Capers and her staff at the Mississippi Archives Department. All these people are now deceased. Christopher Calkins, who until his retirement from the staff of Petersburg National Battlefield is likewise deserving of acknowledgment. As noted above, Chris was behind the publication in 1985 of *The Battle of Five Forks*, my in-house Petersburg report. More important, Chris played a vital role in March 1991 bringing closer Superintendent Brooks' early 1960s dream of adding a Five Forks unit to Petersburg National Battlefield.

Edwin C. Bearss
Historian Emeritus
National Park Service

*   *   *

There are many people who have helped make this project a reality. If I miss someone, you know who you are, and please know I appreciate all you have done.

I would like to thank Theodore P. Savas of Savas Beatie for his eagerness to publish this book and for all his help along the way. At Ted's suggestion, Patrick Brennan, musician and composer extraordinaire and the author of the excellent *Secessionville: Assault on Charleston* (1996), agreed to write the chapter on The Crater, a missing link that was sorely needed to complete this first volume. Many others from Savas Beatie also helped on a variety of fronts: Production Manager Lee Merideth by working overtime with all the issues that crept into play, and in fielding my emails and calls after hours; Marketing Director Sarah Keeney by hitting all the promotional fronts and proofing a late version of the manuscript; and Veronica Kane, who has been working hard on our web presence and who also proofed the final incarnation. Thank you one and all.

Lamar Williams ensured the text adhered to the house style sheet and proofed an early version of the transcribed original Bearss manuscript. David Van Dusen worked with the Savas Beatie team to create an outstanding book trailer, which really captured the thrust and intent of this volume and can be found on the Savas Beatie home page, and on Youtube.com.

Many others typed computer files from the original manuscripts, proofed them, or made certain there was uniformity in the chapters: Alice J. Gayley, Shelley Lewis, Debbie McMahon, Donald R. Parker, Keith and Terri Saunders, and Becky Waid.

Bryce A. Suderow
Washington, DC

Chapter 1

The Attack on Petersburg

June 9, 1864

Editor's Introduction

By the evening of June 3, 1864, Lt. Gen. U. S. Grant's Overland Campaign had lasted thirty days. Grant, the general-in-chief of all Union armies, made his headquarters in the field and guided Maj. Gen. George G. Meade's Army of the Potomac during that long brutal month. Together, the two generals hammered Gen. Robert E. Lee's Army of Northern Virginia in an effort to cripple it and, if not break it up entirely, force it back into the Richmond defenses. The battles stretched from just below the Rapidan River all the way southeast to the Chickahominy River.

The Union army crossed the Rapidan on May 4 and plunged into the heavy terrain known as the Wilderness. Lee attacked Grant on May 5, triggering the battle of the same name. Despite some of the heaviest losses in the war, Grant had no intention of withdrawing as his predecessors had done. Instead, he maneuvered southeast in an effort to insert the Army of the Potomac between Lee's army and the Southern capital at Richmond. By dint of outstanding marching and good luck, however, the Confederates assumed a position that blocked the Union advance, triggering nearly two weeks of bloodshed known as Spotsylvania. Despite major attacks against breastworks, breakthroughs, counter-attacks, and flanking maneuvers, the primary result added nothing but tens of thousands of casualties to the respective army's ledgers.

Petersburg Court House before the battle and siege of Petersburg.
Library of Congress

Undaunted, Grant maneuvered a second time, sliding around Lee's right flank once again and meeting up with him along the North Anna River during the last week of May. The Confederates devised a powerful defensive arrangement that offered a good possibility of inflicting a substantial defeat upon a portion of the Union army, but Lee was too ill during this period and his subordinates not up to the task. Grant sidestepped yet again to the southeast and met Lee and his men at Cold Harbor at the end of May for a general static battle that would stretch nearly as long as Spotsylvania. Believing Lee's army was weak and exhausted, Grant ordered his now-infamous attack that lost thousands of men to no purpose. Instead of standing still or withdrawing, however, Grant conceived of a plan to cross the James and move against Petersburg which was lightly defended by one regular infantry regiment, one cavalry regiment, some artillery, and a handful of militia.

On June 6, while still in front of Cold Harbor, Grant notified Maj. Gen. Benjamin Butler that he planned to send the Army of the Potomac south across the James to seize Petersburg. Grant sent two staff officers to Butler to obtain maps and select the best site on the banks of the James to install pontoon bridges for the crossing.[1]

While putting together the pieces of his complex operation, Grant decided to destroy the Virginia Central Railroad, Richmond's main supply line to the west. On June 5 he ordered cavalry commander Maj. Gen. Philip Sheridan to ride to Charlottesville, and join there with Maj. Gen. David Hunter and his Army of the Shenandoah (which was moving up the Shenandoah Valley). Sheridan's and Hunter's combined force would then destroy the railroad bridge over the Rivanna River and head back to Union lines, destroying the tracks as far east as Hanover Junction and eventually join the Army of the Potomac.[2]

Meanwhile on June 5 at Piedmont Hunter defeated the Confederate force defending the Valley. Lee learned of the defeat the next day and on June 7 sent Maj. Gen. John C. Breckinridge's command, borrowed originally from the Shenandoah Valley to reinforce his own army, back west to repulse Sheridan. Four days later Lee sent his II Corps under Gen. Jubal Early to help with this effort.

Ben Butler was not idle during this period. He revived a plan for a coup de main against Petersburg by his army holding the Bermuda Hundred line. It is not clear whether he mentioned this plan to Grant and received permission, or whether he went ahead with the plan on his own.

*   *   *

Reports from Union informants reached Maj. Gen. Benjamin Butler's Spring Hill, Virginia, headquarters at the end of the first week of June 1864, that the Confederates had stripped the defenses of Petersburg to reinforce Lee's Army of Northern Virginia and to man the Howlett Line, the earthworks that kept Butler's army corked in the Bermuda Hundred bottle. Lee's army continued, as it had since June 1, to hold General Grant's powerful "Army Group" at bay in front of the Cold Harbor lines. Butler's spies stated that the only Rebel troops left in Petersburg were soldiers of the 7th North Carolina Infantry, about 700 troops of the 7th Confederate Cavalry, and a "few pieces of artillery." This force picketing the roads leading into Petersburg was scattered. In an emergency, the Petersburg

---

1   John Horn, *The Petersburg Campaign* (Conshohocken, PA, 1993), 35-37.

2   Horn, *The Petersburg Campaign*, 38.

Major General Benjamin F. Butler
Library of Congress

Major General Godfrey Weitzel
Library of Congress

defenders expected help from the local militia, "consisting from exempts from physical disability from the army, boys under 17 and men between fifty and fifty-five . . ." Butler's sources placed the strength of the militia at between 1,000 and 1,200.[3]

The Petersburg defenses were known to consist of a single line of earthworks, nine miles in length, forming a perimeter, about two and a half miles east, south and west of the city. Butler evaluated these reports and decided to storm the rifle pits and capture the city. The expedition would be entrusted to columns led by Generals Hinks and Kautz. Hinks at the head of his division of African Americans, supported by two sections of artillery, was to carry the Rebel rifle pits on either side of the lunettes guarding the eastern approaches to Petersburg via the City Point and Jordan's Point Roads. Colonel Duncan's black brigade would be pulled out of the rifle pits north of the Appomattox to increase the strength of Hinks' striking force. Kautz's horsemen—1,200 to 1,400 strong— were to leave camp under the cover of the infantry, swing to the southeast, and approach the city by way of the Jerusalem Plank Road.[4]

---

3 *The War of the Rebellion: A Compilation of the Official Records of the Union and Confederate Armies,* 128 vols. (Washington, D.C., 1880-1901), Series 1, vol. 36, pt. 2, 274–275. Hereafter references are to Series 1 unless noted.

4 *Ibid.,* 275. Edward Hinks was a Massachusetts state legislator before answering his country's call. On August 3, 1861, Hinks was commissioned colonel of the 19th Massachusetts Infantry. Hinks fought in numerous battles in the eastern theater of operations from Ball's Bluff to Antietam, where he was seriously wounded. He was on court-martial duty and in charge of the Camp Lookout prison pen till April 1864, when he was assigned to lead the 3rd division, XVIII Army Corps. Mark M. Boatner, *The Civil War Dictionary* (New York, 1959), 402. Ezra Warner, *Generals in Blue: Lives of Union Commanders* (Baton Rouge, 1964), 229-30. August Kautz, after serving in the War with Mexico, had received an appointment to the U.S. Military Academy at West Point, from which he graduated in 1852. Wounded twice by Indians while serving on the

Final plans were hammered into shape by Generals Butler and Hinks, assisted by Chief Engineer Godfrey Weitzel, on the morning of June 8. While they talked, they were joined by General Gillmore, commander of the X Corps. The newcomer listened attentively.[5] Soon after the staff-meeting broke up, General Weitzel called Butler aside, and explained to his friend and superior that Gillmore wished to command the attacking force. Gillmore pegged his argument on "the great importance of the expedition to the Union cause, the necessity of having tried troops to cover the retreat in case of disaster, or who would be more to be depended upon in making the assault upon the enemy's lines." When Butler questioned Gillmore about this, the corps commander said that he would like to employ one of the white brigades from his line, rather than Colonel Duncan's African Americans, and with it "make the real infantry attack." Although it was against his better judgment, Butler was "unwilling to decline an offer to have the expedition led by an officer of General Gillmore's rank and experience." Gillmore, at noon, was placed in charge of the expedition. Butler took it upon himself to see that General Hinks had one of his black brigades ready to march at the appointed hour.

Before parting, Butler and Gillmore reviewed the plan. As they did, Butler unfolded and spread a copy of the map of the Petersburg defenses found on the person of captured Confederate Brig. Gen. William S. Walker.[6] Gillmore was to march the brigade withdrawn from his Bermuda Hundred lines at midnight and cross the pontoon bridge at Point of Rocks. After crossing the Appomattox, Gillmore was to halt the brigade in "some convenient spot until near daybreak." The two infantry brigades (one white and the other African American) would then be put in motion. A three-mile march along the Point of Rocks Road, which had been frequently reconnoitered by Hinks' cavalry, would bring the Union foot soldiers up against the Rebel picket line. The outposts were to be driven in and followed by the bluecoats into the Confederate fortifications.

---

frontier, Kautz held the rank of captain in the 3rd U.S. Cavalry in May 1861. Kautz had seen action both east and west of the Appalachians. June 1864 found Kautz commanding the Army of the James' cavalry. Boatner, *Civil War Dictionary*, 448-449; Warner, *Generals in Blue*, 257-58.

5   OR 36, pt. 2, 275. Quincy Gillmore graduated from the U.S. Military Academy in 1849, and as No. 1 in his class was assigned to the Corps of Engineers. Prior to the Civil War, Gillmore supervised construction of coastal fortifications and taught engineering and served as quartermaster at West Point. Gillmore commanded the X Corps from June 13, 1863, in operations directed against Charleston, South Carolina, and at Drewry's Bluff and Bermuda Hundred. Boatner, *Civil War Dictionary*, 343, Warner, *Generals in Blue*, 176-177.

6   OR 36, pt. 2, 275-76. General Walker was wounded and captured by Butler's troopers on May 20.

Lieutenant General Ulysses S. Grant
Library of Congress

General Robert E. Lee
Library of Congress

As soon as the infantry had uncovered a road leading to the left toward the Jerusalem Plank Road, General Kautz's cavalry was to turn into this byway, execute a detour well out of sight of the Rebel pickets, and charge up the Jerusalem Plank Road. Gillmore and Kautz were informed by Butler that the distance the cavalry would have to travel before attacking was from 15 to 20 miles.

The great benefits to accrue to the Federal cause by the fall of Petersburg were made known to Gillmore. The destruction of the bridges across the Appomattox, he was made to understand, would seriously impede the flow of supplies of men and materiel to Lee's army. With the railroad bridges down, all rolling stock between the Appomattox and James would be bottled up at Richmond. Butler opined, and so told Gillmore, that the capture of Petersburg "would be cheaply purchased at 500, and not too dearly with the sacrifice of 1,000 men killed and wounded."

Butler emphasized to Gillmore the importance of moving promptly, thereby insuring that his troops would be back in their entrenchments by daybreak on the 10th, prepared to resist a Confederate counterstroke against the Bermuda Hundred lines. If successful in his attack on Petersburg, Gillmore could send back 1,000 blacks, with whom Butler would endeavor to hold the entrenchments. Knowing their marching capabilities, Butler had confidence in the African Americans' ability to carry out their mission. If Gillmore destroyed the Appomattox bridges, thus placing the river between Kautz and the Union lines north of the river, the cavalryman was to ride south down the Petersburg & Weldon Railroad, destroying it as he advanced. Upon encountering Rebel forces in strength, Kautz was to retrace his steps.[7]

Returning to his X Corps headquarters, General Gillmore moved to organize his strike force. According to his understanding with Butler, the combat-ready brigade that was to cross the Appomattox was to muster 1,800 fighting men. Gillmore called on the commander of his First division, Brig. Gen. Alfred H. Terry, for a brigade. Terry designated his 2nd Brigade, led by Col. Joseph R. Hawley.

Learning from Terry that Hawley's brigade numbered about 1,400 effectives, Gillmore asked Butler for permission to form a "composite brigade," which would alleviate the need of recalling Hawley's men on picket, and thus running a risk of letting the Confederates know something big was impending. Butler was agreeable, whereupon, Gillmore called on Brig. Gen. John W. Turner of his Second division to name a 400 man regiment to accompany the expedition. Gillmore also suggested that it might be wise to take along a battery. Before returning to Butler's Spring Hill headquarters, Gillmore planned to discuss the situation with General Kautz.[8]

Butler was willing for Gillmore to take two sections of a battery, while Hinks' brigade would be accompanied by two guns. "This is not to be artillery work," Butler pointed out, "but a quick, decisive push."[9]

7   *Ibid.*, 276-77.

8   *OR* 36, pt. 3, 705; pt. 2, 277, 292, 297.

9   *Ibid.*, pt. 3, 705.

Contrary to Butler's instructions, General Terry determined to recall Hawley's pickets, soldiers of the 7th New Hampshire. Orders were issued for Col. Harris M. Plaisted to have one of his regiments, as soon as it was dark, relieve Hawley's outposts. Butler was unaware of this development.

Meanwhile, Gillmore had outlined to Terry the route he wished Hawley's brigade to take to the pontoon bridge—the troops were to move down the entrenchments to Point of Rocks. Terry, shaking his head, remarked that the movement of so "large a body of men" along the earthworks could attract the attention of Rebel sentinels. Since the expedition was cloaked in secrecy, he thought it best for the brigade to march via the road to Hatcher's. Gillmore saw the wisdom in Terry's suggestion, and Hawley was told to take that road.[10]

By 9:00 a.m. on June 8, three of Hawley's regiments—the 3rd New Hampshire and 6th and 7th Connecticut—fell in on the color line. Each man carried two days cooked rations in his haversack and 40 rounds of ammunition in his cartridge box. A few minutes later, the 7th New Hampshire, having been relieved on the picket line, marched up, and Colonel Hawley reported his brigade ready to march. As yet, the promised guide had not put in an appearance to show the column the way to Point of Rocks. A staffer was sent to division headquarters to learn what had happened to the guide. When he returned and reported that he could not secure a satisfactory answer to his request, a second aide galloped off on the same quest, but he was no more successful than the first.[11]

General Terry (at 10:20 p.m.) issued orders for Colonel Hawley to "move at once with your brigade across the Appomattox, by way of the pontoon bridge near General Butler's headquarters, calling there for a guide." On the high ground south of the river, Hawley was to be joined by the 62nd Ohio and Company D, 1st U.S. Light Artillery, and there he would receive additional instructions from General Gillmore. The troops were cautioned to hold down the noise as they moved out. The orderly, who delivered this dispatch, was to guide Hawley's column as far as Butler's headquarters.[12]

Hawley (at 10:30 p.m.) passed the word to take up the march. Orders were given in whispers, and the column moved out. Leaving two staff officers with instructions to bring the brigade to Gillmore's headquarters, Hawley rode ahead and reported to Brig. Gen. Robert S. Foster, the X Corps' Chief of Staff. The colonel asked about the roads, and Foster called for a cavalryman who as an orderly had made frequent rides from Gillmore's headquarters to Point of Rocks. This

10 *Ibid.*, pt. 2, 297, 298; pt. 3, 706-707. Plaisted commanded Terry's 3rd Brigade.

11 *Ibid.*, pt. 2, 297, 298.

12 *Ibid.*, pt. 3, 706, 707.

man, the general said, would show the column the way to the crossing. The head of the brigade, within a few minutes, came tramping up the road. Hawley, accompanied by his staff and a guide, assumed his post and led the troops down the road toward Bermuda Hundred Landing. After following the roadway some distance, the guide turned to the right, following the telegraph line. Before the column had traveled far, mud and water to a depth of two feet was encountered, and the road became all but impassable. Accompanied by one of the guides, Colonel Hawley rode ahead and gained the open country near Point of Rocks. Not knowing what to do next, Hawley dispatched the guide to Butler with a plea for help.[13]

Valuable time was lost while Hawley waited impatiently for the guide to return. Shortly thereafter, the head of the brigade marched up, accompanied by two members of Butler's staff, who had found the column floundering about in the swamp. Because of the rough going, entire units had straggled. While the column closed up, additional time was squandered. It was after 2:00 a.m. before the vanguard started crossing the Appomattox, and it was 3:00 a.m. before the last infantryman reached the south bank. Ascending the hill beyond, Hawley and his troops found the 62nd Ohio and the artillerists. The men took a break, while Hawley reported to General Gillmore's command post.[14]

The aimless march through the swamp had taken its toll. If the column had followed the road it should have, it would have crossed the Appomattox by midnight, and the troops could have rested and caught their second wind before pushing on.[15]

At dark, General Hinks, in accordance with his instructions, had turned out the 4th and 6th U.S. Colored Infantry and Company B, 2nd U.S. Colored Light Artillery, about 1,300 strong. The troops marched from their camp to Copsa's, where Hinks told the regimental commanders to have their men fall out, cautioning them to remain near the colors so they could be formed and mustered on a moment's notice. After placing the senior officer in charge, Hinks (at 9:00 p.m.) rode to the pontoon bridge to await General Gillmore's arrival. While there, Hinks received a communication from General Butler, alerting him to expect Gillmore's and Hawley's column sometime between 11:00 p.m. and midnight. A staff officer stood by to guide Hawley's brigade to a site on the Jordan's Point Road within the

---

13 *Ibid.*, pt. 2, 298-99, 302, 305; Henry F. W. Little, *The Seventh Regiment of the New Hampshire Volunteers in the War of the Rebellion* (Concord, 1896), 264.

14 OR 36, pt. 2, 299, 302, 303, 305; Stephen Walkley, *History of the Seventh Connecticut Volunteer Infantry, Hawley's Brigade, Terry's Division, Tenth Army Corps, 1861-1865* (Southington, 1905), 145.

15 OR 36, pt. 2, 278.

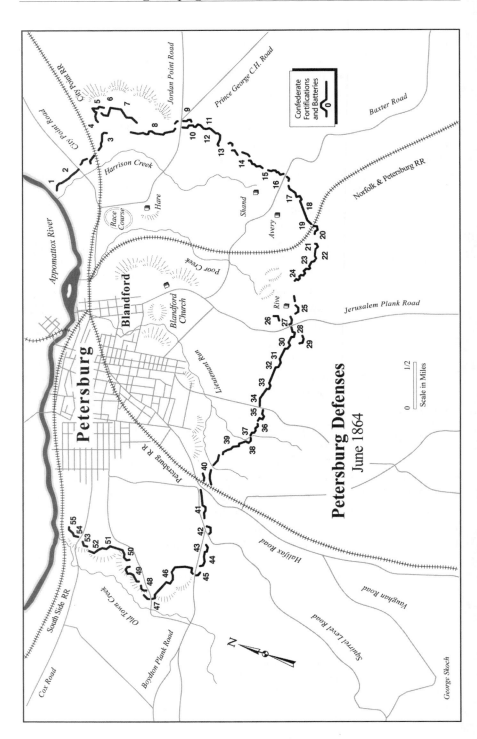

Confederate Fortifications and Batteries

Petersburg Defenses June 1864

Scale in Miles

N

George Skoch

Major General August Kautz
Library of Congress

Union picket line, so the exhausted troops could rest up for the impending hard march they faced.[16]

As the hours passed, General Hinks grew more frustrated. Not only had Hawley's brigade gone astray, so had General Gillmore and his party.

General Foster awakened Butler at 2:00 a.m. to inquire what road led to the pontoon bridge. Butler was aghast, because he felt that the road in question ought to have been as familiar to Gillmore and his people as the path to their beds. It was 2:45 a.m. before Gillmore and his staff crossed the bridge. While Gillmore established his command post in a house on the hillside overlooking the crossing, Hinks kept watch for Hawley's rear guard. He waited until the last foot soldier was across before returning to Copsa's. The men of the African American brigade were aroused, formed, and mustered.[17]

Thirteen hundred picked troopers of Kautz's cavalry division spent the late afternoon of the 8th drawing ammunition, rations, and forage. Each man was issued three days' rations and 20 quarts of oats. At 11:30 p.m., the troopers of the 11th Pennsylvania Cavalry swung into their saddles and rode out of their camp near Point of Rocks, to be followed by Lt. Peter Morton's section of the 8th Battery, New York Light Artillery, the 5th Pennsylvania Cavalry, and the 1st District of Columbia. The horse soldiers found their way obstructed by Hawley's bluecoats,

---

16 *Ibid.*, pt. 2, 306; pt. 3, 707; Frederick H. Dyer, *A Compendium of the War of the Rebellion*, 2 vols. (New York, 1959), vol. 2, 942.

17 *OR* 36, pt. 2, 278, 306.

Major General Quincy A. Gillmore
Library of Congress

and day was breaking before the last of the cavalry reached the south bank of the Appomattox.[18]

As soon as Kautz reported his division across the Appomattox, Gillmore (at 3:40 a.m.) dashed off a message to General Butler. He reported that some of his command had been "delayed by losing the road." In addition, Gillmore feared the Confederates, on alert, would have heard the noise as the cavalry's mounts crossed the bridge, the planks not being muffled. The engineers had spread ten bales of hay on the planking, but Hawley's troops had collected the hay and used it to wipe mud off their shoes and trouser legs.[19]

After Kautz had reported, General Gillmore put his column into motion. Kautz's horse soldiers took the lead as the little army took the road to Copsa's, where it was to be joined by Hinks' black soldiers. It was 5:00 a.m. and the sun was up before the vanguard reached the rendezvous. Gillmore called a halt to confer with Hinks. In the advance on Petersburg, Hinks' column was to follow Kautz's cavalry until it reached the Jordan's Point Road. The African American infantry would then take the lead. Unless the attack was made promptly and vigorously, Gillmore cautioned Hinks, there was danger of failure, as the Rebels would pull troops out of their Howlett Line to reinforce the Petersburg garrison. If his column entered the city first, Hinks was to put the torch to the public buildings, military stores, bridges spanning the Appomattox, the depot, and rolling stock.

---

18 OR 36, pt. 2, 308; pt. 3, 708; Kautz organized his strike force into two brigades, Spear's and Conger's. Spear's command consisted of the 11th Pennsylvania (640 men and two mountain howitzers) and the 5th Pennsylvania (450 men and two mountain howitzers). Conger's brigade was composed of the 1st District of Columbia and Morton's guns. OR 36, pt. 2, 311, 314.

19 OR 36, pt. 2, 278; pt. 3, 718.

Before resuming the march, Gillmore (at 5:30 a.m.) notified Butler that Hawley would approach Petersburg via the City Point Road, while Hinks' blacks bore in on the Jordan's Point Road. To facilitate his attack, Gillmore asked that Terry, on the Bermuda Hundred front, be directed to strengthen and throw forward his pickets beyond Rushmore's.[20]

Meanwhile, Kautz's cavalry had forged ahead. The vanguard—the 11th Pennsylvania—on reaching the City Point Road surprised and captured four bewildered Rebels. Questioned, the Confederates swore they had heard nothing to arouse their suspicion that the Yanks had dispatched a strong column across the Appomattox. This made Kautz feel better. The march continued, the horse soldiers following little frequented byroads parallel to, but about four miles east of, the Petersburg defenses. As they approached the Prince George Court House Road, the bluecoats were fired on by sharpshooters of the 7th Confederate Cavalry. Kautz was compelled to halt and deploy his troopers, thus delaying his march.

Colonel Samuel Spear, riding with the vanguard, had the carbineers of the 11th Pennsylvania dismount and advance into the woods to his front, while two squadrons of the 5th Pennsylvania pressed ahead on the left and right of the carbineers. The Confederates shelled the squadron of the 5th Pennsylvania—Capt. George J. Ker's—that was skirmishing to the left with a howitzer. Only two shells had been fired, when the Rebels were charged by Capt. Bardele Galliseth's squadron of the 5th and routed from their camp and entrenchments. The butternuts, in their wild flight, abandoned arms, saddles and bridles, and clothing, which the Federals destroyed before resuming the march. Several prisoners questioned by General Kautz stated that their regiment mustered between 300 and 400. Pushing ahead, Kautz's column was fired on by Confederate pickets near the Norfolk & Petersburg Railroad. The Union advance charged and scattered the grey clads. Kautz's horse soldiers struck the Jerusalem Plank Road at 5:00 a.m., four miles south of the Petersburg fortifications. The distance that his division had traveled was greater than anticipated. When the general turned his horsemen into the Plank Road, he looked at his watch. It was after 11:00 a.m. To make matters worse, Kautz knew that Confederate pickets had seen his column and had sounded the alarm. Except for the men captured, these outposts had made for previously designated assembly areas.[21]

---

20 OR 36, pt. 3, 719; pt. 2, 288.

21 OR 36, pt. 2, 308, 311, 315; John L. Roper, Henry C. Archibald, and G. W. Coles *History of the Eleventh Pennsylvania Volunteer Cavalry, Together with a Complete Roster of the Regiment and Regimental Officers* (Philadelphia, 1902), 121; August V. Kautz, "Operations South of the James," in Robert U. Johnson, and Clarence C. Buel, eds., *Battles and Leaders of the Civil War*, 4 vols. (New York, 1887-1888), vol. 4, 534.

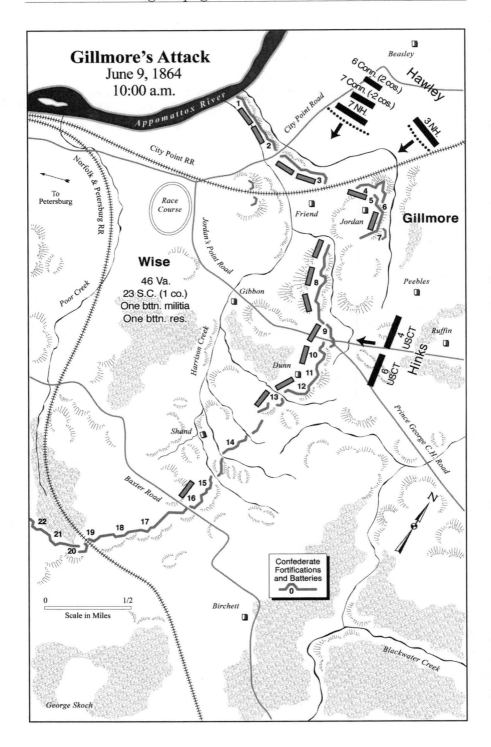

Gillmore's Attack
June 9, 1864
10:00 a.m.

Appomattox River

City Point Road

Beasley

Hawley

6 Conn. (2 cos.)
7 Conn. (-2 cos.)
7 NH.

3 NH.

City Point RR

Norfolk & Petersburg RR

To
Petersburg

Race
Course

Jordan's Point Road

1

2

3

4
5
6
7

Friend

Jordan

Gillmore

Wise

46 Va.
23 S.C. (1 co.)
One bttn. militia
One bttn. res.

Gibbon

Peebles

8

9

4
USCT

Ruffin

Poor Creek

Harrison Creek

10

Dunn

11

6
USCT

Hinks

Shand

12

13

14

Prince George C.H. Road

Baxter Road

15

16

17

18

19

20

21

22

N

Birchett

Confederate
Fortifications
and Batteries
0

0   1/2
Scale in Miles

Blackwater Creek

George Skoch

General Gillmore and his staff accompanied Hawley's brigade as it tramped down the City Point-Petersburg Road. A detachment from the 4th Massachusetts Cavalry led the way. A few Confederate pickets were sighted, but they kept their distance, and the general did not have to call on Hawley's infantry until he neared A. Jordan's. Just beyond Jordan's, the road turned sharply right, crossed the City Point & Petersburg Railroad, and descended onto a broad plain. Gillmore swept the low ground to his front with his glasses and saw plantation roads branching off the main road. These country lanes were flanked by hedges, while the plain was crisscrossed by drainage ditches with underbrush choked banks. It was an area that could be used to advantage by a small but resolute defending force. While the general studied the terrain to his front, his escort clashed with Confederate pickets. One of the Massachusetts cavalrymen was killed. Gillmore called for Colonel Hawley to deploy his lead regiment, the 7th New Hampshire. Responding with his characteristic vigor, Col. Joseph C. Abbott formed his regiment into line of battle. At the same time, one company of the 7th Connecticut was deployed as skirmishers, while a second company moved to the left on the double. The remaining soldiers of the Connecticut unit were massed in support of the 7th New Hampshire.[22]

General Hinks' brigade trailed Kautz's cavalry to Bailey's. There Hinks received a copy of Gillmore's 5:00 a.m. order for his column to approach Petersburg via the Jordan's Point Road. Earlier Hinks had asked Gillmore, "If it was the intention to hold on to the enemy's works as long as possible." Gillmore answered, "No. Unless we take them within an hour it will be useless to attempt it, and you must use your own discretion in the attack."

With these instructions for his guidance, Hinks ordered his column forward. A member of Gillmore's staff—Lt. James H. Barnard—rode beside Hinks, so he could communicate with his General the moment the blacks deployed.

It was 7:00 a.m. when Hinks' lead regiment, having gained the Jordan's Point Road, crossed Bailey Creek. Confederate pickets were encountered and driven across Jordan's and Friend's fields. While the Confederates took cover in Batteries No. 8-12, Hinks deployed the 4th and 6th U.S. Colored Infantry to the left and right of Ruffin's house. As soon as the officers reported that they were ready, Hinks waved his African Americans forward. Letting go fierce cheers for the Union, the blacks advanced to the crest of the ridge. Here Hinks called a halt, when he saw that his right flank could be enfiladed by cannon emplaced in Battery No. 7, 600 yards away. To neutralize this position, Hinks sent for artillery. Lieutenant Barnard, at the same time, galloped off to find General Gillmore and report that Hinks "was in

---

22 *Ibid.*, pt. 2, 299, 303, 305; Little, *The Seventh Regiment of the New Hampshire Volunteers*, 264, 266; Walkley, *History of the Seventh Connecticut Volunteer Infantry*, 145.

position; that his right flank was in a precarious position; and that the black brigade would advance as soon as Hinks could bring his artillery—Company B, 2nd U.S. Colored Artillery—to bear on Battery No. 7." The artillerists reported that it would be impossible to bring their guns into action, unless they were supported by a strong force of infantry. This Hinks was not prepared to do, so the battery was ordered back to Ruffin's house. The infantry at the same time advanced another 50 yards.[23]

To create a diversion in favor of Gillmore's expedition, a pair of gunboats, the *Commodore Perry* and *William C. Putnam* stood up the Appomattox River and took position in the reach below Fort Clifton. Guns were cast loose, and the fort methodically shelled. The Confederates replied with the fort's big guns, but their projectiles fell short of the vessels. Gun spotters aboard *Commodore Perry* claimed that shells from their big, long-range 100-pounder Parrott dismounted one Rebel gun and sundered a second. The gunboats ceased fire at 6:00 p.m. and returned to their anchorage, having expended a large number of shells in the bombardment.[24]

At the time of the first Union thrust against Petersburg, the lines guarding the approaches to the city south of the Appomattox formed an 8-mile perimeter, with the flanks anchored on the river. With the exception of the lunettes and redans, located at commanding and strategic points, little work had been done on the rifle pits connecting the strongholds. A horseman could ride over the rifle pits, Brig. Gen. Raleigh E. Colston (of General Beauregard's command) recalled, "without the least difficulty."[25]

By June 9, 1864, the Petersburg defenses, because of heavy demands elsewhere, had been stripped of defenders. The only troops remaining in and around the city belonged to Brig. Gen. Henry A. Wise's command. Wise, at this stage of the conflict, commanded the First Military District, Department of North Carolina and South Virginia. Wise's command and Capt. Nathaniel A. Sturdivant's four-gun battery were camped near the river, east of Petersburg, while Col. V. H. Taliaferro's 7th Confederate Cavalry picketed the roads toward City Point and Broadway. Every other regiment earmarked for the defense of Petersburg had been

---

23 *Ibid.*, pt. 2, 295, 306-307.

24 *Official Records of the Union and Confederate Navies in the War of the Rebellion*, Series 1, Volume 10, 138-139; R. E. Colston, "Repelling the First Assault on Petersburg," in *Battles and Leaders of the Civil War*, vol. 4, 536.

25 Colston, "Repelling the First Assault on Petersburg," 535. At the end of April 1864, Colston transferred from the Department of Georgia to Virginia, where he was assigned to the provisional command of the post of Petersburg, which he held from January to March, 1865.

Brigadier General Henry A. Wise
Library of Congress

called north of the James to bolster Lee's Army of Northern Virginia in its battle with Grant's "Army Group." [26]

According to the plan worked out by General Wise, the regular infantry units were to hold the one-half mile section of line from Battery No. 1 to Battery No. 3. Several skeleton companies of home guards and the cannoneers of Capt. Edward R. Young's Virginia Artillery Company (less than 150 men) manned the guns mounted in Batteries No. 4 through No. 7. Then came an undefended gap of a mile and one-half. Battery No. 16, which covered the Baxter road, was held by 30 home guards and four field guns. One-half mile farther to the right at Battery No. 22 were posted two of Captain Sturdivant's 12-pounder howitzers. From Battery No. 22 to the river above Petersburg there were neither men nor cannon.[27]

As soon as the pickets of the 7th Confederate Cavalry reported the Federals advancing in force, General Wise had the city alarm bells tolled. It was 8:30 a.m. when the bells began to clang, and every man in Archer's and Hood's Battalions of Virginia Reserves able to shoulder a weapon hurried out to the lines. Major Fletcher H. Archer, a veteran of the Mexican War who had fought under General Colston in 1862, commanded a battalion of Virginia Reserves. Accompanied by 125 officers and men, Archer posted his troops in Batteries No. 27 and 28, covering the Jerusalem Plank Road. Archer's command was composed of men exempted from

---

26 *Ibid.*, 308; OR 36, pt. 3, 892. Wise's command at this stage of the war included the 44th Virginia Infantry Battalion and 46th Virginia Infantry Regiment; Lee A. Wallace, *A Guide to Virginia Military Organizations 1861-1865*, (Richmond, 1964), 141, 166-167, 168-170, 247, 253.

27 Colston, "Repelling the First Assault on Petersburg," 535-536.

field service because of age or infirmities, and boys under the conscription age. They had spent two weeks in camp and then had been allowed to return to their homes, but were required to hold periodic drills. Very few of Archer's men wore uniforms, and they were armed with muskets and substandard rifled-muskets.[28]

At the first alarm, General Colston, who since Wise's return to duty on June 1 had been awaiting a new assignment, mounted his horse and galloped to Wise's headquarters. There he offered his services to the general. Wise thanked Colston and told him to take position at Battery No. 16, which must be "held at any hazard." Wise, with Colston on the field, would cross the Appomattox and collect what reinforcements he could to bolster the Petersburg defenders. As the two generals parted at 9:30 a.m., Wise remarked, "For God's sake. General, hold out till I come back, or all is lost!"[29]

At Battery No. 16, Colston found 30 home guards and four guns, but the foe was nowhere in sight. Toward the northeast there was sporadic firing, but no crashing volleys, such as to indicate an assault. The militia thought that the cavalry had exaggerated the danger.[30]

The shooting over on the City Point Road flared as Hawley's skirmishers of the 7th Connecticut pressed Virginia infantrymen of the 44th Battalion and 46th Regiment back across Jordan's field. Crossing the railroad, the skirmishers, supported by three regiments, passed down a ravine and entered an open meadow extending for one-half mile to the right of the road, while to the left of the road were fields and scattered woods. The rest of the brigade—the 3rd New Hampshire, 62nd Ohio, and Company D, 1st U.S. Light Artillery—held the high ground at Jordan's, to be prepared for a Confederate counterthrust down the railroad.

Colonel Hawley began to have second thoughts. He was unfamiliar with the country to his front, and his superiors—Generals Gillmore and Foster—had failed to brief him as to the whereabouts of the Rebel fortifications. While he had been told that there were few Confederates in Petersburg, there were known to be thousands of combat-hardened Rebels within a day's march of this vital Cockade City.

One of Gillmore's aides now called on Hawley "to push the rebel skirmishers who [had] appeared on the meadow to his front." Pressing on, the bluecoats routed a picket force of Rebel sharpshooters from Beasley's house and outbuildings. The

---

28 *Ibid.*, 36; P.H. Drewry, "The Ninth of June, 1864," in *Confederate Veteran*, 40 vols. (Wilmington, 1927), vol. 35, 290.

29 Colston, "Repelling the First Assault on Petersburg," 536; *OR* 36, pt. 2, 317.

30 *Ibid.*, 317.

City Point Road served as the axis of Hawley's line of advance and now turned to the left.

As the bluecoats moved down into the meadow, unseen cannon sent a projectile whistling overhead. Hawley called a halt, and told the colonel of the 6th Connecticut to send a company of skirmishers into the woods flanking the railroad. Company D, Capt. Charles H. Nichols commanding, moved out on the double and deployed as skirmishers to the left and right of the tracks. A second company, G, from the 6th Connecticut soon joined their comrades on the railroad. Meanwhile, General Gillmore had committed the 3rd New Hampshire. Led by Lt. Col. Josiah I. Plimpton, the New Hampshire boys followed Captain Nichols' skirmishers. It was impossible for one man to control the two columns into which his brigade had broken, so Hawley asked General Foster to oversee the movement along the railroad.[31]

Orders now came for Hawley to "simulate an attack." Hawley had his skirmishers out on the meadow change their front to the left to conform to the road's alignment, thus narrowing the gap separating the wings of the brigade. Driving in the Confederate pickets, Plimpton's and Nichols' bluecoats reached a wooded ravine within 200 yards of Battery No. 5, the guns of which were harassing Hawley's men out on the meadow.

Gillmore now issued instructions for Hawley "to make no unnecessary exposure of . . . [his] men, but to crowd the enemy whenever there was opportunity." From the right of Hawley's line, the Confederate works (distant about 500 yards) were visible. To assail Batteries No. 4 and 5 from the meadow would be suicidal, the Federal leaders believed, because the ground over which they would charge was swept by at least three canister-belching cannon. Reports reached Hawley from Plimpton indicating the terrain south of the railroad was more favorable for the attacker. But, before undertaking anything in that direction, Hawley must withdraw his three regiments from the plain and redeploy his brigade. To do this, he needed authority from Gillmore. All the while, brisk firing from Hinks' front was heard off to the south.[32]

General Hinks was distressed by the relative quiet to his right, where he expected Hawley's brigade to be battering the foe. An aide was dispatched to tell Gillmore that the Confederates were holding Batteries No. 8 through 12 in "considerable force," and it would be impossible to storm these works with the force at Hinks' disposal. As if this were not bad enough, the right flank of his battle

31 OR 36, pt. 2, 299-300, 302-303, 304, 305; Charles K. Caldwell, *The Old Sixth Regiment, its War Record, 1861-1865* (New Haven, 1875), 94-95.

32 *Ibid.*, pt. 2, 299-300, 302-303, 305; Walkley, *History of the Seventh Connecticut Volunteer Infantry*, 264.

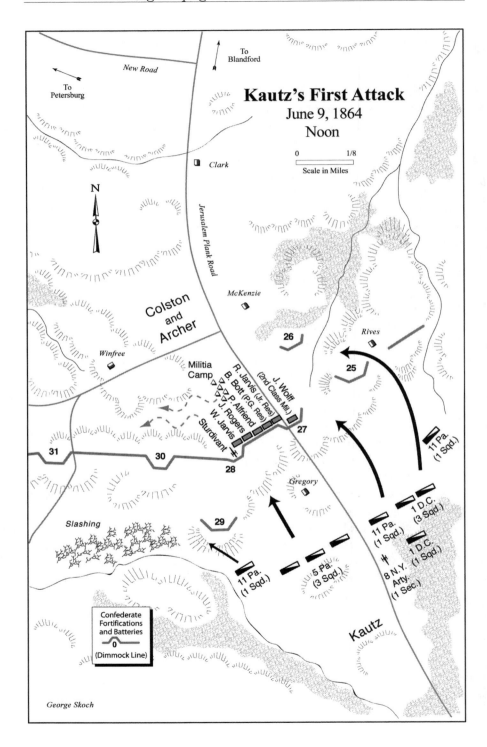

To Blandford

New Road

To Petersburg

Clark

Kautz's First Attack
June 9, 1864
Noon

0   1/8

Scale in Miles

N

Jerusalem Plank Road

McKenzie

Rives

26

25

Colston
and
Archer

Winfree

Militia
Camp

R. Jarvis (Jr. Res)
B. Bott (P.G. Res)
P. Alfriend
J. Rogers
W. Jarvis
Sturdivant

J. Wolff
(2nd Class Mil.)

27

11 Pa.
(1 Sqd.)

31   30

28

Gregory

29

1 D.C.
(3 Sqd.)

11 Pa.
(1 Sqd.)

1 D.C.
(1 Sqd.)

8 N.Y.
Arty.
(1 Sec.)

Slashing

11 Pa.
(1 Sqd.)

5 Pa.
(3 Sqd.)

Confederate
Fortifications
and Batteries

(Dimmock Line)

Kautz

George Skoch

line was exposed to a scathing fire from Rebels posted in the rifle pits on either side of Battery No. 7. If nothing were done to relieve that flank, it must be pulled back. Within a few minutes, Hinks received a verbal message that Hawley's brigade would drive the sharpshooters into their works and keep them pinned down. Hinks accordingly told his African Americans to hold fast. Checking the time, Hinks saw that it was 10:00 a.m.[33]

Gillmore, at an early hour, was satisfied by what he had seen and heard from Hinks and Hawley that an assault on the Confederate defenses "would, in all probability, fail." He, however, ordered the brigades to hold their ground, as he expected at any minute to hear Kautz's guns. Gillmore, about noon, fearing the Confederates would send a column into the gap separating Hawley's and Hinks' units, directed them to withdraw to the road junction near Baylor's.[34]

Shortly thereafter, Gillmore (at 12:30 p.m.), wrote Butler that it would be impossible for the Union infantry to fight their way through the fortifications to their front. According to the reports from Hinks, the Confederates within the past several hours had reinforced their position with two regiments. Distant firing to the south led to the belief that Kautz had also run into opposition. Butler was informed that Gillmore was about to withdraw.[35]

Hinks was notified by Gillmore that the Confederates had advanced a strong line against Hawley's left. At 12:00 p.m. one of Gillmore's aides rode up and told Hinks that Hawley was withdrawing his brigade, whereupon Hinks retired his reserve and artillery across Bailey Creek to Bryant's clover field. One hour later, on orders from Gillmore, Hinks withdrew his battle line from in front of the Confederate defenses and rejoined the artillery east of the creek. Here instructions were received to return to Baylor's Mill, where the black brigade fell in behind the main column.[36]

It was about 1:00 p.m. when orders to pull back reached Colonel Hawley. Preparatory to disengaging his men, Hawley recalled the troopers of the 4th Massachusetts Cavalry and assembled the skirmishers of the 7th Connecticut in the road to act as a rear guard. Colonel Plimpton was told to hold his ground, until the regiments out in the meadow regained the high ground. The 62nd Ohio was posted in line of battle to the right of Jordan's house, while Lieutenant Joseph Sanger had his cannoneers throw their four guns—two 3-inch rifles and two 12-pounder howitzers—into battery nearby. As they retired, the soldiers "heard distant artillery

33 OR 36, pt. 2, 307.

34 *Ibid.*, 289.

35 OR 36, pt. 3, 719.

36 OR 36, pt. 2, 307.

and musketry" to the southwest. As soon as the three regiments passed the 62nd Ohio, Hawley threw one of them into line and notified Colonel Plimpton to retire the 3rd New Hampshire. No attempt was made by the Confederates to harass the bluecoats as they moved back. When all but a rear guard of 20 horse soldiers had passed the 62nd Ohio, that regiment filed into the road and the artillery limbered up. One mile from Jordan's, the brigade, on order from General Gillmore, halted in a large field near Baylor's Sawmill, stacked arms, rested an hour, and ate dinner. Here they were joined by Hinks' column.[37]

While at the sawmill, Gillmore received a terse answer to his 12:30 p.m. dispatch to Butler. The commanding general grieved "for the delay in getting off the expedition . . ." and he trusted that Kautz's horse soldiers had been more successful that the infantry.[38]

Gillmore reported that no sound of Kautz's column had been heard since then. Both he and Hinks opined that Kautz had gone to cut the Petersburg & Weldon Railroad. As he had been directed to be back with the Union lines by nightfall, Gillmore did not feel justified in remaining any longer at Baylor's. The column was accordingly put in motion, and Hawley's brigade re-crossed the Appomattox at sunset.[39]

General Kautz's cavalrymen, about the hour that Gillmore made his decision to recall his infantry, were riding up the Jerusalem Plank Road. As the advance guard of the 11th Pennsylvania forged ahead, they drove in and captured several Rebel pickets. Topping a rise a short distance beyond a crossing of one of the tributaries of Blackwater Swamp, the bluecoats sighted Confederate earthworks. Colonel Spear reined up his horse and studied the fortifications through his glasses. They consisted of five lunettes (Batteries No. 25 thru 29) and a connecting line of rifle pits extending some distance to the right and left of the road. Spear shouted for a squadron of the 11th Pennsylvania to charge with drawn sabers up the road. Amid a clatter of hoofs against the planks, the horse soldiers, riding boot-to-spur, surged forward in column by twos. A crashing volley delivered by Archer's Battalion of reserves sent the Pennsylvanians recoiling. As they fell back, they deployed to the left and right while awaiting the arrival of the rest of the column.

General Kautz joined Spear, and they carefully reconnoitered the Confederate position. It was apparent to Kautz that the works to his front were held by only a small force. Turning to Spear, the general told him to form his brigade for attack.

---

37 *Ibid.*, 298, 300-301, 303-304, 305; Little, *The Seventh Regiment of the New Hampshire Volunteers,* 264, 266; Walkley, *History of the Seventh Connecticut Volunteer Infantry,* 145.

38 *OR* 36, pt. 3, 719.

39 *Ibid.*, 719-720.

Spear dismounted and deployed as skirmishers the 11th Pennsylvania's carbineers to the right of the Plank Road. One squadron of the 11th was sent to the extreme right and a second to the left, with orders to advance "in concert" with the dismounted skirmish line. The remainder of the 11th was posted in the center and right center, "with orders to charge mounted on the appearance of wavering or confusion among the enemy." Horse soldiers of the 5th Pennsylvania were posted west of the Jerusalem Plank Road, with instructions to storm Batteries No. 28 and 29. As the troopers were being formed, their right was shelled by a Confederate gun. To counter this fire, cannoneers of the 5th Pennsylvania unlimbered their mountain howitzers and hammered away at the lunette sheltering the Rebel cannon. Two squadrons of the 1st District of Columbia were dismounted and reinforced the carbineers on the skirmish line.[40]

A courier had reached General Colston's Battery No. 16 command post about noon with a note from General Wise, stating that the Yankees were advancing via the Jerusalem Plank Road and were threatening Major Archer's position. Reinforcements were known to be on the way, but it would be some time before they arrived. Colston determined to ride to the point of danger. As he mounted his horse, the general called for his aide, Lt. J. T. Tosh, whom he placed in charge of Battery No. 16, with orders "not to leave that position until relieved."

Colston galloped toward the Jerusalem Plank Road, and when halfway there he heard the rattle of small-arms. As he passed the area where two of Sturdivant's 12-pounder howitzers were parked, the general hailed the sergeant in charge and told him to bring one of his pieces to Battery No. 28. Colston did not wait for the artillerists but hurried on. As he approached Battery No. 27, he sighted Union cavalry advancing up the Plank Road. Reaching Batteries No. 27 and 28, Colston found that Major Archer "had disposed his small force very judiciously." A wagon had been overturned across the road, and together with a hastily built rail fence, formed a satisfactory barricade.

At the time of Colston's arrival, Archer's Reserves had just repulsed the initial charge by the advance squadron of the 11th Pennsylvania Cavalry. Several dead horses, some sabers and carbines, and a couple of prisoners were trophies of that limited success, and the men's spirits had soared. It was evident to Colston and Archer that the Federals were preparing another and more formidable attack. Their lines were visible in the edge of the woods behind Gregory's house, and the Confederates' slender ranks were extended to the right and left to present a front of equal length. The 12-pounder howitzer now came up, its arrival cheered by the

---

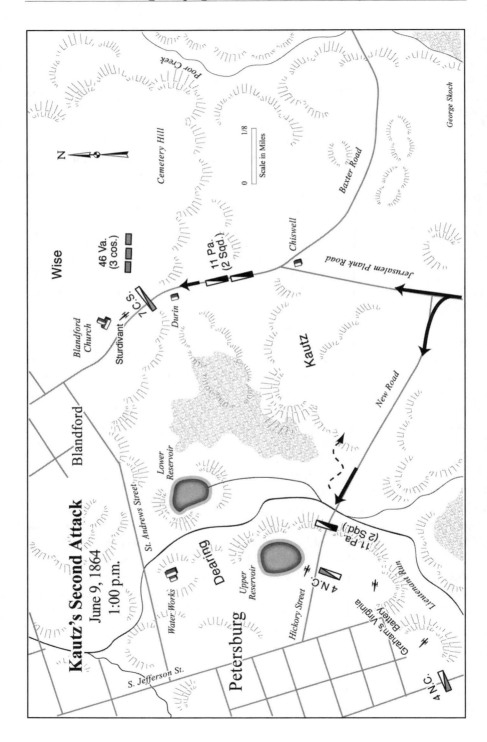

Kautz's Second Attack
June 9, 1864
1:00 p.m.

46 Va.
(3 cos.)

11 Pa.
(2 Sqd.)

Wise

Cemetery Hill

Poor Creek

Baxter Road

George Skoch

N

0   1/8
Scale in Miles

Chiswell

Jerusalem Plank Road

Kautz

New Road

Blandford
Church

Sturdivant

7 C.S.

Durin

Blandford

St. Andrews Street

Lower
Reservoir

Water Works

Dearing

Upper
Reservoir

Hickory Street

Petersburg

S. Jefferson St.

11 Pa.
(2 Sqd.)

4 N.C.

Graham's Virginia
Battery

Lieutenant Run

4 N.C.

Reserves. Colston placed the gun in Battery No. 28, taking his station at the same time in the rifle pits, which were not more than waist high.

The dismounted carbineers from the 11th Pennsylvania and the skirmishers of the 1st District of Columbia pressed forward, while a mounted line from the 5th Pennsylvania appeared behind Gregory's house. Colston called for the Reserves to hold their fire until the Yankees were "at close range, and this direction was well observed." The howitzer, however, bellowed, and the blue clad skirmishers retired, took cover, and blazed away. A number of Kautz's sharpshooters occupied Gregory's house and fired from the windows and garret, some shooting through openings made by knocking off shingles.

Colston told the sergeant of artillery to shell the house, but the distance was so short that the projectiles ripped through the building before exploding, and failed to set the structure on fire as the general had hoped. Seeing that the 5th Pennsylvania's line presented an inviting target, Colston shouted for the artillerists to shift target and give them canister. The general was shocked when the sergeant reported that there was no canister in the limber. Colston then ordered him to shell the mounted line, but too much elevation was used, and the projectiles overshot their mark and burst harmlessly beyond. Whereupon, Colston ordered the sergeant to "cut the fuse at the closest notch," and, pointing the piece very low, he had "the satisfaction of seeing the shell explode just in front of the 5th Pennsylvania and make a great gap in its ranks . . ."

All the while, the minies whistled uncomfortably thick and close. Holding their fire, the Confederates hugged the low breastworks. Union artillery now went into action, first the 12-pounder mountain howitzers of the 5th Pennsylvania and then Lt. Peter Morton's two 3-inch rifled guns, emplaced within 600 yards of Battery No. 28. Undaunted by this turn of events, brave civilians, with Major Archer at their head, volunteered to charge the guns. Colston knew that as soon as they left the cover of the trenches, the Virginia Reserves would be destroyed by the breech-loading carbines, so he shook his head. "Our only hope is in delay," he told the citizen-soldiers.

Colston called for a volunteer to find General Wise, and let him know that time was running out for Archer's Battalion. Eighteen-year-old Lt. Wales Hart of the Junior Reserves stepped forward. After receiving the message, Hart mounted Colston's horse and thundered off. Bullets kicked up dust around him and under his horse's hoofs.

Now the time the Confederates could hold the combat-ready Federals at bay was measured in minutes. But on these few minutes, Colston recalled, "hung the rescue or the capture" of Petersburg. If they were driven from Batteries No. 25-29 before reinforcements crossed the Appomattox, Kautz's horsemen would thunder into the city and burn the bridges. With Petersburg would be lost the railroads upon which General Lee was dependent for his supplies.

But the end was near. Covered by the fire of the artillery and the sharpshooters posted in Gregory's house, carbineers of the 11th Pennsylvania and skirmishers of the 1st District of Columbia worked their way to within 50 yards of the earthworks. Kautz's mounted line now moved forward—the 11th Pennsylvania east of the Plank Road and the 5th Pennsylvania to the west. The horsemen overlapped the Confederate position. General Colston called for the Reserves to fire. As they blazed away, a number fell dead or wounded. Before the survivors could reload, horsemen of the 11th Pennsylvania turned the Rebels left. Occupying Battery No. 26, which Archer had not had enough men to garrison, Union sharpshooters swept Battery No. 28's gorge with destructive volleys.

Troopers of the 5th Pennsylvania forged ahead. Seeing that obstructions made a mounted charge impossible, Lt. Col. Christopher Kleinz halted and dismounted his unit in a defiladed area. As soon as horse-holders had been detailed, Kleinz waved his men forward, and they secured ground close to the works. Immediately after the charge of the 11th Pennsylvania, Kleinz's troopers leapt to their feet and dashed forward. In a futile effort to beat back the blue clad wave, General Colston picked up and discharged several muskets dropped by "our fallen men." Now the Confederates were hemmed in on three sides, and "only a narrow path leading through an abrupt ravine offered a way of escape." As the cannoneers sought to limber up their howitzer, they were fired on by the 5th Pennsylvania—the horses were shot down in their traces, and two artillerists killed. The gun was captured. For as long as there were reunions, troopers of the 5th and 11th Pennsylvania and the 1st District of Columbia argued as to which unit reached the howitzer first. Some of the Reserves were killed or wounded with bayonet or carbine butts, and many captured.

After they had secured the area, Union officers reported finding the bodies of 30 dead Rebels sprawled in the dust and 40 prisoners. The shattered remnants of Archer's Battalion made their way down and across the ravine and retired to Reservoir Hill, where they halted and reformed. After driving the Rebels from the lunettes, Kautz called a halt to recall his dismounted troopers and to send to the rear Confederate wounded and prisoners. "Boots and Saddles" soon sounded, and the mounted column rode out, taking the Jerusalem Plank Road. Several files were thrown forward as skirmishers. Many Federals were confident that they had broken the back of Confederate resistance and would enter Petersburg without further opposition.

The time purchased by Archer's Battalion at a fearful price gave the cannoneers of the Petersburg Artillery, commanded by Capt. Edward Graham, time to drive the teams pulling their four guns across the Appomattox Bridge. A boy's school was in session on Sycamore Street above Fillmore. The teacher had just dismissed his pupils, and the boys came trooping out into the street in time to hear the rumbling of gun carriages up the street. It was the Petersburg Artillery, coming up at a gallop. Excited women and children got in the way, and Captain Graham was "so irritated when he came near to running over one of his own lady friends, who took her time in crossing Bollingbroke Street, that he cried out: 'Damn the women! Run over them if they don't get out of the way!'"[41]

Graham and his cannoneers drove their teams up Sycamore Street, and dropped trail on the military crest of Reservoir Hill, two cannon at Cameron's and the other two south of the reservoir. Hardly had the trails struck the ground before Kautz's vanguard—a squadron of the 11th Pennsylvania—having turned off the Plank Road and into New Road, descended the opposite slope into the hollow through which Lieutenant Run meanders. The Rebel cannoneers opened fire, as did their small supporting force of infantry. A storm of canister and shell swept the Union advance. Shocked Federals reined up their horses.

Colonel Spear, riding with the vanguard, found the bombardment severe and he shouted for his troopers "to wheel to the left about" and retired about 50 yards to the cover afforded by a deep cut. Morton's section of the 8th New York Battery had followed the 11th Pennsylvania. At the time that the Rebel artillery roared into action, the New Yorkers were driving their guns through a deep cut. When Spear's horse soldiers retreated, they passed over the battery at a gallop. Two of the horses on the lead piece were killed. While Morton attempted to cut them loose, one more was shot, and the remainder of the terrified animals became entangled in the traces. About ten minutes had elapsed since the Rebel artillerists had opened this phase of the engagement. Brigadier General James Dearing's cavalry brigade utilized this time to cross the Appomattox and reinforce the artillerists and militia.[42]

41 Colston, "Repelling the First Assault on Petersburg," 536-537; OR 36, pt. 2, 308, 310, 311-312, 315, 316, 317-318; OR 51, pt. 1, 127; Roper, Archibald, and Coles, History of the Eleventh Pennsylvania Volunteer Cavalry, 121. Drewry, "The Ninth of June, 1864," CV, 291. Besides the 12-pounder howitzer, and its caisson, a number of stand or arms fell into the Federals' hands. The small-arms were substandard so Kautz ordered them destroyed, along with 40 or 50 tents, some huts, and a large house in which there were some military stores and ammunition. In the grim fight, Archer lost more than one-third of his command—65 out of 150. According to the regimental historians of the 11th Pennsylvania, "Sergeant [Augustus S.] Malcolm of Company A was the first to reach the guns. Putting his hands on one of them, he exclaimed, 'They are ours!' and rushed on after the retreating enemy. On his return, he found a lieutenant astride one of the guns and loudly claiming their [capture]. He seemed to fear some one would deprive him of the honor of their capture, and it took some preemptory orders to overcome his excitement, and cause him to rejoin his battalion." Roper, Archibald, and Coles, History of the Eleventh Pennsylvania Volunteer Cavalry, 121.

42 Ibid., 537; Drewry, "The Ninth of June, 1864," CV, 292-293; OR 51, pt.1, 1271; 36, pt. 2, 308, 310, 317-318. Excluding the 7th Confederate which was picketing the Petersburg approaches, Dearing's brigade included the 62nd Georgia Cavalry, 4th and 6th North Carolina Cavalry, Barham's Virginia Cavalry battalion, and the Petersburg Virginia Light Artillery. OR 36, pt. 3, 893.

Dearing's brigade had returned to Petersburg in response to General Wise's 10:15 a.m. call for help. General Pierre G. T. Beauregard, Commander of the Department of North Carolina and Southern Virginia, was responsible for the defense of Petersburg. His command post was at Dunlop's, north of the Appomattox. Responding to Wise's report that the Federals were in front of the Petersburg defenses, Beauregard pulled two units out of the Howlett Line, Dearing's cavalry and the four-gun Petersburg Artillery. Relaying this news to Richmond, Beauregard (at 10:45 a.m.), warned, "Have sent . . . [Wise] all I can spare from the lines. Without the troops sent to General Lee, I will have to elect between abandoning lines on Bermuda Neck and those of Petersburg."[43]

Two hours later, Beauregard notified Richmond that according to the latest news from Petersburg, the Federals had "taken works on Jerusalem Plank Road and are advancing into town." No more reinforcements could be sent, he warned, without evacuating the Howlett Line, the fortifications that kept Butler's army corked up on Bermuda Hundred. Beauregard asked the War Department to let him know its "wishes."

General Dearing, who reached Petersburg at 2:30 p.m., telegraphed Beauregard that if the city were to be saved more men were needed immediately.[44] Beauregard had none to send unless the government authorized him to yield the Bermuda Hundred line. To add emphasis to the danger, Beauregard at 3:00 p.m. warned: "Delay in sending reinforcements will be fatal to that city [Petersburg] and to Richmond for its supplies."

Meanwhile, Colonel Spear had observed that, upon the arrival of Dearing's cavalry, the Confederates seemed to be bracing for a counterattack. Taking into consideration the fact that the rest of the division had not come up, Spear passed the word to retire. Before proceeding far, Spear met General Kautz. When asked by his general to explain why he was falling back, the brigade commander explained that the foe had been heavily reinforced by artillery and cavalry. Kautz, unable to hear any firing from the northeast, correctly deduced that Gillmore had retired. Satisfied that with the Rebels pouring reinforcements into Petersburg, it would be impossible for his command to carry out its mission, Kautz gave word to retreat.

Dearing's cavalry by this time had crossed Lieutenant Run and had closed to within 300 yards of the cut. To save his men, Morton ordered the gun with the disabled team to be spiked and abandoned. All the while the blue-coated artillerists were exposed to heavy fire from the Petersburg Artillery. As they retreated down the road, Morton and his men came upon their other 3-inch rifle—this piece had

43 *OR* 36, pt. 3, 884.

44 *Ibid.*, 885.

been disabled earlier in the day when its wheels had locked. The wheels were unlocked, but before the New Yorkers had gone very far both wheels dropped off. With the Confederates closing in, the Federals lifted the tube off the carriage and slung it under the limber and drove off, abandoning the broken stock and trail in Jackson's field.

As the bluecoats rode south down the Plank Road, covered by a strong rear guard from the 11th Pennsylvania, they came under fire from a section of Sturdivant's guns. The Confederates followed the Union rear guard for two miles. After crossing the Blackwater Swamp tributary, southeast of where Fort Davis was subsequently erected, Kautz called a halt. Before resuming the march back to his base, Kautz had a detachment of the 1st District of Columbia relieve the 11th Pennsylvania of responsibility for watching the division's rear.[45]

Kautz's column, bringing with it the captured howitzer and 42 prisoners, re-crossed the Appomattox at dark. Reporting to General Butler, Kautz told his general that his division had been compelled to retire from Petersburg after having carried the "outer and only line of entrenchments." Upon mustering and dismissing their men, the officers found that cavalry casualties in the day's fighting numbered 36: 4 killed, 26 wounded, and 6 missing.[46]

Butler was embarrassed by the failure to capture Petersburg, for which he held General Gillmore responsible. When Gillmore filed his "After Action Report" on the 10th, Butler, in a petulant and abusive mood, picked it apart. Whereupon, Gillmore asked that a court of inquiry be convened to investigate his conduct of the Petersburg expedition. Pending the convening of the court, Gillmore on June 14 was relieved by Butler as commander of the X Corps and directed to proceed to Fort Monroe.[47]

When General Grant learned of Butler's actions, he wrote Butler on the 17th. If Butler had "no objections to withdrawing [his] order relieving General Gillmore," Grant would relieve him at his own request. As matters stood, Grant believed it to be "a severe punishment to General Gillmore, even if a court of inquiry should hereafter acquit him."[48]

---

45 OR 36, pt. 2, 308-309, 312, 313, 314, 316; 51, pt. 1, 1271; Colston, "Repelling the First Assault on Petersburg," 537. While shelling the Confederates holding Battery No. 28, the gun carriage was disabled, the iron axle bands and under straps snapping. Before resuming the advance Morton had the crew lash and lock the wheels over the gun to keep them from dropping off.

46 *Ibid.,* pt. 2, 309; pt. 3, 720.

47 *Ibid.,* pt. 2, 274-282; Walkley, *History of the Seventh Connecticut Volunteer Infantry,* 146.

48 OR 36, pt. 2, 286-287.

General Pierre G. T. Beauregard
Library of Congress

Butler was agreeable, and Grant issued a special order, announcing that Gillmore had been relieved at his own request and was to proceed to Washington and report to Adjt. Gen. Lorenzo Thomas. The court of inquiry that was to be called to investigate Butler's charges against Gillmore never convened.[49]

General Beauregard on the evening of June 9 advised the War Department that for the moment the crisis had passed, with the Federals driven from Petersburg and his soldiers again in possession of the works. Nevertheless, the need for additional troops south of the Appomattox remained urgent, as the Federals could be expected to renew the attack at their first opportunity.[50]

Both Generals Wise and Colston praised the conduct of Archer and his battalion. Colston in his "After Action Report" observed that Archer's command "stood to the breast-works like veterans and did not fall back until ordered to do so, when they were surrounded on three sides . . . Knowing how important it was to hold the position to the last minute, and expecting reinforcements every moment, I delayed giving the order to retreat until it was evident that a minute or longer would have rendered inevitable the capture or death of every man in the breastworks." The salvation of the city of Petersburg is undoubtedly due in the first place to the brave militia of the City; for, had they retreated five or ten minutes sooner, the artillery, which was first to check the enemy's advance, instead of meeting them at the heights, on the south side of the city, would have been intercepted before they could cross the bridge, and the city would probably have remained in the enemy's hands.[51]

Editor's Conclusion

The failure of General Gillmore's assault against Petersburg cost the Federals 60 men and the Confederates 100. The attack had significance far beyond these minor losses because it alerted General Beauregard to Petersburg's vulnerability. Beauregard pressed hard for reinforcements from President Jefferson Davis, Davis' chief of staff Braxton Bragg, and the War Department in Richmond. On June 11, Bragg reluctantly agreed to release Archibald Gracie's Alabama brigade from the Department of Richmond. Beauregard shifted the balance of Henry Wise's Virginia brigade

---

49 *Ibid.*, 286; Walkley, *History of the Seventh Connecticut Volunteer Infantry*, 146.

50 *OR* 36, pt. 3, 885.

51 *OR* 36, pt. 2, 318.

from the Howlett Line on Bermuda Hundred to Petersburg and replaced the Virginians with the Gracie's Alabamians. In other words, if the Federals launched another assault, instead of facing only one of Wise's regiments, they would meet Wise's entire brigade of seasoned infantry.

Chapter 2

The Second Assault on Petersburg

June 15 – 18, 1864

Editor's Introduction

The failure of the heavy attacks at Cold Harbor left U. S. Grant and George Meade with few options. The Federal army had sidestepped all the way southeast to the Chickahominy River. The possibility of a stalemate loomed. Grant, however, decided on a bold plan, and one apparently General Lee was not expecting: instead of more attacks or moving back the way he had come, the Army of the Potomac would cross the wide James River and strike at Petersburg, a critical logistical center below Richmond. The capture of Petersburg and severing of its many railroads would make holding Richmond nearly impossible.

Union army engineers began work in earnest late on the afternoon of June 15 on what would be the longest pontoon bridge of the entire war (2,200 feet), and finished around midnight. The bridge spanned the deep James River from Windmill (Weyanoke) Point to Fort Powhatan on the far bank.

Most of the Federal infantry used boats to cross the James. The IX Corps, a division of the VI Corps, much of its artillery, and all the animals (nearly 60,000 horses and mules and nearly 3,000 beef cattle) and army supply wagons tramped or rolled across on floating bridge on June 15 and 16. By the early morning of June 17, about 100,000 men and 5,000 wagons and ambulances were on the distant bank. The conduct of the entire operation was remarkably smooth, and Lee did not know his determined enemy was no longer in his front. Much of the credit belongs to the faultless planning and execution by Gen. Andrew A. Humphreys, George Meade's Chief of Staff.

The strategic coup that was Grant's crossing of the James, however, began to unravel along the outskirts of Petersburg. The Army of the Potomac was still in the act of crossing the James when William F. Smith's XVIII Corps, followed by Winfield Hancock's II Corps, marched ahead to strike, and hopefully capture, the largely undefended city. The result was not what Grant or Meade had in mind.

Part I

General Smith Prepares to Strike

Early on June 12, 1864, the commander of the XVIII Army Corps, Maj. Gen. William F. Smith, received an important message from Lt. Gen. Ulysses S. Grant's headquarters. General Smith, who was known throughout the Old Army as Baldy, was to march his corps to White House. There he would embark his troops and rejoin the Army of the James at Bermuda Hundred. The XVIII Corps at this time was under temporary assignment to the Army of the Potomac and was posted in the rifle pits at Cold Harbor, Virginia.[1]

"No intimation" was given Smith that on arriving at Bermuda Hundred his troops were to be given a most important assignment—the assault on the fortifications guarding the eastern approaches to Petersburg.[2]

Before contacting his division commanders, Smith addressed a short note to Maj. Gen. George G. Meade, the officer in charge of the Army of the Potomac. Smith wanted to know if Meade had any objection to his "relieving such [of his troops] as may be moved without attracting the attention of the enemy, and sending them to the White House today?"[3] Meade's headquarters replied at 8:15 a.m., granting Smith's request.[4] Measures were promptly instituted by Smith for withdrawing his troops from the rifle pits in proximity to the line of fortifications held by the hard-bitten soldiers of Gen. Robert E. Lee's Army of Northern Virginia. Orders were given for Chief of Artillery Samuel S. Elder to withdraw his batteries, as the second line moved up to relieve the first in the entrenchments. The batteries were to be started for Tunstall's Station, where they would join the corps train. Accompanied by the train, the batteries were to march to the James River. Upon reaching the James, Captain Elder would await further orders from Smith, unless he was contacted by higher authority.[5]

---

1   William F. Smith, "The Movement Against Petersburg June, 1864," in *Papers of the Military Historical Society of Massachusetts*, 15 vols., (Boston, 1906), vol. 5, 79. Two divisions of the XVIII Corps and one division of the I Corps had accompanied Smith to the north side of the James River.

2   *Ibid.*, 79-80.

3   OR 36, pt. 3, 766.

4   *Ibid.*, 766.

5   *Ibid.*, 767.

Major General William F. Smith
Library of Congress

Since the lines of the XVIII Corps were nearer to those held by the Confederates than those of the other corps at Cold Harbor, the task of pulling back the troops could be quite delicate. The brigades not on duty in the front lines were started for White House by noon. As soon as it was dark, the brigades occupying the forward rifle pits were recalled. After the units had packed their gear and were mustered, they marched to an assembly area and started for the landing. The only soldiers now holding the sector formerly defended by the XVIII Corps were the men manning the outposts. Colonel Guy V. Henry, a brigade commander in the First Division, as corps officer of the day, was charged with collecting and bringing off the pickets. Henry's orders were explicit: He was "to hold the lines or delay the enemy, if they advanced, as long as possible and at daybreak to move to the rear."[6]

By daybreak on June 13, all of Smith's XVIII Corps, except Colonel Henry and the rear guard, had reached White House. While en route to the landing, the soldiers of the XVIII Corps encountered large numbers of men from the Army of the Potomac. Writing his wife from on board the steamer *Metamora*, General Smith complained:

> I am once more away from the Army of the Potomac, and Meade is, I suppose, as glad
> as I am. I once more go to Butler under the old system, and that is very unpleasant, but
> there is always an air of brains about Butler.... Such nights I marched all night, and
> found that with all its renown the Army of the Potomac is a straggling, disorderly set,
> compared to the 18th Corps, to which I never yet have had time to do justice in the
> matter of discipline. The trains and the men of the 2nd, 9th, and 6th Corps were all

---

6   OR 51, pt. 1, 1262, 1265; Smith, "The Movement Against Petersburg, June 1864," 105, 106.

over my road and in my way . . . I am trying to make up today, by sleeping, for a terrible night of headache and unrest.[7]

Colonel Henry (at 2:00 a.m.) on the 13th quietly withdrew his pickets and skirmishers. As soon as Henry and his aides could form the men, the march for White House was started. Henry's adjutant recalled, "We moved at a very rapid rate, so as to get a good start of the Rebs in case of pursuit . . . On reaching the White House we sent away those of our rear guard who did not belong to our brigade and then put our own five regiments on transports as rapidly as possible."[8] The troops "gratefully embraced the opportunity for a few hours rest after their late exhausting labors."[9]

Soon after his arrival at White House, Smith was handed a telegram signed by Grant's chief of staff, Brig. Gen. John A. Rawlins. Rawlins wanted Smith to forward his "troops to Bermuda Hundred as fast as they embark without waiting for divisions, the object being to get to Bermuda Hundred at the earliest possible moment."[10]

This seems to have been the first notice received by Baldy Smith that there was any degree of urgency to his movement to the James. The first units of the XVIII Corps to embark belonged to Brig. Gen. William T. H. Brooks' First Division. After boarding the *Metamora*, which would accompany the convoy carrying Brooks' troops, General Smith drafted an order placing Brig. Gen. Adelbert Ames in charge of the troops remaining at White House. Ames was to remain at the landing until the entire corps had been shipped, or until he had made the necessary arrangements for its embarkation.[11]

It was mid-afternoon before the quartermaster people notified Brig. Gen. John H. Martindale that the transports on which he was to embark his Second Division were ready. By 4:00 p.m. all of Martindale's troops had boarded, and a second convoy cast off and started down the Pamunkey River.[12] The next vessels to reach the landing were used by Ames' division. It was daybreak on June 14 before the last

7   Smith, "The Movement Against Petersburg June, 1864," 108.

8   *Ibid.*, 107. The regiments constituting Colonel Henry's brigade were the 21st Connecticut, the 40th Massachusetts, the 92nd New York, and the 58th and 188th Pennsylvania. OR 40, pt. 1, 235.

9   OR 40, pt. 1, 717.

10   OR 40, pt. 2, 17.

11   *Ibid.*, 17.

12   OR 51, pt. 1, 1255, 1262, 1265.

ship with personnel from the reinforced XVIII Corps aboard had pulled away from White House landing.

The convoys with the troops of the XVIII Corps aboard passed from the Pamunkey into the York. Rounding the Peninsula, the vessels steamed by Fort Monroe and started up the James River. As the *Metamora* approached Fort Powhatan, General Smith and his aides saw that the leading elements of the II Corps of the Army of the Potomac were already crossing to the south side.[13]

It was late on the afternoon of June 14 when the *Metamora* tied up at Bermuda Hundred. After going ashore, General Smith, at sunset, reported to his immediate superior, Maj. Gen. Benjamin F. Butler, the commander of the Army of the James. Butler told Baldy Smith that he was "to move at daylight on Petersburg." To carry out this undertaking, Smith's corps would be reinforced by the cavalry division led by Brig. Gen. August V. Kautz and the division of Negro troops under Brig. Gen. Edward W. Hinks. Since no plan had been formulated by Butler's people for the projected operation, Smith at once called for all the maps of the area. After studying the maps and intelligence reports, Smith began issuing "orders for the movement, so that the various commands should not impede each other, and should be properly concentrated at the point" he had designated.

General Butler told Smith of Kautz's June 9 attack on Petersburg. Kautz's troopers at that time had encountered no trouble in riding over the works. Kautz, when questioned by Smith, agreed with Butler that the Petersburg fortifications were not particularly formidable. From the information gleaned at Butler's headquarters and from refugees, Smith was led to believe that his columns as they closed in on Petersburg from the northeast wouldn't encounter any defenses until they reached the main line of works near Jordan's Hill.

Smith then asked Butler for information regarding the troops which the Confederates had available to oppose his thrust. Butler replied that "there was no force of any consequence at Petersburg."[14]

According to the plan of attack mapped out by Baldy Smith, Kautz's cavalry was to begin crossing the Appomattox River at 1:00 a.m., to be followed by such troops of Brooks' and Martindale's divisions as had arrived at Bermuda Hundred from White House. Kautz's horsemen were "to proceed with as little delay as possible to threaten the line of fortifications near the Norfolk & Petersburg Railroad and at the same time protect the left flank of the infantry." General Hinks' division was to march from Spring Hill in rear of Kautz's cavalry, taking post across the Jordan's Point Road as near as possible to the Confederates' works. General

---

13 Smith, "The Movement Against Petersburg June, 1864," 80.

14 *Ibid.*, 80-81.

Brooks' division was to follow Hinks and form line of battle on his right, while Martindale was to march on the River Road to a point near the Petersburg & City Point Railroad and await orders.[15]

After maturing his plans, General Smith determined that it would facilitate matters, if the transports with Brooks' and Martindale's divisions aboard were diverted from Bermuda Hundred to Point of Rocks. Instructions to this effect were communicated to the officer in charge of the Bermuda Hundred docking area. Before this order arrived, the transports with the officers and men belonging to Col. Griffin A. Stedman's brigade of Martindale's division had gone ashore at Bermuda Hundred. Marching to a spot near General Butler's headquarters, the brigade camped.[16] When the convoy with Martindale's other brigade, Brig. Gen. George J. Stannard's, appeared off Bermuda Hundred, the quartermaster succeeded in diverting it to Point of Rocks. All of Stannard's men and gear were ashore and in camp by 9:00 p.m.[17]

The steamboats with General Brooks' division landed most of the troops at Point of Rocks,[18] while those ferrying General Ames' division tied up at Bermuda Hundred.[19] With transports arriving and disembarking units of the XVIII Corps throughout the night of June 14, it was impossible for Smith and his staff to know with certainty just what troops they would be able to employ in the drive toward Petersburg.[20]

General Kautz's troopers spent the late afternoon and evening of the 14th getting their gear squared away, so they would be prepared to take the field at a moment's notice. Each man in the division was issued three days' rations, which he and the members of his mess cooked. All men not having 60 rounds of ammunition were sent to the ordnance tents to draw the stipulated ammunition.[21]

During the day General Hinks received an important dispatch signed by Butler. Hinks carefully read the order:

15 *Ibid.*, 81.

16 OR 40, pt. 2, 43; OR 51, pt. 1, 1263. The transports which landed troops of the XVIII Corps at Bermuda Hundred were: the *Nellie Pentz, Eagle No. 2, Claymont, Webster,* and *Albany.*

17 OR 51, pt. 1, 1262. The vessel with the 2nd Pennsylvania Heavy Artillery and the 9th New Jersey Infantry aboard was delayed in her run up the James. These two regiments didn't rejoin Martindale's division until late on the 15th. *Ibid.*, 1255-1256.

18 OR 40, pt. 1, 715, 717.

19 OR 51, pt. 1, 1246-1247.

20 Smith, "The Movement Against Petersburg June, 1864," 81.

21 OR 40, pt. 2, 46.

Brigadier General John H. Martindale (seated) and his staff.
Library of Congress

You will report with your force in such position that you will be ready to move with General Smith just before daybreak. You will report personally to him at Broadway at 2 a.m. precisely. I think he will not keep you waiting; and General Smith will march on the City Point Road.[22]

At this stage of the conflict, one of Hinks' brigades, Col. John H. Holman's, was camped at City Point, while the other, Col. Samuel A. Duncan's, was posted near Point of Rocks. To insure that Hinks' troops would be ready to march at the designated hour, General Butler on the afternoon of June 14 ordered Duncan's brigade to break camp, cross the Appomattox, and report to General Hinks. Duncan had his troops formed and on the road within a short time. It was starting to get dark as the long column marched from its camp and started for the pontoon bridge crossing the Appomattox at Broadway. By 11:00 p.m. all of Duncan's infantrymen had reached the right bank of the Appomattox and, in accordance with instructions from Hinks, bivouacked.[23] Since Holman's soldiers were already on the south side of the Appomattox, Hinks saw no need to bring them closer to the marshaling area.[24]

22 *Ibid.*, 43-44.

23 *Ibid.*, 45; OR, 51, pt. 1, 265.

24 OR 51, pt. 1, 263-264.

*   *   *

Confederate General Pierre G. T. Beauregard, as commander of the Department of North Carolina and Southern Virginia, was responsible for the defense of Petersburg. Prior to the battle of Cold Harbor, one of Beauregard's divisions, Maj. Gen. Robert F. Hoke's, had been rushed to the assistance of General Lee's Army of Northern Virginia. This left Beauregard with a greatly reduced force with which to resist Smith's attack.

General Beauregard (who established his headquarters at Dunlap's house on Swift Creek, about half way between Howlett's on the James and Petersburg) had placed Brig. Gen. Henry A. Wise in charge or the Petersburg defenses. To carry out his mission Wise had his own brigade and some light artillery, with 22 pieces, besides a few men manning the three or four heavy guns in position. He also had Brig. Gen. James Dearing's cavalry brigade and the local militia. All told, Wise's command numbered about 2,200 effectives.[25]

Until June 11 the Virginia regiments of Wise's brigade had been posted in the lines across Bermuda Hundred Neck. About 11:00 a.m. that day, the Virginians had been relieved by the soldiers of Brig. Gen. Archibald Gracie's Alabama brigade and had been marched into Petersburg, where the senior regimental commander, Col. P. R. Page, reported to General Wise. Page was told to have his men take charge of the batteries along the Petersburg perimeter. The soldiers of the 26th Virginia were assigned to garrison Batteries No. 3, 4, 7, and 8.[26]

Wise's infantry and artillery held the earthworks covering the approaches to Petersburg from the east. These works began near the Appomattox River at Battery No. 1, and passing over level ground ran a little south of east to the Petersburg & City Point Railroad. Turning sharply, the rifle pits mounted the high ground and ran south along a series of crests for about a mile and one-half from Battery No. 5 to Battery No. 12. After crossing Jerusalem Plank Road, the Petersburg fortifications

---

25 Alfred Roman, *The Military Operations of General Beauregard in the War Between the States 1861 to 1865*, 2 vols. (New York, 1883), vol. 2, 229; G. T. Beauregard, "Four Days of Battle at Petersburg," in *Battles and Leaders of the Civil War*, vol. 4, 540; G. T Beauregard, "Letter of General Beauregard to General C. M. Wilcox," in *Papers of the Military Historical Society of Massachusetts*, vol. 5, 119. Wise's brigade consisted of the 26th, 34th, 46th, and 59th Virginia Infantry regiments. Dearing's brigade included the 7th Confederate Cavalry, 4th and 6th North Carolina Cavalry, 8th Georgia Cavalry, and the Petersburg Virginia Cavalry. Non-brigaded troops attached to Wise's command were: Major F. H. Archer's Petersburg Militia, Company F; 24th South Carolina Infantry, Major W. H. Wood's; 3rd Battalion Virginia Reserves; the 44th Virginia Infantry Battalion; Sturdivant's and Young's Virginia Batteries.

26 William Russell, Diary (typescript), n.d., Petersburg National Battlefield. On Tuesday, June 14, Company H, 26th Virginia was shifted from Battery No. 7 to Battery No. 2.

turned sharply to the west. One-half mile beyond the Petersburg & Weldon Railroad, the line veered to the right and abutted on the Appomattox River west of Petersburg.

Because of insufficient manpower, Wise could only guard a portion of the Petersburg perimeter which was laid out to accommodate a garrison of 25,000 men. At the time of Baldy Smith's advance, the only section of the Petersburg line occupied by Wise's troops was the portion between Battery No. 1 and the Butterworth Bridge across Jerusalem Plank Road—about three miles in all. Even so, manpower was so short that there was but one man for every four and one-half yards of earthworks. The remainder of the Petersburg perimeter, seven and one-half miles in length from the Jerusalem Plank Road to the Appomattox west of the city, was undefended.[27]

General Wise on June 15 still had part of his force deployed north of the Appomattox. At the same time, the fortifications across Bermuda Hundred Neck were defended by Maj. Gen. Bushrod Johnson's division of Beauregard's command. Johnson and his troops were charged with the mission of keeping Butler's Army of the James hemmed up in the area between the James and Appomattox rivers.

General Beauregard's scouts had spotted the Union forces soon after they had abandoned the Cold Harbor lines and started for the James. At 7:00 a.m. on June 14, Beauregard telegraphed Gen. Braxton Bragg (who was serving as military adviser to President Jefferson Davis) that the movement of the Army of the Potomac across the Chickahominy and the increase of Butler's force had rendered his position critical. Unless reinforced he could not answer for the consequences. "Cannot my troops [Hoke's division and Ransom's brigades] sent to General Lee be returned at once," Beauregard inquired?[28]

Several hours later Beauregard, bypassing Bragg, wired Lee:

"Petersburg cannot be reinforced from my small force [Johnson's division] in lines of Bermuda Hundred Neck without abandoning entirely that position. Reinforcements should first reach there before detaching these troops, which possessing local knowledge, should be preferably retained where they are. Should you not have a pontoon bridge below Chaffin's Bluff?"[29]

27 Roman, *Military Operations of General Beauregard*, vol. 2, 229; Beauregard, "Four Days of Battle at Petersburg," *Battles and Leaders*, vol. 4, 540; Thomas L. Livermore, "The Failure to Take Petersburg, June 15, 1864," in *Papers of the Military Historical Society of Massachusetts*, vol. 5, 52.

28 *OR* 40, pt. 2, 652.

29 *Ibid.*, 653.

In response to Beauregard's urgent pleas for assistance, General Lee issued instructions for General Hoke to move his 6,000 man division to a point on the east side of the James River above Drewry's Bluff. Hoke, on reaching the James, would be prepared to execute any orders which President Jefferson Davis might see fit to send him.[30]

Hoke lost no time in putting his troops into motion. Crossing the Chickahominy and White Oak Swamp, Hoke's columns headed for the James. As soon as the last of his troops had marched out of the Cold Harbor lines, Hoke tersely wired Beauregard, "My troops are on the march. Will camp half a mile from Drewry's Bluff, on the river road."[31]

Beauregard, during the afternoon of the 14th, was handed an interesting report signed by Lt. Joseph R. Woodley of the Signal Corps. The lieutenant, who was stationed on the lower James at Fort Boykin, had been watching as the transports with the soldiers of the XVIII Corps aboard had passed. Woodley had telegraphed Beauregard that "four large ocean steamers and seven large river steamers" crowded with troops had chugged by his station at 6:00 a.m. On the previous day, the lieutenant had watched as several vessels with large pontoons had ascended the river. No time was lost by Beauregard in forwarding this vital intelligence to General Bragg.

Shortly before dark a Union deserter was being questioned by Beauregard's officers. Replying to the Confederates' questions, the soldier said that Butler's army on Bermuda Hundred had been reinforced by units from the X and XVIII Corps. Beauregard (at 8:10 p.m.) forwarded this interesting information to Lee's headquarters.

Before leaving his office at the War Department for the night, General Bragg telegraphed Beauregard. A forced reconnaissance by Lee, Bragg observed, demonstrated that the Union army had abandoned its depot at White House on the Pamunkey and had moved south to the James River and was probably near Harrison's Landing, where Maj. Gen. George B. McClellan had established his army in the summer of 1862 following the Seven Days' Battles and the defensive victory at Malvern Hill. At the moment, Lee's army was posted with its left resting on White Oak Swamp and its right on Malvern Hill. Bragg noted that Lee had sent Hoke's division "to Drewry's Bluff, with a view to reinforce you in case Petersburg is threatened."[32]

---

30 Douglas S. Freeman, *R. E. Lee: A Biography*, 4 vols. (New York, 1934-1935), vol. 3, 405-406.

31 *OR* 40, pt. 2, 654.

32 *Ibid.*, 653.

Part II

Baldy Smith Scores a
Breakthrough and Then Hesitates

Valuable time was lost by the Federals early on June 15 in getting Kautz's cavalry division across the Appomattox River pontoon bridge at Point of Rocks. Four hours had passed, and it was starting to get light before the last of the troopers reined up their horses on the south side of the Appomattox. Kautz's 2nd Brigade, Col. Samuel F. Spear commanding, had crossed the river first. While waiting for Col. Simon H. Mix's 1st Brigade to reach the right bank, Spear's horsemen had pushed inland about three miles toward the City Point Road. As soon as all his men were across the Appomattox, Kautz sent word for Spear to resume the advance. Colonel Spear, in putting his column into motion, told the 11th Pennsylvania Cavalry to take the lead. Lieutenant Colonel George Stetzel of the Pennsylvania Regiment detailed an advance guard of 12 men.

At 6:00 a.m. Spear's vanguard approached the Petersburg & City Point Railroad and encountered a Confederate outpost. The Yanks charged the Rebels, driving them back into a line of entrenchments. In this little clash near Perkinson's Sawmill, the first in the battle for Petersburg, the Federals captured four butternuts and wounded several, at a cost of one corporal wounded and two privates captured.

Hurrying to the point of danger, Colonel Spear called up and deployed as skirmishers to the right and left of the City Point Road the 1st District of Columbia Cavalry. The horsemen closed to within 800 yards of the Rebel fortifications, a long line of rifle pits. Here, the Federals were fired on by two pieces of artillery which commanded the City Point Road, where it debouched from the woods. These guns were manned by the cannoneers of the Petersburg Virginia Artillery. Spear halted his troopers and told them to hold their ground.[33]

The cannoneers of the 4th Battery, Wisconsin Light Artillery unlimbered their two guns near the head of a ravine occupied by Spear's troopers. Since they were unable to see the Confederate field pieces because of the woods, the Union gunners were told that the range was about 1,800 yards. Giving their elevating screws the

---

33 OR 40, pt. 1, 729, 739; OR, 51, pt. 2, 1270. Kautz's division was organized into two brigades; Colonel Spear's brigade consisted of: the 11th Pennsylvania and the 1st District of Columbia Cavalry regiments. Mix's brigade included: the 1st New York Mounted Rifles, the 5th Pennsylvania, and the 3rd New York Cavalry regiments. A section of guns manned by the 4th Battery, Wisconsin Light Artillery reported directly to General Kautz. OR 40, pt. 1, 728-729.

desired number of turns, the gun captains pointed their pieces and opened fire. After letting off 14 rounds, the bluecoats were compelled to limber up their pieces and retire. Already, the Virginians of the Petersburg Artillery had found the range; one of the Union cannoneers had been injured by shrapnel from an exploding shell.[34]

General Smith had been notified immediately that Kautz's cavalry had found and engaged the foe. Turning to General Hinks, and pointing toward the sound of the guns, Smith told him to march his division through the woods and attack the Confederates. Smith then sent one of his staff officers racing ahead with orders for Kautz to recall his horsemen and move to the left. In making this decision, Baldy Smith evinced a determination to reach the Rebels' main line of works guarding the approaches to Petersburg as quickly as possible. Although his resolution to attack at this point was to cost several hundred men, which might have been avoided by a reconnaissance and a flank attack that the grey clads would have been unable to withstand, yet it saved time, which was at the moment more important than the sacrifice of men.[35]

Kautz, upon the receipt of the communication from General Smith, sent a courier to get in touch with Colonel Spear. Glancing at the scrap of paper handed him by the messenger, Spear found that he was to recall his men. A detachment of carbineers was left to hold the City Point Road, pending the arrival of Hinks' infantry. As the horsemen pulled back, they were shelled by the Confederate artillerists. The iron shells from the Virginians' rifled pieces hissed through the hot air and exploded with great precision among the unfortunate troopers of the 11th Pennsylvania.[36]

The Confederates who contested Kautz's cavalry advance at Perkinson's Sawmill belonged to Brig. Gen. James Dearing's cavalry brigade, and were supported by the Petersburg Virginia Artillery. Dearing, at 7:35 a.m., warned General Wise that he was confronted by Union troopers, and that his scouts had sighted a large force of bluecoats moving toward his position via the Broadway Road. The two Northerners captured by his men in the brisk skirmishing had told Dearing that he was confronted by Winfield Hancock's II Corps.

Before relaying this news to General Beauregard, Wise took personal command of the center sector of the Petersburg perimeter, from Battery No. 14 to Battery No. 23; Brig. Gen. Raleigh E. Colston was placed in charge of the right,

34 OR 40, pt. 1, 743.

35 Livermore, "The Failure to take Petersburg, June 15, 1864," 50.

36 OR 40, pt. 1, 729, 738; OR 51, pt. 1, 1270.

from Batteries No. 23 to Butterworth's Bridge; Colonel Page would command on the left from the Appomattox to Battery No. 14.[37]

Meanwhile (at 7:00 a.m.) Beauregard wired General Bragg. Answering Bragg's message of the previous evening, Beauregard pointed out that the return of the XVIII Corps and the advance of the Army of the Potomac to Harrison's Landing had made his disposition "more critical than ever." If he was not immediately reinforced, Beauregard warned, the Federals would do one of two things: they could force his lines at Bermuda Hundred Neck, capture Battery Dantzler, which was almost completed, or they could take Petersburg before the troops from Lee's army or those at Drewry's Bluff could intervene.

Beauregard, two hours later, forwarded to General Bragg a copy of Dearing's 7:35 a.m. dispatch to Wise.

At 9:30 a.m. Beauregard dashed off two more telegrams to General Bragg. According to the latest news from General Dearing, his force at Perkinson's Sawmill had been assailed by eight Union regiments—four infantry and the rest cavalry. Prisoners had told Dearing that it was "on to Petersburg." The roar of the cannons and the rattle of the small-arms from the fighting at Perkinson's were audible to the Confederates at Fort Clifton.[38]

In view of these developments, Beauregard notified Bragg he had ordered Hoke's division from Drewry's Bluff to Petersburg. Hoke was to leave one brigade at Port Walthall Junction, until it could be relieved by another. Beauregard wanted Bragg to order Ransom's Brigade, which had been sent to the Army of Northern Virginia, to do so.[39]

*   *   *

Kautz, after regrouping his division, turned his column into a plantation road which soon brought his troopers out on the Jordan's Point Road. Here, Kautz's vanguard (troopers of the 3rd New York) was fired into from ambush. Dismounting, the regimental carbineers charged and routed the Confederates from their roadblock. The grey clads fled, leaving the body of a young lieutenant sprawled in the dust. Pressing on, the bluecoats crossed the Prince George Courthouse Road and gained the Norfolk & Petersburg Railroad without difficulty. The column now swung into a road leading northwest. A squadron of the 11th

---

37 Roman, *Military Operations of General Beauregard*, vol. 2, 567.

38 *OR* 40, pt. 1, 655.

39 *Ibid.*, 665. Ransom's brigade of Johnson's division had been ordered to join the Army of Northern Virginia on June 3.

Pennsylvania, which had advanced, met a 50-man Confederate patrol. The Yankees charged and compelled the Rebels to fall back. The bluecoats forged ahead until they came within range of the field pieces emplaced in the Petersburg earthworks. Thereupon, Colonel Spear halted his brigade while awaiting additional instructions from General Kautz. It was almost noon when Kautz caught sight of the frowning Rebel fortifications.[40]

The cannoneers of the 4th Wisconsin Battery unlimbered one of their guns on the Jordan's Point Road. Although they couldn't see the Confederate strong points, which were about 1,600 yards to their front, the Yanks engaged the Rebel guns, which were registered on the road, in a sharp duel. Within a few minutes, Capt. George B. Easterly's gunners had emplaced their second piece about 200 yards farther to the front, and in the verge of a belt of timber facing and commanded by the Confederates' works. A slow, deliberate fire was maintained by the Union artillerists.[41]

Several hours were spent by Kautz in reconnoitering the Rebels' fortifications and bringing up all his men. Two or three miles of the Petersburg perimeter could be seen; the ground in front of the entrenchments was "comparatively level" and afforded little cover for the attacker. As soon as the Federals appeared to their front, the butternut cannoneers had opened with the pieces emplaced in five of their redoubts. Subsequently, the bluecoats were able to pinpoint two more redoubts to their extreme right. From all that he could see, it was apparent to Kautz that the works weren't strongly manned by infantry. Kautz accordingly determined "to make a demonstration, and if possible, to get through the line."

At 3:00 p.m. orders were issued for the brigade commanders to dismount and advance their carbineers. Colonel Mix's 1st Brigade was deployed to the right of the Baxter Road, Spear's 2nd Brigade to the left. One regiment, the 1st New York Mounted Rifles, would be held in reserve.[42]

To cover his troopers, General Kautz had Captain Easterly shift his two guns. A general advance was ordered. Manhandling their pieces forward, the gunners emplaced them at the edge of a field. Here, they came under a heavy shelling from the Rebel guns. As soon as the trails struck the ground, the Yanks began to hammer away at the Confederate earthworks with shot and shell.[43] Covered by this bombardment, Kautz's skirmishers drove forward. The ground over which the carbineers advanced was difficult, being covered with briars and vines.

40 OR 40, pt. 1, 729, 736, 738.

41 *Ibid.*, 743.

42 *Ibid.*, 729.

43 *Ibid.*, 743.

Nevertheless, the cheering skirmishers were able to press to within 500 yards of the Rebel entrenchments. The terrain yet to be crossed was level and cleared of underbrush. To the right of the Baxter Road, Mix's skirmishers charged the Confederate works. Their advance was quickly checked when grey clad riflemen in the trenches north of the road, which had heretofore been masked from the Yanks' view, were able to catch Mix's skirmishers in a deadly enfilade. Repulsed, the bluecoats retired into the edge of the "chaparral," from where they maintained a long-range fire at the Confederates.[44]

About the same time, one of the 4th Wisconsin's guns was disabled by a shell jamming in the bore. The gun was sent to the rear. As soon as it was cleared, the piece was put back into action.[45]

Since only a portion of his troopers were armed with carbines, and so many men had to be detailed as horse-holders, Kautz now calculated that the Rebels probably had more men in the rifle pits than he had in his battle line. Kautz therefore decided not to renew the attack. Spear's and Mix's battle lines by this time had closed to within 1,500 yards of the Petersburg perimeter. Spotting the Union battle line, the Rebel cannoneers switched targets. Shells were soon bursting among the trees, filling the air with deadly fragments.[46]

The Federals held their ground until 5:30 p.m. All the while, General Kautz anxiously waited "to see some indications that General Smith had carried the enemy's line" on his right. Several hours had now passed without any firing in that direction. Now Kautz's brigade commanders approached and warned him that their skirmishers were running short of ammunition. Already, Mix's skirmishers on the right had started to withdraw. Because of this situation, Kautz sent a staff officer to direct Colonel Spear on the left to recall his carbineers. When Spear joined the General, he reported that his men could not have held their position much longer.[47]

As soon as the officers had assembled their units, the division retired to the Jordan's Point Road and bivouacked. It had been a fatiguing day for Kautz's division, especially as the men and animals had had no rest on the night of the 14th. On checking their rolls, the Federal officers found that their losses had been small, "as the enemy's artillery was very badly served." If the 12 guns mounted in his works to his front had been manned by skilled artillerists, Kautz felt certain that his men would never have been able to make the advance they had. Among the Union

44 *OR* 51, pt. 1, 1268-1269.

45 *OR* 40, pt. 1, 743.

46 *Ibid.*, 729, 738.

47 *Ibid.*, 729.

casualties was Colonel Mix who had been mortally wounded and left in front of the Confederates' works north of the Baxter Road.[48]

*   *   *

General Hinks (at 2:00 a.m.), in accordance with a directive from General Butler, reported to Baldy Smith at Broadway. Smith told Hinks to concentrate his division near the Cope house, a mile southeast of Broadway, on the City Point-Petersburg Road. Hinks was to have his men at Cope's and be ready to push for Petersburg at daylight. According to Smith's master plan, Hinks' division was to follow Kautz's cavalry.

In accordance with Hinks' instructions, Holman's brigade marched out of its City Point encampment at 2:00 a.m. Since he didn't have as far to go to reach the rendezvous, Duncan put his troops into motion one hour later. Duncan's soldiers found the road from Broadway to Cope's somewhat obstructed by units from the XVIII Corps.[49]

As directed, Hinks' division was massed alongside the City Point-Petersburg Road at the time scheduled. It was starting to get light before Kautz's cavalry came jogging down the road from Point of Rocks. By 5:00 a.m. the last of the troopers had passed. At a word from Hinks, the brigade commanders put their units in motion.

As the head of the column approached the Petersburg & City Point Railroad, the soldiers found the road blocked by Kautz's cavalry. Hinks, who was riding with the vanguard, heard the roar of cannon and the rattle of musketry to the front. It was apparent to the infantry officers that Kautz's horsemen had found the foe. After telling his brigade commanders to have their men stand at ease, the general and his staff made a personal reconnaissance. Hinks ascertained that the Rebel force (Dearing's cavalry), which was delaying Kautz's advance, had opened fire from several field pieces unlimbered in Baylor's field. These guns commanded the road as it debouched from the woods and swamp near Cabin Creek. Sensing that

---

48 *Ibid.*, 729, 736, 738-739; OR, 51, pt. 1, 1269. According to Colonel West, who succeeded Mix as commander of the 1st Brigade, "The works of the enemy demonstrated upon were a line of square redoubts, connected by covered ways, which later also served as rifle pits. The force defending them was not large, but sufficient, I think, to have held them against any effort we could have made with our available force." OR 51, pt. 1, 269.

49 OR 40, pt. 1, 720, 721; 51, pt. 1, 263-264, 265. Duncan's brigade consisted of: the 4th, 5th, 6th, and 22nd regiments of U.S. Colored Infantry. Holman's provisional brigade included the 1st U.S. Colored Infantry, two companies of the 4th Massachusetts Cavalry, a battalion of the 5th Massachusetts Cavalry (dismounted), and Battery B, 2nd U.S. Colored Infantry.

the blue clad horsemen would be unable to smash the Rebel roadblock, Hinks retraced his steps and told General Smith what he had seen.

The Confederates, he reported, had selected their ground wisely. It was on the crest of a ridge about 300 yards west of the woods. The woods were about 600 yards in depth and were "traversed by a turnpike and railroad in directions diagonal" to the direction from which the Federals would have to mount their attack. In places the road and railroad passed through deep cuts which would constitute a serious obstacle to the advancing Yankee battle lines. Dearing had posted his dismounted troopers and the Petersburg Light Artillery behind a line of hastily constructed earthworks which crossed the City Point-Petersburg Road at right angles. Hinks was satisfied that the Rebels occupation of this position constituted a serious obstacle to farther progress by the Union columns.[50]

Smith, after listening to Hinks, determined to recall Kautz's cavalry and employ Hinks' infantry to smash the Confederate force holding up the advance. While waiting for the cavalry to get out of his way, Hinks deployed his division into double lines of battle—Duncan's brigade in front and Holman's in support. There was considerable delay as the battalion of dismounted troopers from the 5th Massachusetts Cavalry encountered difficulty in deploying from column into line. The battalion was made up largely of recruits who had received little instruction beyond the basic school of the cavalryman. Finally, the brigade commanders were able to report that they had completed their dispositions.

Skirmishers were advanced by Colonel Duncan. Supported by the overhead fire of the six 3-inch rifled guns of Capt. James R. Angel's Battery E, 3rd New York Light Artillery, the black regiments pressed forward with a shout. The thick woods and swamp which bounded Cabin Creek slowed the Union advance. To ford the stream it was necessary for the regiments to break formation. All this time, the Yanks were being "furiously assailed with spherical case, canister, and musketry." Several units on the left of Hinks' battle line were thrown into confusion, and a number of men took to their heels.[51]

The 22nd U.S. Colored Infantry, Col. Joseph B. Kiddoo commanding, had advanced to Cabin Creek with the 5th U.S. Colored on its right and the 4th and 6th U.S. Colored on its left. Wading the stream, Kiddoo's foot soldiers found they had lost contact with the units to the left and right. The 4th U.S. Colored was first to emerge from the woods which bounded Cabin Creek. As they did, the Yanks looked across 300 yards of open field and saw their tormenters posted in rifle pits.

---

50 *OR* 40, pt. 1, 720, 721; 51, pt. 1, 264, 265.

51 *Ibid.*, 264.

Two guns of the Petersburg Artillery had been unlimbered on the crest of a hill to the Federals' right.

The center companies of the 4th U.S. Colored, without waiting for orders, started for the works, cheering wildly. Lieutenant Colonel George Rogers called for the men to come back. This attracted the Confederates' attention. Pointing their guns at the 4th U.S. Colored, the Rebel artillerists sprayed the regiment with deadly charges of canister. The unit was thrown into confusion and retired into the woods, leaving 120 dead and wounded on the field.

The 6th U.S. Colored had lost its way in the swamp. When it debouched from the morass, it partially overlapped Colonel Rogers' unfortunate regiment. To make matters worse for them, the soldiers of the 6th found themselves exposed to a deadly enfilading fire from the left. Consequently, the left wing of Duncan's battle line was knocked out of action for the time being. Duncan's two right flank regiments, the 5th and 22nd U.S. Colored now surged out of the swamp.

Colonel Kiddoo of the 22nd recalled that Duncan had told him not to charge until ordered. But, the regimental commander reasoned, a staff officer would have a difficult time getting in touch with him in face of the broken terrain. Without hesitating, Kiddoo shouted for his men to charge the Rebel rifle pits. The regiment forged ahead. Not waiting to cross bayonets with the onrushing bluecoats, Dearing's dismounted cavalrymen took to their heels. Other Union regiments now emerged from the woods. The race for the Confederate rifle pits was won by Colonel Kiddoo's regiment, and the colors of the 22nd U.S. Colored Infantry were proudly planted on the abandoned rifle pits. In their hurry to get away, the cannoneers of the Petersburg Artillery left a 12-pounder howitzer.[52]

General Hinks, on reaching the captured works, glanced at his watch. It was a little after 8:00 a.m. Within a few minutes, General Smith joined Hinks. Smith, after discussing the situation with his division commander, directed Hinks to reassemble his command, move to the left, and use the Jordan's Point Road as his line of advance.

It was 9:00 a.m. before the troops had been reformed and mustered. Taking a plantation road west of the one pioneered by Kautz's cavalry, Hinks' division (Holman's brigade in the van) marched across to the Jordan's Point Road. Turning into the Jordan's Point Road, the column drove rapidly toward Petersburg. As the advance guard (the 1st U.S. Colored Infantry) was preparing to cross Bailey Creek, near Bryant's house, it was fired on by Confederate pickets. Hinks called for Holman to deploy his brigade. This time there were no hitches; Holman's troops

---

52 OR 40, pt. 1, 721, 724; 51, pt. 1, 265-266; Livermore, "The Failure to Take Petersburg, June 15, 1864," 50-51.

forded Bailey Creek and drove the Rebel horsemen beyond the woods surrounding the Ruffin house.[53]

Hinks' division resumed the march and soon arrived on the high ground in front of the fortifications covering the approaches to Petersburg via the Jordan's Point Road. The division was formed for battle (Holman's brigade to the right and Duncan's to the left). Hinks anchored his left on the Prince George Courthouse Road, while his right extended beyond Peebles' house.[54]

General Brooks' division of the XVIII Corps broke camp near Bermuda Hundred at 3:00 a.m. on June 15. The division marched to the pontoon bridge at Point of Rocks. A soldier in the 13th New Hampshire recalled:

> While crossing the pontoons, a regiment in our rear takes up the "cadence-step," as if marching to music and soon sets the bridge in rapid vibration, and a number of its men are seen to lose step, stumble, and plunge off headlong into the mud and water; and as they drawl laboriously up out of the infamous mud, and thoroughly bedaubed with it from head to foot, they are greeted with shouts of laugher from the other troops.[55]

As the troops of Brooks' division ascended the road leading up from the crossing, one of the soldiers recalled, "a wide prospect of fine, well-tilled farm lands lay before us, extending to the James, and the morn, in russet mantle clad, walked over the dew of the high eastward hills."[56]

Falling in behind Hinks' column, Brooks' infantry marched inland. Soon after leaving Broadway, the soldiers heard the distant roar of artillery, but they didn't come within range of the Confederate guns until shortly before 8:00 a.m. At that time the men watched as a solid projectile struck the ground and bounded along. They were now within killing range. The head of Brooks' column came up with Hinks' black troops immediately after they had driven the Confederates from their earthworks on Baylor's farm. A diarist fighting in the 13th New Hampshire observed:

---

53 *OR* 40, pt. 1, 705, 721; *OR* 51, pt. 1, 264.

54 *Ibid.*, pt. 1, 721-722; 51, pt. 1, 226. Seven companies of the 1st U.S. Colored Infantry held the section of the lines assigned to Holman's brigade; part of the 5th Massachusetts Cavalry (dismounted) was held in reserve and the rest was deployed to protect Holman's left flank. *OR* 51, pt. 1, 264.

55 S. Millett Thompson, *Thirteenth Regiment of New Hampshire Volunteer Infantry in the War of the Rebellion, 1861-1865* (Boston, 1888), 382.

56 William Kreutzer, *Notes and Observations made During Four Years of Service with the 98th N. Y. Volunteers, in the War of Rebellion, 1861-1865* (Philadelphia, 1878), 210.

A number of the dead Negroes are lying about—and a dead Negro is the most ghastly corpse ever seen—and their wounded are coming back shot in all sorts of ways, in legs, arms, heads and bodies, but hobbling along and bringing their guns with them. Negroes will keep on their feet, and move on, with wounds that would utterly lay out white men, and they stick like death to their guns. A white man severely wounded throws his gun away.[57]

After Hinks' black troops had broken the Confederate roadblock at Baylor's and had marched for the Jordan's Point Road, Brooks turned his lead brigade (Burnham's) into the City Point-Petersburg Road. About one mile beyond the captured works, Brig. Gen. Hiram Burnham called for Capt. Charles M. Coit of the 8th Connecticut. Coit was told to deploy Roberts' battalion to the left of the road. This precaution was taken none too soon, because within a few minutes Confederate pickets were encountered. Whereupon, Coit deployed his other battalion to the right and sent his color guard to the rear. Forging ahead, the Union skirmishers drove the Rebel pickets through a wooded area. As the soldiers of the 8th Connecticut emerged from the timber, they sighted to their front a strong line of redoubts connected by rifle pits.

Confederate artillerists began shelling the bluecoats as soon as they came into view. The skirmishers took cover in a "ravine pretty close up to the works," while the rest of Burnham's brigade sought shelter in the woods. Here, they were bombarded by Rebel artillery. Among the casualties was the commander of the 118th New York, Maj. Charles E. Pruyun, who, while standing up surveying the works, was struck in the chest by a shell.

Captain Coit, in accordance with instructions from General Burnham, waved his men forward. Working their way cautiously toward the redoubts, the soldiers on the left dashed from tree to tree while those advancing on the right infiltrated a dense thicket. From the cover afforded, they sniped away at the Confederates posted in the earthworks. North of the City Point-Petersburg Road, the Federals all but silenced the guns emplaced in Battery No. 4. About noon, a grey clad patrol undertook a sortie to dislodge the Yankee sharpshooters. This counterthrust was easily repulsed.[58]

Meanwhile, the other units constituting Brooks' division had arrived in front of Petersburg. The brigade commanders massed their units in "line of battle by regiments." Each regiment was formed into column by division. Colonel Henry

---

57 Thompson, *Thirteenth Regiment of New Hampshire Volunteer Infantry*, 382.

58 OR 40, pt. 1, 713; John L. Cunningham, *Three Years with the Adirondack Regiment: 118th New York Volunteer Infantry* (Norwood, 1920), 132.

formed his brigade in rear of Brig. Gen. Gilman Marston's; Burnham's massed his brigade on Marston's left. The brigade commanders were admonished to hold their men ready to advance at a moment's notice.[59]

The 13th New Hampshire was sent forward to act as skirmishers by General Burnham. On the left the skirmishers from New Hampshire established contact with outposts from Hinks' division, while on the right they joined the skirmish line held by the 8th Connecticut. Later in the day, the skirmish line was reinforced by a pair of companies of the 118th New York, and another 150 men from the 92nd New York. As senior officer present, Colonel Aaron Stevens of the 13th New Hampshire assumed command of Brooks' skirmish line.

An amusing incident occurred as the skirmishers worked their way through the pines. "We unearthed about a round dozen of rebels in rifle pits dug among some thick brush not far away to our right front, and they open fire most spitefully," a soldier wrote:

> We are quickly safe behind trees, and they hit no one, excepting a little, wiry Irishman in the Thirteenth; a rebel bullet just glancing across the top of his thumb, a little back of the first joint. The affair is a mere bruise. For a moment the thumb is numb, and Paddy stands still, contemplating it most studiously; and then he suddenly belches out a most distinguished mixture of groan, scream and yell combined and loud enough to raise the dead, throws his gun as far as he can, shoots about six feet into the air, throws his roll of blankets a couple of rods away; and for fully a minute turns himself into a perfect little spinning gyration of sprawling, flying legs and arms, flopping haversack, banging canteen, and rattling tin-cup and cartridge-box, all the time yelling as man never yelled before—in our hearing. He jumped, whirled, laid down, rolled, kicked, struck out, screamed, swore and bawled all at once. Meanwhile the little squad of rebel pickets—either thinking that we have invented a new yell, and are going to charge, or else we have with us the veritable "Yankee Devil" himself, horns and all—cease firing instantly upon the Irishman's first compound scream, seize their loose clothing and blankets in the hands, and make off towards [sic] Petersburg, running as for dear life. A most amusing scene to all of the Union troops—excepting Paddy.[60]

General Martindale had been alerted on the evening of June 14 to have his division ready to follow Brooks' infantry across the Appomattox River at daylight. When he worked out his order of march, Martindale issued instructions for

---

59 *OR* 40, pt. 1, 714, 717.

60 Thompson, *Thirteenth Regiment of New Hampshire Volunteer Infantry*, 383-384.

Stannard's brigade to take the lead. The division commander spent the night of the 14th at Bermuda Hundred. Shortly after daybreak, he started for the front.[61]

Reveille sounded in the camps of Martindale's command at 2:00 a.m. on June 15. As soon as the troops had been formed and mustered, and Brooks' division was out of the way, Stannard put his column into action. Crossing the Appomattox on the Point of Rocks pontoon bridge, the head of the brigade (the 25th Massachusetts in advance) turned into the Spring Hill Road. The 89th New York was deployed as skirmishers and thrown forward to screen the march. Stedman's brigade started crossing the Appomattox the moment Stannard's foot soldiers were out of the way.[62]

Martindale, riding like the wind, overtook Stannard's vanguard before it had gone very far. About a mile and one-half beyond the pontoon bridge, the 89th New York encountered Rebel pickets. Martindale directed Stannard to deploy his brigade and continue the advance. As soon as the regiments had been formed into line of battle to the left and right of the road, the offensive was resumed. Skirmishers from the 89th New York continued to have the lead. A Confederate battery, supported by a small force of cavalry, harassed Martindale's march. The Rebels would mask their guns in the edge of the pines and wait for the bluecoats to approach. After firing a few rounds, the grey clads limbered up their pieces and retired a short distance. The guns would again be put into battery, and the operation would be repeated. Martindale fretted over his lack of cavalry, which kept him from permanently eliminating these will-o'-the-wisp riders.

Nevertheless, Stannard's troops forged ahead until they reached the junction of the Spring Hill and City Point-Petersburg roads. General Smith sent a staff officer with instructions for Martindale to halt and form a junction with Brooks' division on his left. From this point a broad flat extended about a mile to the Appomattox. This plain was commanded by Archer's Hill, on the west bank of the river.

Within a short time, Smith notified Martindale to advance Stannard's brigade on the left. Before pressing forward, Stannard was to make certain that his front was covered by a strong force of skirmishers. Stannard, as he pressed ahead, was to regulate his movements by Brooks'. The Petersburg & City Point Railroad would guide the direction of the advance.

Resting his left flank on the railroad, Stannard pressed ahead in conjunction with Brooks' skirmish line. Stannard's troops advanced until they came under fire

61 OR 51, pt. 1, 1256.

62 Ibid., 1267; W. P. Derby, Bearing Arms in the Twenty-Seventh Massachusetts Regiment (Boston, 1883), 330.

from the Rebel guns emplaced in the Petersburg defenses. This proved very disconcerting to the right flank units which were compelled to halt in an open field; the soldiers on the left of the battle line were more fortunate, because they were screened from the Southerners' view by a thick wood.[63]

By this time, Stedman's brigade had arrived on the field. Martindale sent Stedman to the right, with orders to extend his skirmishers to the Appomattox. Stedman, upon completing his dispositions, advanced his battle line one-half mile. His troops halted when they came under fire from the Rebel guns emplaced in the redoubts covering the approaches to Harrison Creek.[64]

Martindale's division was now ready to assault the Confederate works, but he hesitated to send his men charging across the broad, low valley to his front, cut up as it was by ditches and ravines, and swept by the guns emplaced in Battery No. 5, which jutted some 600 yards in front of the Confederate lines along Harrison Creek. Pending a thorough reconnaissance, General Smith refused to hurl his men against the Petersburg fortifications.[65]

General Ames' division broke camp at 4:00 a.m. Moving out of their camps at Bermuda Hundred, the troops followed Martindale's column across the Point of Rocks pontoon bridge. After reaching the south bank of the Appomattox, the division pushed inland and turned into the City Point-Petersburg Road. The division found itself trailing Brooks' bluecoats. As the column neared the Petersburg defenses, loaded ambulances and the "hobbling wounded" were encountered. These men, who belonged to Hinks' black division, were highly elated. Even the severely wounded greeted their white comrades with, "Tell you boys, we made um get."

"We druv em."

On that occasion, even those who were the most conservative, "suddenly experienced, an accession of respect for the chattel on this discovery of its 'equal' value in a possible emergency."[66]

It was noon before Ames' division reached the area in front of Battery No. 5. The brigade commanders halted their troops in the woods. Colonel Lewis Bell massed his brigade on the left side of the City Point-Petersburg Road. Here, his troops were "under cover of a wood and sprout clearings, which skirted the open

---

63 *OR* 51, pt. 1, 1256, 1262.

64 *Ibid.*, 1256.

65 *Ibid.*, 1256. Andrew A. Humphreys, *The Virginia Campaign of '64 and '65*, (New York, 1882), 207.

66 J. A. Mowris, *A History of the One Hundred and Seventeenth Regiment, N. Y. Volunteers, (Fourth Oneida)* . . . (Hartford, 1866), 114.

fields before the enemy's works, across which the range was unobstructed." When the line had been "extended sufficiently," the men were directed to lie down. Two hundred picked men were deployed and advanced to bolster Brooks' skirmish line.

Colonel A. Martin Curtis formed his brigade about 20 paces in rear of Bell's command and anxiously awaited the word to advance. Cannoneers of Battery C, 3rd Rhode Island Light Artillery unlimbered their guns and maintained a "well-directed fire" upon the Confederate fortifications throughout the long, hot afternoon. The Rebel artillery roared into action as Bell's skirmishers sought to work their way across a clearing. A number of the projectiles overshot their mark and landed in the pines beyond, striking down a number of the blue clads massed there.[67]

Up until the time that his infantry arrived in front of the Petersburg defenses, no one could deny that General Smith had acted with anything but "great promptness and spirit." His columns had marched five or six miles, fought a sharp engagement, drove in the Rebel skirmishers, and had pinpointed the foe's main line of defense.

The Confederate works confronting Brooks' and Hink's divisions presented a very formidable profile to the troops. From Battery No. 5 to Battery No. 10, the Rebel fortifications ran along commanding crests, the forest to their front had been felled so as to expose the Union battle lines if they advanced to a deadly sweeping fire for one-half hour or more. Numerous pieces of artillery were registered on this ground, while a strong line of skirmishers posted in rifle pits, well out in front of the Petersburg perimeter, kept up a spirited and effective fusillade. These circumstances had compelled Baldy Smith and his generals to form their troops for battle under the cover of the pines "at such a distance from the works that difficulty was encountered in making connections, as the lines converged, from a very extended arc." To reconnoiter with any effect, and to place batteries where they could assist the assailing formations, required that the lines should be advanced to eminences and that these positions should be held. This work was fraught with difficulties.[68]

No engineer officer had reported to him, so General Smith was obliged to make the reconnaissance in person. Much time was accordingly lost. Only a few soldiers were visible in the works, but General Smith felt that was not positive proof that Rebel infantry wasn't there in force. It just didn't seem feasible that the Confederates would emplace the number of guns they had in the redoubts without

---

67 OR 40, pt. 11, 70; OR 51, pt. 1, 1246-1247; Isaiah Price, *History of the Ninety-Seventh Regiment, Pennsylvania Volunteer Infantry, During the War of the Rebellion, 1861-1865* (Philadelphia, 1875), 291.

68 Livermore, "The Failure to take Petersburg, June 15, 1864," 52-53.

adequate support. Although Smith and his generals did not know it, the entire Rebel force in the Petersburg entrenchments on the afternoon of the 15th, in addition to the artillery, consisted of Wise's brigade (2,400 strong), the militia, and Dearing's Brigade of cavalry.[69]

General Smith reconnoitered personally on the skirmish line, all the while subjected to the fire of Confederate sharpshooters. About noon, Smith told General Hinks to see if his skirmishers could advance and pin down the Rebel artillerists. If they could, Hinks was to see that his batteries were pushed well out in front and turned on the Confederate redoubts. In considering the question of delay, it can hardly be argued that this action was not in line with a judicious preparation for the assault.[70]

Hinks lost no time in contacting Colonel Duncan. The brigade commander was told to advance the 5th U.S. Colored, which was deployed as skirmishers to the left of the Jordan's Point Road. Advancing through a dense thicket for about one-half mile, the black troops took cover in front of Batteries No. 9 and 10. Colonel James W. Conine told his men to snipe at the Rebel artillerists in the redoubts. If they could not silence the field pieces, the officers hoped that their men would annoy the gunners. The distance separating the redoubts from the edge of the woods was too great, fully 600 yards—for the sharpshooters to accomplish much beyond distracting the butternuts' attention.[71]

Calling for Colonel Duncan, Hinks told him to see if he could secure a position in the open field to the right and rear of the 5th U.S. Colored from which the Union Artillery could shell Batteries No. 9 and 10. Batteries B, 2nd U.S. Colored, and K, 3rd New York Light Artillery reported to the colonel. Although Duncan and the two battery commanders thoroughly scouted the area, they were unable to find a place where their cannoneers could emplace their pieces, as the Rebel guns seemed to sweep every crest with a deadly crossfire. They returned with long faces to report to Hinks that they had failed. All the while, the Confederate artillerists hammered Hinks' battle line with shot and shell. Many of the bluecoats were killed or wounded by the shelling.[72]

It was about 1:00 p.m. when Duncan, in obedience to his instructions from General Hinks, withdrew the 5th U.S. Colored troops, which had suffered considerably from the intense and accurate fire of the Confederate guns. Two

---

69 OR 40, pt. 1, 705; Humphreys, *The Virginia Campaign of '64 and '65*, 207.

70 Livermore, "Failure to take Petersburg, June 15, 1864," 53.

71 OR 40, pt. 1, 721-722; 51, pt. 1, 266.

72 OR 40, pt. 1, 722, 725; 51, pt. 1, 266-267.

companies were left behind to continue the demonstration and to screen the brigade's left flank.[73]

The way the situation had developed up until 2:00 p.m. will hardly admit of unfavorable criticism upon Baldy Smith for delay in assaulting the Petersburg perimeter. Until then there had been no connection between Brooks' and Hinks' divisions, and the battle line was incomplete. Moreover, it is apparent that persistent and courageous attempts had been made to place the units in position from which they could assail the Rebel works.[74]

In addition, the reconnoitering of two or three miles of works under fire from points by woods, hills, and hollows might well require three hours. The selection of probable approaches to fortifications pronounced by General Smith to be stronger than those stormed by the Army of the Cumberland at Missionary Ridge were also described by Grant as the strongest encountered on the drive southward from the Rapidan. That Baldy Smith performed this duty in person and with great activity and exposure of his person was attested to by many eyewitnesses.[75]

*   *   *

Dearing's Confederate troopers, unable to stem the advance of Hinks' division, secured their mounts and retired into the Petersburg perimeter. Reporting to General Wise, Dearing informed him that his cavalrymen had been driven from their position at Baylor's farm by three brigades of infantry. At the moment, these Union foot soldiers and a considerable force of cavalry were apparently striking for the Baxter and Jerusalem Plank Roads. Before dismissing Dearing, Wise complimented him for delaying the Yankees long enough to enable the Petersburg defenders to take position in the earthworks.[76]

Wise, on forwarding this news to Beauregard's Swift Creek headquarters, called for reinforcements. Beauregard (at 11:45 a.m.) relayed this information to General Bragg. On doing so, he warned, "We must now elect between lines of Bermuda Neck and Petersburg. We cannot hold both."[77]

Bragg replied immediately that Hoke's division "early this morning" had been ordered to report to Beauregard. At 11:30 a.m., Bragg observed, he had received a

---

73 OR 51, pt. 1, 267.

74 Livermore, "The Failure to take Petersburg, June 15, 1864, 54.

75 *Ibid.*, 54-55.

76 OR 40, pt. 1, 656; Roman, *Military Operations of General Beauregard,* vol. 2, 567-568; Beauregard, "Four Days of Battle at Petersburg," 540.

77 OR 40, pt. 1, 656.

telegram from Hoke announcing that his division was crossing the James.[78] Bragg felt certain, since he was on the spot, Beauregard would be able to judge better than he as to "the movements necessary to be made by the troops" belonging to the Department of North Carolina and Southern Virginia.[79]

Acknowledging Bragg's message, Beauregard at 1:45 p.m. wrote, "I did not ask advice with regard to the movement of troops, but wished to know the preference of the War Department between Petersburg and lines across Bermuda Hundred Neck, for my guidance, as I fear my present force may prove unequal to hold both."

No answer was received by Beauregard's headquarters to this dispatch.

Meanwhile, Beauregard had made his decision: He would hold Petersburg in preference to the Bermuda Hundred Neck. He had telegraphed Bragg (at 1:00 p.m.) that he had ordered Hoke to Petersburg. The lines across Bermuda Hundred Neck would be held as long as practicable, but if worse came to worse he would evacuate and rush Johnson to reinforce Hoke. Beauregard suggested that it might be wise if a strong division was withdrawn from Lee's Army of Northern Virginia and sent to the Walthall Junction area as a strategic reserve.[80]

Beauregard, having determined to hold Petersburg, notified General Wise that Hoke's division was en route from "Drewry's Bluff and would be in time to save the day, if our men could stand their ordeal, hard as it was, a little while longer."

Wise accordingly issued orders "to hold on at all hazards!"[81]

About noon, Wise observed the approach of Kautz's cavalry against the Baxter Road sector defended by the 34th Virginia. Dismounting and deploying, the bluecoats beat their way slowly toward the Rebel defenses. Once again, Wise called for help.

For two hours, from 12:00 to 2:00 p.m., Kautz's skirmishers pressed the Confederates hard. To cope with this threat, Wise had his line close from the right to bolster the 34th Virginia. The 3rd Battalion, Virginia Reserves was called up and sent to reinforce Colonel Page's command on the left.[82]

Between the Petersburg & City Point Railroad and the Appomattox River, the soldiers of the 26th Virginia watched while Martindale's bluecoat infantry appeared in their front. A Confederate diarist grimly noted, "We had such a small force here, that it made me tremble to see them. Advancing on us; in such larger and

---

78 *Ibid.*, 658.

79 Roman, *Military Operations of General Beauregard*, vol. 2, 574.

80 *OR* 40, pt. 1, 656.

81 Beauregard, "Four Days of Battle at Petersburg," 540.

82 *Ibid.*, 540. Roman, *Military Operations of General Beauregard*, vol. 2, 568.

overwhelming numbers; I said to myself, that our Batteries would fall before night."[83]

Wise, on witnessing the continued Union build-up to his front, again called for reinforcements. Beauregard replied that one of Johnson's brigades had been ordered to Petersburg, and that Hoke's division, which had marched from Drewry's Bluff (at 12:15 p.m.), should reach Petersburg by 5:00 p.m.[84]

*   *   *

Baldy Smith was engaged in making a personal reconnaissance of the Confederate works until about 4:00 p.m. At that time, while still anxiously riding along in front of his lines and surveying the Rebel redoubts, Smith dispatched word to General Hinks that he was satisfied there were very enemy few foot soldiers manning the works. Consequently, since the Confederate cannoneers could tear a battle line to pieces, Smith felt that the Federals might be able to storm the defenses with a skirmish line. Hinks, therefore, would at once "form a very heavy skirmish line, which should go into the works, followed by the line of battle, if successful—the assault to be made when orders were received, or when General Brooks' line advanced."

For some unknown reason, several hours passed before orders were issued for Brooks' division to advance. Meanwhile, General Smith had found, or at least resolved to take advantage of, a flaw in the Rebel defenses in Brooks' sector.

The ground in front of the works south of the Petersburg & City Point Railroad is cut by deep hollows, and although it was difficult to pass over the intervening crests which were denuded of timber, some of these ravines ran close against the fortifications and offered a covered line of approach to a commander bold enough to exploit them. It was subsequently learned by the Unionists that General Beauregard entertained the opinion that the line of works was badly located, and especially vulnerable in the sector from Battery No. 5 to Battery No. 7. Baldy Smith likewise detected this weakness. In making his after-action report, General Brooks observed, "It was determined by General Smith to throw forward his line of skirmishers (Burnham's) if possible to the ravine just in front of the enemy's line, from which position it was supposed they might keep down the artillery fire while the main column would cross the opening in our front."[85]

83 Russell, *Diary*, n.d.

84 Roman, *Military Operations of General Beauregard*, vol. 2, 568.

85 Livermore, "The Failure to take Petersburg, June 15, 1864," 56; Smith, "Movement Against Petersburg, June, 1864," 83.

The battle plan, as worked out by General Smith, called for Chief of Artillery Capt. Frederick Follett to mass his artillery and direct the gun captains to hammer the Jordan's Hill Salient and Battery No. 5. As soon as the artillery had softened up the Confederate position, he would send a strong skirmish line to carry the works, which could be done if they were weakly held by infantry as Smith suspected.[86]

*   *   *

About 4:00 p.m. the Confederates placed two long-range rifled artillery pieces on Archer's Hill. From this key height, they were able to enfilade and take in reverse Stedman's battle line. The shells struck down a number of men in the brigade. Even more frustrating for the Federals was the fact that they had no guns with which to counter this fire. Stedman was compelled to retire about 800 yards. At the time that the bluecoats pulled back, a 15-man reconnaissance patrol was feeling its way toward Harrison Creek. Before they knew what was up, the bluecoats found themselves surrounded by a superior number of butternuts from the 26th Virginia and were captured.[87]

To the left of Brooks' division, General Hinks early in the afternoon started forming his division for the attack. Colonel Duncan massed his brigade in double line of battle in Jordan's field—the 4th U.S. Colored on the right and the 22nd U.S. Colored on the left of the first line; the 5th U.S. Colored on the right and the 6th U.S. Colored on the left of the second line. The 1st U.S. Colored of Holman's brigade rested its left on the right of Duncan's brigade. As soon as he had completed his dispositions, Colonel Duncan led his brigade forward. He planned to occupy the crest in Jordan's field, which heretofore had been weakly held by skirmishers from Holman's command. Since the field was swept by guns emplaced in Batteries No. 6, 7, 8, 9 and 10, the black regiments found the going difficult. Their advance was supported by the overhead fire of Captain Angel's 3-inch rifles. The New Yorkers had manhandled two guns into battery to the right of the Peebles' house and another section to the left. It was 2:00 p.m. before the Federals gained the crest. Now, in accordance with orders from Baldy Smith, Hinks saw that Duncan extended his right to link up with the left flank of General Brooks' division. The connection between the two divisions was made near a point of woods.

For the next several hours, Hinks' troops hugged the ground, as shot and shell crashed and exploded about them. A number of the soldiers were killed and

---

86 Humphreys, *The Virginia Campaign of '64 and '65*, 208.

87 *OR* 51, pt. 1, 1256.

wounded by the bombardment. Since the Rebels were protected by earthworks, the bluecoats held their fire.[88]

About 5:00 p.m., a staff officer galloped up to General Hinks' command post and informed the general that Baldy Smith "intended to charge the works with the skirmish line, and directed . . . [Hinks] to cause the proper disposition to be made to advance as soon as General Brooks' line commenced to advance." Hinks, in turn, relayed this information to his brigade commanders. Duncan and Holman were directed to strengthen their skirmish line and make sure that the skirmishers "advanced to gain the most favorable position . . . and to drive in all the enemy's sharpshooters."[89]

Upon receipt of this order, Colonel Duncan reinforced his skirmish line with three companies from the 4th U.S. Colored and four companies of the 22nd U.S. Colored. The skirmishers advanced, took position at one pace intervals, and worked their way cautiously ahead. As they pushed forward, the blacks drove the Confederate sharpshooters before them. All the while, the officers kept one eye cocked to the right to be ready to cooperate the moment Brooks' troops took up the advance.[90]

Brooks' skirmish line by 5:00 p.m. had closed the distance to as near the abatis as it deemed prudent. Colonel Stevens of the 13th New Hampshire called to the men to halt, find cover, cease firing, and keep hidden. Tired from the "long day's actions," the men rested on their arms, "settling down behind the large logs and stumps."

For the next two hours, one of the soldiers recalled:

We were so near to Battery Five, that we can occasionally, when the wind serves, distinctly hear the commandant's orders, "Load," "Fire," and can look right into the muzzles of his guns, as they are run up to the embrasures; and fired straight at us, "puff-bang;" sometimes singly, sometimes all at once. Our cover is so secure, however, that this firing is more interesting than harmful. Away to our left, near to Mr. . . . [Peebles'] house, is a long and strong line of skirmishers—colored troops—working forward over dusty, plowed land, among numerous apple or peach trees. They are in full view, and are having a hard time of it. They rush forward, and are then driven back; and then try again, and again; but without success, and quite a number of them are stretched out on the ground, dead. Battery Five shells them severely, and they and the shells drive up a great deal of dust. The scene is very interesting to us; for a

88 *Ibid.*, 264, 267; OR 40, pt. 1, 722, 724-725.

89 *OR* 40, pt. 1, 722.

90 *Ibid.*, 722, 725; OR 51, pt. 1, 264, 267.

determined charge by the enemy upon these Negroes would expose the Thirteenth . . . The Negroes are doing wretched skirmishing. Now drums are heard in our rear—a dozen loud taps—and all is still. Immediately a full regiment of colored infantry, with colors flying . . . and in a splendid line of battle, move up toward a rail fence on our left and rear. In a moment Battery 5 gives them—over our heads—three or four shells right in their faces. Snap—and back go they like wild men. Somebody's fool has blundered. A good, thorough, handsome, elegant blunder too![91]

General Brooks, whose division was to spearhead the attack, kept a close watch on his brigade commanders. At 6:00 p.m. the two companies of the 8th Connecticut (G and K) armed with Sharps rifles notified Captain Coit that they had expended the 60 rounds of ammunition they carried on their persons. More embarrassing, the ordnance sergeants reported that there were no Sharps cartridges in the ammunition wagon. Coit accordingly had no choice but to relieve the two companies. Their places on the skirmish line were taken by two companies of the 118th New York.[92]

Preparatory to making the attack, Brooks called on his brigade commanders for units to reinforce his skirmish line. Colonel Henry of the Third Brigade sent his general the 92nd New York. Henry's four remaining regiments were alerted to be ready to support the skirmish line and "meet any counter-charge of the enemy in the event of a repulse."[93]

Prior to the beginning of the attack, General Marston rode backward and forward behind the regiments of the brigade. He stopped every rod or two, and counseled his men to keep steady, saying, "Don't be afraid; we are ten to one of the enemy."[94]

After several ineffectual attempts to find positions for the corps artillery, it had been withdrawn and sent to the rear. Now that it was necessary for the guns to be massed to support the assault on the Jordan's Hill Salient and Battery No. 5, a call was sent for the batteries. Chief of Artillery Follett, on his own responsibility and without consulting anyone, had had his gunners unhitch their teams and send them to the rear for water. Upon learning what had occurred, Baldy Smith decided it would be impossible to dispense with the artillery, and there was nothing to do but wait for the cannoneers to collect and hitch up their teams. Much time was lost; it

---

91 Thompson, *Thirteenth Regiment of New Hampshire Volunteer Infantry*, 386-388.

92 *OR* 40, pt. 1, 713.

93 *Ibid.*, 714, 717.

94 Kreutzer, *Four Years of Service in the War of Rebellion, 1861-1865*, 211.

was almost 7 o'clock before the artillerists had unlimbered their guns to cover the advance.[95]

General Smith, however, must assume the responsibility for the failure to get the artillery in position as scheduled.

When Smith gave the word, three Union batteries finally opened on the Jordan's Hill Salient. Covered by this bombardment, Brooks' skirmish line (the 13th New Hampshire, eight companies of the 8th Connecticut, and detachments from the 92nd and 118th New York) prepared to charge. The usual distance between skirmishers, about five paces, was taken. On the left, the 13th New Hampshire was directly in front of Battery No. 5, its flanks extending a considerable distance to the right and left. The regimental historian of the 13th New Hampshire reported:

> The flankers under Lieut. [S. Millett] Thompson of [Company] E, on the left of the Thirteenth, are directed to come up on the line, to extend to the right and to deploy as skirmishers in the same manner as the rest of the Thirteenth. As these flankers rise to their feet in the low slashing, and hence come into full view, the men need at first a little encouragement. They come up into line . . . , and by so doing the most of them are brought to the very edge of the slashing and some of them out of it altogether and into the clear open ground at the field in front, a very exposed position.

At the command, "Forward!" the Union skirmishers rushed ahead with a shout. The guns emplaced in Batteries No. 5 and 6 remained silent as the blue clad skirmish line drove toward them. As they closed to within small-arms range, the Federals encountered a sharp fire from Confederate infantry. Soldiers began to fall. Lieutenant Thompson of the 13th New Hampshire was hit in the left ankle and knocked off his feet. The 13th New Hampshire dashed toward Battery No. 5 "in a long thin line, narrowing front" as it advanced. A line of "French rifle pits" running across the middle of an open field was overrun.

Within a few minutes "a little party of officers and men" of the 13th New Hampshire reached the bottom of the deep ravine fronting Battery No. 5. Captain Nathan D. Stoodley called to Capt. George N. Julian, "If we follow this thing right up now, we can take this battery."

"Then we can take it." Julian answered. Accompanied by Capt. Enoch W. Goss and a few other men from the 13th New Hampshire who had joined them in the ravine, the two captains scrambled up the embankment. "Some straight up over the front walls, others up the north side, on bayonets stuck in the sand, grasping

---

95 Humphreys, *The Virginia Campaign of '64 and '65*, 208; Smith, "Movement Against Petersburg, June, 1864," 90.

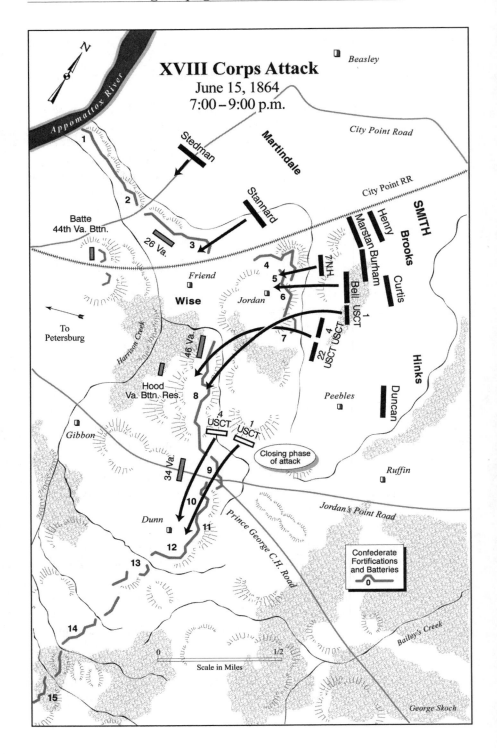

XVIII Corps Attack
June 15, 1864
7:00 – 9:00 p.m.

Appomattox River

1

Stedman

Martindale

City Point Road

2

City Point RR

Stannard

SMITH

Marstan

Henry

Burham

Brooks

Batte
44th Va. Bttn.

26 Va.

3

4 N H

Curtis

Friend

4

5

Bell USCT

Wise

Jordan

6

1
USCT

To
Petersburg

Harrisont Creek

46 Va.

7

4
USCT

Hinks

22 USCT

8

Peebles

Duncan

Hood
Va. Bttn. Res.

Gibbon

4
USCT

1
USCT

34 Va.

9

Closing phase
of attack

Ruffin

10

Jordan's Point Road

Dunn

11

12

Prince George C.H. Road

Confederate
Fortifications
and Batteries

0

13

14

Bailey's Creek

0   1/2
Scale in Miles

15

George Skoch

grass and weeds to assist in climbing, striking their boots into the gravel—anyhow so as to be the quickest way in; and as these few Northern soldiers look from the parapet down into the battery they see a full hundred of the enemy." The Confederates had been thrown into confusion by the men who had abandoned the "French rifle pits" and had taken refuge in the redoubt—they seemed to be waiting for something to happen.[96]

Meanwhile, Colonel Bell's skirmishers, a detachment of 100 men led by Capt. William J. Hunt of the 117th New York, had charged by the flank and crossed the Rebel rifle pits between Batteries No. 5 and 6. Captain Hunt, having penetrated the Confederate line, redeployed his men into line of battle behind Battery No. 5. A volley was sent crashing into the rear of the grey clad defenders.[97]

The detachment from the 13th New Hampshire at the same time charged into the works. Captain Julian called upon Lt. Col. James C. Councill of the 26th Virginia to surrender and received his sword. Captain N. A. Sturdivant of the Confederate artillery handed over his sword to Captain Stoodley. Within a few seconds all was over, the 211 prisoners, including 16 officers, were lined up by their captors—Hunt's detachment and the men of the 13th New Hampshire. Besides the personnel, the Federals captured two stands of colors, and five guns (one iron gun and four 12-pounder howitzers) in Battery No. 5.

As to be expected, the prisoners were a glum lot. A number of them were found to be members of the Petersburg militia and armed with smoothbore muskets. When Captain Sturdivant discovered the small size of the force which captured Battery No. 5, he was beside himself with anger and chagrin, and was heard to exclaim, "Here are my guns double-shotted for infantry, and all of us captured by a ____ Yankee skirmish line."

Discovering that the guns were loaded, the Federals prepared to turn them on the retreating foe—but the fuses were gone. Captain Stoodley asked Captain Sturdivant for the fuses. The Confederate artillerist replied, "Don't want to be a party in this matter."

Captain Stoodley didn't press the matter.

Sergeant John F. Gibbs of Company E, 13th New Hampshire, who besides being one of the first to enter Battery No. 5 had served for a time in the artillery, soon located some fuses.[98] The artillery pieces were accordingly manhandled about

---

96 Thompson, *Thirteenth Regiment of New Hampshire Volunteer Infantry*, 386-388.

97 OR 51, pt. 1, 1247-1248.

98 Thompson, *Thirteenth Regiment of New Hampshire Volunteer Infantry*, 388-390. The prisoners taken in Battery No. 5 were turned over to Colonel Bell's provost marshal, Lt. George W. Ross.

so they faced toward "Petersburg and fired—just as a 'Here-we-are' greeting to that city."[99]

After helping to secure Battery No. 5, the 8th Connecticut was advanced and occupied a hill in rear of the captured redoubt. Captain Coit put his men to work throwing up breastworks. Skirmishers of the 92nd New York reached Battery No. 5 on the heels of Burnham's and Bell's troops. Colonel Stevens at the same time collected the soldiers of the 13th New Hampshire and moved them to the left, posting them on "the steep, high bluff-side near and just west of Charles Friend's house.

Within a few minutes after the Union skirmishers had swarmed over Battery No. 5, General Brooks ordered Colonel Henry to advance his brigade. Moving forward at the double quick, Henry's column reached a point nearly abreast and to the right of Battery No. 5. Here he halted and deployed his brigade to the right. Henry now gave the word to press on; his battle line crossed the now deserted rifle pits, and reached a road leading directly into Petersburg. Halting his battle line, Henry had his men entrench. A patrol from the 21st Connecticut found and brought in "two fine pieces of artillery, with caissons and limbers," which the Rebels in their haste had abandoned.[100]

Colonel Bell's massed brigade, preceded by Hunt's skirmishers, had advanced on Henry's left flank. Captain Martin S. James' gunners of Battery C, 3rd Rhode Island Artillery steadily shelled the redoubt (Battery No. 6), against which Bell directed his attack. Bell's skirmishers closed in on some "French rifle pits" from which Confederate marksmen had harassed them throughout the afternoon. Most of the defenders grounded their arms as the cheering bluecoats closed in. Pushing on, the left flank of Bell's battle line struck Battery No. 6 at the same time as the black troops.

The Confederates (many of whom were members of the Petersburg militia and had been "engaged at their usual avocations in the city" until a few hours before) expressed surprise to their captors at the suddenness of the advance. A number of the Rebel dead and prisoners were clad in citizen's attire. Curtis' brigade, which was deployed to the left of Bell's command, was crowded out, and didn't enter Battery No. 6 until well after Bell's bluecoats.[101]

---

99 Cunningham, *The Adirondack Regiment*, 132.

100 OR 40, pt. 1, 714, 717-718.

101 OR 51, pt. 1, 1248; Price, *History of the Ninety-Seventh Regiment, Pennsylvania Volunteer Infantry*, 291; Mowris, *History of the One Hundred and Seventeenth Regiment, N. Y. Volunteers*, 114-116.

It was around 7:00 p.m. when one of General Smith's aides galloped up to Hinks' command post and warned the general that Brooks' division was in motion. Hinks notified Duncan and Holman that they were to begin the assault.[102]

A powerful skirmish line, strengthened much beyond tactical numbers, swept toward the Petersburg perimeter. Lieutenant Colonel Elias Wright of the 1st U.S. Colored Infantry led his cheering soldiers against Battery No. 6. Colonel Holman at the same time called for the two companies of the 5th U.S. Colored deployed on the left of Colonel Wright's regiment to assail the Rebel works to their front. These companies, however, refused to do as Holman ordered. The ground in front of the left of Holman's command was covered with timber and undergrowth, while to the right the terrain was smooth and open. Holman therefore placed himself in charge of the left of the skirmish line; Wright led the right wing. Wright's soldiers reached and carried Battery No. 6 in cooperation with Bell's storming column. Meanwhile, Holman had veered off to the left. Followed by two companies of the 1st U.S. Colored, Holman advanced against Battery No. 9.[103]

Seven companies of skirmishers from the 4th and 22nd U.S. Colored advanced on the left of Colonel Wright's men. As they did, the cheering soldiers came under a heavy fire from Battery No. 7 to their front. Since the bluecoats were running, they soon passed through the beaten zone and entered a defiladed area in front of the redoubt. At this moment, the officer in charge of the four companies of the 22nd U.S., Maj. John B. Cook, shouted for his line to "break to the right and left." Passing around the flanks of the battery, the Yanks gained its rear. To Capt. Jacob F. Force and Lt. William D. Milliken fell the honor of being the first to enter Battery No. 7. Within the redoubt, the soldiers of the 22nd U.S. Colored captured three guns— two 12-pounder howitzers and an iron gun. Soldiers from the 4th and 1st U.S. Colored entered Battery No. 7 close on the heels of Major Cook's battalion.[104]

Meanwhile, the rest of Duncan's troops had moved out on the double-quick. When he reached Battery No. 7, Col. Joseph B. Kiddoo of the 22nd U.S. Colored was delighted to find that Cook's men had reached the works first. Kiddoo, after reforming his regiment, prepared to exploit the breakthrough by moving against Battery No. 8. As the 22nd U.S. Colored marched to the left, Colonel Kiddoo ran into Colonel Wright with a portion of the 1st U.S. Colored. Wright's bluecoats had just occupied a small lunette between Batteries No. 7 and 8, which had been hurriedly evacuated by the Rebs. Kiddoo proposed to Wright that they unite their

102 OR 40, pt. 1, 722.

103 OR 51, pt. 1, 264.

104 Ibid., 267; OR 40, pt. 1, 725.

commands and charge Battery No. 8, "a strong work advantageously posted on a considerable elevation behind a difficult ravine."

Wright shook his head, remarking that such a plan bordered on rashness. But, he added, he would support the 22nd U.S. Colored if Kiddoo persisted.

Kiddoo quickly formed his regiment into column of assault. While his men were taking position, they were fired on by Confederates sheltered in Battery No. 8. A number of men were detached and left at the lunette to harass the Rebel gunners in the redoubt.

Kiddoo bellowed, "Charge!" The column dashed down into the ravine and waded a swamp. Deserting their cannon, the Rebel artillerists took up small-arms and rushed to the parapet. Kiddoo's men faltered as the grey clads ripped their ranks with several well-aimed volleys. They, however, took heart and rallied when they saw that the color guard had reached the opposite side of the hollow. Colonel Wright and his soldiers of the 1st U.S. Colored rushed to Kiddoo's assistance. Pressing on, the two black regiments stormed Battery No. 8, capturing one 12-pounder howitzer.[105]

Kiddoo called for volunteers with knowledge of field guns. These men were put in charge of the 12-pounder which they turned on Battery No. 9. Lieutenant William B. Short was detailed to bury the dead and take care of the wounded.[106]

After retreating to the cover afforded by Battery No. 9, the Confederate officers re-formed their men and counterattacked. Kiddoo didn't panic easily. Deploying the 1st and 22nd U.S. Colored, he advanced to meet the oncoming grey clads. The blacks checked the Confederates and compelled them to retire into their strongholds. Kiddoo now shouted for his men to get ready to storm Battery No. 9. A number of officers dashed up to the colonel and reported that most of their soldiers had shot up the 40 rounds of ammunition carried in their cartridge boxes. This news caused Kiddoo to cancel his order. The two regiments retired into Battery No. 8.[107]

By this time, Colonel Rogers had regrouped his regiment—the 4th U.S. Colored. Baldy Smith had directed Rogers to capture Battery No. 8. Finding Battery No. 8 in Union hands, Rogers' regiment passed in front of it. Marching up a deep ravine, Rogers' troops headed for Battery No. 9, a work 500 yards away, and commanding the section of line already taken. As Rogers' foot soldiers approached Battery No. 9, two companies from another of Hinks' regiments were working their

105 *Ibid.*, 725.

106 *OR* 40, pt. 1, 725. Lieutenant Short's party buried 11 men and evacuated 43 wounded from Battery No. 8.

107 *Ibid.*, 752.

way through an abatis. Fired upon by the Confederates, the two companies charged, and the garrison abandoned Battery No. 9 and retired into Battery No. 10. There, they were charged by Rogers' command and compelled to retire, leaving one gun, with its caisson and team in the hands of the 4th U.S. Colored.

Following the loss of Battery No. 10, the Confederates also pulled out of Battery No. 11, at the Dunn House.

Duncan's second line of battle, the 5th and 6th U.S. Colored, was of little assistance in the capture of Batteries No. 6 through 11 by their comrades. It proved impossible for these units to follow the line of advance pioneered by the 22nd and 4th U.S., consequently, they were directed toward Batteries No. 9, 10, and 11. General Smith rode up and told Colonel Duncan to assault these works. A column of battalion front was formed, the 6th U.S. Colored leading. Skirmishers were thrown out and the advance commenced. A battery was ordered up to assist the movement.

To reach the redoubts, the bluecoats had to cross a wide ravine. As they did, they found their way obstructed by stumps, piles of wood, fallen timber, bushes, and pools of water. Darkness was enveloping the area, so that the soldiers' only guide was the flashes from the Rebel's guns. The column advanced as best it could, receiving only an occasional round. The Confederates' attention was focused upon the storming parties threatening their left flank. Duncan's column had reached the bottom of the hollow, when shouts ahead told that their comrades were in possession of the redoubts.

It was now 9:00 p.m. Duncan reformed his brigade in rear of Battery No. 10. Details were turned to refacing the captured earthworks, as a precaution against a Confederate counter thrust.[108]

General Hinks on January 1, 1866, wrote General Smith concerning this brilliant feat of arms. It was Hinks' considered opinion that "An assault made in any other mode would have resulted in disaster." Hinks went on to explain why he believed this. "No column," he continued,

> or line of battle which General Smith could have arrayed could have marched over the long and difficult approaches under the direct and enfilading fire of the enemy, and that, as it was, notwithstanding we had been maneuvering for several hours in front of two miles of the enemy's line, he was completely surprised by the dash of the skirmish line, which he could not break up with artillery, and which had possession of the guns almost as soon as he could see our supporting lines, which were in the works before the skirmishers could be dislodged.

108 *OR* 51, pt. 1, 267-268.

The Dunn house in Petersburg and the trenches surrounding it.
Library of Congress

"Full credit," historian Thomas L. Livermore wrote in 1878:

> Ought to be given to General Smith for first using on an extended scale the tactics which the Germans . . . [adopted in the Franco-Prussian War], of assaulting with heavy lines of skirmishers in lieu of lines of battle; and his delay enabled him to charge in the Russian fashion of later days, at nightfall, so as to avoid long-range missiles; yet his own judgment that he could take the works with a skirmish line, uttered at four o'clock, convicts . . . [Smith] of wasting three precious hours at least. He waited for reinforcements, perhaps,—but needlessly, as it now seems.[109]

Preparatory to advancing to the attack, General Martindale on the Union right had instructed Stannard to press ahead along the Petersburg & City Point Railroad and Stedman via the City Point Road. These lines of advance were dictated by a desire on Martindale's part to partially shelter his troops from the fire of the Rebel rifled guns emplaced on Archer's Hill. Before moving forward, Stannard reinforced his skirmish line with two companies of the 25th Massachusetts.

Martindale's attack jumped off at 7:00 p.m. On the right, Stedman's troops drove the Confederate skirmishers back into the rifle pits covering Harrison Creek,

---

109 Livermore, "The Failure to Take Petersburg, June 15, 1864," 60-61.

while Stannard's men compelled the Southerners to evacuate Battery No. 3, where they captured two light 12-pounder guns, three caissons, and a considerable amount of camp equipage.

It was getting dark. One of Smith's staff officers galloped up and told Martindale to suspend his attack and withdraw his division to the Spring Hill Road in rear of Brooks' and Ames' divisions. Before recalling his men, Stannard established a strong picket line held by the 55th Pennsylvania and the 25th Massachusetts.[110]

*   *   *

When the Federals scored their massive breakthrough between Batteries No. 5 and 11, General Wise issued instructions for his troops on the right to close to the left on Battery No. 14. The 59th Virginia, reaching Petersburg at this time from north of the Appomattox, was rushed eastward toward Battery No. 2 to bolster the units of the 26th Virginia opposing Martindale's attack.[111]

Meanwhile, General Hoke's division had gained the Richmond-Petersburg Pike. Near Chester Station, General Hoke was notified that there were enough locomotives and rolling stock at that point to provide transportation for part of his division. Hoke ordered two of his brigades, Brig. Gen. Johnson Hagood's and Alfred Colquitt's, to move to the station and entrain. Hoke and his other brigades, Clingman's and Martin's, continued to march down the pike.

Hagood's South Carolinians, upon reaching the tracks of the Petersburg & Richmond Railroad, clambered aboard waiting cars. Colquitt's Georgians would follow as soon as additional rolling stock became available. The train with Hagood's troops chugged into the Petersburg depot about dark. Notified by a staff officer that General Beauregard had reached the city, Hagood hastened to the General's headquarters, while his men were getting off the cars and forming in the street. At Beauregard's headquarters in the post office, Hagood learned that the general was on the lines. Chief Engineer D. B. Harris told Hagood to march his column out the Jerusalem Plank Road and "take position where it issued from the fortifications."

Before Hagood rejoined his brigade, a courier arrived with shocking news that the Yanks "had carried the defenses from [Batteries] No. 3 to No. 7 . . . , and that our troops were retreating." Harris, turning to Hagood, told him to march his South Carolinians out the City Point-Petersburg Road and take position to cover

110 OR 51, pt. 1, 1262-1263.

111 Roman, *Military Operations of General Beauregard*, vol. 2, 568; Beauregard, "Four Days of Battle at Petersburg," 541; Russell, *Diary*, n.d.

Brigadier General Alfred H. Colquitt
Library of Congress

that approach to the city, and upon which a new defense line might be established. It was a critical moment. Routed troops were flowing back into Petersburg, spreading alarm on every hand. Upon making an inquiry, Hagood learned that the only organized troops available in the city to resist the Union thrust were his South Carolinians and the 59th Virginia of Page's Brigade.

Since it was dark and he was unacquainted with the area, Hagood hoped that his "volunteer guides" would be of some assistance. He was soon disenchanted with these people as they gave confused and contradictory directions. Finally, Hagood halted his brigade at the junction of the City Point and Price George Courthouse Roads. Leaving the senior regimental commander, Col. C. H. Simonton, in charge, Hagood, accompanied by two members of his staff, made a personal reconnaissance. The general and his party rode out the Prince George Courthouse Road. As the officers approached the ford across Harrison Creek, they were hailed by a wounded Reb and told not to go any farther as there were Yankees at the ford. Reining up their horses, they turned and started riding across a field toward the City Point Road. Here, Hagood was hailed by a courier from Chief Engineer Harris with a map, who had also "the foresight to send a bit of tallow candle and matches." With the aid of the map, Hagood determined to post his brigade along the line of Harrison Creek. This stream emptied into the Appomattox behind Battery No. 1, while its west fork crossed the line near Battery No. 15. The line taken up by Hagood was a chord of the arc of the captured works. It ran along the west side of Harrison Creek and its western prong, and commanded the cleared and cultivated valley to its front. [112]

---

112 OR 40, pt. 1, 801; Butler Hagood, *Memoirs of the War of Secession from the Original Manuscripts of Johnson Hagood* (Columbia, 1910), 265-267; Roman, *Military Operations of General Beauregard*, vol. 2, 578.

The trains with Colquitt's Georgians reached Petersburg during the evening. Marching out to Harrison Creek, the Georgians filed into position on Hagood's right. Before digging in across the Prince George Courthouse Road, Colquitt's grey clads drove the Federal pickets away from the Harrison Creek ford. General Hoke reached Petersburg about midnight with Clingman's and Martin's troops. Clingman's North Carolinians entrenched on Colquitt's right, while Martin's troops marched out the City Point Road and halted a short distance behind the line taken up by Hagood's butternuts. Meanwhile, soldiers from the 59th Virginia had crossed Harrison Creek and relieved the companies of the 26th Virginia garrisoning Batteries No. 1 and 2.[113]

General Beauregard had reached Petersburg from Swift Creek at 6:00 p.m. Shortly thereafter, while Beauregard was inspecting the lines, the Federals stormed the Petersburg perimeter. At first, Beauregard intended to employ Hoke's troops in a counterattack, but on observing their jaded condition, after their forced march, he decided not to and ordered Hoke to dig in.

Returning to his headquarters in the post office, Beauregard (at 9:20 p.m.) wired Richmond, "Reinforcements not having arrived in time, enemy penetrated lines from Battery 5 to 8, inclusive." He promised to try to recover the lost redoubts by daybreak. To assist with this work, Beauregard observed, he had issued instructions for Johnson's division to abandon the Bermuda Hundred Neck lines and march to Petersburg. General Lee would now have to look to the defenses of Drewry's Bluff and the lines across Bermuda Neck.[114]

Beauregard waited 70 minutes before forwarding to Johnson a directive outlining the steps he was to take in abandoning the lines across Bermuda Hundred Neck. Troops, trains, and artillery were to be withdrawn at once. Pickets and skirmishers were to remain till daylight or later, if necessary, to cover the movement.[115]

At 11:15 p.m., Beauregard telegraphed Lee that he had abandoned the lines across Bermuda Hundred Neck to concentrate all his forces for the defense of Petersburg. Skirmishers and pickets would hold the earthworks until daybreak. "Cannot these lines be occupied by your troops?" Beauregard inquired.[116]

---

113 Hagood, *Memoirs of the War of Secession*, 267; Frank E. Peabody, "Some Observations Concerning the Opposing Forces at Petersburg on June 15, 1864," in *Papers of the Military Historical Society of Massachusetts*, vol. 5, 156.

114 Roman, *Military Operations of General Beauregard*, vol. 2, 580, 581; *OR* 40, pt. 2, 656.

115 *OR* 40, pt. 2, 657.

116 *Ibid.*, 657.

Major General David B. Birney
Library of Congress

*   *   *

General Smith's troops on the evening of June 15 had scored a decisive breakthrough. A mile and one-half of entrenchments and 16 guns had been captured. If Smith renewed the attack, Petersburg in all probability would be in Union hands by morning. But at this moment, with victory in his grasp, Smith hesitated.

Reinforcements were already in the field. On the previous evening, the 14th, Maj. Gen. Winfield S. Hancock was directed by General Meade to hold the II Corps ready to march. Since it was probable that his corps would be sent to Petersburg, Hancock would look to City Point for his rations.[117]

About one hour before midnight, a telegraphic dispatch was received from Meade announcing that:

> General Butler has been ordered to send to you at Wind-Mill Point, 60,000 rations. Soon as these are received and issued you will move your corps by the most direct route to Petersburg, taking up a position where the City Point railroad crosses Harrison's [sic] Creek at the cross-roads indicated on the map at this point, and extend your right toward the mouth of Harrison's [sic] Creek where we now have a work.[118]

Hancock, on receipt of Meade's directive, drafted his plans. At 10:00 a.m. on June 15 or as soon thereafter as rations had been issued to his command, Maj. Gen. David B. Birney was to march with his division, accompanied by such of "his ammunition wagons, ambulances, etc. as may have been ferried over the river, on the direct road to Petersburg, taking post near where the City Point Railroad crosses

117 *Ibid.*, 27.

118 *Ibid.*, 29.

Harrison's [sic] Creek." Gibbon's and Barlow's divisions were to follow Birney's in the order named, "with such part of their transportation as may be across the river, taking position to the right as they come up, extending toward the mouth of Harrison's [sic] Creek, where we have a work."[119]

General Hancock dispatched his Chief Commissary, Col. Joseph S. Smith, to the south bank of the James River to make necessary arrangements for the receipt and delivery of the rations. At the same time, Hancock's Chief of Staff, Lt. Col. Charles H. Morgan, told Quartermaster Charles S. McEntee to send the transport with the rations as soon as it arrived at the upper landing.[120]

At 3:30 a.m. General Hancock addressed a note to General Meade's headquarters announcing that all the infantry of the II Corps, except one regiment of heavy artillery, had disembarked on the south side of the James. The corps artillery had started crossing, and, at that hour four batteries, except four caissons and several horses, had been landed. As yet, he pointed out, the rations which were to be forwarded from City Point hadn't arrived. Hancock feared that when the rations did show up, it would take considerable time to issue them, because of a wagon shortage. At the moment, two of his divisions were camped two miles from the landing. The third was massed nearby.

Hancock waited anxiously for two and one-half hours for the ration-loaded transport to arrive. When she didn't, the general sent another wire advising General Meade of the situation. Since his last communication, all the equipment and horses belonging to the four batteries had been put ashore. Hancock, at the moment, had returned three ferryboats which would greatly facilitate the crossing of the rest of the corps artillery and the trains.[121]

Meade lost no time acknowledging his corps commander's wire. Hancock was directed to see that the crossing of his artillery and trains was expedited. Since General Meade needed the larger ferryboats to take care of his headquarters, Meade wished to know when Hancock would release them.

It would be noon, Hancock replied, before the last of his artillery and trains reached the south side, and he would have no further use for the large ferries.[122]

Colonel Morgan had left corps headquarters at 2:00 a.m. and had ridden down to the landing to see if he could expedite the crossing. About 7:00 a.m. Maj. Wesley Brainerd of the Corps of Engineers, who had been in charge of a fatigue party which was repairing the wharf where the rations were to be received, returned to

119 *Ibid.*, 61.

120 OR 51, pt. 1, 269-270.

121 OR 40, pt. 2, 56.

122 *Ibid.*, 57.

the north bank of the James. Brainerd told Morgan that Colonel Smith was at the wharf with his commissary people, and that the transport with the rations aboard had tied up. Looking across the James, Morgan saw a steamboat anchored at the wharf in question. Morgan notified General Hancock that the anxiously awaited rations had finally arrived.[123]

Hancock (at 7:15 a.m.) relayed this information to Meade's headquarters.

Replying, Meade informed Hancock not to wait on the rations to be distributed, but to march his troops to Petersburg, taking position where the Petersburg & City Point Railroad crosses Harrison Creek. A staff officer would be sent to direct the transport with the rations to return to City Point or to proceed to the Appomattox to a more suitable point from where Hancock's troops could be supplied.[124]

Colonel Morgan now made an embarrassing discovery—Major Brainerd had been mistaken. The boat in question didn't have the rations aboard. General Hancock delayed this order for his troops to take up the march till 9:00 a.m., while waiting to receive the rations from City Point.[125]

Unfortunately for himself and the Federal cause, General Hancock hadn't been notified that Baldy Smith was to make an attack on Petersburg and that great results might depend on his reaching his destination an hour earlier or later. He had been simply told to move toward Petersburg, and there take up a position. Like any good commander, Hancock preferred to march with his troops rationed. "And not knowing—what General Meade himself did not know—that Petersburg was to be assaulted," he took advantage of the alternative offered him, until it was discovered that the information received regarding the arrival of commissary stores at Windmill Point was erroneous.[126]

At 9:00 a.m. Hancock gave the order by "signal telegraph" for his lead division, Birney's, to move out. Hancock, not wishing to take any chances, sent Colonel Morgan to General Birney's command post with an identical order.

On the morning of June 15 nothing seemed to go right for the II Corps. The boat in which Morgan crossed the James grounded. Morgan was delayed one-half hour. When Morgan finally reached Birney's headquarters, he found the troops standing in ranks waiting for rations. When he questioned Birney, Morgan found that the order to take up the march hadn't been received—the message sent by

123 *OR* 51, pt. 1, 270.

124 *OR* 40, pt. 2, 57

125 *OR* 51, pt. 1, 270; 40, pt. 1, 303.

126 Francis A. Walker, *History of the Second Army Corps in the Army of the Potomac* (New York, 1886), 527.

"signal telegraph" had miscarried. Consequently, it was 10:30 a.m. before the column was put in motion.[127]

Meanwhile, Hancock (at 9:40 a.m.) had notified Meade's headquarters that he had been "deceived about the rations." Orders had been issued for the corps to take up the march and for the rations when they arrived to be forwarded to City Point. Hancock assured Meade that everything was "getting along here as fast as possible," but it was slow work getting the artillery and wagons aboard the ferries. Within the next several minutes, unless Meade should order differently, Hancock planned to cross the James and join his corps as it drove toward Petersburg.

Shortly after sending this dispatch, Hancock was notified by Meade that a wagon and ambulance train belonging to the XVIII Corps had crossed the James River pontoon bridge and would accompany the II Corps "to City Point or some place on the Appomattox . . . "

Meade, in acknowledging Hancock's 9:40 a.m. telegram, sanctioned his plan to push on without waiting for the rations. Hancock was to accompany his infantry, leaving a staff officer to bring up the corps artillery and trains. When the wagons overtook the infantry, Hancock was to see that the ordnance wagons were unloaded and sent to City Point for rations.

Soon after Hancock crossed to the south bank of the James, the schooner *Susan* and another boat tied up with the rations earmarked for the II Corps. Colonel Smith, in view of Hancock's latest instructions, would take the two vessels to City Point and there await further directions as to their disposition.[128]

Prior to leaving Hancock's headquarters, Colonel Morgan had been furnished a map prepared at army headquarters on which the Union position behind "Harrison Creek" had been plotted. According to the map, these earthworks were about four miles east of Petersburg on the Petersburg & City Point Railroad. Subsequently, much to their embarrassment, the officers of the II Corps found that the map was inaccurate. The position Hancock was ordered to take didn't exist as described in his instructions. Harrison Creek, at the same time, proved to be inside the Confederate lines and not within miles of the location indicated on the map furnished by army headquarters. General Hancock recalled that the map was "utterly worthless, the only roads laid down on it being widely out of the way."[129]

Harrison Creek was inside the Confederate earthworks, and was such an insignificant rivulet as probably not to be known by any such name beyond the eastern fringes of Petersburg. There was a run marked on the map as Harrison's

127 OR 40, pt. 1, 303; 51, pt. 1, 270.

128 OR 40, pt. 2, 58.

129 OR 40, pt. 1, 303-304.

Creek, but erroneously laid down. This stream, according to the map, was crossed by the Petersburg & City Point Railroad about three and one-half miles from the city. There was a small stream, Cabin Creek, crossed by the railroad halfway between City Point and Petersburg, and this watercourse emptied into the Appomattox near General Butler's pontoon bridge at Broadway Landing, where there was a bridgehead, as there was at the site of the pontoon bridge, a mile and one-half above. These works appear to be the ones referred to in the dispatch by the phrase "where we now have a work," for there were no Union fortifications where the railroad crossed the run.[130]

Sent wrong by these orders, Hancock's line of march increased several miles, after his time of starting had been delayed. When Hancock did put his corps in motion, he had no intimation that his troops were to be "imperatively required at Petersburg."[131]

Fortunately for the Federals, Colonel Morgan was able to obtain an "intelligent" black, who was familiar with the area, to serve as guide. The II Corps, spearheaded by Birney's division, took "the nearest and most direct route" from Windmill Point to Petersburg. Reaching a point on the Suffolk Stage Road, within two miles of the courthouse, Morgan had Birney call a brief halt. Here, the colonel made "diligent inquiry" as to the location of Harrison Creek. Morgan was unable to find anyone who knew the whereabouts of the stream.[132]

Morgan notified Hancock of his difficulties. At the same time, Morgan pointed out that his black guide had indicated that the best way for the II Corps to secure the position Meade had directed was for the head of the column to turn off the Suffolk Stage Road toward Old Courthouse, and then by utilizing a crossroad, get behind Harrison Creek (actually Cabin Creek). As soon as Colonel Morgan gave the word, Birney's division, closely followed by Gibbon's, turned to the right. As the head of Birney's column resumed the march, Morgan looked at his watch. It was 3:00 p.m. Hancock at the same time turned Barlow's division, which was accompanied by the corps train, into a road veering to the right, a short distance west of Powell's Creek. If all went according to plan, the three divisions would rendezvous near Old Courthouse.[133]

The plantation road on which Birney's and Gibbon's divisions marched struck the Jordan's Point Road about two and one-half miles from the Suffolk Stage Road.

130 Humphreys, *The Virginia Campaign of '64 and '65*, 211-212.

131 Walker, *History of the Second Army Corps*, 529.

132 *OR* 51, pt. 1, 270.

133 *Ibid.*, 270; *OR* 40, pt. 2, 59; 40, pt. 1, 304; Charles H. Weygant, *History of the One Hundred and Twenty-fourth Regiment, N.Y.S.V.* (Newburgh, 1877), 349.

Just as the head of Birney's column was entering the Jordan's Point Road, one of Brig. Gen. Francis C. Barlow's aides thundered up with a dispatch from General Grant. Glancing at the scrap of paper, Morgan learned that Baldy Smith's XVIII Corps had attacked the Petersburg defenses. Grant wanted the II Corps to hasten to Smith's assistance. Whereupon, Morgan took upon himself the responsibility of abandoning the march to the apocryphal "Harrison's Creek [sic]" and turned Birney's vanguard down the Jordan's Point Road.[134]

Meanwhile, General Hancock, who was riding with General Barlow, reached Old Courthouse. There, a courier with a dispatch signed by General Grant and addressed to "General Gibbon or any division commander of the Second Corps," hailed Hancock. Unfolding the message, Hancock learned that General Smith's troops had attacked and carried the outer works guarding the approaches to Petersburg from the east. The II Corps was to proceed to Smith's assistance as rapidly as possible. Before riding on, Hancock told his adjutant to note the time. It was 5:25 p.m.

Thirty minutes later, Capt. Thomas L. Livermore of Baldy Smith's staff came thundering down the road. Livermore handed Hancock a communication signed by Smith.[135] Hancock studied the paper and found that, at the moment, there didn't appear to be many Confederate infantry in the Petersburg defenses. "The wide open spaces along my entire front," Smith reported, in conjunction with the Rebels' "heavy artillery fire" had prevented his troops from making an assault and from getting his artillery into position. If the II Corps could come up in time to make a night assault on the Rebel fortifications in the vicinity of the Norfolk and Petersburg Railroad, Smith believed, the Federals would be able to capture the city. Smith wanted Hancock to let Captain Livermore know when the head of the II Corps would reach the Petersburg area. To guide Hancock in making his dispositions, Smith reported that his left flank rested on the Jordan's Point Road.

To add an air of urgency to the situation, Smith announced that information gleaned from Confederate prisoners indicated that General Lee's Army of Northern Virginia was crossing the James River at Drewry's Bluff.[136]

These messages were the first and only intimation Hancock had received that Petersburg was to be attacked that day. Up to 5:30 p.m. Hancock hadn't been "notified from any source" that he was expected to assist Smith in assaulting the city. Sporadic firing by artillery had been audible from the direction of Petersburg for hours. When he had questioned the local farmers, they had reported that

134 OR 51, pt. 1, 270.

135 OR 40, pt. 1, 304, 317.

136 OR 40, pt. 2, 59.

General Kautz's cavalry had passed toward Petersburg. Hancock therefore attributed the firing to a reconnaissance or a raid by Kautz's troopers.[137]

As soon as General Grant's note directing him to hasten to Smith's assistance was received, Hancock sent Colonel Morgan racing ahead to inform General Smith of the whereabouts of his column, and to assure him that the II Corps "was marching to his support with all dispatch." As the troops swung down the road, they could hear the roar of the cannons in their front.

Leaving the black guide to show Birney the way, Colonel Morgan had put his spurs to his horse. Morgan's orders were to contact General Smith and perfect arrangements for bringing the II Corps into action.

It was after 6:00 p.m. when Morgan reported to Smith. After exchanging greetings, Morgan explained to Smith "the exact position" of the II Corps. Next he asked Smith where, under the circumstances, should the II Corps deploy.

"On my left," Smith replied.

Morgan was disappointed when Smith failed to indicate where his left was or send a staff officer to show him. Finally, Smith told Morgan to go see General Hinks.

Accompanied by Capt. William P. Wilson, Morgan went to look for Hinks' command post. On doing so, they encountered one of General Birney's staff officers, who had been sent ahead to report to Baldy Smith. Morgan told the staff officer to retrace his steps and conduct Birney's column to such point on the field as General Hinks might indicate. The Chief of Staff did this knowing that Hancock would have great difficulty in getting to the front in time to give the necessary orders.[138]

When he discussed the local road network with General Smith, Morgan learned that there was a crossroad leading from the Jordan's Point Road, along which Barlow's division was supposed to be marching, that would bring the column in on the XVIII Corps' left. Morgan started out the Jordan's Point Road, hoping to contact Barlow's vanguard. If successful, he might be able to get Barlow's division up about the same time as Gibbon's, and thus have the II Corps massed in time to cooperate in any offensive operations which Generals Smith and Hancock might undertake.[139]

At 6:30 p.m. General Birney's vanguard reached Bryant's house on Bailey Creek, a mile in the rear of Hinks' division.

---

137 *OR* 40, pt. 1, 304.

138 *OR* 51, pt. 1, 270.

139 *Ibid.*, 270-271.

General Birney's troops had been on the road since 11:00 a.m. A 30-minute halt had been called at 4:00 p.m. Foraging had been poor so the troops had little to eat except fresh beef. Throughout the afternoon, the roar of the guns from the fighting on the eastern approaches to Petersburg had been heard. As Birney's troops approached Petersburg, they encountered a number of wounded black soldiers from Hinks' division making their way to the rear.[140]

Hancock, accompanied by Maj. William G. Mitchell, rode ahead to see Baldy Smith. Instructions were left for Birney and Gibbon to move their divisions forward as soon as they could ascertain at what point their assistance was required. When Hancock and Mitchell arrived near Battery No. 5, they encountered Generals Smith and Brooks. Smith tersely explained that his troops had stormed forward and captured a number of Confederate redoubts. He pointed out as best he could, in the failing light, the sector of the Rebel line his men had carried.

Hancock informed Smith that he had two divisions (Birney's and Gibbon's) close at hand, and they were ready for any services which Smith, "in his judgment and knowledge of the field," wished undertaken. Replying, Smith cautioned Hancock that he was afraid the Confederates were throwing fresh troops into Petersburg. He accordingly wanted the II Corps to relieve his troops in the works which they had just carried, so that the grey clads, in case they counterattacked, would encounter fresh units.

The meeting of the two corps commanders probably occurred about 9:00 p.m., as the assault had just concluded.

Smith, Hancock, and Brooks, accompanied by their staffs, rode off toward the captured works. On the way, Hancock called to Major Mitchell, telling him to return to Bryant's House and bring up Gibbon's division; a second staff officer was sent to General Birney with similar instructions.

As soon as they received the word, Gibbon and Birney put their troops in motion. When they took position, Gibbon's troops filed into the earthworks to the left of the Friend house, while Birney's relieved Hinks' black regiments. By 11:30 p.m. all of Gibbon's and Birney's troops were in the captured earthworks, but by then it was "too late" to resume the offensive. It was a "lovely moonlight night." The roofs and spires of Petersburg could be distinctly seen by the troops which were posted at Battery No. 5.[141]

---

140 Gilbert A. Hays and William H. Morrow, *Under the Red Patch, Story of the Sixty Third Regiment Pennsylvania Volunteers, 1861-1864* (Pittsburgh, 1908), 255; Alfred S. Roe and Charles Nutt, *History of the First Regiment of Heavy Artillery Massachusetts Volunteers, Formerly the Fourteenth Regiment of Infantry, 1861-1865* (Worcester, 1917), 172.

141 OR 40, pt. 1, 305, 317; Cunningham, *The Adirondack Regiment*, 132.

It was early the next morning before Barlow's division reached the area. Taking the wrong road, Barlow's troops had marched almost to City Point before the error was discovered.[142]

Following the arrival of Birney's and Gibbon's divisions, Baldy Smith could have advanced on the crumbling Petersburg defenses with at least 15,000 men. It is doubtful the Confederates could have withstood this force, if indeed they were willing to rally for another stand. While Birney's and Gibbon's troops were weary, they were combat veterans. Although General Smith had lost perhaps a tenth of his forces in the day's fighting, and one-third of those remaining were blacks who had received their first taste of combat, all had behaved with great courage and steadiness. Much could have been trusted to soldiers who had proved themselves by holding their ground for five hours under a fierce bombardment and then storming the strong works protecting the guns which had tormented them.[143]

It is not a part of this paper to go into the arguments as to whether General Smith could have occupied Petersburg on the night of June 15. The pros and cons of this dispute are adequately covered in volume 5 of the Papers of the Military Historical Society of Massachusetts. It, however, seems to this military historian that the odds were strongly in favor of Smith achieving his mission, if he had pushed on.

JUNE 16

On the night of June 15, after the Federals seized the center of the Dimmock Line, Beauregard considered ordering Hoke's division to launch an assault to regain the line but changed his mind when he realized those troops were exhausted by their march to join him. He decided instead to postpone any attacks until the arrival of Johnson's division. Also that night he withdrew Johnson's division from the Howlett Line on Bermuda Hundred in order to help hold the line at Petersburg, leaving Bermuda Hundred undefended except for a picket line.[144]

At 12:25 a.m. on June 16 Hancock told his division commanders John Gibbon and David B. Birney that the Confederate line was to be attacked and taken before daylight. However, Gibbon and Birney did not reconnoiter

---

142 *OR* 40, pt. 1, 318.

143 Livermore, "The Failure to Take Petersburg, June 15, 1864," 67.

144 Thomas J. Howe, *Wasted Valor* (Lynchburg, 1988), 38.

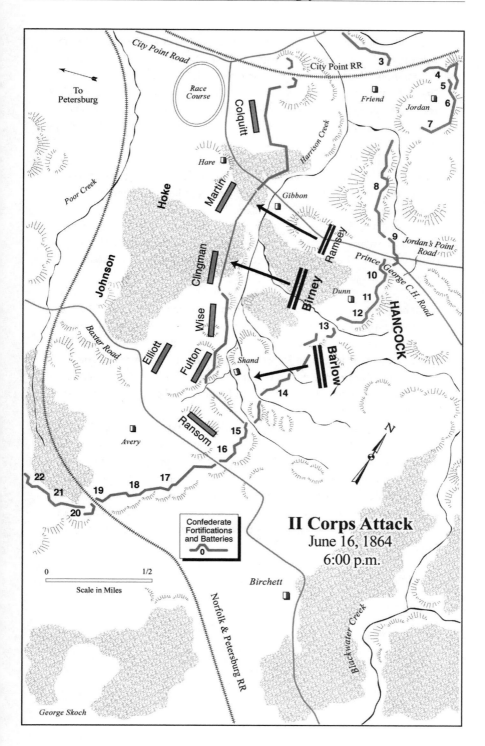

II Corps Attack
June 16, 1864
6:00 p.m.

Confederate
Fortifications
and Batteries

0

Scale in Miles
0   1/2

George Skoch

their fronts for weak spots until 6:00 a.m., well after dawn. At dawn Barlow's division, having lost its way en route to Petersburg, began straggling in.[145]

Gibbon's division's right flank joined the left of the XVIII Corps at the Friend house. Birney's division held the center of Hancock's II Corps line from the Prince George Court House Road to the area south of Battery No. 12. As Barlow's men dribbled onto the battlefield, they formed on Hancock's left.

In front of Gibbon was Colquitt's and Martin's brigades from Hoke's division. In front of Birney were Clingman's and Wise's brigades, also from Hoke's division. In front of Barlow the lines were lightly defended by newly arriving troops from Johnson's division.[146]

After Gibbon and Birney had examined the rebel line Hancock ordered a reconnaissance in force. Egan's brigade of Birney's division captured Battery No. 12 but failed to break the Confederate line defended by Clingman's Brigade.[147]

At 10:30 a.m. Grant left City Point for the front, after ordering Meade to leave his headquarters at the pontoon bridge spanning the James River and ride to City Point and take command of the attack on Petersburg. He also urged Meade to hurry Warren's corps to the front so it could anchor the Union left at the Jerusalem Plank Road. Meade and his staff reached City Point at 11:30 a.m. only to find Grant gone. Riding forward they met Grant returning from the front lines. Grant told Meade that if possible he wanted an assault at 6:00 p.m.[148]

Barlow observed that Johnson's division had arrived and formed opposite him on Hoke's right. Here, he believed was an opportunity to flank the Confederate right. Hancock rejected Barlow's suggestion and did not pass it along to Meade. By 4:00 p.m. Meade had also come up with a plan. Birney would assault the Confederate lines at the Hare Farm. Gibbon's division would support the attack. Baldy Smith's XVIII corps would make a strong demonstration in its front. Barlow would attack the position opposite the Shand and Avery houses.[149]

145 *Ibid.*, 43.

146 *Ibid.*, 43, 54.

147 *Ibid.*, 44-46.

148 *Ibid.*, 48.

149 *Ibid.*, 49.

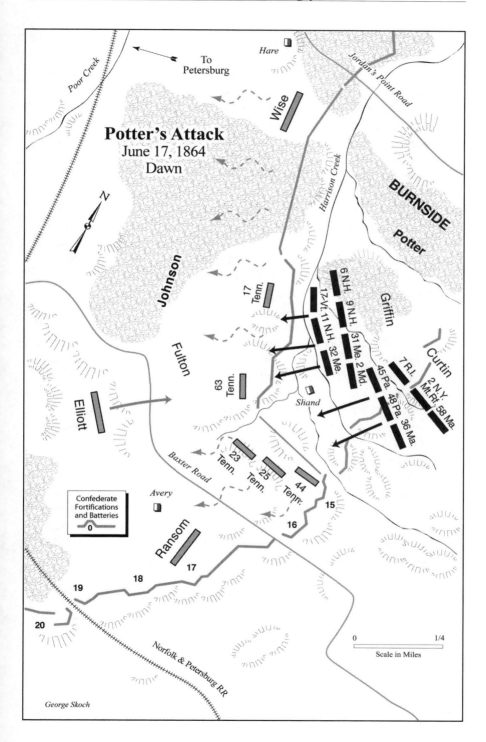

Potter's Attack
June 17, 1864
Dawn

To
Petersburg

Hare

Poor Creek

Wise

Jordan's Point Road

Harrison Creek

BURNSIDE

Potter

N

Johnson

Fulton

17
Tenn.

6 N.H.
9 N.H.
17 Vt.
11 N.H.
31 Me.
32 Me.
2 Md.

Griffin

Curtin

7 R.I.
2 N.Y.
Mt. Rf.
45 Pa.
58 Ma.
48 Pa.
36 Ma.

63
Tenn.

Shand

Elliott

23
Tenn.
25
Tenn.
44
Tenn.

Baxter Road

Avery

15

16

Confederate
Fortifications
and Batteries
0

Ransom

17

18

19

20

Norfolk & Petersburg R.R.

0   1/4
Scale in Miles

George Skoch

The attack took place on schedule. Smith's corps kept Hagood's brigade engaged during the main attack, which was carried out almost entirely by the II Corps. Ramsey's brigade of Gibbon's division formed in two lines on the Prince George Road facing the Hare Farm. Despite heavy fire many reached the edge of the woods by the farm, and some got as close as forty yards from the Confederate position. On their left, brigades under Tannant and Mott of Birney's division formed with their right flanks on the Prince George Road and charged forward. The brunt of the attack fell on Clingman's brigade. The federals entrenched close to his line.[150]

On Barlow's right Nelson A. Miles' brigade got as far as some of the Confederate rifle pits and fortifications. On Barlow's right Beaver's brigade made it to some protective ravines in front of Johnson's Tennessee brigade where its men were safe from Confederate fire. The 44th Tennessee came out of their lines and forced 500 men of the 7th New York Heavy Artillery to surrender. In the center MacDougall's brigade attacked the trenches at the Shand house but was repulsed.[151]

Meade expected Burnside to support the attack. As early as 10:00 a.m. the first of Burnside's troops had begun arriving at Petersburg. By 2:00 p.m. two of his three divisions were in position on Barlow's left. (The Third division did not arrive until 6:00 p.m. However, Simon Griffin's brigade of the IX Corps attacked and captured some rifle pits). The rest of the corps was too tired to join in the attack.[152]

The 6 o'clock attack netted the Federals Batteries 3, 13 and 14, but the Confederate line remained intact. With fewer than 14,000 men Beauregard had held his ground against 50,000 Federals. However, since the attacks were mostly launched by Hancock's II Corps, only a fraction of the rest of Meade's forces were employed.[153]

On the night of June 16, Beauregard launched several vigorous attacks to retake lost batteries and to drive the Federals back. Although these attacks failed, they prevented the Federals from launching their own new attacks and kept the Federals (already exhausted from the long march to Petersburg and the fighting) from getting much needed sleep.[154]

---

150   *Ibid.*, 53-55.

151   *Ibid.*, 56.

152   *Ibid.*, 48-49, 57.

153   *Ibid.*, 57.

154   *Ibid.*, 58-59.

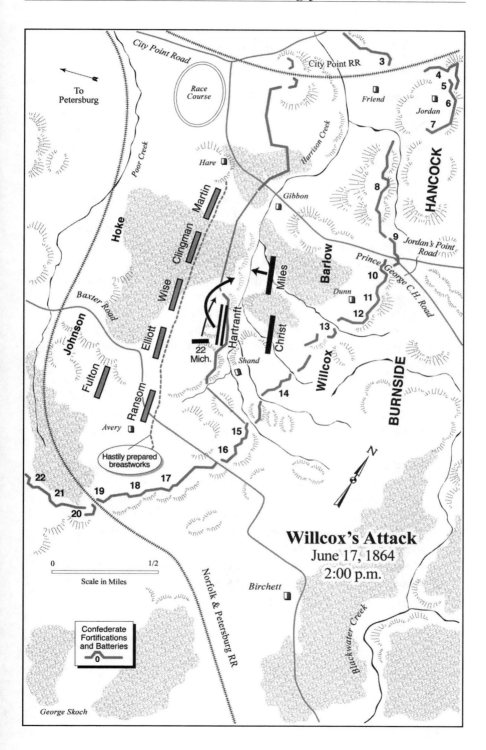

To Petersburg

City Point Road

Race Course

City Point RR   3

Friend

Jordan

4
5
6
7

Poor Creek

Hare

Gibbon

Harrison Creek

HANCOCK

8

Hoke

Martin

Clingman

Wise

Elliott

Baxter Road

Johnson

Fulton

Ransom

Avery

Hastily prepared breastworks

Hartranft

22 Mich.

Shand

Miles

Christ

13

BARLOW

Dunn

10
11
12

Jordan's Point Road

Prince George C.H. Road

9

WILLCOX

14

BURNSIDE

15

16

22
21
19
18
17
20

N

Willcox's Attack
June 17, 1864
2:00 p.m.

0   1/2
Scale in Miles

Birchett

Norfolk & Petersburg RR

Blackwater Creek

Confederate
Fortifications
and Batteries

George Skoch

JUNE 17

Meade believed one more attack would break Beauregard's line and he ordered Burnside to select a spot in front of his lines for the assault. Burnside chose the Shand house where ravines led right up to the Confederate position defended by Johnson's Tennessee Brigade. To make the attack Burnside selected Simon Griffin's and Curtin's brigades from Robert Potter's division. They were in position by 1:00 a.m.[155]

The Federals charged forward just before dawn broke and struck a gap between Wise's Virginia brigade and Fulton's Tennessee brigade. In one of the most remarkable successes of the war, Potter drove back the Tennessee troops and seized a mile of front (and may have captured Petersburg if Ledlie's division had supported him as ordered, and if Barlow had attacked on his flank). Beauregard employed Elliott's brigade to erect a new line a few hundred yards behind the breach. The Confederates fell back to this line and repulsed Potter's further attacks.[156]

At dawn on June 17, Warren's V Corps began arriving and by mid-morning the corps was in place on Burnside's left, giving Meade a total of twelve divisions to assault the city. Unfortunately, although Grant did not directly command troops on June 17, he interfered with Meade enough on at least two occasions to lessen Meade's chances of winning. In response to a request from Butler, Grant relieved Kautz's cavalry of its task of guarding the Union left against a flank attack and sent it to Bermuda Hundred to help man the intrenchments. He replaced it with Warren's V Corps, thus tying down an entire corps for the whole day. Also on the 17th, mistakenly believing there was a chance to break through the Confederate lines on Bermuda Hundred, Grant landed most of Wright's VI Corps there. When he learned the Confederate position was stronger than Grant anticipated, Wright decided not to attack and remained idle for two days. If the V and VI Corps had been used at Petersburg on June 17, Meade may well have taken the city.

Meade's second attack on the 17th consisted of another assault by Burnside, scheduled for 2:00 p.m., this time by Willcox's division. Once

155 *Ibid.*, 62-63.

156 *Ibid.*, 65-67.

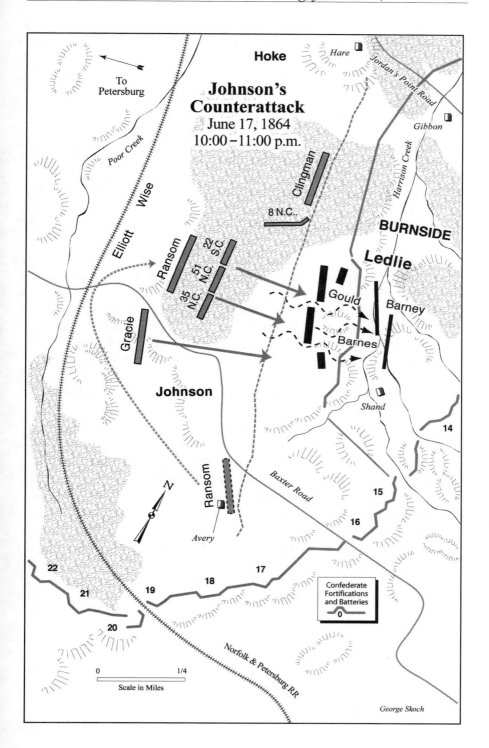

Hoke

Johnson's Counterattack
June 17, 1864
10:00–11:00 p.m.

To Petersburg

Hare

Jordan's Point Road

Gibbon

Poor Creek

Wise

Elliott

Clingman

8 N.C.

Harrison Creek

BURNSIDE

Ransom

22 S.C.

51 N.C.

35 N.C.

Ledlie

Gould

Barney

Gracie

Barnes

Johnson

Shand

14

N

Ransom

Baxter Road

15

Avery

16

22

17

21

18

19

Confederate Fortifications and Batteries

20

0

Norfolk & Petersburg RR

0   1/4

Scale in Miles

George Skoch

again the objective was the ravines by the Shand house. Willcox selected for his attack the brigades of John Hartranft and Benjamin Christ.[157]

Hartranft's brigade led the attack, supported by Christ. Miles' Brigade from the II Corps advanced on Hartranft's right. Because Warren was tied down there was no support for the IX Corp's left. Consequently Hartranft's left was pummeled so hard that his line veered to the right, charging across the Confederate front in a perpendicular direction. This presented its left flank to the fire from the main Confederate line, and the Federals broke and fled to the rear. Upon seeing the disintegration of Hartranft's line, Christ veered to the left in his attack, but was pinned down. Ledlie's division following Willcox clawed its way through the Confederate slashing, and occupied Batteries 15 and 16, but could go no further. Miles' attack had failed.[158]

Burnside decided to make a third attack on the area near the Shand house that evening with his last fresh division under Ledlie. The attack was to be supported by Barlow's division of the II Corps. In Ledlie's front line were the brigades of Jacob P. Gould and Joseph H. Barnes. Lt. Col. Benjamin B. Barney's brigade formed a second line. Three-quarters of the attack was directed at Bushrod Johnson's division. Defending the Confederate right south of the Baxter Road were Johnson's Tennessee brigade and Ransom's North Carolina brigade. In the center were parts of Wise's Virginia and Elliott's South Carolina brigades. On the left was Clingman's brigade of Hoke's division.[159]

North of the road Ledlie launched the attack at 6:00 p.m. and broke through Johnson's front. One of Willcox's brigades came to Ledlie's support and seized ground as well. To the north Barlow's division attacked to widen the breach. It looked as though the Confederate line would crumble.[160]

Then the tide turned. Colquitt's brigade stood firm and repulsed Barlow while Beauregard directed a series of counterattacks by parts of Ransom's, Clingman's, Colquitt's and Wise's brigades. The battle lasted from 6:00 p.m. until 10:00 p.m. The Federals withdrew from the captured works, leaving

157 *Ibid.*, 75.

158 *Ibid.*, 75-79.

159 *Ibid.*, 94.

160 *Ibid.*, 96.

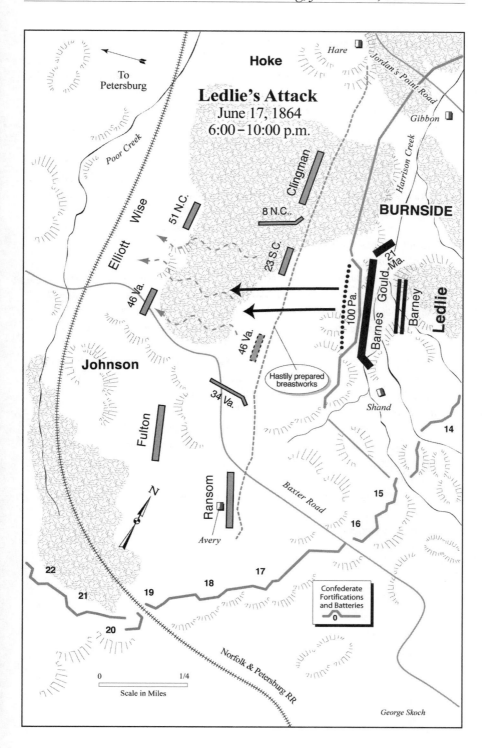

To Petersburg

Hoke

Hare

Jordan's Point Road

Gibbon

Ledlie's Attack
June 17, 1864
6:00–10:00 p.m.

Clingman

Harrison Creek

Poor Creek

51 N.C.

8 N.C.

BURNSIDE

Wise

Elliott

23 S.C.

21 Ma.

Gould

Barney

Ledlie

46 Va.

100 Pa.

Barnes

46 Va.

Hastily prepared breastworks

Johnson

34 Va.

Shand

14

Fulton

N

Baxter Road

15

Ransom

16

Avery

22

17

21

19

18

Confederate
Fortifications
and Batteries

20

0

0   1/4

Scale in Miles

Norfolk & Petersburg RR

George Skoch

behind many prisoners. Overall Ledlie lost one-third of his strength in the assault.[161]

Once again the Confederates held their positions despite overwhelming Union numbers. Once again Meade cancelled out his superiority in numbers by committing only one corps and a tiny fraction of another corps to the attack. June 16 had been the II Corps' turn to be battered and bloodied, and the IX Corps' on the 17th.

On the night of the 17th Meade issued an order for a 4:00 a.m. attack by the II, V, and IX corps. The XVIII Corps and the newly arrived division of Martindale from the VXIII Corps were to remain ready to support the other corps or launch their own attacks if an opportunity presented itself.[162]

During the night Beauregard's soldiers fell back to a new line located 500-800 yards in rear of the previous one. The line began on the Appomattox River 200 yards west of the Hare house and ran south to the Petersburg & City Point Railroad. After crossing the railroad it followed a ditch running behind the New Market Race Course. Johnson Hagood's brigade defended this part of the line. From the race course the center of the line ran south along the west side of Hare Hill and across Poor Creek to a point southwest of the Hare house. General Alfred Colquitt's Georgia brigade defended this part of the line. After crossing Poor Creek the line traversed the Norfolk and Petersburg Railroad and followed a high ridge toward the Rives Farm. This part of the line was defended by the brigades under Generals Martin and Clingman.[163]

The new Southern line continued south, crossing the Baxter Road at nearly right angles until it joined the Dimmock Line at Battery No. 25 on the Rives Farm just east of the Jerusalem Plank Road, where it continued west along the Dimmock Line. This sector of the line was thinly manned by the depleted ranks of Johnson's division and Wise's brigade. The extreme Confederate right was defended by Dearing's cavalry brigade. In many places the trenches did not exist and had to be thrown up by the weary troops.[164]

---

161 *Ibid.*, 94-99.

162 *Ibid.*, 106.

163 *Ibid.*, 107.

164 *Ibid.*, 107.

Part III

Meade's June 18 Assault on Petersburg Fails
and the Investment Begins

Major General George G. Meade of the Army of the Potomac, at 11:00 p.m. on June 17, 1864, ordered three of his four corps commanders to be ready to make a "vigorous assault" on the Rebel works guarding the approaches to Petersburg at 4:00 a.m. Corps commanders were to make necessary arrangements to insure that their attacks would get under way simultaneously, and "to make it in strong columns, well supported," so that if a breakthrough occurred it could be exploited. Brigadier General Thomas H. Neill of the VI Corps and the officer in charge of the units from the XVIII Corps, posted on the Spring Hill Road, were to hold their troops ready to attack to their front, or to march to the left to bolster the assaults of the other corps. If the men of the IX Corps had actually breached the Rebel fortifications as he had been led to believe in the day's final thrust, Meade felt that one more blow would sweep the Confederates out of Petersburg and across the Appomattox.[165]

Upon the receipt of Meade's circular, Maj. Gen. Winfield S. Hancock of the II Corps discussed the projected onslaught with his staff. Hancock, on questioning his officers, found that all of his troops were in line, and none could be withdrawn to beef up an attack in a specific sector. To assault a given point, Hancock notified Meade before retiring, he could probably mass three or, at the most, four battle lines of a brigade front. Unless this force made a breakthrough, it would be unsafe to commit his other units, because in event of a repulse, Hancock would have no troops to contain the Rebel counterthrust.[166]

Hancock, like the good soldier he was, proceeded to work out plans for the dawn attack. Since the thrust would have to be on a restricted front, it was decided to attack at a point in front of the sector held by Maj. Gen. David B. Birney's Third division. Birney's troops were to be supported by "such part" of Maj. Gen. John Gibbon's and Brig. Gen. Francis C. Barlow's divisions as it was possible to utilize for that purpose. Gibbon and Barlow were to send to Birney all their surplus units. These troops were to be preceded by staff officers who were to ascertain the

---

165 OR 40, pt 2, 120.

166 *Ibid.*, 163.

Brigadier General Thomas L. Clingman
Library of Congress

positions they were to occupy. Birney was cautioned that the assault was to be made on the narrowest possible front. The attack was to begin at 4:00 a.m.[167]

Two hours before the day's action was scheduled to commence, General Hancock was compelled to relinquish his command. For some months, the wound which he had received the previous July at Gettysburg had been suppurating and giving him great pain. The pain now became unbearable. Hancock was compelled to relieve himself from duty and place General Birney in charge of the II Corps. Hancock planned to spend the day in his tent. With Birney in charge of the corps, Brig. Gen. Gershom Mott took charge of the Third Division.[168]

Major General Ambrose E. Burnside of the IX Corps was unenthusiastic about the prospects of the projected attack. The previous evening Brig. Gen. James H. Ledlie's First division, which had penetrated the Rebel defenses near the Shands house, had been caught in a counterthrust. Ledlie's bluecoats had been driven from the captured rifle pits and compelled to retire to the crest occupied before the advance. Telegraphing Meade's headquarters at 3:15 a.m., Burnside reported that "scarcely anything" was left of Ledlie's division. At the same time, two of his three other divisions (Potter's and Willcox's) were "very much wearied as we made three assaults yesterday." Burnside allowed that he could attack the Confederates, but he warned that he wasn't "confident of doing much." In closing, Burnside inquired, "Shall I attack them?"[169]

---

167 *Ibid.*, 170.

168 *Ibid.*, 170-171; *OR*, 40, pt. 1, 308; Walker, *History of the Second Army Corps*, 539.

169 *OR* 40, pt. 2, 191.

When he acknowledged Burnside's communication, Meade told him that he wanted the attack to begin as scheduled. Burnside was to commit all the men he had available.[170]

*   *   *

General Pierre G. T. Beauregard foresaw on June 16 that, unless he was reinforced, he would have to contract his lines covering the eastern approaches to Petersburg or see them ruptured. Beauregard and his Chief Engineer, Col. D. B. Harris, spent considerable time on the 17th selecting a new and shorter defense line along Poor Creek. The two officers issued instructions that this new line be "clearly marked out with white stakes, so that it might be occupied at night without confusion," whenever the troops were directed to retire upon it. Major Generals Robert F. Hoke and Bushrod Johnson were instructed to see that their staff officers and those of the brigades under their command examined and learned the new positions to be occupied by their units. This they did with "their usual care and precision" while resisting the Federals' onslaught.[171]

Late in the afternoon, Beauregard addressed a circular to his division commanders. As soon as it was dark, they were to begin withdrawing their troops to the positions previously determined upon. A "strong line of skirmishers" would be left to hold the works and cover the movement. General Hoke's new main line of resistance was to begin on the Appomattox River east of Poor Creek, following the ditch along the "race course." After crossing Poor Creek, Hoke's right was to join "Johnson's left toward the Baxter Road." Johnson's line was to cross the Baxter Road "nearly at right angles," continue to the Jerusalem Plank Road, and from that point follow the original perimeter as far west as numbers would permit. One of Johnson's brigades would be held in reserve about his center or near Jerusalem Plank Road. Brigadier General James Dearing and his horsemen were to guard the sector from Johnson's right to the Appomattox west of Petersburg.[172]

As soon as the fighting had died out along the lines, the soldiers, in accordance with Beauregard's instructions, began kindling campfires. Outposts were advanced.

About 1:00 a.m. the Confederate soldiers started their retrograde movement. Beauregard recalled that "notwithstanding the exhaustion" of the men and "their sore disappointment at receiving no further reinforcements," the withdrawal was "safely and silently executed, with uncommonly good order and precision, though

170 *Ibid.*, 192.

171 Roman, *Military Operations of General Beauregard*, vol. 2, 233.

172 *OR* 40, pt. 2, 666.

the greatest caution had to be used . . . to retire unnoticed from so close a contact with so strong an adversary." Upon being posted along the new line, the grey clads were put to work digging rifle pits. Entrenching tools were in short supply, so the troops used "such utensils as had been hastily collected" in Petersburg. Many of the Rebs used their bayonets, their knives, and even their mess plates. By daylight, in spite of "nearly insurmountable difficulties," the Confederates had covered themselves behind earthworks.[173]

The troops of Brig. Gen. Johnson Hagood's South Carolina brigade were posted on the left of Hoke's line. Hagood's left rested on the Appomattox, about 200 yards west of the house owned by the younger Hare. Running at nearly right angles to the river, the rifle pits dug and occupied by the South Carolinians crossed the City Point Road and extended over the western slope of the eminence known as Hare's Hill. The New Market Racecourse was in front of Hagood's right; the approaches to the trenches held by South Carolinians were over "generally level" ground. Brigadier General Alfred Colquitt's Georgia brigade was posted on the right of Hagood's butternuts.[174]

Beauregard had 51 pieces of artillery organized into four battalions: Read's, Moseley's, Coit's, and Boggs'. A portion of Coit's Battalion (the cannoneers of the Confederate Guards Artillery and Capt. Samuel T. Wright's Virginia battery) had emplaced their guns on the north side of the Appomattox. The gunners had sighted their 8 pieces (including three 20-pounder Parrotts), to sweep with an enfilading fire, the left flank of Beauregard's new main line of resistance on the opposite side of the river. The rest of Beauregard's guns were posted along the line and at commanding points in its rear to aid in the defense of Petersburg.[175]

*   *   *

Colonel John C. Tidball, the II Corps' Chief of Artillery, had been alerted by Hancock that an attack was impending. The cannoneers turned infantrymen of the 4th New York Heavy Artillery were mustered at dawn and sent into the earthworks to relieve Mott's foot soldiers. At 4:00 a.m., the II Corps artillery roared into action; the gunners manning the smoothbores hammered the Confederate fortifications, while those serving the rifled guns shelled Petersburg.[176]

---

173 Roman, *Military Operations of General Beauregard,* vol. 2, 233.

174 Hagood, *Memoirs of the War of Secession,* 268-269; OR 40, pt. 1, 802.

175 *Ibid.,* 755-757.

176 *Ibid.,* 423. Batteries C and I, 5th U.S. Light Artillery had moved to the front at daybreak and had relieved the 10th Massachusetts Battery. Upon being relieved, the Massachusetts

Shortly after 4:00 a.m. Birney and Mott gave the signal. Amid the rattle of drums and blare of bugles, massed battle lines of the II Corps surged forward. North of the Prince George Courthouse Road, Gibbon's division advanced in double line of battle. The Rebel works to their front were clouded in dust and exploding shells.[177] As Gibbon's blue clad formations approached the beaten zone, the Federal artillerists shifted target. Except for scattered shots fired by Confederate pickets, the Yanks encountered no opposition. The Rebel outposts retired rapidly in the face of the Union thrust. Gibbon's troops entered the Confederate earthworks and found them deserted.

Officers halted and reformed their units; scouts moved out to see if they could pinpoint the Confederate's new main line of resistance. Within a short time, patrols returned with news that the Southerners were dug in about one-half mile to their front.[178]

Mott's line of advance lay south of the Prince George's Courthouse Road. As they pressed ahead, Mott's soldiers beat their way through the pines. Like Gibbon's division on its right, Mott's encountered no resistance beyond an occasional shot from a Confederate sharpshooter. Reaching the Rebel works at the O. P. Hare house and along the Plank Road, Mott's bluecoats found that the Rebs had pulled back during the night. The officers promptly put their men to refacing the abandoned earthworks. A detachment from the 1st Brigade (soldiers of the 124th New York) was advanced to within 200 yards of the Confederates' new line before it entrenched.[179]

A soldier in the 17th Maine recalled:

On the right of our line, was an elegant residence, formerly occupied by Mr. O. P. Hare, a southern sporting gentleman of wealth, who was "not at home" when we arrived. The men, in their customary style of protecting sesesh property, procured some very elegant horse-trappings and equipments, from his establishment. His house and the adjacent buildings were completely riddled with shot and shell. His furniture

---

cannoneers had shifted their pieces farther to the left into the sector held by Barlow's division. *Ibid.*, 429, 442.

177 *Ibid.*, 366. Gibbon's first line of battle consisted of Col. B. R. Pierce's and Col. John Fraser's brigades, while Smyth's brigade constituted the second line. Colonel Frank's brigade of Barlow's division followed Smyth's troops.

178 *Ibid.*, 366, 375, 377, 382; David Craft, *History of the One Hundred Forty-First Regiment, Pennsylvania Volunteers 1862-1865* (Towanda, 1885). 215-216; Edwin E. Houghton, *The Campaigns of the Seventeenth Maine* (Portland, 1866), 203.

179 *OR*, 40, pt. 1, 184, 391, 396, 416; Weygant, *History of the One Hundred Twenty-Four Regiment*, 350; Houghton, *The Campaigns of the Seventeenth Maine*, 203-204.

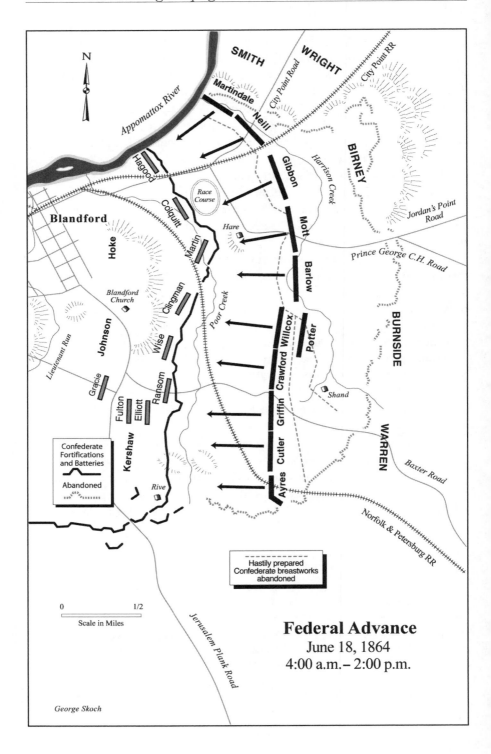

Federal Advance
June 18, 1864
4:00 a.m. – 2:00 p.m.

George Skoch

was sadly "demoralized," and soon distributed along the works. Costly stuffed chairs, and sofas of plush and damask, furnished Yankee soldiers luxuriant repose; and a fine rosewood piano, which a rebel-shell had "played upon," was made to do duty in a portion of the works we had thrown up across his garden.

The initials of this gentleman's name furnished some wag with an opportunity to perpetrate a joke, which no soldier can resist, even though under fire. On one of the walls of a room had been inscribed, for the information of the curious, the following line: "The proprietor is OPH."[180]

During the advance, soldiers of the II Corps captured 40 Confederates. When they questioned these men, the Federal officers learned that the Rebs had evacuated their earthworks near the Hare house about 2:00 a.m. and had retired to a shorter line, "said to envelop the railroad bridge and to be about one mile" east of Petersburg. General Meade, at 5:30 a.m., relayed this information to his immediate supervisor, Lt. Gen. Ulysses S. Grant. On doing so, he reported that his troops were still pressing ahead and would continue to do so until the Southerners were "found and felt." Additional movements of the Army of Potomac would, Meade informed Grant, be governed by what these forced reconnaissances developed.[181]

As soon as the troops of the II Corps reported that the Confederates had fallen back, General Meade addressed a "circular" to the Army of the Potomac. Since information garnered from prisoners indicated that the Rebels had retired to an inner belt of fortifications nearer Petersburg, corps and other "independent commanders" were to advance their units. As they did, they were to keep contact with the troops on their left and right, and develop the Confederate's new defense line.[182]

General Barlow (at 6:00 a.m.), upon receipt of Meade's "circular," sent his troops into the pines to his front. Foraging ahead, Barlow's brigades experienced no difficulty in reaching and occupying the abandoned Rebel rifle pits to Mott's left, south of the Hare house.[183]

*   *   *

The soldiers of the IX Corps had taken up the attack at 4:30 a.m. Brigadier General Orlando B. Willcox's Third division had been assigned to spearhead the

---

180 Houghton, *The Campaigns of the Seventeenth Maine*, 204.

181 OR 40, pt. 1, 156.

182 OR 40, pt. 1, 161.

183 OR 40, pt. 1, 180, 327, 339, 342.

advance and saw that a strong force of skirmishers were pushed out to feel for the Confederates. Within a short time, the officer in charge reported that the Rebs had abandoned their earthworks in front of the IX Corps. Upon receipt of this news, Willcox directed the commander of his 1st Brigade, Brig. Gen. John F. Hartranft, to send his troops forward. Hartranft's soldiers were told that they were to advance to the Norfolk & Petersburg Railroad and drive the grey clads from the shelter afforded by the railroad cuts and embankments.

Screened by a formidable skirmish line, Hartranft's brigade crossed the fields to its front. Entering the woods beyond, the blue clads pressed toward the ridge crowned by the Taylor house.[184]

In the pines, the Federals encountered Confederate sharpshooters. As if this weren't bad enough, Rebel artillery emplaced west of the Norfolk & Petersburg Railroad went into action. Shells exploded in the tops of trees, showering the Yanks with needles, branches, and flying pieces of iron. Undaunted, the grim infantrymen pressed ahead, driving the Confederate skirmishers before them. The Rebels, as they retired, took cover in a deep cut through which the railroad passed.

Debouching from the woods, Hartranft's troops entered a broad, open field of grain "near the Taylor house." Here, they saw a heartbreaking sight. The Southerners had thrown up a strong line of rifle pits beyond the railroad cut and the winding ravine, through which Poor Creek flowed. General Willcox observed that the banks of Poor Creek to his front were steep and covered with trees and dense underbrush. To reach the Confederates' new main line of resistance, Willcox's foot soldiers would have to cross two formidable obstacles—the cut and the hollow. Moreover, if the Federals were to reach the railroad, they would have to cross the open field while exposed to a sweeping fire.

As he studied the Confederate defenses through his glasses, Willcox saw that their rifle pits were about 800 yards west of the Taylor house, and ran along the foot of "Cemetery Hill" and veered to his right toward Hare House Hill.

A Rebel artillery emplacement had been erected to cover the railroad cut. To try to knock out this position, which contained one gun, Willcox sent a staff officer to bring up the 34th Battery, New York Light Artillery. The cannoneers drove their pieces forward at a gallop. At the edge of the pines, Capt. Jacob Roemer halted his battery. The fire of the foe was "so hot" that Roemer was obliged to leave his team in the woods. General Willcox showed Captain Roemer where he wished him to

---

184 *Ibid.*, 523, 575, 577. Hartranft had formed his brigade into double line of battle. From left to right the first line was composed of the 50th Pennsylvania, 2nd and 20th Michigan. The other two regiments were to guide on the 2nd Michigan. The second line from left to right included the 37th Wisconsin, 109th New York, and 27th Michigan. Colonel Raulston's brigade was massed in close supporting distance of Hartranft's. *Ibid.*, 557.

emplace his four 3-inch rifles. One section of the New Yorkers' guns were manhandled into battery to register on several Rebel pieces firing on the Yanks from the left, while the other pointed its guns at the Confederate piece which commanded the railroad cut.

By this time, reinforcements were at hand. Brig. Gen. Samuel W. Crawford's division of the V Corps had advanced through the pines. As they forged ahead, Crawford's right flank units kept pace with Hartranft's battle line.[185] Brigadier General Robert B. Potter's division of the IX Corps now came up and took position in the woods behind Willcox's troops. As yet, Barlow's division, which was supposed to be on Willcox's right, hadn't put in an appearance.

Willcox told Hartranft to "carry the railroad cut." As soon as the gunners of the 34th New York Battery had knocked out the Rebel gun covering the cut, Hartranft waved his men forward. Letting go with a wild cheer for the Union, Hartranft's blue clads stormed the railroad cut in "good style, "although they suffered "very severely from a galling cross-fire." Crawford's soldiers of the V Corps kept abreast of Willcox's battle line. After occupying the cut, the Federals were disconcerted to discover that Confederate sharpshooters from the rifle pits on the right commanded the cut. To keep down casualties, Hartranft put a large detail to work throwing up a traverse across the cut on the right of his brigade's front. Track and ties were ripped up and used to build the traverse.[186]

Since Barlow's division, which was supposed to support his right, was nowhere in sight, Willcox asked General Potter for assistance. General Potter called up his 1st Brigade, Col. John I. Curtin's, which moved into position on Hartranft's right.[187]

Several soldiers of the 36th Massachusetts of Curtin's brigade recalled:

---

185 *Ibid.*, 572, 577, 585, 589, 609; Committee of the Regiment, *History of the Thirty-Sixth Massachusetts Volunteers, 1862-1865* (Boston, 1884), 210-211.

186 William H. Powell, *The Fifth Army Corps (Army of the Potomac), A Record of Operations During the Civil War in the United States of America, 1861-1865* (New York, 1896), 700. Major General Gouverneur K. Warren of the V Corps, preparatory to attacking, deployed Crawford's division to the right and Brig. Gen. Lysander Cutler's to the left. As the V Corps battle line pressed ahead through the pines, Warren rushed one of Brig. Gen. Romeyn B. Ayres' brigades to Cutler's assistance. Like their comrades of the II and IX Corps to their right, Crawford's and Cutler's troops swept over the abandoned rifle pits. A number of stragglers belonging to Hoke's and Johnson's divisions were picked up by the bluecoats. By 7:30 a.m. Crawford's and Cutler's divisions had developed the Confederates' new main line of resistance. Relaying this information to army headquarters, Warren reported that the Confederates were dug in on the crest west of Poor Creek. Cutler's skirmishers on the left drove the Rebel outposts across the Norfolk & Petersburg Railroad, while on the right Crawford's were fighting to do so.

187 OR 40, pt. 1, 572, 577, 585, 589, 609.

The line of the railroad crossed our front diagonally, and on our right, at the point where the enemy's main line crossed the railroad, a small redoubt had been erected, in which was placed a single piece of artillery. This gun had perfect range of the railroad cut, and completely enfiladed our line of fire with a severe fire of . . . canister. While our line in this position was well protected from the fire in front, it was exposed to this hot fire from the right flank. The attention of our batteries was soon bestowed upon this gun in the redoubt; and the men tore up the railroad ties, and erected a barricade which afforded them ample protection from the fire.

It was now comparatively easy to hold the railroad cut, but to advance was quite another matter. The railroad bank was high, and so steep that the men had to dig holes in the side of it to place their feet, and as soon as a man showed his head above the bank he was a target for the Rebel sharpshooters.[188]

Shortly after Curtin's soldiers had filed into position on Willcox's right, General Barlow's division resumed its advance. Covered by a strong skirmish line, the division beat its way through the pines. Except for the fire of the Confederate snipers, which inflicted a number of casualties, Barlow's troops encountered no resistance. As the blue clads approached the railroad, the 140th Pennsylvania drove the Rebs from a large brick culvert which passed under the road bed. Drawing abreast of the IX Corps troops, Barlow called a halt. Outposts were established, the troops put to work entrenching. Barlow on inspecting his front was delighted to discover his troops had dug in along a ridge fronting and commanding the railroad cut.[189]

In their advance to the Norfolk & Petersburg Railroad, the soldiers of the IX Corps captured 355 Confederates. These men, along with the ones taken by the II Corps, were rushed to army headquarters to be questioned by the Provost Marshal and his people. The prisoners sent in by Generals Birney and Burnside all claimed to belong to Beauregard's army or to Hoke's division, which reached Petersburg on the night of the 15th. Nine brigades in all were represented. None of the soldiers admitted to having seen any units belonging to the Army of Northern Virginia in the Petersburg trenches.

The men bagged by the II Corps reported that early on the 17th a portion of Martin's Brigade, two regiments of Gracie's Brigade, and Evan's Brigade had pulled out of the trenches north of the Appomattox River and marched into Petersburg. According to these men, the only troops left along Swift Creek to oppose Maj. Gen. Benjamin F. Butler's advance were cavalry.

---

188 Committee of the Regiment, *History of the Thirty-Sixth Massachusetts Volunteers*, 211.

189 OR 40, pt. 1, 337, 339, 342, 344, 349.

Most of the prisoners had been assigned to outpost duty, or had fallen asleep and had been left behind when their units pulled back during the night. One of the Confederates had told his interrogators that in passing through Petersburg and out to the front, no interior line of works had been seen. Most of the other captives, however, claimed that their comrades had retired about one mile to a position just east of town. None of them, when pressed, were able to describe Beauregard's new main line of resistance.[190]

When they were questioned, the butternuts captured by the IX Corps explained that their officers had told them to hold their ground, because reinforcements were en route and "they must be of good courage." Several of the grey clads reported that Lt. Gen. Richard S. Ewell's Corps was close at hand. But when the Union intelligence officers pressed the point, they were unable to find any Confederates who had actually seen soldiers from the II Corps of the Army of Northern Virginia.[191]

*   *   *

When the decision to expand the scope of the forced reconnaissance was made, one of General Meade's staff officers handed a message to one of the headquarters telegraphers. General Neill was to have his batteries fire on the Confederates and employ his infantry to feign an attack. If, however the troops of the II Corps scored a breakthrough, Neill was to have his division ready to take up the advance. Neill was to see that Brig. Gen. John H. Martindale, on his right, was apprised of the contents of this message.[192]

The telegrapher didn't know the whereabouts of Neill's command post. Consequently, valuable time was lost while a staff officer carried Meade's 5:00 a.m. dispatch to Neill. Meanwhile, the soldiers of the II Corps had taken up the advance. At 5:15 a.m., Meade notified Neill that the soldiers of Birney's corps had reached the Confederate "works of last night" and had found them evacuated. Neill was to advance his skirmish line and determine the situation to his front. Neill was to relay this information to General Martindale.[193]

---

190 OR 40, pt. 2, 158, 159.

191 *Ibid.*, 158. Apparently, news that Jubal Early had succeeded Ewell as commander of the II Corps, Army of Northern Virginia, hadn't reached the Federals. At this time, Early's Corps was in the Shenandoah Valley.

192 *Ibid.*, 190.

193 *Ibid.*, 191.

Very little time was lost by General Neill in putting his division into motion. Screened by a skirmish line, the men of Neill's division left the protection afforded by their earthworks. The opposition encountered by Neill's troops was characterized by a staff officer as "trifling." Crossing the abandoned rifle pits to their front, the advance by 7:15 a.m. had reached Harrison Creek. Here, Neill called a halt to consolidate his gains. His left flank brigade, Brig. Gen. Frank Wheaton's, occupied the ground on Gibbon's right.[194]

Meade now began to fret about what might happen on his right, where he had Neill's division of the VI Corps and two divisions of the XVIII Corps under Martindale. He accordingly asked one of his aides to check to see which of the two was senior. If General Martindale ranked Neill, he was to take charge of the three divisions and advance till he encountered the Confederates new defense line. As the troops pressed ahead, Martindale was to maintain contact with the troops of the II Corps on his left.[195]

At 7:50 a.m. the staff officer telegraphed Meade's headquarters that, as ranking officer, Martindale had assumed command of the divisions on the right.

Martindale moved promptly to carry out Meade's directive. The brigade led by Col. Griffin A. Stedman was deployed across the City Point-Petersburg Road. Brigadier General George J. Stannard's brigade and two battalions of the 2nd Pennsylvania Heavy Artillery were to support Stedman's advance. One of Brig. Gen. Edward W. Hinks' brigades, Col. Samuel A. Duncan's, would press forward along the Petersburg & City Point Railroad. General Hinks, accompanied by his artillery and his 1st Brigade, was posted at the junction of the Spring Hill and City Point Roads.

As soon as Martindale's troops started up the valley of the Appomattox, they were shelled by Confederate guns emplaced on Archer's Hill on the opposite side of the river. Hinks' artillery went into action and soon silenced the Reb's pieces. No further difficulty was encountered by Martindale's columns in reaching Harrison Creek. Observing that the foe (Hagood's South Carolinians) was strongly posted on the west side of the stream about Page's house, Martindale called a halt. Martindale, while awaiting additional instructions, adjusted his lines.

Neill's division was on the left, with Wheaton's brigade thrown forward to connect with the II Corps. When the advance was resumed, Neill was to rest his right on the City Point Road. Stedman, reinforced by a battalion of the 2nd Pennsylvania Heavy Artillery, was on Neill's right, with skirmishers extended to the

---

194 *Ibid.*, 191. OR 40, pt. 1, 495, 496.

195 OR 40, pt. 2, 203.

river. Stedman's battle line was supported by Stannard's and Duncan's brigades and a battalion of the 2nd Pennsylvania Heavy Artillery.[196]

*   *   *

Soon after the Federals had occupied the deserted Rebel rifle pits, General Meade notified General Birney, "There is every reason to believe the enemy has no regularly fortified line between the one abandoned and Petersburg." If the Rebels weren't pressed, Meade knew they would soon complete a new belt of earthworks covering the eastern approaches to the key city. Meade had therefore ordered the entire army forward and had directed the officers on the right and left of the II Corps to communicate with Birney. If it were at all possible, Meade wanted the Rebels driven across the Appomattox River. Up to this moment, Meade wrote, the only troops to his front that had been identified belonged to Beauregard's Army. The latest intelligence reports placed the Confederates' strength in the Petersburg area at 30,000 as opposed to 55,000 bluecoats.[197]

Meade, at 10:00 a.m., addressed a note to Birney requesting information as to how the situation was developing in the II Corps sector. A short time before, Meade had received a dispatch from Martindale reporting that his troops would be unable to cross Harrison Creek until Gibbon's division advanced. Consequently, Meade wanted to know at what hour Birney would be able to assault so he could direct Martindale "to make a simultaneous attack." Meade in closing chided, "I think there is too much time taken in preparations, and I fear the enemy will make more of the delay than we can."

Within less than one-half hour Meade had his reply. Birney announced that he had pinpointed the Rebels' new defense line and had driven in their outposts. A reconnaissance of the grey clads' position had disclosed that it was as strong as the one abandoned and that artillery would be of no use in the impending attack. Birney pronounced himself ready to cooperate with Martindale's troops.

At 10:30 a.m. Birney notified Meade that he was advancing his left flank. Two of Barlow's brigades (Miles' and Hasting's) and Brewster's brigade of Mott's division were to close the gap which had opened in the Union line between the II and IX Corps. To make matters more difficult, Mott had notified Birney that because of the terrain, his right flank units would be at a marked disadvantage in the

---

196 *Ibid.*, 203; OR 51, pt. 1, 1257, 1263. A third battalion of the 2nd Pennsylvania Heavy Artillery reported to Hinks at the junction.

197 OR 40, pt. 2, 165.

forthcoming assault. Birney, in view of this situation, would employ only one division (Gibbon's) in the attack.[198]

General Meade (at 11:00 a.m.) addressed telegrams to Generals Birney, Burnside, Martindale, and Warren. They were alerted that a general assault was to begin at 12:00 p.m. Each officer was to make "the columns of assault strong, have them well supported, and push them vigorously, endeavoring to have them advance rapidly over the ground without firing until they have penetrated the enemy's line." The generals involved were to telegraph army headquarters for a time-check to insure that their attack would be launched simultaneously.[199]

Instead of attacking in line of battle, points were to be chosen which might be attacked in column, the columns to be followed by the lines in rear as reserve. Meade, on June 18, was confronted by two new factors. First, the defenses into which the Confederates had withdrawn, and which there had been no opportunity to reconnoiter; second, the arrival during the day within the Petersburg lines of heavy reinforcements from the Army of Northern Virginia.[200]

From the time they had reached Harrison Creek until noon, Martindale's troops had clashed with Hagood's pickets. First one side then the other would gain the upper hand.

Before sending his men across Harrison Creek, Martindale redeployed his troops. Three of Stannard's regiments were called up and filed into position between Stedman's right and the river. When Martindale gave the order, his men scrambled to their feet with a shout. After wading the stream, Stedman's and Stannard's bluecoats worked their way slowly up the opposite ridge. One of Stannard's regiments on the right, next to the river, pressed ahead in column of attack. The Federal officers were confident that the grove of trees and the buildings of the younger Hare would screen this movement. As soon as the head of the column debouched from the grove, the officers sought to deploy their men. At the same time, Stedman's and Stannard's other units advanced in line of battle. Soldiers of the 11th, 21st, and 27th South Carolina opened fire on the column as soon as it showed itself and at the battle line at 300 yards. A few of the bluecoats penetrated to within 250 yards of the South Carolinians' defenses, before crashing volleys compelled them to recoil. Falling back a short distance, the Federals took cover on

---

198 *Ibid.*, 165.

199 *Ibid.*, 176.

200 John C. Ropes, "The Failure to Take Petersburg on June 16-18, 1864," in *Papers of the Military Historical Society of Massachusetts*, vol. 5, 178.

the ridge west of Harrison Creek and began to entrench. At the cost of several hundred casualties, Martindale had gained about 150 yards.[201]

South of the City Point Road, troops of two of Neill's brigades (Wheaton's and Edwards') flushed grey clad sharpshooters of the 7th South Carolina Battalion and the 25th South Carolina from shallow rifle pits, underbrush, and fences. The Confederates retired, leaving about 40 prisoners. His troops had outdistanced Gibbon's division on the left, so Martindale called a halt as soon as his men had secured the Page house ridge. Martindale, on examining his sector, was distressed to discover that as his "provisional corps" swept towards Petersburg, its front had been constricted. To correct this situation, Martindale redeployed Neill's division. Colonel Oliver Edwards' brigade was pulled out of the battle line and reformed behind Wheaton's command.[202]

As soon as the Federals had occupied the abandoned Confederate rifle pits near the Hare house in the morning, Colonel Tidball rode forward. Reconnoitering the area, he selected a position near the turn of the Prince George Courthouse Road and put a fatigue party to work throwing up an advanced artillery emplacement. The working party, however, was compelled to take cover when Rebel guns began to pound the ridge. Three batteries (Ricketts', Dow's, and Ames') were ordered up. The gunners parked their pieces on the road in rear of the Union earthworks. Tidball now spotted what looked like a good artillery position on a hill near the Hare house. Orders were sent for Capt. Bruce R. Ricketts to put his four 3-inch rifles into battery at that point. Within a few minutes, the rugged Pennsylvanians had manhandled their four guns into position. Pointing them toward Petersburg, they opened fire. Along toward mid-morning, Tidball brought up the 1st Battery, New Hampshire Light Artillery. The gunners placed their four 3-inch rifles in battery about 100 yards south of the Hare house, and opened fire on the Confederate earthworks beyond the Norfolk & Petersburg Railroad.[203]

Prior to Gibbon's noon assault, instructions were sent for Capt. Edwin E. Dow to go into battery as soon as the infantry had marched from the marshaling area. Captains J. Henry Sleeper and John E. Burton were to unlimber their guns behind Barlow's division. After the infantry were out of the way, the gunners of Burton's, Sleeper's, and Ricketts' batteries opened fire. Dow's cannoneers put the spurs and whips to their teams. Thundering forward, the artillerists emplaced their

---

201 OR 51, pt. 1, 1258, 1263; Hagood, *Memoirs of the War of Secession*, 269.

202 OR 40, pt. 1, 495, 496; pt. 2, 204.

203 OR 40, pt. 1, 423, 430, 438. Ricketts commanded Battery F, 1st Pennsylvania Light Artillery, Dow the 6th Battery, Maine Light Artillery, and Ames Battery G, 1st New York Light Artillery.

four Napoleons south of the Hare house and within 200 yards of the Confederates' trenches. Almost as soon as the trails struck the ground, the cannoneers began hammering the Rebs with shot and shell. Within a few moments, they had dismounted two Confederate guns which were sweeping the ground with canister across which Gibbon's troops were charging. Dow's artillerists grimly held their ground, although ten were cut down by grey clad sharpshooters.[204]

General Gibbon's troops advanced in double line of battle toward the rifle pits held by Colquitt's Georgians. The right flank brigade (Pierce's) sought to maintain contact with Martindale's "Provisional Corps" to the right. Because of the thick woods through which they were compelled to charge, it was necessary for the officers to halt their units and re-form their lines. As they pressed ahead, the Yanks drove back the Confederate sharpshooters. The dense timber and the fire of the Rebel marksmen, however, took their toll. Among the wounded were several popular officers—Brig. Gen. Byron R. Pierce and Col. Joseph F. Ramsey. Pierce refused to leave his men. By the time the Unionists had closed to within small-arms range of the Confederates' main line of resistance much of the steam had been taken out of Gibbon's thrust. In an attempt to bolster his striking force, Gibbon called up Col. Thomas A. Smyth's brigade from the second line, employing it to prolong his front to the right. This proved a vain gesture, as the Confederates repulsed Gibbon's division without much difficulty.[205]

Gibbon's assault was directed against the rifle pits defended by the 27th Georgia. A soldier in this regiment, Washington Dunn, kept a diary. He recorded:

> At daybreak here they came yelling as they thought that Petersburg they were bound to have. They shelled us very much as they came on and charged our brigade with several columns; but they were repulsed with heavy loss. They came up and established their line in 200 yards of our line of battle and their batteries came up right in front of four pieces of ours and planted them, in spite of our boys. The sharp shooters were very bad all day; we lost a good many by sharp shooters today.[206]

Birney (at 1:55 p.m.) sadly notified General Meade that Gibbon's attack had been unsuccessful. The II Corps commander proposed to regroup and make another attack with another unit later in the day. Birney had been unimpressed by Gibbon's assault, which he described as lacking in spirit, although the Rebels' position, he admitted, was strong. When the next thrust was made, it would be

---

204 OR 40, pt. 2, 166; pt. 1, 184, 318, 366, 373; Craft, *History of 141st Pennsylvania*, 215.

205 Washington L. Dunn, *Diary*, n.d., Georgia Dept. of Archives and History.

206 Dunn, *Diary*, n.d.

directed against another sector. Gibbon's operation was not a complete failure, Birney observed, because the troops had held their ground and had "gained a good crest for artillery."

Acknowledging Birney's communication, Meade coldly observed, "You will attack again, as you propose, with the least possible delay." Birney was reminded that Meade's order of the morning required "strong columns of assault." Since General Martindale was about to renew his advance, Meade pointed out the necessity of the cooperation of the II Corps. Birney was to select the point of attack, but he was cautioned not to lose any time in reconnoitering.

When Birney replied, he observed that Gibbon had assaulted "by columns in support of lines." Meade's directive did not give him time to shift his point of attack, so Birney proposed to make a second thrust against the sector where Gibbon had been beaten back.

Meade was taken aback by Birney's message. At 2:30 p.m. he telegraphed his corps commander that he had sent "a positive order to Generals Burnside and Warren to attack at all hazards with their whole force." Since the general now found it impossible to set an hour "to effect cooperation," he therefore found himself compelled to issue Birney "the same order." Meade in an effort to play upon Birney's vanity wrote, "You have a large corps, powerful and numerous, and I beg you will at once, as soon as possible, assault in strong column. The day is fast going, and I wish the practicability of carrying the enemy's line settled before dark."

Upon receipt of Meade's communication giving him more freedom of action, Birney determined to attack along the front held by Mott's division. Orders were issued for brigade commanders to mass their units. If all went well, Birney informed Meade, it would be 4:00 p.m. before he could concentrate the nine brigades which he proposed to hurl against the Rebel earthworks.

Meade (at 3:10 p.m.) approved Birney's plan to assault on Mott's front. When he notified Birney of this, Meade urged him to "hasten matters as much as possible."[207]

Birney (at 4:10 p.m.) wired Meade that Mott was forming his troops for the onset. The advance would be made "in columns, covered by a heavy skirmish line," and would be sustained by pressure from Gibbon's and Barlow's divisions. Birney cautioned Meade the impeding onslaught "would probably be successful had . . . [he] enough good officers left to lead the attacking columns." Heavy losses of "good officers" in the past six weeks had sapped the effectiveness of the II Corps.

207 OR 40, pt. 2, 166,167.

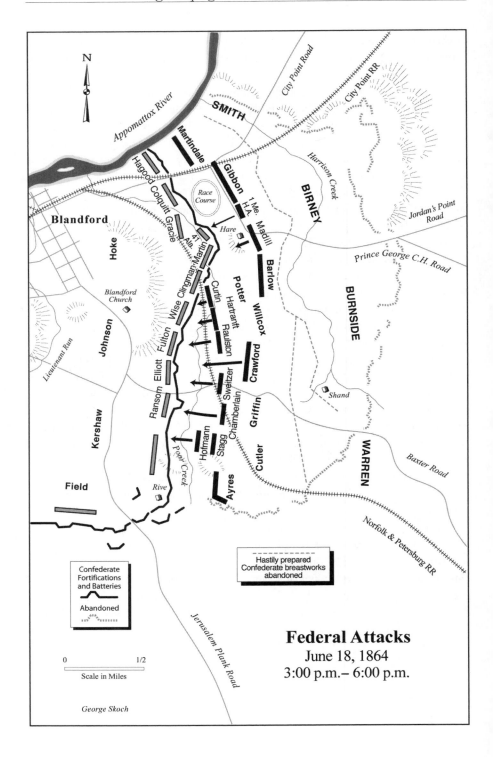

Confederate
Fortifications
and Batteries

Abandoned

Hastily prepared
Confederate breastworks
abandoned

Federal Attacks
June 18, 1864
3:00 p.m. – 6:00 p.m.

0   1/2

Scale in Miles

George Skoch

If nothing out of the way developed, Birney assured Meade that Mott would be ready in about 25 minutes.[208]

*   *   *

Meade (at 1:30 p.m.) had confirmed what Martindale already knew—Gibbon's assault had failed. Martindale was advised that another attack by the II Corps had been scheduled. Meantime, Martindale's "Provisional Corps" would continue to press the Confederates.

Upon receiving Meade's go ahead, Martindale called up two batteries. The gunners emplaced their pieces on the bluff overlooking the confluence of Harrison Creek and the Appomattox River. By 2:10 p.m. the battery commanders notified Martindale that their artillerists were about ready to open fire.

Martindale (at 2:40 p.m.) was informed that Meade had been unable to set an hour when all the corps would attack simultaneously, consequently, each corps commander was to hurl his troops forward "at once at all hazards and without reference to each other." Meade hoped that Martindale would be able to carry out his assignment without waiting for Birney to launch a new blow.[209]

Within 20 minutes, Martindale had communicated the order to resume the attack to his division commanders. The advance was to be taken up by successive units from right to left. Supported from the fire of the guns emplaced on the bluff, the troops of the "Provisional Corps" pressed slowly toward Petersburg. As soon as Martindale's right wing started forward, Neill's troops left the protection of their shallow rifle pits. A storm of small-arms missiles and canister greeted the Federals. As if a foe to the front weren't bad enough, Wheaton's brigade, which spearheaded Neill's division, found its left flank enfiladed. After advancing less than 150 yards, Wheaton's bluecoats were pinned down.

Up till the time that Neill's troops were checked, Stedman's and Stannard's brigades had gained about 200 yards. The well-aimed volleys delivered by Hagood's South Carolinians caused them to pause. Stedman and Stannard warned Martindale that it would be suicidal for their battle lines to push on unless they were supported on the left. To make matters worse, Confederate sharpshooters posted in the woods on the north bank of the Appomattox River began to take a grim toll. Martindale told his two brigade commanders to hold their ground and entrench, while he contacted General Meade.

208 *Ibid.*, 168.

209 *Ibid.*, 205.

At 3:55 p.m. Martindale notified Meade's headquarters that he had attempted "to advance immediately in front," but had found it impossible to do so, because of the enfilading fire his troops were receiving from the sector in front of the II Corps. If he were to succeed in his mission, Martindale warned Meade, it was vital that Birney's troops take up the attack.[210]

*   *   *

The troops of Col. Daniel Chaplin's brigade of Mott's division had taken cover in the Prince George Courthouse Road. Rebel sharpshooters were able to rake the road and picked off a few officers and some of the men. Meanwhile, news circulated through the brigade that a charge would be made. As they examined their surroundings, the troops didn't like the looks of what they saw. Creeping up the embankment, the soldiers saw they would have to cross a level plain to reach the Rebel works, 600 yards to their front. The outlook was anything but reassuring.

"Attention!" Orders came for the 93rd New York, the 84th and 150th Pennsylvania to form in advance, the 5th Michigan, the 1st Maine Heavy Artillery, and the 1st Massachusetts Heavy Artillery were to be in support. Many of the New Yorkers and Pennsylvanians at this cried, "Played out! Let the 1st Maine go!" This was reported to General Birney. Soon orders came for the 1st Maine to be deployed in advance.[211]

It was 4:30 p.m. before Mott completed his preparations for the attack. The onslaught, as Meade had ordered, would be made in "strong columns of assault." Colonel Henry J. Madill massed his brigade in column by regiments in rear of the Hare house. The troops were kept standing in ranks from 1:00 p.m., while the other brigade commanders formed their units. Between the brigade and the Confederate works was "a rise of ground which, while it sheltered and concealed the movements of the brigade was found when the commanding officers of the regiments in company with Colonel Madill went upon it for the purpose of viewing the ground over which they would be required to pass to the works they were to assail, to be swept by a terrible fire of shot, shell and musketry." When the reconnaissance was completed, the officers rejoined their units.[212]

Colonel Chaplin's brigade assembled by the side of the Prince George Courthouse Road north of the Hare house. When his column advanced, it would be

---

210 *Ibid.*, 205-206; *OR* 40, pt. 1, 496; 51, pt. 1, 258, 1263.

211 Roe and Nutt, *History of the 1st Regiment of Heavy Artillery*, 180-181.

212 Craft, *History of the One Hundred Forty-First Regiment*, 216. The 141st Pennsylvania was massed at the rear of Madill's column.

spearheaded by the 1st Maine Heavy Artillery. Mott, in selecting the 1st Maine Heavy Artillery to lead one assaulting column, was guided by several considerations—the regiment was numerically strong, while its combat effectiveness had not been sapped by repeated failures when assailing earthworks. The 16th Massachusetts and the 7th New Jersey, as named, took position behind the men of the 1st Maine.[213]

The artillerists turned infantrymen formed along the Prince George Courthouse Road, where the road made a sharp turn to the right, and ran northwest past the New Market Race Course. Here, the road was nearly parallel with and about 500 yards from the Confederate earthworks. The road at this point was partly planked and sunken, the spoil being thrown up on either side. The embankments were covered with small trees and underbrush, thus affording shelter from the missiles while the bluecoats awaited orders to advance. Waiting for the word to attack seemed like an "eternity" to the Yanks.

According to the plan sketched by Colonel Chaplin, the 1st Maine was to charge in three lines. The three battalions (Maj. Russell B. Shepherd's, Christopher V. Crossman's, and Capt. William S. Clark's), 850 strong, were formed in that order.[214]

Mott's two remaining brigades (McAllister's and Brewster's) were concentrated behind Madill's and Chaplin's closely packed columns. Prior to the hour scheduled for the assault, Gibbon pulled two of his brigades (Fraser's and McIvor's) out of the line and sent them to reinforce the attacking force. Mott massed these two brigades in close column, by division, in rear of Brewster's and McAllister's men.[215]

Meanwhile, soldiers of the 1st U.S. Sharpshooters had infiltrated the Hare house grounds. Besides affording protection to Dow's Napoleons, the sharpshooters banged away at Confederate artillerists. So effective was their fire that they compelled the Rebel gunners to desert two of their pieces.[216]

Mott (at 4:30 p.m.) gave the signal; the two powerful columns of attack started forward. To the right of the Hare house, the 16th Massachusetts failed to follow the 1st Maine Heavy Artillery as ordered. Seeing this, Maj. Frederick Cooper of the 7th

213 OR 40, pt. 1, 182, 185, 366, 377, 379, 380, 391, 394, 410, 418.

214 Horace H. Shaw and Charles J. House, *The First Maine Heavy Artillery, 1862-1865* (Portland, 1903), 121-122; Walker, *History of the Second Corps*, 541-542.

215 OR 40, pt. 1, 182, 185, 366, 377, 379, 380, 391, 394, 410, 418.

216 *Ibid.*, 410.

New Jersey waved his troops ahead. Not being "properly supported," the New Jersey regiment failed to advance beyond the Hare house.[217]

The 1st Maine Heavy Artillery stormed up out of the Prince George Courthouse Road. Union artillery posted on Hare House Hill opened over the heads of the charging blue clad columns. The cannoneers were to keep firing until the infantry entered the beaten zone near the Rebels' line. Major Shepherd's wave was to break down the abatis and gain the ditch fronting the Confederate works. Major Crossman's battalion was to follow close behind and, with well aimed volleys, keep the grey clads pinned down, while Shepherd's troops were regrouping for the final rush. As soon as Shepherd's battalion entered the trenches, Crossman's was to follow and assist in driving out the Rebs. Clark's battalion was to support the other two.

The 1st Massachusetts Heavy Artillery left the protection afforded by the road soon after the Maine men. According to the regimental historian of the 1st Massachusetts:

> Bullets whistled like rain. The Maine boys fell fast. "Forward, men," could be heard from their line … canister is let loose by the Rebels and dirt is flying, yet the Maine men who crept up the bank do not flinch, but sullenly close up ranks, now decimated. For over four hundred yards the lines . . . clung together, but it seemed a fruitless attempt, much more so than it did at the onset.

After advancing fifty or seventy-five yards the column broke in the center, the troops falling back and taking cover in the woods.[218]

Five hundred yards of open ground, all of it under Confederate observation, had to be crossed before the 1st Maine Heavy Artillery closed with the foe. The regiment's line of advance was within easy canister range of the Rebel artillery posted in the works to its front. On the north side of the Appomattox, the cannoneers of Wright's and the Bradford Virginia Batteries had registered their pieces to sweep the field with a deadly enfilade fire. According to one of the participants, if the rush by the 1st Maine had been "promptly" supported all along the line as ordered, the Confederates would have been unable to focus their attention on the single onrushing column. The veteran troops massed behind the 1st Maine and those constituting Madill's column of assault on the left "had not forgotten their experiences in assailing breastworks at the Wilderness, at

217 *Ibid.*, 418.

218 Roe and Nutt, *History of the First Regiment of Heavy Artillery Massachusetts Volunteers Heavy Artillery*, 181.

Spotsylvania and at Cold Harbor." While they started forward with a rush, they found the fire so terrific that they retired into their rifle pits.

The 1st Maine, however, was undaunted. All the Rebel batteries along a mile front seemed to concentrate on the field across which the Maine men advanced. The air was filled with flying fragments of lead and iron.

One of the officers recalled, "The field became a burning, seething, crashing, hissing hell, in which human courage, flesh, and bone were struggling with an impossibility, either to succeed or to return with much hope of life."

Within ten minutes it was all over. Most of the men of the 1st Maine who had not been killed or wounded, had retreated from the field and were striving to reform under cover of Prince George Courthouse Road.

Shooting from the Confederate and the Union lines continued for some time after the repulse. The five acres of ground over which the regiment had charged was covered with fallen men of the 1st Maine Heavy Artillery. Many of those lying helpless on the field were wounded again or killed by flying missiles.[219]

A participant recalled:

> I doubt if a man on the Union side saw a Confederate during the charge. They were completely sheltered by a strong earthwork. It is a positive fact that wounded men lay in the open field in front of their works throughout the remainder of the day under a burning sun, dying for want of water.

Detachments of men succeeded in a few instances in getting within seventy-five yards and in a few instances within fifty yards of their line, where some of their wounded lay for twelve hours. These were all Maine men from the front line. The colonel of their regiment is reported to have cried like a child that night.[220]

Led by Colonel Madill, the left column of assault (massed in ten lines of regimental front) with fixed bayonets flashing had charged to the left of the Hare house. In crossing the ridge which had heretofore sheltered them, the bluecoats suffered fearfully. A barn located between Madill's column and the Rebels' works "afforded too tempting a shelter to the men of the brigade; and after they had become satisfied that the assault was impracticable, the larger portion of the troops soon congregated in disorder behind it; and the attempt to storm the position was abandoned."

The regimental historian of the 141st Pennsylvania recalled:

219 Shaw and House, *The First Maine Heavy Artillery*, 121-122, 408.

220 Roe and Butt, *History of the First Regiment of Heavy Artillery Massachusetts Volunteers*, 181.

The result was only the repetition of the story so frequently told during the campaign—a dash against works strengthened by all the appliances of military skill and defended by men subjected to the severest military discipline, fighting with desperation and using the best appliances of modern warfare:—a horrible slaughter of the assailants, a disheartening repulse, a falling back of shattered and bleeding columns to a place of shelter to gather up the remnants of commands, perhaps to renew a like fruitless assault.

In the savage onset, Madill's brigade had lost nearly 200 killed and wounded. Captain Dow of the artillery reported that the heads of the charging columns were unable to penetrate more than 50 yards in front of his guns.[221]

Although the Confederate artillery and Colquitt's Georgians had the major role in smashing Mott's onslaught, Hagood's right flank regiment—the 25th South Carolina—got in a few licks. As Colonel Chaplin's column stormed forward, the South Carolinians "fired volleys obliquely into the assaulting column" as it advanced over Hare House Hill.[222]

Among the men of the 1st Maine trapped in front of the Confederate works was Sgt. Frederick O. Talbot of Company K. To protect himself from the hail of flying iron and lead, the sergeant threw himself to the ground and placed his "full haversack on the middle" of his backing, believing that it might turn the path of a minié ball.

The sun was bright and hot. Already, the sun "was getting in its work on the dead and dying" who were sprawled near the sergeant. A "steady low murmur filled the air." This, Talbot took to be the groans of "many wounded men."

"The wicked, cruel sound" which he heard all too often, as a minié ball tore into a man already wounded or dead, unnerved Talbot. A number of balls struck the ground near the sergeant, kicking dirt over him. He thought of digging a hole with his bayonet, but the ground was too hard and the bayonet was a slow tool to dig with. To make matters worse, the Johnnies would undoubtedly sharpen their marksmanship on Talbot while he dug. He therefore decided it would be best if he lay quiet, and perhaps they would think him dead.

Talbot hugged the ground and wished he "was as flat as a postage stamp." After about three hours of suspense, during which time the sergeant lay perfectly flat on his face, listening to the zip of bullets, it started to get dark. Confederate

---

221 Craft, *History of the One Hundred Forty-First Regiment*, 216; OR 40, pt. 1, 318, 391, 409, 427; Weygant, *History of the One Hundred and Twenty-fourth Regiment*, 350; Houghton, *The Campaigns of the Seventeenth Maine*, 205. One of Madill's regiments, the 124th New York, advanced to the attack with but 82 muskets.

222 Hagood, *Memoirs of the War of Secession*, 269.

sharpshooters continued to bang away. Another sergeant lay on his side with an arm thrown over his blanket roll a few feet in front of Talbot. The chevrons on his sleeve, being red, could be seen a considerable distance. He was a large stout man.

Talbot called, "Sergeant, are you wounded?"

"Yes," he answered.

"Can't you lie in any other position? Your chevrons are so bright that they can be seen easily by the Johnnies."

"No," he answered, "I have a bullet in my hip. I can't lie in any other way."

Next, Talbot heard voices to his rear, one of which he recognized as Lt. Hiram F. Sweet of Company K. Talbot called to Sweet. The two men agreed to remain quiet until the Confederates stopped sniping.

A band somewhere in the rear of the Rebs' line now started playing. Talbot tried to make out the tune, but he was unable to do so. Soon a band over in the Union line struck up an air. Talbot listened, but it was likewise too far away for him to recognize the number. The stars came out. Off to his left, Talbot heard the heavy, deep boom of a cannon; he saw a bright streak ascend, describe an arc, and fall into the grey clads' works. He identified it as a mortar projectile and was glad to see it. First one, then another followed the first.

Suddenly, a wounded soldier who was sprawled nearby pulled his pipe from his pocket, deliberately filled it, and lighting a match began to smoke. The match as it flared lighted the field for several feet around the soldiers. Another wounded soldier called for the smoker to douse his match or the Johnnies would fire on them. The smoker answered coldly, "Let them fire and be d—d, I will never have another smoke," and continued to enjoy his pipe.

Finally the bombardment ceased and all was quiet. Talbot called to Lieutenant Sweet, "Now is our time."

"Come on," Sweet replied.

With a bullet in his leg and a buckshot in his wrist, Sweet jumped up and was "off like a deer" before Talbot could scramble to his feet. At the same time, the Confederate and Union pickets, hearing the commotion, opened fire. Shielded by the darkness, both men succeeded in reaching Union lines.[223]

At 5:00 p.m. General Birney confessed sadly to Meade that Mott's assault had been "repulsed with considerable loss."

Meade reported that he was "sorry" to hear that the II Corps had been unable to carry the works. Birney was to occupy the best possible position and get his troops ready to repel a Confederate counterthrust. Upon the failure of this attack,

---

223 Shaw and House, *First Maine Heavy Artillery*, 408-411.

Meade was ready to admit that his attempt to score a breakthrough at Petersburg had failed.

Acknowledging Meade's message, Birney reported that his line was "strong and mostly entrenched." He promised to hold the ground gained.[224]

Meade at the same time notified Martindale that Mott's assault had failed. If he were unable to carry the Rebel works to his front, Martindale was authorized to have his troops dig in, and take steps to close the interval which had been opened between Neill's left and Gibbon's division of the II Corps.[225]

A quick reconnaissance convinced Martindale that it would be suicidal for his troops to press any closer to Petersburg, unless the II Corps was able to dislodge the Rebels holding the high ground west of Hare House Hill. Moreover, it was apparent that the Petersburg defenders were being heavily reinforced. This could mean only one thing—General Lee's Army of Northern Virginia had reached the point of danger. Orders were issued for the troops of the "Provisional Corps" to entrench.[226]

*   *   *

Early in the afternoon, General Willcox had approached Crawford and Barlow and proposed that they make a general assault on the fortifications to their front. Crawford was agreeable, but Barlow replied that he had no orders to attack. Willcox was taken back, because he considered a "vigorous attack on Barlow's front" essential to his success, since his flank was exposed to a "heavy enfilading fire" from the works which curved around to his right. Although traverses had been thrown up in the cut, Rebel sharpshooters continued to inflict heavy casualties on the IX Corps troops who had taken cover in the cut.[227]

When he learned of the situation, Burnside notified Meade that Barlow's left did not connect with Willcox's right. Until such time as it did, the Confederates posted in the railroad cut to the right of the IX Corps would continue to embarrass the Federals.[228]

---

224 OR 40, pt. 2, 168.

225 *Ibid.*, 206.

226 *Ibid.*, 157.

227 OR 40, pt. 1, 572.

228 OR 40, pt. 2, 166.

Meade lost no time in relaying this information to Birney. At the same time, the army commander notified Burnside that Gibbon's assault had failed. Burnside was reminded that "the best way to get out of enfilading fire" was to go ahead.[229]

At 2:00 p.m., General Warren of the V Corps telegraphed Meade's headquarters that his divisions had been close enough to the Rebels since 1:15 p.m. to assault. According to his interpretation of Meade's orders, the 12:00 p.m. attack "was to be a rush." But at that hour, the left flank of Warren's corps wasn't close enough to the Rebel lines for a charge. Valuable time had been wasted while Warren got his flank division (Ayres') into position. As soon as everything was ready, Warren had ridden to the right, where he discovered that Crawford's soldiers had kept pace with the IX Corps. Willcox's IX Corps troops, however, had been unable to advance beyond the cut, because Barlow had halted too soon and their right was enfiladed by Rebel guns along the II Corps front. Warren was of the opinion that it would be "safe for us all to make a rush at, say, 3:00 p.m." This would allow sufficient time for Meade to notify all officers concerned that they were to make another effort. From what Warren was able to observe, the Confederates didn't seem to have much infantry in the rifle pits to his front.

General Burnside agreed with what Warren had to say. He felt that Birney's left should be advanced, because, at the moment, the IX Corps' line seemed perpendicular to the "general direction" of the II Corps' battle line.

Meade was shocked by the contents of Warren's 2:00 p.m. dispatch. "What additional orders to attack do you and Burnside need?" Meade inquired. He testily informed the commanders of the V and IX Corps that his orders, which he now repeated, were that "you each immediately assault the enemy with all your force." If there were any additional delays, Meade warned, "the responsibility and the consequences will rest with you."[230]

The commanding general's message was in Burnside's hands at 2:35 p.m. Burnside and several of his staff told Meade's representative at their command post that if Birney advanced his left and center, they could carry the Rebels' works to their front. As the situation now stood, the II Corps' line was at nearly a right angle to Burnside's. Nevertheless, Burnside and Warren had alerted their division commanders to attack at 3:00 p.m.

Meade forwarded the communication to Birney with a request that "if he can advance Barlow, as well as the attack of Gibbon's front, it will be well to do it."[231]

229 *Ibid.*, 193.

230 *Ibid.*, 179.

231 *Ibid.*, 194.

By 3:00 p.m. Willcox was ready to attack. Hartranft's and Curtin's brigades, supported by Col. William C. Raulston's, were to spearhead the assault on the Confederate line, which was about 300 yards to their front. A small stream (Poor Creek), flowing through a ravine, with trees on the west side, intervened. The cut of the Norfolk & Petersburg Railroad where the Federals had taken cover was about 15 feet deep, with almost perpendicular sides. Steps had to be dug into the embankment to enable the troops to get out of the cut. To add to the Federals' difficulties the cut was commanded by the Rebel rifle pits. This led to "vexatious labor and delay" to assure that the troops scaled the bank simultaneously.

Fortunately for the Federals, the pines on the opposite side of Poor Creek partially sheltered them from the Confederates' view. Nevertheless, large numbers of bluecoats were cut down. The regiments of Willcox's division were in no condition to make a powerful onslaught. The hard-campaigning of the past six weeks had eroded the strength of the regiments—the units scarcely averaging 100 strong. Losses in dead and wounded on the morning of the 18th and on the previous day had been heavy; large numbers had straggled.

On the extreme left of Willcox's front, where the embankment wasn't so steep, the troops had less trouble. There, the soldiers reached Poor Creek and, assisted by Crawford's men on their left, mopped up the Confederates.

By 5:30 p.m. Willcox had all his troops in position and ready. When he gave the word, his division, supported on the right by Curtin's brigade, stormed ahead into a murderous fire. The ground between the railroad and Poor Creek was crossed, bluecoats falling at every step. Poor Creek was waded, and the crest beyond reached. Willcox's and Curtin's troops had fought their way to within 125 yards of the Confederates' main line of resistance. At this point, the battle line was exposed to a sweeping fire. Any farther advance would be suicidal. Among the hundreds of casualties was Colonel Curtin. A quick check by General Willcox showed that he had less than 1,000 men in the ranks available for another rush. Orders were issued for the men to entrench. The soldiers of the IX Corps had won for themselves the distinction of gaining and holding the nearest point to the Rebel earthworks seized by the army during that bloody day.[232]

Soldiers in the 36th Massachusetts of Curtin's brigade recalled:

Nothing could exceed the heroic daring of the advance, under the fearful fire of the enemy at point-blank range, covering every inch of the ground from the railroad-cut to their earthworks. The line was strong and well defended, yet, notwithstanding, all the

232 OR 40, pt. 1, 547, 573, 577, 578.

ground from the railroad to the ravine [Poor Creek] was carried; the ravine was crossed and the crest beyond secured.

During this gallant attack Colonel Curtin, our brigade commander, was severely wounded in the shoulder, and the command devolved upon Lieutenant-Colonel [Henry] Pleasants of the Forty-eighth [Pennsylvania].

After the last attack the firing slackened somewhat, and was confined to the front line of battle, and it was fondly hoped that the record for sacrifice and bloodshed for that day was fully made up. The company cooks brought up the coffee—the only refreshment the regiment had received since daylight. The men were huddled behind the low breastwork eating supper, when the attention of Captain [Amos] Buffum was attracted by some movement in front, and he rose to ascertain the cause. He had just remarked that he was the only member of the large mass that had crossed the Rapidan who had escaped death or wounds, and laughingly said, "It is the rule for all to be struck; but every rule has an exception."

He had scarcely risen to his feet when the fatal bullet, directed by the unerring arm of the watchful Rebel sharp-shooter, struck him. He uttered a piercing cry, sprang into the air, fell back, and in a few moments passed beyond the reach of pain. The scene was witnessed by nearly all the regiment, and sent a thrill of horror to every heart.[233]

General Burnside (at 6:50 p.m.) telegraphed Meade's headquarters that Willcox had assaulted, but had failed to take "the enemy's works." At the moment, Burnside reported, Willcox's and Potter's troops were west of the railroad and could hold their ground.[234]

General Warren's V Corps advanced in conjunction with Burnside's troops. As soon as Crawford's troops on the right left the protection afforded by the railroad cut, they encountered a galling fire. Crossing the eastern prong of Poor Creek, Crawford's foot soldiers scaled the ridge, but they were unable to work their way across the crest.[235]

Griffin's division struck with more élan than Crawford's. When Griffin's command moved to the attack, Col. Jacob B. Sweitzer's (91st Pennsylvania) brigade was deployed to the right, Col. Joshua L. Chamberlain's to the left, and Brig. Gen. Joseph J. Bartlett's in reserve. Supported by Crawford's left flank brigade (Col. James Carle's), Sweitzer's and Chamberlain's blue clads stormed across the ridge separating the east and west branches of Poor Creek. Although hammered by the Rebel artillery and ripped up by well-aimed infantry volleys, the Yanks fought their

233 Committee of the Regiment, *History of the Thirty-Sixth Massachusetts Volunteers*, 211-213.

234 *OR* 40, pt. 2, p.195.

235 *OR* 40, pt. 1, p.190.

way through the pines, and into the ravine beyond. Here, the advance was checked. These gains, which had carried the battle flags of Griffin's division and Carle's brigade to within 150 yards of the Rebs' main line of resistance, had been made at a heavy cost. Among the desperately wounded was Colonel Chamberlain.[236]

Cutler's two-brigade division assaulted to Griffin's left. Colonel J. William Hofmann's brigade spearheaded the thrust. Preparatory to moving forward, Hofmann had formed his troops into line of battle on the crest of a ridge east of Blackwater Swamp and about 700 yards from the Confederate defenses. Hofmann's battle line and its supporting brigade (Col. Edward S. Bragg's) were subjected to a fearful bombardment as soon as they started forward. At first, it was musketry and spherical-case, but as the Yanks drove closer, the Rebel cannoneers switched to canister. Hofmann and Bragg were able to hold their units together until they started to move down the slope into the west fork of Poor Creek, which at this point was about 200 yards in front of the Confederate works. Here, Hofmann's horse was shot from under him, and his brigade fell to pieces. About 200 men pushed on and reached a defiladed area between the stream and the rifle pits. The rest of the survivors retreated in confusion. The officers finally rallied these men behind the ridge where they had massed for the attack. Bragg's troops, seeing what had happened to Hofmann's brigade, halted and took cover.[237]

Ayres' division was posted on Cutler's left. When the V Corps advanced on the afternoon of the 18th, Ayres deployed Col. J. Howard Kitching's brigade to the right, Col. Nathan Dushane's in the center, and Col. Edgar K. Gregory's on the left. Upon moving forward, Ayres' bluecoats ran into "a most terrific fire of artillery and musketry." Ayres' drive was quickly checked. Taking cover on the ridge separating the watershed of Poor Creek from Blackwater Swamp, Ayres' brigades began digging in.[238]

At 6:30 p.m. General Meade, having learned that the V Corps had encountered "a heavy fire" and was suffering severe casualties, notified Warren and Burnside

---

236 *Ibid.*, 455-456, 457. The cannoneers of the 9th Massachusetts and the 15th New York Batteries had taken their guns across the railroad and unlimbered them behind the crest of the ridge, dividing the east and west prongs of Poor Creek. Prior to the attack, Chamberlain's skirmishers had thrown up "slight lunettes" on the ridge. When the attack was launched, the artillerists manhandled their pieces up onto the crest and opened fire on the Confederate works. Within a few minutes, Battery C, 1st New York Light Artillery moved to the front and took position 75 yards to the left of the other two units. Here, the Union gunners were "within easy canister and musketry range of the enemy's works and all suffered severely." The three batteries covered the retreat of Chamberlain's and Sweitzer's troops. After dark, the batteries were withdrawn. *Ibid.*, 482.

237 *Ibid.*, 474, 476.

238 *Ibid.*, 470-471.

that the II Corps had made "a strong attack" and had been repulsed. The commanders of the VI and IX Corps were to exercise their own "judgment as to further operations." Meade was afraid that units from the Army of Northern Virginia had reinforced the Petersburg defenders. Moreover, with it all quiet on the II Corps' front, the Rebel generals would be able to rush troops to counter the movements of Warren and Burnside. As soon as the corps commanders concluded that nothing further could be accomplished, they were to straighten their lines and secure their flanks.[239]

Warren determined to make another effort, just at dark, to smash the Confederate defenses to his front. Before he could do so, he received a telegram from Meade, pointing out that it was "useless to make another attack." Strong fears had been voiced at headquarters on the army's ability to follow up and exploit any success scored by the V Corps. Warren would therefore "secure" his lines and look to his left.[240]

Upon the receipt of Meade's message, Warren cancelled his orders for another attack. Though his troops hadn't succeeded in penetrating the Confederates' new defense line, Warren reported, they "held firmly all the ground they gained," which at some points was very close to the Reb's rifle pits.[241]

General Meade at 6:30 p.m. had telegraphed Grant that all was quiet on Martindale's and Birney's fronts. At the moment, Burnside's and Warren's troops were still advancing, and Meade hoped that a breakthrough might yet be scored. Everything seemed to indicate, Meade warned, that Lee had reinforced Beauregard.

Inside of 30 minutes Meade had a reply. Grant was of the opinion that if the assault then in progress didn't succeed, it might be wise to allow the troops to rest and protect "themselves as well as possible."[242]

At 9:50 p.m. Meade sent a message to Grant summarizing the day's activities. According to Birney and Martindale, the Confederates to their front were present "in very strong force, with heavy reserves masked in rear." From this information, Meade concluded that Lee had reinforced the Petersburg defenders. Meade assured Grant that his men had held their gains and were entrenching. During the past 72 hours, Meade reported, his men had driven the Confederates from the lines of fortifications, captured four guns, four stand of colors, and about 500 prisoners. While the Federal losses, especially "to-day," had been severe, they were not more than would be expected when cognizance was taken of the numbers engaged.

239 OR 40, pt. 2, 180.

240 Ibid., 181.

241 Ibid., 182.

242 Ibid., 156.

Meade in closing observed, "It is a source of great regret that I am not able to report more success, but I believe every effort to command it has been made."

General Grant assured Meade that he was "perfectly satisfied that all had been done that could be done, and that the assaults today were called for by all the appearances and information that could be obtained." While waiting for a new opening, Grant wanted Meade to rest his men and "dig in." As soon as Brig. Gen. James H. Wilson's cavalry had rested, Grant planned to use his mounted arm to raid the Rebel communication lines which linked Richmond and Petersburg with the rest of the Confederacy.[243]

*   *   *

General Beauregard, by late afternoon on June 17, was satisfied that most of the Army of the Potomac, as well as the Army of the James, was before Petersburg. If he were to continue to hold Petersburg, Beauregard would have to have more troops.[244] At 6:30 p.m. Beauregard telegraphed General Lee: The increasing number of the enemy in my front, and inadequacy of my force to defend the already much too extended lines, will compel me to fall within a shorter one, which I will attempt to effect to-night. This I shall hold as long as practicable, but without reinforcements, I may have to evacuate the city shortly. In that event I shall retire in the direction of Drury's [sic] Bluff, defending the crossing at Appomattox River and Swift Creek.[245]

To make certain that Lee understood just how critical his position was, Beauregard during the evening sent three members of his staff successively to acquaint him with the situation before Petersburg. The last of these officers, Maj. Giles B. Cooks, reached Lee's headquarters at Drewry's Bluff at 3:00 a.m.[246]

One-half hour after Cooks' arrival at Drewry's Bluff, Lee telegraphed the Superintendent of the Richmond & Petersburg Railroad, "Can trains run through to Petersburg? If so, send all cars available to Rice's Turnout. If they cannot run through, can any be sent from Petersburg to the point where the road is broken. It is important to get troops to Petersburg without delay."[247]

243 *Ibid.*, 157.

244 Roman, *Military Operations of General Beauregard*, Vol.2, 234.

245 *Ibid.*, 234-235.

246 *Ibid.*, 235, 579.

247 OR 40, pt. 1, 668.

Even before his 3:30 a.m. message to the railroad superintendent, Lee had issued marching orders to Lt. Gen. Richard H. Anderson's I Corps. Anderson was to put two of his three divisions into motion for Petersburg. Major General Joe Kershaw had his division on the road by 3:00 a.m.; Maj. Gen. Charles W. Field's division followed Kershaw's. Major Cooks rode with Kershaw at the head of the column to show the men of the I Corps the shortest way to Petersburg. It was shortly after 7:00 a.m. when the city's defenders saw the glint of the bayonets of Kershaw's division coming through a ravine near Blandford Cemetery, and it was to "their weary eyes the fairest sight of the entire war."[248] Field's division crossed the Appomattox at 9:30 a.m.;[249] Lt. Gen. Ambrose P. Hill's Corps was spread along the Petersburg Pike, fighting dust and thirst and marching at a furious pace.[250]

Kershaw's troops marched out the Baxter Road, and moving into the rifle pits relieved the soldiers of Bushrod Johnson's combat-weary division. When Field's butternuts reached the "trenches" they filed into position on Kershaw's right.[251] It was after dark when Hill's troops crossed the Appomattox River and moved into position on the extreme right, thus extending the front well beyond the railroad that led from Petersburg to Weldon, North Carolina.

Lee reached Petersburg about 11:00 a.m. and rode out to the front to join Beauregard. Together they inspected the line that Colonel Harris had laid out the previous night. It was so close to Petersburg that when Grant organized his front, the city could be bombarded. Otherwise, Lee could find no fault with it. Colonel Harris had excelled himself in selecting the best available ground, when he had scarcely a moment to spare. Beauregard was so elated with the ease with which the evacuation had been carried out, and so reassured by the arrival of Kershaw and Field that he proposed an attack on the left flank of the Army of the Potomac. Lee rejected Beauregard's idea, contending that the troops were too exhausted to seize the initiative.[252]

With the coming of darkness, a dense mist rose from the Appomattox and settled over the battlefield. Several wounded men of the 1st Maine Heavy Artillery succeeded in crawling back to the lines. Others were rescued by their comrades who, as soon as it was dark, ventured out into the field of death.

---

248 Freeman, *Lee*, vol. 3, 425; Roman, *Military Operations of General Beauregard*, vol. 2, 579.

249 OR 40, pt. 1, 668.

250 J. F. J. Caldwell, *The History of a Brigade of South Carolinians, Known First as "Gregg's," and Subsequently as "McGowan's Brigade,"* (Philadelphia, 1866), p.166.

251 OR 40, pt. 1, 761, 766.

252 Freeman, *Lee*, vol. 3, 425.

In the following gray dawn, Lt. Horace H. Shaw, accompanied by Sgt. James A. Dole and Pvt. Ephriam K. Drew, left the protection of the rifle pits and moved forward to rescue Lt. Gardner H. Ruggles and several other men of Company F, who were reportedly lying wounded not far from the Confederates' lines. Taking advantage of the dense fog, the three approached to within 100 yards of the Rebel's breastworks. The fog lifted suddenly; the butternuts spotting the bluecoats opened fire. Lieutenant Shaw and his companions threw themselves into a gully, where "the dead were piled." Screened from the screaming minies, the trio dashed for their rifle pit. By the time they regained the Union lines, the fog had again closed.

So terrible was the fire for the next several days in this sector that no further attempt was made by the Federals to bring off or bury their dead, except under the cover of darkness. The historians of the 1st Maine reported: "It was an appalling sight, to take a desperate chance for life and peer over the breastworks across this field of slaughter, strewn thick with blue coated bodies of those sterling sons of Maine, decomposing in the fierce rays of a Southern sun. What ghastly evidence of the inhumanity of man to man!"

The morning of June 19 was a "sorrowful one" for the surviving remnants of the regiment. A roll call disclosed of the 850 men who charged out of the Prince George Courthouse Road and into the field, fewer than 200 remained. So far as could be ascertained, 115 had been killed, 489 wounded, and 28 were missing— 632 officers and men lost in ten minutes. No such havoc was wrought in such short time on any other regiment, North or South, during the war. In some companies not one commissioned officer was left; only two company commanders were uninjured. Several companies were led by sergeants. Many uninjured soldiers had their uniforms "tattered and torn" by bullets and fragments of exploding shells.[253]

Editor's Conclusion

The failure to capture Petersburg on June 15-18 was one of the few opportunities that would have changed the course of the war. The mismanaged affair cost the Federals nearly 11,000 men from all causes and the Confederates about 4,000. Once it was obvious the attacks had failed and the Southern lines were held in strength, Meade ordered his men to throw up breastworks. The failed attacks and orders to dig in marked the beginning of ten months of long, grueling, and bloody siege warfare.

253 Shaw and House, *First Maine Heavy Artillery*, 123-124.

Chapter 3

The Battle of the Jerusalem Plank Road

June 21 – 24, 1864

Editor's Introduction

Despite growing evidence that the performance of the Union forces had declined, and the morale in the Army of the Potomac had plummeted, Gen. U. S. Grant decided to undertake a new offensive three days after the direct assaults against Petersburg ended in failure.

The goal of this new offensive was to advance the Union battle lines westward all the way to the Appomattox River so that the city of Petersburg would be ringed by a solid half-circle of Union troops and its important railroads and major roadways severed.

Part I

General Meade Sends II Corps across the Plank Road

After their failure to break through the reorganized Confederate Petersburg defense line on June 18, 1864, the Union generals determined to invest the city partially by a line of entrenchments aimed at the South Side Railroad. These earthworks were to consist of redoubts connected by rifle pits, fronted by abatis, from which entire divisions could be withdrawn at any time, leaving a sufficient force to hold the fortifications. The corps pulled out of the works would be free to assail Gen. Robert E. Lee's Army of Northern Virginia "in unexpected quarters south, or even north, of the James."[1]

Major General George G. Meade, on June 20, determined to redeploy his Army of the Potomac. The works assigned his army would be held by the V, VI, and IX Corps, while the II Corps would constitute a mobile strategic reserve. When he notified Lt. Gen. Ulysses S. Grant of this, Meade reported that prisoners and contrabands questioned by his people were of the opinion that Gen. Pierre G. T. Beauregard's command had been reinforced by a pair of divisions belonging to Lt. Gen. Ambrose P. Hill's III Corps of the Army of Northern Virginia. Patrols sent out by Warren's V Corps on Meade's left had discovered that the Confederate fortifications continued to the west farther than they had been able to adequately reconnoiter.[2]

General Meade's information was indeed correct. General Lee had reached Petersburg on June 18 with General A. P. Hill's III Corps and two divisions of Anderson's I Corps under Maj. Gens. Charles W. Field and Joseph B. Kershaw. Kershaw's division, which arrived first, marched out the Baxter Road, and moving into the rifle pits, relieved the soldiers of Maj. Gen. Bushrod R. Johnson's combat-weary division. When Field's butternuts reached the "trenches," they filed into position on Kershaw's right flank.[3] It was after dark when A. P. Hill's Corps crossed the Appomattox River and moved into position on the extreme right of the line,

---

1   Humphreys, *The Virginia Campaign of '64 and '65*, 226; Walker, *History of the Second Army Corps*, 543.

2   *OR*, 40, pt. 2, 231.

3   *OR* 40, pt. 1, 761, 766. At this stage of the conflict, Beauregard commanded the Department of North Carolina and Southern Virginia, with headquarters in Petersburg.

thus extending the front well beyond the railroad that led from Petersburg to Weldon, North Carolina.[4]

General Lee had reached Petersburg about 11:00 a.m. and rode out to the front to join Beauregard. Together they inspected the line that Beauregard's chief engineer, Col. D. B. Harris, had laid out the previous night. It was so close to the city that when Grant organized his front, the city could be shelled. Otherwise, Lee could find no fault with it. Colonel Harris had excelled himself in selecting the best available ground, when he had scarcely a moment to spare. Beauregard was so elated with the ease with which the evacuation had been carried out, and so reassured by the arrival of Kershaw and Field that he proposed an attack on the left flank of the Army of the Potomac. Lee rejected Beauregard's idea, contending that the troops were too exhausted to seize the initiative.[5]

Although "no" was said to him on June 18, Beauregard soon learned that Lee "never lost an opportunity of delivering a blow when he saw a fair opening." For four reasons, it was difficult for the Confederates to strike soon or heavily at Petersburg. Because of the strength of the Federals' position and the weight of numbers, the Rebels could not afford to attack Union entrenchments unless the situation was desperate. The Army of Northern Virginia, at the same time, had to guard the approaches to Richmond as well as of Petersburg. Third, cost what it might, the army must keep open lines of supply from the Southern heartland. "If this cannot be done," Lee wrote, "I see no way of averting the terrible disaster that will ensue." From this statement Lee had to accept that the Petersburg & Weldon was doomed, though sound logistics demanded its protection and use as long as this could be done without excessive loss of life. Whenever other railroads were assailed by Union cavalry, they must be defended to the limit by Rebel horse soldiers. Finally, in the planning and the execution of this difficult military course, the Confederates were crippled by lack of manpower and by the loss of leaders.[6]

Meade, on the 20th, visited Grant's City Point headquarters. There the two generals discussed steps for forcing the Confederates out of Petersburg. To increase the strength of the projected strategic reserve, Grant determined to order the leader of the Army of the James, Maj. Gen. Benjamin F. Butler, to extend his lines to the left and occupy ground now held by VI Corps. When he moved to the

---

4 Freeman, *Lee*, vol. 3, 425.

5 *Ibid.*, 425.

6 Douglas S. Freeman, *Lee's Lieutenants, A Study in Command*, 3 vols. (New York, 1944), vol. 3, 538; *OR* 40, pt. 2, 690.

Major General George G. Meade
Library of Congress

left, Grant cautioned Meade, "it will be advisable to do it by rapid movement, and with as heavy force as possible."

Butler would be told to see that the redeployment of his XVIII Army Corps was completed by noon the next day. The heavy artillery companies ordered to report to the XVIII Corps, Grant hoped, would be able to destroy the railroad bridges spanning the Appomattox, and possibly silence the Confederates' big guns north of the river.[7]

After returning to his headquarters, Meade forwarded a memorandum to Grant, reviewing the master plan agreed upon at the City Point meeting. The left of Maj. Gen. Gouverneur K. Warren's V Corps at the moment was anchored on the Jerusalem Plank Road. During the night, the II Corps would be relieved, the IX Corps extending to the right to relieve the men of the II Corps. The II Corps would then be massed on the left and rear of the Fifth. As soon as the VI Corps was relieved by Butler's troops, Meade would advance westward with his strategic reserve and endeavor to reach the Appomattox west of Petersburg.[8]

Major General David B. Birney (who had assumed charge of the II Corps on June 18, when Maj. Gen. Winfield S. Hancock had been compelled to relinquish command, because his Gettysburg wound had become very painful) had been notified at 8:45 a.m. that the VI Corps was to relieve the division of his corps on the right, while Maj. Gen. Ambrose E. Burnside's IX Corps was to relieve the remainder of his troops. Upon being pulled out of the works, Birney was to camp the II Corps in rear of the fortifications held by the V Corps, "at some point easily accessible from all parts of the position now held by the army, and from the crossing of the Blackwater."[9]

Upon receipt of this message, Birney alerted his division commanders to hold their units well in hand and be ready to march as soon as relieved.[10]

Meade's headquarters (at 10:45 a.m.) notified Birney that it would be after dark before his corps could be pulled out of the lines.[11]

---

7   OR 40, pt. 2, 233. On June 20 Company I, 1st Connecticut Heavy Artillery, with three 30-pounder Parrotts, moved into position along the lines of the XVIII Corps. Company I was followed on June 24 by Company D, 1st Connecticut Heavy Artillery, with four 30-pounder Parrotts and four 8-inch siege mortars. The mortars were turned over to Company I. OR 40, pt. 1, 672.

8   OR 40, pt. 2, 233.

9   Ibid., 238. With Birney in command of the corps, Brig. Gen. Gershom Mott, as senior brigadier commander, took charge of the Third division, II Army Corps.

10 Ibid., 238.

11 Ibid., 239.

Staff officers spent much of the day reconnoitering the area behind the V Corps to select ground where Birney could mass his divisions. Chief of Staff Charles H. Morgan, after studying the terrain, informed Birney that their corps' left should rest on the Norfolk and Petersburg Railroad, which would place it between Baxter Road and the tracks. The only good "camping ground" in this area was near Avery's house.[12]

With the hour at which his soldiers were to be relieved at hand, Birney (at 7:40 p.m.) inquired of Meade, "Is it essential that my corps take position exactly in rear of General Warren's left, or will it do to mass in his rear?" All that he had heard from Colonel Morgan indicated that the terrain to the rear of the V Corps' left was "very much obstructed," and at night it would be difficult to march across.[13] Within 25 minutes Birney had his answer. He would mass his troops at any point behind Warren, provided his divisions could be shifted rapidly and without confusion into position on the left of the V Corps.[14]

General Meade (at 8:15 a.m.) had alerted Maj. Gen. Horatio G. Wright of the VI Corps that he was to have his troops hold their ground until notified differently, as he was to relieve part of the II Corps. Fifteen minutes later, Wright learned what he was to do. He was to replace one of Birney's divisions, and hold the earthworks from Hare's house to the Appomattox. One VI Corps division was to watch the river, while the earthworks facing the Confederate fortified zone were to be strengthened.[15]

By 2:00 p.m. Wright had perfected his plans. As soon as it was dark, troops of Brig. Gen. David A. Russell's and Thomas H. Neill's divisions, currently posted in the rifle pits, were to extend to the left and relieve Maj. Gen. John Gibbon's II Corps. Before undertaking this movement, Russell and Neill were to consult and determine the sector of the line for which each would be responsible. Brigadier General James B. Ricketts' division would continue to be in reserve. Three hundred men were to be detailed by Ricketts to patrol the banks of the Appomattox from the emplacements where the cannoneers of Battery H, 1st Ohio Light Artillery and Battery E, 1st Rhode Island Light Artillery had mounted their guns to the fleet anchorage.

Meanwhile, Meade had got in touch with the commander of his IX Corps, General Burnside. The IX Corps was to extend to the right and relieve Birney's

12 *Ibid.*, 240.

13 *Ibid.*, 241.

14 *Ibid.*, 242.

15 *Ibid.*, 248.

troops as far as Hare's house.[16] Later in the morning, Meade's Chief of Staff, Andrew A. Humphreys, informed Burnside that he would also extend his left and occupy as much ground currently held by the V Corps as possible.

Burnside as his first order of business inquired of General Birney, "How many troops are needed to occupy the trenches from the IX Corps' right to the Hare house?"

"Four thousand men, without any reserves, could hold the first line," Birney replied.[17]

This shocked Burnside, because he had only 3,800 available, and he knew there were two II Corps divisions and six batteries (not less than 10,000 men) posted along that sector of the front. Examining his morning reports, Burnside saw that exclusive of Brig. Gen. Edward Ferrero's division, which was under orders to report to General Butler, his entire corps did not muster 10,000 effectives. Now, to make matters worse, he had received instructions to relieve part of Warren's line. Burnside protested that a too great extension of the frontage held by the IX Corps, such as contemplated by army headquarters, could jeopardize its safety.

Acknowledging Burnside's message, Meade's headquarters observed, the IX Corps was "to hold the position defensively," and that the orders for Ferrero's division to report to Butler had been canceled. Moreover, the directive for Burnside to extend his left to relieve part of Warren's right was "conditional" upon his "finding it practicable to do so."[18]

Burnside (at 7:20 p.m.) notified Meade that the two divisions slated to replace the II Corps troops were ready to march. Once again, he wanted the people at army headquarters to know that he would be unable to throw anywhere near the same number of troops into these rifle pits as had formerly occupied them. At the same time, it was important that a strong force be kept in the works currently held by the IX Corps, which were very important.[19]

Grant, following Meade's departure from City Point, got in touch with General Butler. Butler was informed of the design "to envelop Petersburg so as to have the left of the Army of the Potomac rest on the Appomattox . . . " Such an undertaking would make offensive operations along the Bermuda Hundred Line impracticable until the new position had been taken up and fortified. To release as many VI Corps troops as possible for this movement, Butler was to extend his left. The force

16 *Ibid.*, 249. Like Wright, Burnside would see that his men strengthened their works.

17 *Ibid.*, 250.

18 *Ibid.*, 251.

19 *Ibid.*, 252.

posted between the James and Appomattox was to be reduced "to the lowest number" necessary to hold the trenches. The troops thus relieved were to cross to the south bank of the Appomattox. Butler was urged to see that this redeployment was expedited, so as to relieve the VI Corps by noon on June 21.[20]

In accordance with Grant's directive, Butler (at 7:30 p.m.) directed Maj. Gen. William F. "Baldy" Smith to get the troops of his XVIII Corps "ready to cross the Appomattox at daylight." Units from the X Corps were to relieve soldiers of the XVIII Corps on the Bermuda Hundred Line. When he marched, Smith was to take with him two batteries of artillery.

Orders were drafted at Smith's headquarters for the XVIII Corps division commanders to have their units ready to march at the designated hour.[21]

At 8:00 p.m., on June 20, the telegraph key in Burnside's headquarters tapped out the message, "Relieve General Birney at once. If necessary put your whole corps in position."[22] Burnside, after reading the communication, shouted for several staff officers. One was told to tell Brig. Gen. Orlando B. Willcox that he was to relieve the II Corps' Third division, while Brig. Gen. James H. Ledlie was to put his troops in motion for the sector held by Brig. Gen. Francis C. Barlow's men.

Guided by staff officers, who had previously reconnoitered the line of march, Willcox's division started north from its camp in the pines, east of the ruins of the Taylor house. As the column approached the rear of the trenches held by Brig. Gen. Greshom Mott's II Corps bluecoats, via the Prince George Courthouse Road, the officers cautioned their men to be quiet.[23] Ledlie's troops, at the same time, had moved up from their camp near the Shand house toward Barlow's sector. The IX Corps troops, by midnight, had replaced Barlow's and Mott's veterans.[24] Ferrero's black division had been advanced and occupied the line of rifle pits overlooking Poor Creek. Here the black troops would be in close support of the soldiers of Brig. Gen. Robert B. Potter's Second division, IX Corps, who held the ground west of the Norfolk and Petersburg Railroad, gained by Burnside's people in the bloody fight of June 18.[25]

---

20 *Ibid.*, 258.

21 *Ibid.*, 264-265.

22 *Ibid.*, 252.

23 *Ibid.*, 250; OR 40, pt.1, 107, 573, 578, 585.

24 OR 40, pt. 1, 195.

25 *Ibid.*, 594; Augustus Woodbury, *Major General Ambrose E. Burnside and the Ninth Army Corps* (Providence, 1867), 419-421. On the 17th the army's trains having reached the south bank of the James, Ferrero had crossed the river and camped for the night near Willcox's. The next day,

Simultaneously, General Neill's VI Corps division had extended to the left, relieving Gibbon's II Corps soldiers in the earthworks north of the Hare house.[26] Orders were given in whispers, as the brigades of the II Corps moved back from the ground seized on the 18th. After the division commanders had notified General Birney that all their units had reported, the columns were put in motion for the area Colonel Morgan had selected for the rendezvous. Birney, at 5:10 a.m. on the 21st, notified Meade's headquarters that his corps was "massed in rear of Warren's left," and he was awaiting further orders.[27]

Although nominally "in reserve," the soldiers of the II Corps did not "found on this fact any great expectations for a long rest," for they had never forgotten the remark of a member of the Irish Brigade on the occasion when Brig. Gen. George H. Caldwell formed his division in a line of battalions in mass, behind Maj. Gen. Daniel Sickles' III Corps at Gettysburg, and the men were told that they were to be in reserve. "In resarve; js resarved for heavy fightin'." This remark, emphasized as it was by Caldwell's experience in the Wheatfield, had become proverbial in the II Corps. Consequently, the troops were not surprised in the least, when orders came to move out.[28]

At 7:15 a.m., Meade instructed Birney to shift his corps farther to the south, and to take position on the left of Warren's V Corps. On doing so, Birney was to extend "as far to the left as practicable, enveloping and keeping as close as possible to the enemy's line." When Birney carried out this movement, it was hoped at army headquarters that the II Corps would gain possession of the Weldon Railroad. The VI Corps, during the night, would be pulled out of the works, posted on Birney's left, and endeavor to break through to the Appomattox west of Petersburg.

The only cavalry in the immediate neighborhood was a detachment led by Capt. Benjamin W. Crowninshield. Since these horse soldiers were picketing the V Corps' left, Meade, at 8:45 a.m, directed Warren to turn Crowninshield's detachment over to the II Corps. Birney would have the cavalry advance into the

---

moving in rear of the trains, the USCT division had marched to Bailey Creek, where Ferrero reported to Meade for instructions. Meade replied, directing Ferrero to leave the dismounted cavalry to guard the trains and to report with the rest of his command to General Burnside. Pressing on, the division camped on the night of the 19th a short distance in rear of the IX Corps' sector.

26 OR 40, pt.1, 495.

27 *Ibid.*, 318; OR 40, pt. 2, 273. For the time being, corps headquarters would be at Avery's house.

28 Walker, *History of the Second Corps*, 543.

region between the Jerusalem Plank and Halifax Roads, and see if it could pinpoint the Confederates' defenses.[29]

As soon as Birney passed the word, the corps moved out—Barlow's division, screened by Crowninshield's troopers, took the lead, followed by Gibbon's and Mott's bluecoats. The sun had reached its zenith by the time Barlow's vanguard, which had taken the road leading by Southall's, struck the Jerusalem Plank Road, one-half mile east of R. Williams' house. Here Barlow called a short halt, while he conferred with brigade commanders. The absence of any commanding elevations limited visibility. Before reaching the Plank Road, the Federals had passed three open fields on their right and one on their left. Water was short; many of the soldiers had emptied their canteens. There were several large fields west of Williams'. These fields drained to the south into Second Swamp. The woods to the west and northwest had not been reconnoitered, so Birney was concerned lest he blunder into a trap. He therefore directed Gibbon and Mott to mass their divisions in Williams' fields west of the Plank Road. Barlow was to employ his infantry and Crowninshield's cavalry and undertake a forced reconnaissance toward the Weldon Railroad.[30]

Spearheaded by the horse soldiers, Barlow's division moved out, taking the road to Globe Tavern. By 1:10 p.m. the lead brigade under Brig. Gen. Nelson A. Miles, with which Barlow rode, had penetrated to within two and one-half miles of the Weldon Railroad. For the past ten or fifteen minutes, Crowninshield's troopers had been in contact with dismounted Southern cavalrymen of Brig. Gen. Rufus Barringer's North Carolina brigade. Although the firing was light, Crowninshield called for help. Whereupon, Barlow told Miles to deploy and throw out as skirmishers two regiments—the 61st New York to the right and the 81st Pennsylvania to the left.[31]

Crowninshield and his troopers seemed unwilling to close with the foe, so Barlow used them to cover his flanks, as the rugged foot soldiers of the 2nd U.S. Sharpshooter Regiment took the lead. By the end of another hour, the head of the division had penetrated to within two miles of its goal. To delay the Federals, the Confederates had brought artillery into play. The cannoneers of McGregor's Virginia battery employed two of their guns against the Federals. Barlow's advance guard captured prisoners from three North Carolina cavalry regiments, the 1st, 2nd and 3rd.

29 OR, 40 pt. 2, 274.

30 *Ibid.*, 274-275.

31 *Ibid.*, 275-276.

Barlow, when he had committed his infantry, had been under the assumption that he would be supported by Gibbon's division. Learning now that Gibbon's division had been halted after crossing the Plank Road, Barlow decided that he had better get in touch with Birney. A staff officer thundered off with an inquiry. Barlow would leave it to Birney, "to decide whether it is safe for us to advance so as to separate this division farther from the rest of the corps." It was impossible, Barlow wrote, for his troops to continue to press toward the Weldon Railroad and "keep up connection with the rest of the corps."[32]

Upon the receipt of this message, General Birney recalled Barlow's column. When his troops pulled back, Barlow had them file into position on Mott's left, near Williams' house, and dig in. From right to left, Barlow's brigades were posted: Fraser's, MacDougall's, Moroney's, and Miles'.[33]

Gibbon's and Mott's divisions in the meantime had taken position. Gibbon's bluecoats were on the right and had entrenched west of the Jerusalem Plank Road, connecting on the right with V Corps and on the left with Mott's division. The soldiers had erected a double line of rifle pits in the dense pines fronting the Rebels' works. Brigadier General Byron R. Pierce's and Maj. Timothy O'Brien's brigades held the front line, Pierce on the right; Col. Thomas A. Smyth's and Col. William Blaisdell's brigades occupied the reserve trenches. Under the cover of darkness, the cannoneers of the 12th Battery, New York Light Artillery emplaced their four 3-inch rifles on the left of Pierce's foot soldiers.[34]

Mott, like Gibbon, positioned his division in double line of battle. Colonels Daniel Chaplin's and William R. Brewster's brigades held the front line, with Col. Henry J. Madill's and Robert McAllister's brigades posted in reserve. Soldiers of the 5th Michigan occupied the line of outposts covering Mott's main line of resistance.[35]

When the II Corps marched from Avery's, it was accompanied by six batteries. Except along the front held by Gibbon's division, Chief of Artillery John C. Tidball was disappointed to see that pines and oaks limited his artillerists' fields of fire.

---

32 *Ibid.*, 275-276 OR 40, pt. 1, 758. General Mott, at 10:00 a.m., had been ordered to have the 2d U.S. Sharpshooters report to General Barlow. Birney had established corps headquarters in front of Jones' house. OR 40, pt. 1, 318.

33 OR 40, pt. 1, 333, 335, 337, 339, 340, 342, 348, 354. At dark the 5th New Hampshire moved out and occupied the picket line.

34 *Ibid.*, 366, 372, 374, 375, 382, 386. The earthworks occupied by Pierce's and O'Brien's brigades were along a wood road veering off at an angle of 25 degrees in a southwesterly direction from the Jerusalem Plank Road.

35 *Ibid.*, 391, 394, 396, 401, 402, 418.

Lieutenant James Gilliss of Batteries C and I, 5th U.S. Light Artillery had his men unlimber their Napoleons in the interval between Mott's and Gibbon's divisions. Southwestern Prince George County, being unsuited for the employment of artillery, Colonel Tidball had his four remaining battery commanders park their guns near Jones' house.[36]

General Birney, about dark, had ridden out to inspect the line taken up by his corps. According to reports brought in by scouts, the Rebel works that they had reconnoitered seemed to be a continuation of those stormed by Baldy Smith's corps on June 15th. A salient (Battery No. 32) had been spotted in front of Gibbon's left.

When he visited Gibbon's left, Birney, looking across the fields to his front, sighted a strong column moving through the pines beyond. The grey clads were marching southwest, and Birney theorized that the Rebel generals had dispatched a strong force down the railroad to cope with Barlow's thrust. Relaying this information to Meade's headquarters, Birney observed, it would "not be prudent" for him to throw forward his left until the VI Corps was "in position or ready to go into position."[37]

At 9:10 a.m., on June 21, General Meade had issued orders that as fast as VI Corps units were relieved by elements of the Army of the James, General Wright would march his soldiers into position on the left of the II Corps.[38] At the time that this telegram reached Wright's command post (9:30 a.m.), only one division of the XVIII Corps, Brig. Gen. George J. Stannard's, had arrived from Bermuda Hundred.

Stannard started his division for the Point of Rocks pontoon bridge at 4:00 a.m. When he reached the Appomattox, he was compelled to call a halt to wait for Brig. Gen. James H. Wilson's cavalry to get out of the way. The bridge was free of cavalry within 90 minutes, and the foot soldiers crossed the Appomattox and tramped southward down the Point of Rocks Road. Because of their proximity to the Confederate lines, Wright and Stannard were satisfied that it would be unwise for the XVIII Corps troops to relieve the VI Corps people in the rifle pits before dark. When he notified Meade of this decision, Wright telegraphed that he had ordered staff officers to locate and explore a road to Birney's left. As soon as these

---

36 *Ibid.*, 424, 431, 443. When the corps moved out, the 11th New York and Battery K, 4th U.S. had marched with Barlow; Battery B, 1st New Jersey and the 12th New York with Gibbon; Battery A, 1st Rhode Island and Batteries C and I, 5th U.S. with Mott.

37 *OR* 40, pt. 2, 275-276.

38 *Ibid.*, 281.

officers returned with their report, Wright promised to put his reserve division, Ricketts', in motion.[39]

At 11:45 a.m. Meade notified Wright that he "need not move any part" of VI Corps "until the whole is ready to move."[40] This message, however, arrived too late, because Ricketts had already put his two-brigade division on the road.

Apparently, the Confederates suspected the Federals were up to something. At 1:30 p.m. the batteries emplaced to the right and front began hammering the VI Corps' lines with shot and shell. Union cannoneers replied with all their guns that would bear.[41]

After a short while the guns fell silent, and Wright and his officers went back to work preparing for the night's march. A request was forwarded to the chief engineer for a guide, who could show Wright the "shortest road to Chieves' house, on the Jerusalem Plank Road."

Just before dark, Wright was handed an urgent message from Meade's headquarters. As soon as his corps was relieved by Baldy Smith's troops, it was to move to the left of the II Corps, "and take position there, pressing up against the enemy and driving them into their main works, but not taking the offensive so far as to assault their works." For his guidance, Wright was informed that the II Corps was forming on Warren's left, which rested on the Jerusalem Plank Road, and would extend as far to the west as feasible. The object of this move to the west and the extension of the lines, Meade informed Wright, was to invest Petersburg and cut ingress and egress via the Weldon and Lynchburg Railroads. Wright would therefore extend his line from Birney's left "as far as practicable consistent with its security as a defensive line."[42]

Ricketts' division reached the area to the left and rear of Barlow's command at a most opportune time for the Federals. Just as it was getting dark, Barringer's North Carolinians, who had followed Barlow's column as it retraced its steps, charged Crowninshield's cavalry. There was a great amount of powder burned, but very few casualties as the Union horse soldiers retreated. Barlow shouted for General Miles to countermarch his brigade and deploy to the left and right of the Globe Tavern Road. Several crashing volleys from Miles' foot soldiers rocked the

---

39 *Ibid.*, 281; *OR*, 51, pt. 1, 1250. General Stannard had assumed command of the First division, XVIII Corps, on the evening of June 20.

40 *OR* 40, pt. 2, 281.

41 *Ibid.*, 281.

42 *Ibid.*, 282.

Confederates, and they drew back. Ricketts' vanguard by this time had reached Williams' house.

Hailing Ricketts, Birney told him to move his division out the Globe Tavern Road. Colonel Benjamin F. Smith's 2nd Brigade took the lead as the column started forward. The 6th Maryland and the 9th New York Heavy Artillery advanced on the double and relieved the hard pressed cavalry, while Colonel Smith formed the rest of his brigade into double line of battle across the road. The soldiers broke out their entrenching tools and began throwing up earthworks. At 10:00 p.m., the 110th Ohio reported to Col. John W. Horn of the 6th Maryland on the picket line. The New York heavy artillerists turned infantrymen were armed with smoothbores, so Horn had the Ohioans relieve them.[43] Ricketts' 1st Brigade, commanded by Col. William S. Truex, was positioned to close the gap that had opened between Barlow's left and Smith's right and dug in.[44]

Colonel Tidball heard the firing occasioned by the attack by Barringer's dismounted cavalry on the Union left and rear. Not knowing that Ricketts' VI Corps troops had intervened and had checked the Confederates, Tidball was understandably concerned lest the foe reach his artillery parked at Jones' house. To guard the rear, the cannoneers of Battery B, 1st Rhode Island Light Artillery, unlimbered their six Napoleons at the forks of the road. Infantrymen of the 4th New York Heavy Artillery were posted in support of the guns. There was little rest for the cannoneers during the night as their battery commander had them throw up a parapet and cut embrasures.[45]

The thrust by the Confederates against the Union left caused Birney to get in touch with General Mott. The commander of the Third division was told to "keep up" his connection with Barlow on the left and Gibbon on the right. Mott was to hold his two reserve brigades ready to march to Ricketts' assistance should it become necessary.[46]

Barlow, in obedience to orders from Birney, had put three of his brigades into line of battle, with his left in contact with Ricketts' right. To do this, Barlow was compelled to spread his men so thin that he feared he would be unable to resist an attack, if made in strength. Barlow, shortly after midnight, protested that his division had to cover a mile front, while Ricketts was responsible for about

43 *Ibid.*, 275-276; OR 40, pt. 1, 506-508.

44 OR 40, pt. 1, 505.

45 *Ibid.*, 424, 429, 430, 433, 435, 436, 439, 441, 443.

46 OR 40, pt. 2, 277.

one-fourth mile. At the moment, there was a gap between Barlow's right and Mott's left, which he understood Mott was to close.[47]

It was after dark when the 15,000 soldiers and eight batteries of Baldy Smith's corps advanced and relieved Wright's First and Second divisions. Stannard's division moved to the right, assuming responsibility for the rifle pits between the Appomattox River and the Petersburg & City Point Railroad, formerly held by Russell's VI Corps troops. Brigadier General Hiram Burnham's 2nd Brigade replaced Brig. Gen. Emory Upton's in the trenches next to the river, while Col. Guy V. Henry's 3rd Brigade filed into the rifle pits on the left, heretofore occupied by Col. William H. Penrose's 1st Brigade. The soldiers of Col. Edgar M. Cullen's 1st Brigade, except for one regiment, were assigned to the second line. The detached regiment was detailed to support the 7th Battery, New York Light Artillery on the right of the ravine.[48]

Brigadier General John H. Martindale's division replaced Neill's bluecoats in the sector between the railroad and Hare's house.[49]

In compliance with Baldy Smith's instructions, Brig. Gen. Edward W. Hinks camped his USCT division a short distance behind the rifle pits held by Stannard's and Martindale's reserve brigades. The XVIII Corps would look to Hinks for fatigue parties and for details to picket the south bank of the Appomattox downstream to the gunboats' anchorage. Moreover, Hinks' division would constitute a strategic reserve in case of a Rebel counterstroke in this sector.[50]

During the day there had been a change in the command of Wright's Second division. General Neill was relieved and directed to report to the Army of the James. For the time being, the senior brigade commander, Brig. Gen. Frank Wheaton, would lead the division, while Col. John F. Ballier of the 98th Pennsylvania took charge of the 1st Brigade.[51]

General Wright, as soon as Russell and Wheaton had reported all their troops off the line, passed the word to take up the march. With a guide detailed by the chief engineer leading the way, the long column moved out. Progress was slow; it was

---

47 *Ibid.*, 310-311.

48 *OR* 40, pt. 1, 712, 715, 718; *OR*, 51, pt. 1, 1250.

49 *OR* 51, pt. 1, 1259. Martindale's division had been relieved by the VI Corps on the night of June 19. The next day, the division returned to Bermuda Hundred. Once there, Martindale's division was reorganized. On the morning of the 21st, Martindale was ordered to return to Petersburg.

50 *OR* 40, pt. 1, 215, 216.

51 *Ibid.*, 496.

after 2:00 a.m. when the advance crossed the Norfolk & Petersburg Railroad. The eastern horizon was starting to pale by the time the rear guard passed the Jerusalem Plank Road. Wright (at 4:00 a.m.) called a halt near Jones' house, and he told Russell and Wheaton to allow their soldiers to take a well deserved break. Within a few minutes, the men had stacked their arms, shucked their knapsacks, and had turned to preparing breakfast.[52]

General Warren was not to be left undisturbed by the redeployment. At 7:15 a.m., on June 21, Warren was notified that Birney's II Corps was to take position on the left of his V Corps, "enveloping the enemy." The V Corps' role in the forthcoming offensive was to be passive, but Meade wanted Warren to extend his left to hold as much ground as possible.[53]

Three of Warren's divisions, (Ayres', Crawford's, and Cutler's) were in trenches at this time, and a fourth under Brig. Gen. Charles Griffin was in reserve. Warren made his plans accordingly. Orders were issued for Griffin to move forward and take position on Brig. Gen. Romeyn B. Ayres' left, "reaching out to the Plank Road."[54]

Griffin's troops had broken camp by 10:00 a.m. As they moved out, the columns headed south, and two hours later they halted on Chieves' plantation. After the division had been formed into line of battle with Brig. Gen. Joseph J. Bartlett's brigade on the right, Col. William S. Tilton's on the left, and Col. Jacob B. Sweitzer's in support, Griffin called for skirmishers to be advanced.[55] The officer in charge of the skirmish line was told that his mission was to drive the Rebel outposts to his front into their works. As he advanced, his left was to anchor on the Plank Road and his right on Ayres' left. Griffin's battle line was to give the skirmishers close support and seize ground as near the foes works as possible, "without suffering from random bullets and overshooting." At dark Griffin was to see that his men entrenched.[56]

When Griffin gave the word, his skirmishers swept toward the foe. The Confederate pickets were forced back about one-half mile, before Griffin, seeing that his men were getting too close to the frowning Rebel breastworks, called a halt. Entrenching tools were issued, pickets posted, and rifle pits dug. Riding to his left,

---

52 *Ibid.*, 495, 496.

53 OR 40, pt. 2, 278.

54 *Ibid.*, 279. Powell, *The Fifth Army Corps*, 703.

55 OR 40, pt. 1, 457, 461.

56 OR 40, pt. 2, 280.

Griffin was delighted to see that Gibbon's II Corps division was holding the ground west of the Jerusalem Plank Road.[57]

General Meade (at 9:00 a.m.) had written Grant that the II Corps was en route to take position on the left of the V Corps, "the Fifth extending as far as the Jerusalem Plank Road." West of the Plank Road, Meade's scouts had reported the Confederates occupying earthworks previously marked out. As these rifle pits were about three miles south of Petersburg, Meade, after studying his maps, saw that the Rebel line from the Plank Road to the Appomattox above Petersburg would be considerably longer than from the Plank Road to the river below. To check his enveloping columns, Meade forecast, Lee would have to throw the entire Army of Northern Virginia, except the units holding the Howlett Line, south of the Appomattox.[58]

Meanwhile, Grant, back at his City Point headquarters, had been studying a map on which the engineers had plotted the troop positions. Grant's attention was drawn to Jerusalem Plank Road. There the Confederate line, which had been running south, turned west, creating a salient angle. Writing Meade of what he had discovered, Grant (at 10:00 a.m.) suggested that Meade have Warren mass his artillery and use it to pin the Rebels in their earthworks, while the II and VI Corps crossed the Plank Road. As soon as the two corps had taken position, Grant felt confident the Confederates would be unable to hold their present line, because the Federals would be able to take it in reverse.

Meade was unable to understand what Grant intended, and at 11:00 a.m. so informed him. Replying, Grant telegraphed Meade that he wanted Petersburg "enveloped as far as possible, without attacking fortifications, and the way the position of the two armies is marked [on the engineer's map] it looks as if the front of the enemy can be swept from about Warren's left or left center, thereby giving out troops the position desired without exposure, unless the enemy exposes himself equally."[59] This message reached Meade's headquarters about the same time as Chief Engineer John G. Barnard. The engineer explained to Meade that Grant wanted him to occupy ground from which the Confederate works covering the Jerusalem Plank Road could be enfiladed. Meade (at 1:00 p. m.) notified Grant that he was riding to the front to see that this was done.[60]

---

57 OR 40, pt. 1, 457, 461, 465, 469.

58 OR 40, pt. 2, 267.

59 Ibid., 268.

60 Ibid., 269. Meade, at 11:00 a.m., had asked Grant to send either General Barnard or Col. Cyrus B. Comstock to explain what he wished.

Grant, besides keeping up with the activities of the Armies of the Potomac and James, had other important business. His commander-in-chief, President Abraham Lincoln, had decided to visit the troops before Petersburg. Disembarking at City Point from the steamboat that had carried him up the James, the president called on his general. Grant (at 11:40 a.m.) telegraphed Meade that he and the president planned to leave for the front at 3:00 p.m. They would go as far as the house where Baldy Smith had had his headquarters on the 16th.[61]

Part II

Mahone Staggers the II Corps

General Birney about daybreak on June 22, 1864, called for Colonel Morgan and told him "to order the advance of the lines until the position of the enemy was enveloped," in accordance with Meade's master plan. Both Meade and Birney had been apprised by this hour that General Wright had massed Russell's and Wheaton's divisions at Jones' house, and was preparing to move out along the road to Globe Tavern reconnoitered by Barlow. Birney therefore planned to advance his left and center divisions. Barlow, whose First division constituted the II Corps' left, was to "conform" to the movements of the VI Corps, advancing his line as General Wright advanced his. As the Union line swept forward, it was presumed at corps headquarters that it would be "considerably contracted," consequently, Birney wanted Barlow "to close in to the right from time to time to give General Mott an opportunity to get part of his command in reserve."[62]

Mott was directed to advance his division in conjunction with Barlow's, particularly his left, so his new position would be nearly parallel with the earthworks to his front defended by the Confederates.[63]

The advance of the II Corps, being dependent upon the VI Corps, Colonel Morgan rode over to Jones' house. When he reached Jones', he found General Wright and his staff busy redeploying the VI Corps. General Russell's First division was advanced and took position on Ricketts' right. This enabled Barlow, whose II

61 *Ibid.*, 269.

62 *OR* 40, pt. 1,325, 327-328.

63 *OR* 40, pt. 2, 311.

Corps division held a mile of front, to close to the right. After occupying the breastworks thrown up by Barlow's left flank brigade, Russell covered his front with a strong force of skirmishers and turned his men to deepening and strengthening the rifle pits.[64]

General Wheaton's Second division was marched down the Plank Road until the head of the column reached Globe Tavern Road. Here Wheaton called a brief halt while he conferred with Colonel Ballier. The colonel was told to mass his brigade, the 1st, in rear of Ricketts' division.[65] As soon as Ballier's brigade had fallen out, the march was resumed. A staff officer now rode up and told Wheaton that he was to have two of his brigades take position on Ricketts' left. Brigadier General Lewis A. Grant's "Green Mountain Brigade" filed to the left and formed into line of battle perpendicular to the rifle pits held by Ricketts' bluecoats. Brigadier General Daniel D. Bidwell's 3rd Brigade was posted in support of the Vermonters, with its left refused toward the Jerusalem Plank Road.[66] Wheaton's 4th Brigade, Col. Oliver Edwards', marched down the Plank Road another one-half mile before halting and establishing a roadblock, south of Second Swamp. Edwards' mission was to ward off any Confederate columns that might come rolling in from the southeast.[67]

One of Wright's aides explained to Colonel Morgan that the VI Corps officers were encountering some difficulty in pushing out their skirmish lines. Meanwhile, General Birney (at 7:30 a.m.) had dictated a second dispatch addressed to General Barlow. The commander of the First division was notified that Mott had been "directed to take the position pointed out to him yesterday," and to advise Barlow when he advanced. Barlow in turn would begin closing in on Mott, and swinging forward his left, keeping Wright advised as to his movements.[68]

Before Barlow could act on this order, Colonel Morgan received a report from Captain Crowninshield of the cavalry. The horse soldier wrote that (at 7:15 a.m.) his men were picketing the Plank Road to a point two miles beyond Williams' house. No Confederates had been seen since midnight. Information gleaned from local planters led the captain to conclude that Dearing's cavalry was holding the Weldon Railroad. Confederate vedettes were said to be operating within one mile of the

---

64 OR 40, pt. 1, 328, 492, 493, 494, 501.

65 *Ibid.*, 497.

66 *Ibid.*, 501, 504.

67 *Ibid.*, 495.

68 *Ibid.*, 325.

Plank Road. To check on this report, Crowninshield had sent a patrol westward along the Globe Tavern Road.[69]

About 9:30 a.m. Colonel Morgan, as he rode through the woods, encountered General Barlow. The general looked worried. He showed Morgan the 7:30 a.m. order from II Corps headquarters. A glance was all that was needed to satisfy the chief-of-staff that this message was quite different in its tenor from the order he had drafted at 4:50 a.m. Morgan began to fret, because it appeared to him "that the later order imperiled the corps." There must be a mistake, he told Barlow, as he wheeled his horse about, preparatory to returning to corps headquarters to ascertain what had happened.

On his arrival, Morgan learned from General Birney that the II Corps would "make our movement independent of any by the Sixth Corps." When he returned to Barlow's command post at 10:00 a.m., Morgan carried a message:

> The major-general commanding directs that you move forward your division, connecting with General Mott on your right, swinging forward until your whole line is in close proximity to that of the enemy. You will not be dependent on any movement of the Sixth Corps. Having attained the position above indicated, you will strengthen it by entrenching. If General Wright is not able to connect with you, you will have to look out for your left.[70]

Prior to Morgan's arrival at the First division's command post, General Meade had been there. When Barlow explained that there was a misunderstanding as to whether he should hold his connection to the right or left, Meade becoming impatient replied, "You cannot connect with both, keep your connection to the right; each corps must look out for itself."[71]

With the question as to whether General Barlow should guide left or right finally settled, the II Corps and VI Corps prepared to march their separate ways. According to Birney's revised battle plan, his right flank division under John Gibbon would remain in the earthworks, while Mott's and Barlow's lines wheeled toward the Confederate fortifications that extended westward from the Jerusalem Plank Road.

---

69 *OR* 40, pt. 2, 310. Crowninshield complained at this time that his command was nearly out of ammunition, while the horses hadn't been unsaddled for four days. 12,000 rounds of Sharps' carbine cartridges, 6,000 of Burnside, 1,000 of Spencer, and 3,000 rounds for Colt's army revolvers were needed.

70 *OR* 40, pt. 1, 326, 328.

71 *Ibid.*, 328.

Covered by a strong skirmish line, Mott's and Barlow's divisions left the protection afforded by the barricades and advanced into the pines to their front. As the troops scrambled over the low parapets, a number of officers glanced at their watches: it was 2:00 p.m.[72]

Mott, like Gibbon and Barlow, had two brigades (McAllister's and Chaplin's) in advance and two (Madill's and Brewster's) in support. Screened by the skirmishers from the 5th Michigan, Mott's bluecoats forged ahead—McAllister's brigade on the right gained nearly three-quarters of a mile.[73] It was soon apparent to Barlow, whose right flank brigade (Fraser's) guided on Mott's left, that it would be impossible to maintain contact with VI Corps. Throwing his line forward, Barlow effected nearly a "right half-wheel" through the dense woods. But as his men swept ahead, the gap which had opened between his left brigade (MacDougall's) and the VI Corps troops increased. To guard his left and rear which had been exposed by this movement, Barlow refused his two small, left flank brigades—MacDougall's and Moroney's. Barlow rode with his skirmishers.[74]

A mile advance was registered before Barlow's skirmishers encountered any resistance. Rebel sharpshooters now opened on the skirmishers covering the left. Barlow urged his men on; they responded with their characteristic élan. The Confederate snipers were rolled back by the bluecoats protecting the division's refused flank. Barlow, however, was worried. He sent word for MacDougall to deploy several regiments as skirmishers to prolong the "return," and endeavor to re-establish contact with the VI Corps. The firing having ceased along the skirmish line, Barlow wheeled his horse about and rode toward his reserve brigade, Miles', which during the advance had followed several hundred yards behind Fraser's battle line. Barlow wanted Miles to change his formation.[75]

One of Meade's staff (Lt. Col. Theodore Lyman), in the meantime, had galloped up to General Wright's command post. Wright at this hour (12:10 p.m.) was with Ricketts' advance brigade. From Wright, the aide learned that Ricketts' left extended about 200 yards south of the Globe Tavern Road. Wheaton's division was massed behind Ricketts, "ready to act in the required direction . . . " Scattered shots could be heard off to the north along Russell's skirmish line. Wright told Lyman to

---

72 *Ibid.*, 326.

73 *Ibid.*, 388, 391, 401, 402, 411. At 11:00 p.m. Madill's brigade had been called up from the reserve and sent to the left to relieve one of Barlow's brigades.

74 *Ibid.*, 328-329, 330, 333, 350, 354.

75 *Ibid.*, 330.

tell Meade that he was "advancing his picket line preparatory to a general advance."[76]

Before ordering a general advance by his corps, Wright told Ricketts and Russell to move their skirmish lines forward. The skirmishers pressed ahead through a heavily forested area. Ricketts' men had gained about one-half mile, when they were assailed by a strong force of Rebels deployed as skirmishers. The bluecoats recoiled a few steps, recovered their wits, and pressed cautiously ahead. Within a few minutes, the fighting which had begun along Ricketts' front had extended to the left of Russell's picket line.

Wright and his officers, after conferring briefly, decided that the Confederates had advanced to the attack, because scouts, who had just returned from the area where contact had been established, reported that they had seen no Confederates. Wright instructed Ricketts and Russell to have their skirmishers carry the fight to the enemy, and to advance their battle lines.[77]

*   *   *

Two divisions of General Hill's III Corps and a part of a third had reached Petersburg on the afternoon of June 18. After crossing the Appomattox, Hill's division commanders placed their men in the works. Major General Cadmus Wilcox's division was posted on the right; its right flank brigade anchored on the Weldon Railroad and its left on Wilcox Creek.[78] Brigadier General William Mahone's five-brigade division relieved Maj. Gen. Charles Field's right flank units in the rifle pits between Wilcox Creek and Battery No. 29.[79] Two of Maj. Gen. Henry Heth's four brigades had accompanied the corps to Petersburg. The brigades (Kirkland's and Fry's) which had accompanied the corps to Petersburg were responsible for the defense of the Rives Salient. General Heth, with Davis' and Cooke's brigades, had remained with Pickett on the Howlett Line.[80]

76 OR 40, pt. 2, 313. Wright's command post at this time was on the Globe Tavern Road. The staff-officer informed Wright at this time that Col. Edward S. Jones' cavalry and General Meade were at VI Corps headquarters.

77 *Ibid.*, 313, 314; OR, 40, pt. 1, 506, 508, 511, 512. At this time, Wright's line was "somewhat over a mile beyond the Jerusalem Plank Road," on the Globe Tavern Road.

78 Caldwell, *The History of a Brigade of South Carolinians*, 163.

79 Sergeant John F. Sale, Diary, n.d., Virginia State Library.

80 OR 40, pt. 1, 680; OR, 51, pt. 2, 1024, 1026. Heth, with Cooke's and Davis' brigades, on June 21, was sent back across the James to Chaffin's Farm.

Hill's artillery was placed along the earthworks to the right of the I Corps' guns. Lieutenant Colonel Charles Richardson's Artillery Battalion, less Lewis' Virginia battery, occupied the Rives Salient. The other III Corps artillery battalions, reinforced by the Washington Artillery Battalion, mounted their guns along the fortifications from the Jerusalem Plank Road on the left to the Weldon Railroad on the right.[81]

June 19 was Sunday. A brigade historian in Hill's Corps recalled, "We were not disturbed, but lay and slept or heard preaching as we chose. We were in quite an exposed place to the sun, but we managed to construct arbors which afforded some protection."[82] Not so fortunate, depending on one's spiritual needs, were the men of Col. Daniel A. Weisiger's brigade. John Sale of the 12th Virginia noted in his diary:

> Remained in the same position which we took last night. It's a shame that having 3 chaplains, the brigade can not have services at least on the Lord's Day, and more especially when there is no more danger than there is today, but they are so careful of their precious bodies that they care not for our souls which is their business. No one would expect them to needlessly expose themselves, but many and many a day one is in the position in which there is no danger and they will never come near. Such men can do more good with a musket than otherwise. Our chaplain, on being asked to do so, did manage to carry a gun for about 100 yards and he had no baggage whatever to encumber him. [83]

Hill's troops, on the 20th, remained in or near the works. Nothing of interest occurred to their front, but off to the northeast, they could hear the roar of artillery.[84]

The advance of the Union II Corps across the Jerusalem Plank Road on the afternoon of the 21st had immediate repercussions. General Hill, on learning that Barringer's horse soldiers were in contact with the Yankees east of Globe Tavern, issued marching orders to General Wilcox. Within a few minutes, Wilcox's brigade commanders had turned out their units. When the division moved out, it wheeled into the Halifax Road at the Lead Works and headed south. Wilcox called a halt near Globe Tavern, and the men were soon busy "arranging a temporary

---

81 *OR* 40, pt. 1, 757.

82 Caldwell, *History of a Brigade of South Carolinians*, 163.

83 Sale, Diary, n.d.

84 *OR* 40, pt. 1, 757; Caldwell, *History of a Brigade of South Carolinians*, 163.

breastwork." A number of Barringer's troopers came in and reported that they had been compelled to retire by Union cavalry. The cannoneers of McGregor's Virginia battery threw their 3-inch rifles into battery and shelled the woods east of the tavern.

Reports were now received that the Federal horsemen (Crowninshield's detachment) were retiring. Wilcox ordered his men forward. Crossing the field, the butternuts entered the pines beyond Dr. Gurley's. Skirmishers were advanced, and Brig. Gens. Samuel McGowan and Edward L. Thomas moved their brigades by the flank along a narrow cart road.

McGowan's South Carolinians, as they pressed toward the Jerusalem Plank Road, began to wonder when they would meet the foe. Suddenly there was a sharp volley ahead, "which sent a pretty good shower of balls whizzing over our heads." Here there was a little clearing on the left of the road along which McGowan advanced. Across this opening, the South Carolinians saw Thomas' Georgians advancing in line. The skirmishers in front cheered lustily and fired freely. Most of the soldiers thought that a battle was at hand. Thomas' Georgians advanced into the woods beyond, and the tempo of the firing increased. McGowan shouted to his South Carolinians, "Lie Down!" The troops threw themselves down in the dusty road, "fronting almost at right-angles with the line of Thomas' brigade."

The minies, one of McGowan's veterans recalled, "came over us by spells, sometimes quite thickly; but they were very high." At dark, Wilcox recalled his troops. The division retraced its steps, returning to the sector of the Petersburg defenses from which it had marched ten hours before.[85]

The next morning, the 22nd, when General Lee rode to his right, he learned from the people at General Hill's headquarters that Union infantry was again pressing toward the Weldon Railroad. Lee, who like all great captains, believed that "offensive movements are the foundation of a good defense," had Hill send for General Mahone. As a civil engineer, Mahone had surveyed the area and "knew every inch of the ground hidden by the tangled chaparral."

Mahone thought he saw an opening for a flank attack and asked permission to deliver it. Lee and Hill were agreeable. Instructions were issued at 1:00 p.m. for Brig. Gen. J. C. C. Sanders, Col. Daniel Weisiger, and Col. William Gibson to hold their units ready to move out in light marching order at a moment's notice. To hold the rifle pits vacated by these units, Mahone's two other brigades (Finegan's and Harris') were to extend to the left and right. One of Weisiger's veterans observed,

---

85 Caldwell, *History of a Brigade of South Carolinians*, 163-164; Frank Edwards, "Army Life of Frank Edwards," *Confederate Veteran* (La Grange, 1911), 7-9. Colonel Gibson, as senior unit commander, led Wright's Georgia brigade in the battle of the Jerusalem Plank Road.

"Everyone instantly commenced surmising where was our probable destination. No ones [sic] knows it, everyone could form some idea that it meant a fight."

At 2:00 p.m. Mahone passed the word, and the three brigades took up the march. To screen his approach from Federal pickets, Mahone led his troops up the hollow through which Wilcox Creek meanders. As the head of the column approached Johnston's farm, Mahone was delighted to learn from his scouts that the Union generals had blundered. The ever widening gap that had opened between the left division of the II Corps and the right division of the VI Corps had been spotted by the grey clads. Mahone determined to capitalize on the Yankees' mistake. While aides raced to the rear to urge the men forward, Mahone deployed and advanced his sharpshooter battalion. Moving into the woods beyond, the sharpshooters established contact with Barlow's skirmishers. In accordance with the information supplied by his scouts, Mahone formed his three brigades into line of battle in the field fronting Johnston's house—Sanders' Alabamans and Gibson's Georgians in front, Weisiger's Virginians in support. The cannoneers of the 1st Maryland Battery, who had accompanied Mahone's column, threw their four 12-pounder Napoleons into battery on Sanders' left. While the soldiers were moving into their battle formation, they could hear scattered shots and shouts in the pines to their left and front. This told them what Mahone and his brigade commanders already knew, they had gained a position on the II Corps' left and rear.

Mahone now waved his men forward. As the long battle line entered the woods, Weisiger moved his brigade into position on Gibson's right. Sanders' Alabamans on the left were the first to make contact with Barlow's II Corps division.[86]

General Wilcox had been ordered by General Hill to cooperate with Mahone. As on the previous afternoon, the "Light Division" left the protection afforded by the earthworks and hiked down the Halifax Road. Once again, on reaching Globe Tavern Wilcox turned the head of his column eastward. As the division approached the woods, Wilcox called a brief halt. Skirmishers were deployed and thrown forward. McGowan's sharpshooters screened the division as it moved in route column down the road leading from Globe Tavern to Williams'. Wilcox had told the officer in charge of the sharpshooters, he was to advance till he reached a "small farm house."

The skirmishers covering Wilcox's division had a difficult time beating their way through the tangled brushwood. North of the road, Capt. Charles E. Watson's

---

86 Sale, Diary, n.d.; William Gorden McCabe, "Defense of Petersburg," in *Southern Historical Society Papers*, 52 vols (Richmond, 1876), vol. 2, 272-273.

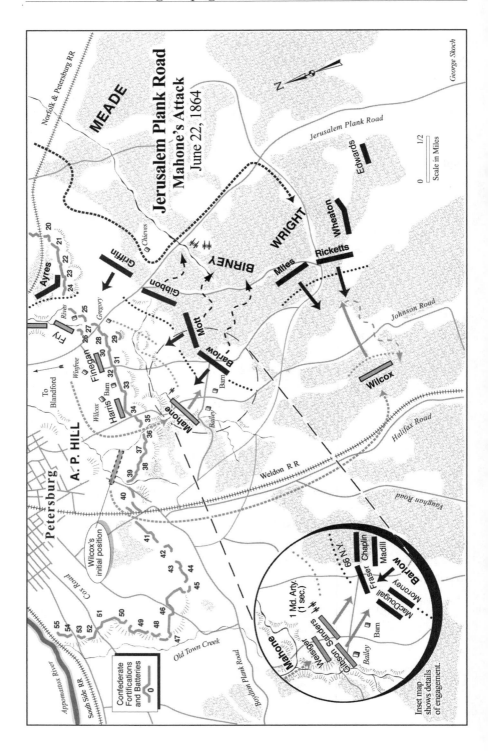

Jerusalem Plank Road
Mahone's Attack
June 22, 1864

company of sharpshooters clashed with Union pickets. Watson and his men drove the bluecoated skirmishers before them.[87]

Within a few moments, Union resistance stiffened. The dense pines and underbrush, along with the absence of any commanding elevations, made the fighting somewhat akin to blindman's bluff. After about 90 minutes of savage combat with Wilcox's sharpshooters, Ricketts' skirmishers had gained perhaps 100 yards. The officer in charge reported that he could advance no farther unless General Wright was willing to commit his battle lines. This, Wright was not prepared to do without Meade's sanction. All that he had seen and heard, however, satisfied Wright that the Rebel skirmish line did not extend very far north of the Globe Tavern Road. Orders were therefore given for Russell to redeploy his skirmishers, so that they would be able to turn Wilcox's left flank. When he notified Meade of his actions (at 2:55 p.m.), Wright pointed out, if his "supposition" that the Rebels had only committed a small force were correct, a frontal attack by Ricketts' skirmishers, in conjunction with Russell's flanking movement, would compel the foe to retire. According to his people on the left, their flank rested on Second Swamp, an impassable barrier. Wright inquired of his chief, "Do you wish me to attack in force?"[88]

Before Meade could reply, disaster had engulfed the II Corps. Barlow's and Mott's skirmishers, closely followed by the battle lines, were now approaching the Confederate fortifications. While Barlow was absent communicating with Miles, Mahone's column penetrated the gap that had opened between Barlow's left and Russell's right. The interval between the II and VI Corps "had become so great as to prevent any timely or intelligent co-operation." General Wright was first to sense that the Confederates were endeavoring to exploit the blunder on Meade's part that had caused the corps to lose contact. Wright forwarded this information to Colonel Morgan. Upon receipt of these evil tidings, Morgan rode to warn Barlow that his division was in grave danger. Morgan, however, was too late. [89]

Preceded by a large number of skirmishers, Mahone's battle line closed in on Barlow's refused flank. The butternuts quickly overran MacDougall's picket line, scattering those who were not killed, wounded, or captured. Pressing on, the Rebels assailed MacDougall's battle line from the front, flank, and rear. Moroney shouted

---

87 W. S. Dunlop, *Lee's Sharpshooters: or The Forefront of Battle* (Little Rock, 1899), 125; Caldwell, *History of a Brigade of South Carolinians*, 164; Spencer G. Welch, *A Confederate Surgeon's Letters to His Wife* (New York, 1911), 100. Caldwell did not accompany the brigade on the 22nd; he was among the group detailed by the brigade commander to picket the works.

88 *OR* 40, pt. 2, 314.

89 *OR* 40, pt. 1, 326, 328.

for his brigade to rush to MacDougall's assistance. It was like trying to sweep back the tide with a broom, as the grim, grey clad infantry drove ahead. First, MacDougall's and then Moroney's brigades dissolved into panic-stricken mobs. Each soldier, intent on saving his own skin, thought only of regaining the safety afforded by the breastworks.

As he galloped through the pines, Colonel Morgan sighted remnants of several shattered regiments fleeing before Mahone's onslaught. He called for the men to reform on their colors, but the men refused to heed; shouting that their units "had been 'captured' or 'cut to pieces.'"[90]

Barlow, as soon as he learned that MacDougall's and Moroney's brigades had been overwhelmed, ordered General Miles to have his troops double-quick back to the rifle pits from which they had advanced. Miles was to deploy his brigade and attempt to reestablish contact with VI Corps. As Miles' bluecoats hurried to the rear, the Confederates closed in on Fraser's brigade. Captain Burton H. Davis of the 66th New York, whose unit was deployed as skirmishers, saw that the Rebels had infiltrated the ground between his New Yorkers and the brigade battle line. He bellowed for every man to fend for himself. It was evident to Colonel Fraser that his brigade was in a precarious situation. Orders were given for the troops to oblique to the left to meet the onrushing Rebels. The regiments on the left of Fraser's line panicked. Fraser, seeing that it was hopeless to remain where he was, passed the order to retire into the rifle pits. As the Yanks faced toward the rear, they came under a scathing fire. Like MacDougall's and Moroney's brigades, Fraser's collapsed in face of Mahone's slashing assault on its left.[91]

In the wild retreat, a large number of Federals, including Colonel Fraser, were surrounded and captured. The survivors emerged from the woods and reached the breastworks shortly after Miles' grim veterans had filed into position. Assisted by Colonel Morgan, Barlow struggled frantically to reform his three shattered brigades. As the general sought to calm the men, he heard them speak of "overwhelming numbers" of Rebels and "three lines of battle." These tales, he discounted. Before Barlow could reorganize his shattered brigades, a Confederate battle line (Weisiger's Virginians) debouched from the pines and advanced against the breastworks. Miles' troops held; the attack was repulsed. As the Virginians retired, Miles ordered the 2nd New York Heavy Artillery to follow. Mopping up the area in front of the barricades, the New Yorkers bagged 40 Rebel stragglers.[92]

90 *Ibid.*, 326, 328, 329, 330, 347, 348, 349, 350, 351, 352-353.

91 *Ibid.*, 354, 357, 359, 360, 363.

92 *Ibid.*, 328, 329-330, 333, 337, 339, 340, 342, 344, 345.

It was mid-afternoon when Colonel Tidball was notified that Barlow's division had broken. To help stabilize the situation, marching orders were issued to the 4th New York Heavy Artillery and Battery K, 4th U.S. Light Artillery. The battery moved out at a trot to the field where Miles' foot soldiers were taking position in the rifle pits. Unlimbering the two Napoleons of the right section, the regulars shelled the woods to their front.[93]

Meanwhile, Sanders' Alabamans and Gibson's Georgians had moved against Mott's left, which had been uncovered by the rout of Barlow's division. Mott's left flank brigades (Chaplin's in advance and Madill's in support) were unable to adjust to an attack from an unexpected direction. It was like rolling up a carpet. The Union officers involved made little effort to change front to meet Mahone's onset. Subsequently, General Mott recalled that his "first intimation of an attack" was when Barlow's panic-stricken men engulfed his left.

Along Mott's skirmish line, the soldiers of the 5th Michigan (at 2:00 p.m.) had "heard heavy picket-firing at some considerable distance" to their left. At this time there was almost no activity to their front. Captain David S. Root was shocked and dismayed to see Barlow's skirmishers take to their heels. To keep his men from being gobbled up by the Rebels, Root called, "Retreat!"

Meanwhile, Mott's two advance brigades (Chaplin's and McAllister's), having gained the day's objective, had started digging in. McAllister's brigade on the right was in contact with Gibbon's division. In reaching this position, McAllister's right flank regiment, the 1st Massachusetts Heavy Artillery, had had a number of men cut down by Rebel snipers. While Gibbon's line ran north and south, the line McAllister's troops were fortifying ran east and west. While entrenching, the brigade "suffered much from the enemy's fire, both artillery and musketry." Near a knoll on McAllister's left, the soldiers found the soil so hard that they had to dig rifle pits with pick and shovel, as it was impossible to chop or drive stakes.

Colonel Chaplin's troops occupied the area to McAllister's left. At the time Barlow's division was overpowered, Chaplin's men had started to entrench, but they had made little progress. The soldiers were understandably startled by the sudden crash of small-arms volleys off to their left. A few minie balls now whistled in from the rear. Dropping their entrenching tools, the bluecoats snatched their rifle muskets. Within a few minutes, soldiers from Barlow's division charged toward Chaplin's yelling, "The Rebels are in our rear!" Chaplin called for his officers to form their regiments for battle. While the soldiers were dressing their

---

93 *Ibid.*, 424, 441. Because of the heavy growth of timber, the battery commander (Lt. John W. Roder) was unable to see how much effect the projectiles had, although the Confederates soon retired from his front.

lines, Gibson's Georgians sent a volley crashing into their rear. The brigade faced about, but the panic was contagious, and Chaplin's troops broke. Moving to the right a short distance, the brigade rallied behind a breastwork thrown up by other troops.[94]

Colonel McAllister had established his command post near the angle. At first, McAllister and his staff believed the heavy firing off to the left resulted from Barlow advancing his line. As the roar and shouts came nearer, McAllister had second thoughts and called his men to attention. "Very soon," he recalled, "a retreating mass of the First division came running along in my rear, with the rebels on their flank and rear." It was impossible for the 2nd Brigade to open fire without cutting down their comrades. With the retreat of Chaplin's brigade, Mahone's battle line bore in on McAllister's left, as well as his front, following the withdrawal of the 5th Michigan. McAllister had only one alternative—he ordered the brigade, except the 1st Massachusetts Heavy Artillery on the right, to fall back into the earthworks from which it had advanced. Upon reaching the rifle pits, McAllister and his officers reformed the troops and braced themselves to await a new Confederate attack.[95]

Mott's reserve brigades (Madill's and Brewster's) likewise melted away and retired to the protection afforded by the earthworks erected during the night.

The Confederates so far had scored heavily—Barlow's division and all of Mott's command, except the 5th Michigan and the 1st Massachusetts Heavy Artillery, had been sent reeling back through the pines. Mahone now directed his grim fighters against the fortifications held by Gibbon's division. Gibbon's bluecoats, unlike Mott's and Barlow's, had held their ground on June 22. Two brigades, O'Brien's on the left and Pierce's on the right, defended the advance line of rifle pits facing west, while Blaisdell's brigade, supportimg O'Brien's and Smyth's, was posted behind Pierce's.[96]

The cannoneers of the 12th New York Battery had unlimbered their four 3-inch rifles in the interval between O'Brien's and Pierce's brigades. Captain McKnight and his artillerists had spent the morning strengthening this emplacement. The 4th New York Heavy Artillery and Battery A, 1st Rhode Island Light Artillery, having returned to the artillery park, near Jones' house, Colonel

94 *Ibid.*, 401, 402, 414, 416-418, 420.

95 *Ibid.*, 401, 402, 403, 404, 412. The soldiers of the 5th Michigan reinforced the 1st Massachusetts Heavy Artillery, as they came in off the picket line.

96 *Ibid.*, 366-367, 369-371. From left to right, Pierce posted his men: the 1st Minnesota, 19th Maine, 19th Massachusetts, 42nd and 82nd New York, 15th Massachusetts, 59th New York, 20th Massachusetts, 36th Wisconsin, and 7th Michigan.

Tidball reinforced McKnight's battery with a detachment from the 4th New York. The ex-heavy artillerists were turned to fashioning gabions. About noon a four-gun Confederate battery emplaced in Battery No. 29 roared into action. Shells burst with uncanny accuracy above McKnight's position, as well as the rifle pits to the artillerists' left and right. McKnight had his men change the embrasures so that their pieces would bear on Battery No. 29.

General Pierce, learning what the New Yorkers were doing, sent word for McKnight to return the Rebels' fire. At 2:00 p.m. the Yanks put their guns in action. The grey clads replied with eight cannons. To make matters more embarrassing for the bluecoats, sharpshooters had infiltrated the woods to their front, and banged away whenever a head popped above the breastworks. General Pierce, who was at the battery, saw that McKnight and his men were hard pressed. Hoping to relieve the pressure on the New York artillerists, Pierce galloped to the extreme right of his brigade. Here where his brigade anchored on the Plank Road, the general hailed Capt. A. Judson Clark of Battery B, 1st New Jersey Light Artillery. Clark was told "to open at once on the enemy's battery." When Clark gave the word, his men began to hammer the Rebel batteries with shot and shell from their Napoleons."[97]

General Pierce reined up his horse in order to better gauge the effect of Clark's opening rounds. Now, instead of the occasional report of a rifle musket off to his left, there came the terrible full-throated roar that informed the general that serious combat had opened. As Pierce rode down his line toward the 12th New York Battery, he found the road jammed with frightened refugees from Mott's division. Pierce called for the officers to rally their men behind the works occupied by Blaisdell's brigade.[98]

The rifle pits defended by O'Brien's brigade had been subjected to an hour's bombardment by Confederate guns emplaced in Batteries No. 29 and 32, before the men picketing the far side of the wheat field fronting the trenches sent word that a Confederate skirmish line had been sighted to their left front. From his command post near the brigade's left, Major O'Brien now sighted Sanders' Alabamians advancing through the pines in front of Mott's sector. Moments later, O'Brien was dismayed to see Mott's division disintegrate. A staff officer pounded off to warn General Gibbon that the division to his left had abandoned its position and was in wild retreat.[99]

97 *Ibid.*, 369, 424, 431-432, 436.

98 *Ibid.*, 369.

99 *Ibid.*, 376, 385-387. From left to right, O'Brien's brigade was deployed: the 69th Pennsylvania, 152nd New York, and the 184th, 106th, and 72nd Pennsylvania.

Within ten minutes, Sanders' battle line came surging across the wheat field. O'Brien's bluecoats, in conjunction with the 1st Massachusetts Heavy Artillery and the 5th Michigan on their left, beat off this frontal assault. The Alabamans pulled back, reorganized, and came on again. Once again, they were repulsed. Meanwhile, Mahone's center and right brigades closed in. O'Brien, to meet this challenge to his left and rear, pulled his left flank regiments (the 69th Pennsylvania and the 152nd New York) out of the rifle pits and filed them to the left oblique. Several volleys delivered at pointblank range by these units caused the Confederates to recoil.

Word now reached O'Brien that McKnight's guns were in danger. When he gained his right regiment, the 72nd Pennsylvania, O'Brien found the soldiers closely engaged with Sanders' Alabamans to their front. He remained with the 72nd until it had repulsed this, the third frontal attack made on the brigade. While O'Brien was thus employed, Gibson's Georgians routed the 1st Massachusetts Heavy Artillery and the 5th Michigan from the rifle pits to the left of the 2nd Brigade. From the protection afforded by these earthworks, the Georgians sent volley after volley crashing into the 69th Pennsylvania and the 152nd New York. These two regiments gave way in confusion. Having broken the 69th Pennsylvania and the 152nd New York, Mahone's butternuts outflanked and smashed the 184th, 106th, and 72nd Pennsylvania.[100]

Captain McKnight, at the time of the Rebel assault on O'Brien's brigade, bellowed for his cannoneers to enlarge the embrasure of his left piece. Opening fire with canister, the New Yorkers enfiladed and helped repulse the initial frontal attacks on O'Brien's infantry to their left. McKnight was unable to employ his other 3-inch rifles against the Rebel infantry to his left, because the embrasures faced Battery No. 29, to his right. The artillerists learned that disaster had overtaken the units to their left, when infantrymen came running past their emplacement, crying, "We are flanked on the left; the left has broken!"

The brave gunners manning the left piece, however, held their ground and sent round after round of canister and case-shot without fuse ripping into the Confederates, until the 72nd Pennsylvania collapsed. The butternuts stormed down the abandoned rifle pits and planted a stand of colors on the parapet protecting the left 3-inch rifle. A Rebel officer called for the cannoneers to surrender. In a final effort to save his guns, Captain McKnight ordered, "Fix prolonges!" It was too late, for Alabamians and Georgians were pouring over the works in overwhelming numbers. McKnight at this time was on the right of the battery with his 1st sergeant.

---

100 *Ibid.*, 375, 376, 385-386, 387.

The 1st Minnesota, to the battery's right, broke on seeing O'Brien's brigade fall to pieces. The troops were quickly rallied by their officers and fired one volley, before taking to their heels a second time. Lieutenant Henry D. O'Brien of the 1st Minnesota collected a handful of his men and joined Captain McKnight and several of the artillerists in a struggle to save the right 3-inch rifle. Just as the Yanks were affixing prolonges, the Confederates poured in a "heavy volley," killing the 1st sergeant and several men who were pulling the piece. Simultaneously, the Rebels called for the Federals to give up. Whereupon, Captain McKnight shouted for the men to scatter.[101]

As he rode toward his left, General Pierce inquired of the frightened troops encountered, "What has happened?"

They replied, "We were flanked."

Pierce urged the men of O'Brien's brigade to reform, but in the woods and in their panic-stricken condition, the soldiers refused to heed. As they came out on the Plank Road, most of them were halted and regrouped in rear of Blaisdell's brigade by Capt. A. Henry Embler of Birney's staff. Pierce now learned from Captain McKnight of the loss of the four 3-inch rifles. An aide was dispatched with orders for Captain Clark to bring up his teams, which had been sent to the rear. As soon as the horses arrived, the left section of Battery B, 1st New Jersey was shifted across the Plank Road, so it could register on the area where McKnight's guns had been positioned.

Intermixed with the artillerists of the 12th New York Battery, Pierce encountered infantrymen of the 1st Minnesota and 19th Maine. Considerable difficulty was experienced by the general in halting the men and getting them to reform on their colors. The two regiments were deployed across the road. Pierce received another blow as Maj. I. Harris Hooper of the 15th Massachusetts rode up and reported that the Confederates (Weisiger's Virginians) had come up in his rear and captured most of his regiment. Grave fears were voiced by Hooper that the regiments to the left and right of his unit (the 19th Massachusetts, and the 42nd, 59th, and 82nd New York) had also been gobbled up by the onrushing Rebels.

When called upon to surrender by the butternuts, these regiments had grounded their arms and surrendered their colors. Much different was the conduct of the 20th Massachusetts, the unit to the right of the 59th New York. Captain Henry L. Patten, taking advantage of a slight turn in the breastworks, had his regiment execute a partial change of front, thus checking any farther advance by Mahone's brigades up the rifle pits toward the Plank Road.

101 *Ibid.*, 436-437.

General Gibbon at this hour joined Pierce. The division commander directed his subordinate to advance a strong skirmish line composed of the 1st Minnesota. He then called up two small regiments (the 155th New York Infantry and the 8th New York Heavy Artillery) from Blaisdell's brigade and directed Pierce to recapture McKnight's battery. The two fresh regiments were posted on the left of the 19th Maine. As soon as the men were in position, Pierce launched his counterattack.

By this time, Mahone had been reinforced by Brig. Gen. Nathaniel Harris' brigade, one of the two that had been left behind when the division moved out, together with a section of guns manned by Clutter's Virginia battery. Harris and his Mississippians were advanced by Mahone and told to hold onto the captured guns and rifle pits, while Sanders, Gibson, and Weisiger reformed their brigades, and detailed fatigue parties worked to collect arms and accouterments thrown away by the Federals in their wild flight to escape death or captivity. Large detachments were organized to guard the many hundreds of bluecoats captured during the impressive advance.

The counterattacking bluecoats drove to within 100 yards of the captured guns before the 1st Minnesota became hotly engaged with Harris' Mississippians posted behind the breastworks. One of the skirmishers reported to Pierce that the Confederates had drawn off the artillery pieces and were in "force behind our works."

Captain Embler now galloped up, and he informed Pierce that the troops he had reformed on the Plank Road were coming up. Pierce had Embler form them as a second line. The charge was sounded, and the "lines went forward with a will until within fifty yards of the works, when they received a volley from the enemy." Whereupon the first line broke and rushed through the second, carrying part of it away. It required the greatest exertion on the part of Pierce and his staff to check the rout.

Just as Pierce succeeded in reforming his battle lines, Colonel Blaisdell reported to him with the 170th New York and the 182nd New York regiments. Pierce informed Blaisdell to have his units take up a position on the right and left of the second line. While Pierce was conferring with Blaisdell, Capt. Walter Gale rode his horse down the line with orders from General Gibbon to attack immediately. Because the first charge against Harris' Mississippians had broken from right to left, Pierce directed Lt. Ansel L. White of his staff to ride to the right with a few soldiers and ascertain the whereabouts of the 20th Massachusetts, which was said to be holding its own astride the works. Pierce hoped to connect with the 20th Massachusetts, "get a flank fire on the enemy, and fill the works in succession from the right."

Before Pierce could perfect his arrangements, Captain Embler galloped up and handed him an order signed by General Gibbon placing him under arrest.[102]

Colonel Blaisdell, who superseded General Pierce, assailed the Mississippians, but he was repulsed. Gibbon, in relieving Pierce, maintained that his failure to counterattack promptly had enabled the Confederates to cement their grip on the captured earthworks. Unless heavily reinforced, Gibbon was now of the opinion that it would be impossible for his battered division to recover the lost ground.[103]

Colonel Tidball was distressed to learn of the loss of McKnight's guns. To stabilize the situation, three batteries (Battery A, 1st Rhode Island and Batteries C and I, 5th U.S.) were rushed from the Jones' house artillery park to Mott's assistance. The guns rumbled down a cart road and were thrown into battery behind the breastworks in which Mott's infantry had taken cover. A short distance in front of the fortifications were the pines out of which Mahone's butternuts had routed the Third division. Hardly had the trails of his six Napoleons struck the ground, before Lt. James Gillis' regulars were engaged in a duel with the 1st Maryland Battery at range of 300 yards. After firing about 50 rounds, the Federals gained the upper hand, and the Confederates brought up their teams and withdrew their guns.[104]

At the time that the Confederates were sweeping all before them, five batteries were positioned along the Plank Road.[105] The cannoneers of the 11th Battery, New York Light Artillery, at dusk moved their four 3-inch rifles into position to the right of Captain Clark's Napoleons.[106] Several hours later, the 6th Battery, Maine Light Artillery was advanced and relieved Clark's exhausted cannoneers.[107]

General Meade, as soon as he learned that the II Corps and VI Corps had encountered the enemy, got in touch with Generals Warren and Burnside. Should the Confederates be present in strength, he explained, the V Corps and IX Corps

---

102 Ibid., 327, 367, 369-370, 372, 374, 382, 432; Dunbar Rowland, The Official and Statistical Register of the State of Mississippi, 1908 (Nashville, 1908), 450, 466, 493, 514; OR, 51, pt. 2, 1026; A Historical Sketch of the Quitman Guards, Company E, 16th Mississippi Regiment, Harris' Brigade (New Orleans, 1868), 69.

103 OR 40, pt. 1, 367. Pierce was released from arrest on June 24 and transferred to the Third division, II Army Corps.

104 Ibid., 424, 439, 443, 758.

105 Ibid., 424. Emplaced along the Plank Road were Battery B, 1st New Jersey; 11th New York; Battery A, 1st Rhode Island; Batteries C and I, 5th U.S.; Battery K, 4th U.S.

106 Ibid., 424, 435.

107 Ibid., 424, 427.

were to be ready to advance against the fortifications to their front or rush reinforcements to the left.[108]

Replying, Warren notified Meade that his two divisions nearest the Plank Road (Griffin's and Ayres') would each send a brigade. Warren was of the opinion that it would be wiser for him to send men to bolster the left, rather than assail the works to his front. Because of the configuration of the terrain in the Rives Salient, Warren felt confident his artillery could keep the foe pinned in position during the daylight hours.[109]

Meade (at 4:00 p.m.) wrote Warren that he had better mass his two reserve brigades behind Griffin's left. The II Corps, in the fighting, had been broken and hurled back. Counterattacks, however, had checked the Confederate surge. If the Rebel generals committed additional troops, the II Corps would require massive assistance. The commander of the relief column was to report to General Birney near Jones' house.

Twenty minutes later, the situation along II Corps' front had deteriorated to the point where Meade messaged Warren to send the two brigades "on the double-quick."[110]

The two V Corps brigades (Col. Nathan T. Dushane's and Jacob B. Sweitzer's) moved out smartly at 5:00 p.m. At Jones' house, they were met by several of Birney's staff officers. Dushane's Marylanders were conducted to Barlow's support, while Sweitzer's brigade was massed behind Gibbon's sector.[111]

Along the front held by Wright's VI Corps there had been heavy skirmishing throughout much of the afternoon between Union skirmishers and Wilcox's sharpshooters. News that disaster had overtaken the II Corps caused Wright to issue instructions for his units to pull back to positions held in the morning. This would enable him to reestablish contact with the II Corps. As Russell's division on the right retired, orders were given by Wright for Wheaton to rush his reserve brigade (Ballier's) "to Russell's right to reinforce him or Barlow." Before the order was received, General Grant on the right of Wheaton's battle line received orders to reinforce the division skirmish line with Walker's battalion of the 11th Vermont. When Ricketts' division on their right started to pull back, Grant's Vermonters did likewise. Orders now arrived for Grant to march to Birney's assistance, but they were immediately countermanded, and the "Green Mountain Brigade" took

108   *OR* 40, pt. 2, 311.

109   *Ibid.*, 311-312.

110   *Ibid.*, 312.

111   *OR* 40, pt. 1, 187-188, 459, 470.

position near Williams' house and entrenched. The 3rd Vermont was thrown out to picket the area from Walker's left to Jerusalem Plank Road. By 5:25 p.m. the VI Corps troops were back where they had been in the morning.[112]

Wilcox's sharpshooters followed Wright's VI Corps skirmishers as they withdrew. As they closed in on the breastworks into which the Yanks had retired, the Confederates were received with a galling fire. Nevertheless, the Rebels pressed on, only to be repulsed with considerable loss. The historian of McGowan's sharpshooter battalion recalled:

> Captain [William H.] Brunson . . . received a painful wound in the foot, which caused him to retire, and from which he was disabled for some two months. The command of the battalion therefore devolved upon Captain [Ingraham] Hasell, who dropped back to a safe position, from which he continued to fire and contented himself with holding the Federals close under their guns.[113]

After the VI Corps had retired, orders were received from Meade authorizing Wright to hold his advance position. Writing Meade at 5:25 p.m., Wright observed, he considered his "present position, on the whole, the better of the two for defensive purposes, though not for attack."

"Indeed," he continued, "an attack from my present lines would be very injudicious," as the VI Corps would be compelled to carry the works constructed earlier in the day.[114]

Meade, upon being notified that the two V Corps brigades were on the field, issued orders for Birney and Wright to "make every arrangement for attacking" with their entire corps. The counterstrokes were to be launched at 7:00 p.m., or as soon as they were ready.[115]

Upon receipt of Meade's message, Wright sent for his three division commanders to give them their instructions. He was afraid; however, he warned Meade (at 6:10 p.m.) that his troops would be unable to advance at the designated hour.[116]

The II Corps moved out first, Gibbon on the right advancing at 7:05 p.m. Barlow on the left took up the advance several minutes later. Because of the dense

---

112 OR 40, pt. 2, 316; OR 40, pt. 1, 492-493, 495, 497, 500, 501, 506.

113 Dunlop, *Lee's Sharpshooters*, 125-126.

114 OR 40, pt. 2, 316.

115 *Ibid.*, 309.

116 *Ibid.*, 316.

woods, Barlow employed a "heavy skirmish line." By 7:25 p.m. Mott had started forward, employing the same formation as Barlow.[117]

Gibbon on the right reported that he had found the Confederates, and they (Harris' Mississippians) were in such force as to preclude an attack. Mott's and Barlow's reinforced skirmish lines encountered only isolated pockets of Confederates, as they drove back into the pines. On the right, Mott's skirmishers charged across a cornfield and took cover in the edge of the woods, while Barlow's on the left gained 400 yards, before darkness put a stop to the clash of arms along the II Corps' front.[118]

General Mahone, by 7:20 p.m., had checked with his brigade commanders. Since establishing contact with Barlow's skirmishers, his troops had rolled back the II Corps "more than a mile to his trenches on the Plank Road." Four 3-inch rifles, along with a large number of small-arms and entrenching tools, had been captured. So far, over 1,600 prisoners had been counted. Scouts, who had made their way through the pines, had returned with information that the position into which the Federals had retreated was "strongly fortified." Relaying this information to General Hill, Mahone reported that he had reformed his division in the captured rifle pits, within 300 or 400 yards of the Plank Road. Several Union counterattacks, which he described as feeble, had been repelled. General Wilcox's division had finally come up, but with darkness closing in, it was "too late to push farther." In addition, "a challenge of mode of attack would be necessary." Mahone was of the opinion that it would be unwise for the Confederates to hold on to the ground gained by his troops.[119]

Hill accordingly issued orders authorizing Mahone and Wilcox to retire into the Petersburg perimeter. Before doing so, however, they were to see that their wounded were collected and evacuated.[120]

At 10:00 p.m., Mahone recalled his four brigades. Covered by Harris' Mississippians, Mahone's column returned to the position held before the attack. The division, as evidence of its sweeping success scored at the expense of the II Corps, brought with it McKnight's four 3-inch rifles, over 2,000 stand of arms, and

117 *Ibid.*, 309.

118 *Ibid.*, 309; *OR*, 40, pt. 1, 363, 402.

119 *OR* 51, pt. 2, 1026.

120 *Ibid.*, 1025-1026.

eight battle flags. 1,742 Union prisoners were escorted into the Confederate lines by a detachment led by Mahone's Inspector-General.[121]

By the time Wright's corps moved forward, Wilcox had recalled his sharpshooters. On the right Russell's division, supported by Ballier's brigade, reoccupied the breastworks on which the soldiers had been working at the time of their recall. [122] Ricketts' bluecoats "moved forward very handsomely and carried the enemy's advance position with little resistance." Pushing on, the Third division continued to forge ahead till darkness compelled Ricketts to call a halt. As soon as lines could be adjusted and outposts established and manned, the soldiers stacked their arms and began erecting breastworks. When he checked with his staff, Ricketts was delighted to learn that his division had gained almost two miles.[123] Grant's and Bidwell's brigades of Wheaton's division cooperated with Ricketts.

Grant's Vermonters were strengthening the rifle pits near Williams' house, when the command to advance was passed. As the brigade moved forward, steps were taken to cover Ricketts' left. It was 11:00 p.m. when Grant posted his troops in good position, about one mile east of the Weldon Railroad. The 4th Vermont was deployed as pickets to connect with the left of Walker's line of outposts. Bidwell's brigade had shifted to the right and followed in close supporting distance of Ricketts' soldiers.[124]

Cannoneers assigned to three VI Corps artillery units (Battery E, 1st Rhode Island Light Artillery; the 3rd Battery, New York Light Artillery; and the 4th Battery, Maine Light Artillery) emplaced their guns in support of Ricketts' division, near Williams' house.[125] The men of Battery A, 1st Massachusetts Light Artillery unlimbered their six Napoleons near Jones' house, on the Jerusalem Plank Road.[126]

The recall of Wilcox's division disturbed the men of McGowan's sharpshooter battalion. It was theorized that the "failure of the Light Division to attack may have been part of the program, to hold Wright while Mahone skinned Birney."

---

121   *Ibid.*, 1025-1026; Sale, Diary, n.d.; John Sale to Aunt, July 9, 1864, Virginia State Library; McCabe, "Defense of Petersburg," 273. Sergeant Sale of the 12th Virginia reported that Weisiger's brigade "did not get as hotly engaged as the Balance of the div. The movement was well planned and executed, we entering the Yankee lines in the rear of their breastworks." Kirkland's brigade of Heth's division spent the afternoon and evening at General Hill's headquarters.

122   *OR* 40, pt. 1, 492, 493, 497.

123   *Ibid.*, 506, 508, 510, 512; *OR* 40, pt. 2, 316.

124   *OR* 40, pt. 1, 495, 501, 504.

125   *Ibid.*, 514, 517, 520.

126   *Ibid.*, 515.

Major General Horatio G. Wright
Library of Congress

When Wright's men moved out at dark, the sharpshooters, who were covering the Light Division as it pulled back, found themselves in deadly peril. For a few minutes, it seemed to the Rebels that the bluecoats would reach the Globe Tavern Road to their rear, if so, their retreat would be cut off. According to the unit historian:

The darkness was intense and the underbrush thick and tangled, yet, when the purpose of the foe was discovered, the sharpshooters delivered a stinging volley and made a dash for the road, with the Federals upon each flank and close upon their heels. A furious race ensued, in which a number of vicious curs from the Federal lines participated, but the light weighted, clean heeled Confederates won by half a neck, and made good their escape . . .[127]

"One little sharpshooter," a veteran recalled:

straggled into my line just after dark. He was still panting and laughing. "L—d G—d!" said he, "you ought to see them fat Yankees run. They run arter me, a-hollin' 'Stop you d—d rebel! Cut off the d—d rebels!' I heerd 'em blow. Say I to myself, 'You too fat Yankee! You get too much to eat over your side. You don't catch me!' And you ought to 'a seed me as I slid past em!'"[128]

General Meade was disappointed that darkness had put a stop to the attack, just as his Army of the Potomac was recovering the initiative. Writing Grant (at 9:00 p.m.) Meade observed, "On the left and the center the enemy have been pressed

127 Dunlop, *Lee's Sharpshooters*, 126-127; Welch, Confederate Surgeon's Letters, 101; Caldwell, *History of a Brigade of South Carolinians*, 164-165.

128 Caldwell, *History of a Brigade of South Carolinians*, 165.

back considerably; on the right no advantage was gained." The II and VI Corps' lines were now secure. A "general advance" had been scheduled for daylight, and Birney's and Wright's troops would endeavor to push the Rebels back into their fortifications. In the day's fighting, the Army of the Potomac had taken about 100 prisoners. Meade at the same time thought that when all the reports were in, he would find that his casualties would be light.[129]

With the situation stabilized, Meade, at 9:03 p.m., notified Warren that the two V Corps brigades rushed to bolster Birney would be returned during the night. It was after midnight before Sweitzer's and Dushane's troops were back in their camps.[130]

Wright, by 10:00 p.m., had made his plans for the next day. His corps would attack at 3:30 a.m., in double line of battle, covered by a strong skirmish line. Ricketts' division was to be on the left and Russell's division, reinforced by Ballier's brigade, on the right. Grant's Vermont brigade would be held in reserve, under orders to guard the left as the battle lines surged toward the Weldon Railroad. Bidwell's and Edwards' brigades of Wheaton's division were to hold their ground. Before taking up the advance, General Russell was to exert himself to link up with the II Corps on his right. Corps headquarters would be in rear of Ricketts' division, near the Globe Tavern Road.[131]

Part III

General Wright is Paralyzed by the Confederates

Birney's II and Wright's VI Corps advanced as scheduled at daybreak on June 23, 1864.

Under the cover of darkness, Gen. A. P. Hill withdrew Mahone's and Wilcox's divisions. The Rebels took their captured booty and prisoners with them. Consequently, no opposition, except on Gibbon's front, was encountered by the blueclad skirmish lines as they pressed ahead. By 6:00 a.m. Barlow's skirmishers had gained a mile without seeing a single Confederate. Gibbon's troops reoccupied the

---

129 OR 40, pt. 2, 304.

130 *Ibid.*, 312; OR 40, pt. 1, 459, 470.

131 OR 40, pt. 2, 316-317.

rifle pits from which they had been driven the previous afternoon, but they were disappointed to discover that Mahone's butternuts had made off with McKnight's 3-inch rifles. In front of Gibbon's left, shots had been exchanged as the Federals closed in on the Confederate picket line covering Battery No. 29.[132]

General Birney (at 6:35 a.m.) notified Meade that, on the right, Gibbon had forced back the Rebel outposts. In this fighting, Colonel Blaisdell was mortally wounded by a sharpshooter. Mott's right, by this hour, had recovered the earthworks from which it had been routed by Mahone's onslaught. At the moment, the II Corps was continuing to advance "as rapidly as possible through the dense woods . . ."[133]

Within the hour, Birney was able to report that Barlow's left was in contact with Russell's VI Corps division. Russell's troops, Birney advised Meade, had not advanced since daybreak, and Barlow would have to hold his ground till they did. Barlow's skirmishers by this hour had passed through the woods and had reached the edge of a field, a mile in advance of the earthworks occupied by their comrades. To their front, they could see spoil and abatis, a sure indication that the grey clads' main line of resistance crossed this field. Their advance had been so rapid that Barlow's skirmishers had outdistanced those from the divisions to their left and right. Barlow, in relaying this information to headquarters, wrote that it would be impossible for his skirmishers to press any farther "without coming upon the enemy's works."[134]

By 8:30 a.m. Meade had seen Barlow's communication. On doing so, he notified Birney that he did "not wish any attack on the enemy's works." As soon as Birney could advance his "line in connection with Wright to envelope the enemy's line," Meade wanted it done. The corps would then entrench "in the strongest manner possible."[135]

Meade also got in touch with General Wright. He wanted the VI Corps' commander to detail "a staff officer to ascertain exactly the position of Barlow's skirmish line . . . " This information would be used to govern Ricketts' and Russell's movements.[136]

---

132 *OR* 40, pt. 2, 338.

133 *Ibid.*, 339, 342; *OR*, 40, pt. 1, 367. With Col. Blaisdell dead, Colonel J. P. McIvor assumed command of the 2nd Brigade, Gibbon's division.

134 *OR* 40, pt. 2, 339, 341.

135 *Ibid.*, 339.

136 *Ibid.*, 348.

Meanwhile, Colonel Lyman was writing Meade. He had reached a point a mile and one-half west of Williams'. Here the road forked, with one branch leading to the Weldon Railroad two miles beyond, and the other route running north toward Petersburg. Colonel Timothy M. Bryan and his cavalry had taken the road leading to the railroad, while Ricketts' division was on the other road with his line facing north. According to all that he had heard, Russell's division looked west. A prisoner from Cadmus Wilcox's division, whom Lyman had just questioned, explained that the Confederate "Light Division" on the 22nd had marched down the Halifax Road to Globe Tavern and had then struck eastward across the open fields north of Aiken's house.[137]

Prior to starting on his raid against the South Side and Danville Railroads, General Wilson, on June 21, had organized a provisional cavalry brigade to be commanded by Colonel Bryan. That evening the units assigned to the provisional brigade were detached and rendezvoused at the camp Colonel Bryan had established in rear of V Corps. On the 22nd Bryan reported to General Wright, and deployed his troopers to cover the left of the VI Corps. Outposts were established and manned on the Jerusalem Plank and Lee's Mill Roads.

Colonel Bryan, on the morning of the 23rd, had taken the field at the head of two battalions of the 18th Pennsylvania Cavalry. Turning into the Globe Tavern Road, Bryan rode westward—his goal was the Weldon Railroad.[138]

Colonel Lyman (at 10:00 a.m.), having examined Ricketts' and Russell's positions, addressed a second note to his chief. He had found the divisions posted as indicated in his letter of 8:30, except that their lines were "rather crooked by reason of going through thick woods." Captain Alexander M. Beattie of the 3rd Vermont, with about 90 sharpshooters, had gained the Weldon Railroad, seeing only a few Confederate horsemen as they pushed ahead. After cutting the telegraph, Beattie had had his men pry loose a number of rails. Ricketts' left at this hour rested on a large field, one and one-half miles east of the tracks. Orders had been given for Ricketts and Wheaton to see that a line of skirmishers was established linking Ricketts' left with Beattie's sharpshooters at Globe Tavern.

---

137 *Ibid.*, 349. Two trains had headed south from Petersburg on the tracks of the Weldon Railroad that morning, Lyman learned from several VI Corps scouts, but they had been compelled to return. This was a certain clue that General Wilson's cavalry had wreaked havoc on the railroad somewhere south of Globe Tavern.

138 OR 40, pt. 1, 640; *History of the Eighteenth Regiment of Cavalry, Pennsylvania Volunteers (163rd Regiment of the Line) 1862-1865* (New York, 1909), 25, 54. Assigned to the Provisional brigade were the 3rd New Jersey Cavalry, two battalions 18th Pennsylvania Cavalry and a detachment 22nd New York Cavalry.

Brigadier General James B. Ricketts
Library of Congress

Colonel Lyman had also resolved the difficulty between Russell and Barlow. Russell had been a little in advance of Barlow and to "resume connection," he had to withdraw his right flank slightly.[139]

Fifteen minutes later, General Wright notified Meade that all that he had seen and heard indicated "the general direction of my line is not far from right, though it will probably be advanced somewhat." Beattie's patrol had reached the railroad, so Wright inquired, "Would it be worth while to attempt destroying the road at that point?"[140]

It was noon before Wright's message was finally read by Meade. Replying immediately, the army commander observed that the part of Wright's dispatch reading "the general direction of my line is not far from right, though it will probably be advanced somewhat" was unclear. It had been Meade's intention to have the VI Corps press ahead until it encountered the enemy, and then press the Confederates back into their works. Barlow's skirmishers were known to be before the Confederate fortifications, consequently, Meade felt that Wright should advance his skirmishers as far as Barlow's men, and then advance his line of battle.[141]

Two hours before, Meade had written Wright that it would be a wise move to put Colonel Bryan's horse soldiers to work wrecking the Weldon Railroad on either

139 *OR* 40, pt. 2, 349.

140 *Ibid.,* 349.

141 *Ibid.,* 351.

side of Globe Tavern. An officer had been sent to Bryan with two wagon loads of tools.[142]

At 11:00 a.m. a signal officer posted in a tall tree near Jones' spotted a Confederate column moving down the Halifax Road toward Wright's left. When he warned Wright of what could be a dangerous development, Meade inquired, "What progress are you making in your advance?"[143]

A staff officer, who had ridden with Bryan' horse soldiers to the railroad, was disappointed to discover that Wright had merely detailed some of the troopers as pickets to guard his left. When Meade was apprised of this, he ordered Wright to "throw out strong parties of the cavalry on the roads crossing the railroad, in advance of your left, and feel for the enemy."[144]

Wright replied at 12:10 p.m., informing his chief that he had detailed a small force of cavalry to watch his left, while dispatching the rest in two columns to "feel the enemy, and get information." At the time that Meade's latest two messages had been received, Wright was en route to see Birney "to arrange an advance, having previously ordered my picket-line forward." Wright was of the opinion that the two corps could not cooperate effectively in an advance, unless the commanders could meet to coordinate their plans. In view of Meade's concern regarding his movements, Wright promised to "continue on with my own command alone, without regarding the connection with any other corps."

Colonel Bryan's column, as it rode westward, had encountered a few Rebel horsemen near Dr. Gurley's. Dismounting, the Federals drove back the butternuts and pushed on toward their objective—the Weldon Railroad.[145] Bryan turned his men to prying up rails. The wagons with the tools having failed to show up, Bryan forwarded a request to Wright to lend him some.[146]

A signal officer at 12:45 p.m. sighted a column of Confederate infantry "at least a mile long, with two batteries of artillery, moving out of the enemy's works along the Weldon Railroad." In order to guard against a repeat of what had occurred on

---

142 *Ibid.*, 350. The tools had been slated to be used by General Wilson's column, but news that the Confederates were hot after the Union raiders had caused Meade to change his mind.

143 *Ibid.*, 350. A Negro had been picked up by Wright's troops and questioned. He told Colonel Lyman that he had left the city via the Halifax Road the previous day. As he had walked south, the Negro had seen about 800 Rebel soldiers near the road about a mile from the City. There were fortifications thereabouts, but no guns mounted therein.

144 *Ibid.*, 350.

145 *Ibid.*, 351.

146 *Ibid.*, 352; *History of the Eighteenth Regiment of Cavalry*, 25, 54.

June 22, Meade wanted General Wright to advance his pickets and "push out parties of cavalry, so as to give you . . . notice of the enemy's position as you advance."[147]

Besides advancing his skirmish line, General Wright made several other changes in the dispositions of his VI Corps brigades. Early in the day orders were given for Ballier's brigade to move up from the reserve and plug a gap that had opened between Russell's and Ricketts' divisions. After the brigade had moved to the point indicated, Colonel Ballier was informed by General Russell that his and Ricketts' troops had readjusted their lines and the opening had closed. The brigade then reported to Wheaton's command post near Ricketts' left. News that a strong Rebel column was tramping south, caused Wheaton to tell Ballier to advance his bluecoats and post them on the left of Grant's brigade. As his troops filed into position, Ballier found that his battle line was within one-fourth mile of Aiken's house and faced west. While the rest of the infantrymen were turned to throwing up breastworks, Ballier ordered out the 62nd New York, with instructions to extend the skirmish line.[148]

General Grant was likewise very busy. Shortly after Beattie and his sharpshooters had arrived on the Weldon Railroad, the brigade pioneers were ordered out to rip up iron rails. Next came a call from General Wheaton "for 200 men, properly officered," to report to the brigade officer of the day—Lt. Col. Samuel E. Pingree. The detail was made from the 11th Vermont, and the men deployed to form a picket line from the right of the 4th Vermont to the Weldon Railroad. Their mission would be twofold—besides protecting the pioneers, they would maintain a connection with the main force. Soon thereafter, Grant received a call for another detachment "to support the line." Major Charles K. Fleming of the 11th Vermont was sent out in charge of this force, which was posted about one-half mile in front and to the left of the brigade. Thus by 3:00 p.m. the strength of the Vermont brigade had been sapped by details to man the picket lines and for fatigue parties.[149]

Bidwell's brigade of Wheaton's division was held in reserve near Williams' house, while Edwards' continued to hold its position across the Jerusalem Plank Road.[150]

---

147 *OR* 40, pt. 2, 351-352.

148 *OR* 40, pt. 1, 497, 499, 500.

149 *Ibid.*, 502.

150 *Ibid.*, 495, 504.

Major General William Mahone
Library of Congress

All of Ricketts' men, except those on the skirmish line, were kept employed entrenching.[151]

The strong Rebel column sighted and reported by personnel of the signal corps belonged to Mahone's command. Mahone's brigade commanders, taking cognizance of the hard work of the afternoon of the 22nd, had let their men sleep in. Sergeant John Sale of the 12th Virginia reported that he "slept till ten o'clock, at which time [we] were waked to go on picket, relieving a portion of the 6th [Virginia] Regt. While on post, we learned that our brigade had been ordered to march out."[152]

General Lee, on learning that the Federals were again feeling their way toward the Weldon Railroad, had got in touch with the leader of his III Corps, A. P. Hill. A strong column was to be pushed down the Halifax Road and attempt to dislodge the Union force that had reached the Weldon Railroad at Globe Tavern. If fortune continued to smile on Confederate arms, the Yankees might well be dealt another punishing blow.

Hill determined to entrust command of the column that was to be ordered out to General Mahone. Wilcox was still in hot water with his immediate superior, because of his failure to cooperate with Mahone in the attack on the II Corps. Wilcox, in his defense, had claimed that his orders from Hill were contrary to Mahone's battle plan, so he held to his instructions and had accordingly done little

151 *Ibid.*, 506, 508.

152 Sale, Diary, n.d.

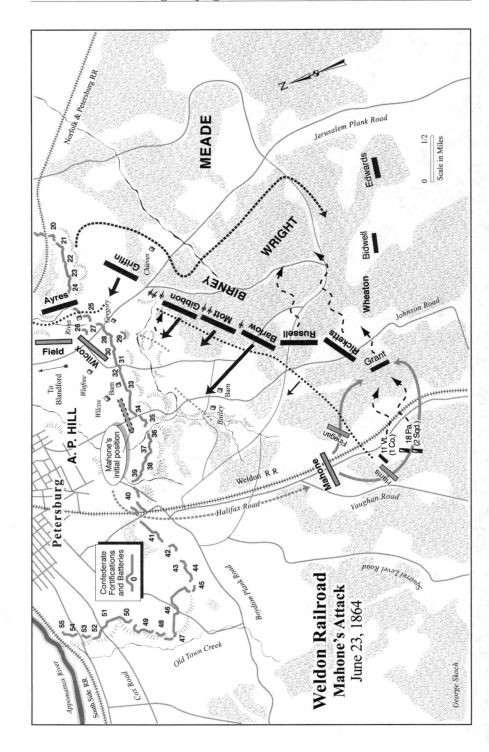

Weldon Railroad
Mahone's Attack
June 23, 1864

George Skoch

to contribute to the sweeping success scored by Mahone's troops at the expense of the II Corps.[153]

Except for the men on picket duty, Mahone was accompanied by his entire division, when he took the field at noon on June 23. Mahone's striking force was materially increased, when Brig. Gen. William W. Kirkland reported to him with his four-regiment North Carolina brigade. After marshaling his troops near the Lead Works, Mahone put his six brigades and two batteries in motion down the Halifax Road.[154]

Upon reaching the woods three-quarters of a mile north of Globe Tavern, Mahone called a halt to form his brigades into double line of battle. It was mid-afternoon before the Rebel officers had completed their dispositions in the cornfield north of the pines and were ready to strike. Covered by a strong force of skirmishers, the butternuts drove down the railroad, scattering Beattie's sharpshooters and Grant's pioneers. As soon as they could collect their wits and regroup, the Federal foot soldiers retired eastward toward Aiken's house. Pressing on, the Confederates cleared Bryan's cavalry from the right-of-way. Bryan's horse soldiers pulled back along the road leading to Dr. Gurley's. Before being routed from the railroad, Bryan reported that his men had wrecked a quarter mile of track and burned one culvert.[155]

To cope with this Confederate thrust, Wright thought it a good idea to recall part of Ricketts' division. Ricketts' men would be deployed to assist Wheaton to hold the Army of the Potomac's left flank. Hoping to gain time, orders were issued for Bryan and his cavalry "to again advance and attack anything but a line of battle."[156]

At 4:00 p.m., Wright warned Meade that according to the latest intelligence from the front, a second Confederate battle line had crossed the railroad, on the left of the one that had driven in Beattie's sharpshooters and Bryan's cavalry. The way the situation was developing, it looked as if his left would be subjected to major attack. If there were any troops in reserve, Meade had better put them in motion, because the VI Corps' left was weak. For the time being, the forward movement by the VI Corps' skirmish line toward the Petersburg defenses had been suspended.

153 Freeman, *Lee*, vol. 3, 453-454; Caldwell, *History of a Brigade of South Carolinians*, 166.

154 Sale, Diary, n.d.; Rowland, *Mississippi Official and Statistical Register*, 450, 466, 493, 514.

155 *OR* 40, pt. 1, 497, 502; *OR*, 40, pt. 2, 352; *History of the Eighteenth Regiment of Cavalry*, 25-26, 54.

156 *OR* 40, pt. 2, 352.

Orders had also been issued recalling Edwards' brigade from Jerusalem Plank Road.[157]

Upon receipt of Wright's message, Meade fired off a barrage of telegrams. Birney was to notify his "division commanders to be prepared in the event of General Wright being obliged to throw back his left to meet the attack of the enemy, to make corresponding movements so as to withdraw to the line occupied last night, should it be necessary." [158] Warren was to rush two of his V Corps "brigades at once to the Williams house . . ."[159] Wright was told to "take the initiative and attack the enemy if, in your judgment, this course is advisable; if not, that you withdraw your left flank so as to secure it . . ." In case his movements affected his right, Wright was to keep Barlow informed. Word that Warren had been instructed to send all the reinforcements he could spare to bolster the VI Corps was relayed to Wright.

Wright's proposal to recall Edwards' troops was frustrated when Union vedettes reported, "Confederates advancing up the Jerusalem Plank Road."[160] Subsequently, it was discovered that this tale was a wild rumor.

Within moments of the receipt of Meade's 4:00 p.m. telegram, Warren had contacted Griffin and Ayres. They were told to turn out their reserve brigades—Sweitzer's and Dushane's. Having been called out on the 22nd, the officers and men knew exactly what to do. After being formed and mustered, Sweitzer's and Dushane's bluecoats moved out, turning into the Jerusalem Plank Road. The V Corps brigades, by 5:40 p.m., had reached Williams' house.[161]

Meanwhile, Bryan's cavalrymen had endeavored to delay Mahone's thrust, but they failed. Skirmishers covering the advance of Harris' Mississippi brigade, by 5:00 p.m., had driven the Union horse soldiers back upon the picket line held by Grant's Vermonters. One of Meade's staff officers (Capt. W. W. Sanders) was so disgusted by the way the troopers behaved that he notified his chief, our cavalry "does not now appear to be worth anything as far as fighting goes." General Wright, who was on the scene, called for Colonel Bryan to dismount his two battalions of the 18th Pennsylvania and put the troopers into the rifle pits. [162]

---

157 *Ibid.*, 352-353.

158 *Ibid.*, 340.

159 *Ibid.*, 343.

160 *Ibid.*, 353.

161 *Ibid.*, 355; OR 40, pt. 1, 459, 470.

162 OR 40, pt. 2, 353-355; *History of the Eighteenth Regiment of Cavalry*, 25-26, 54.

Meade (at 5:40 p.m.) notified Wright that the two V Corps brigades were near Williams' house. Staff officers had been detailed to post the reinforcements in support of VI Corps batteries.[163]

The Rebels now assailed Grant's picket line. As soon as the cavalry had fallen back before Mahone's advance, Major Fleming had had his men strengthen their position by erecting barricades of fence rails. It was believed by Wheaton and Grant that the foe would assail Fleming's skirmish line, but the grey clads (Harris' Mississippians) bore to the "left around a skirt of woods." At the same time, Ricketts advanced his pickets, so they would be abreast of Fleming's right. The 4th Vermont was called forward as skirmishers and took post on Fleming's left. But the Mississippians swept farther to the left, closing in on the right of Walker's battalion of the 11th Vermont. Wheaton committed two of Ballier's regiments to cope with this threat to his left.

General Grant, fearing for the safety of his command, galloped to General Wright's command post. After listening attentively to his subordinate, Wright accompanied Grant to the sector of the picket *line* held by Fleming's battalion and the 4th Vermont. As they rode along, Grant told Wright that if the picket line gave way in front of Walker's battalion, the Rebels would take the 4th Vermont and Fleming's soldiers from the rear. Wright replied, "The division officer of the day has his instructions."

"What are they?"

"In case the Rebels broke through on the left," Wright answered, "the 4th Vermont and Fleming's battalion were to retire to the right and come in on Ricketts' skirmish line."

Shortly after the two generals parted, Harris' Mississippians smashed through Walker's battalion, occupying a field in rear of the 4th Vermont and Fleming's men. When they sought to withdraw to the right as planned, the Vermonters found to their horror that General Mahone had committed Brig. Gen. Joseph Finegan's Florida brigade. Seeing an opening, Mahone had advanced Finnegin's Floridians. Advancing through the pines and dense undergrowth west of Aiken's, Finegan's brigade quickly rolled back Ricketts' skirmish line and infiltrated the woods beyond. The jaws of the Rebel pincers quickly snapped. Except for a few men who were able to hide in the pines, Fleming's battalion and the 4th Vermont, 400 strong, surrendered to Finnegin's Floridians.[164]

163 OR 40, pt. 2, 355.

164 *Ibid.*, 355, 685; *OR*, 40, pt. 1, 495, 497, 502-503; Rowland, *Mississippi Official and Statistical Register*, 450, 466, 493, 514; OR 51, pt. 2, 1028.

Brigadier General Joseph Finegan
Library of Congress

Wright was understandably distressed to learn that the Rebels had broken Wheaton's picket line. Alarmed for the safety of his left and rear, he called frantically for reinforcements. At the same time, General Wheaton was authorized to call up Bidwell's brigade from Williams' house. Meade on being apprised of Wright's fears sought to calm his corps commander. At 6:30 p.m. he sent the message, "Do not let the enemy turn your left flank; either attack or withdraw; the former is most preferable." If there were no Confederates in front of his right, the VI Corps' leader could use troops from Russell's division to beef up his left. If his attack were unsuccessful, Wright could take advantage of the late hour and retire. Only in "case of extreme emergency" would the two V Corps brigades be committed.

Acknowledging Meade's communication, Wright inquired, "Shall I abandon what has been my front line and put all the troops between my left of this morning and the Williams' [house]?" But, Wright cautioned, "the attack on my left may be a feint to cover a major assault on my present front."

Meade, however, urged Wright to attack at once. Bidwell's brigade was en route to support the VI Corps' left, and another could be called up if necessary. There was no time to change position, Meade messaged, and not much for an attack if Wright continued to drag his feet.[165]

At 6:55 p.m. Meade learned from Colonel Lyman, who was at Wright's headquarters, that pickets had reported that the Confederates were advancing south of Second Swamp, and well to the left of the VI Corps. This column, it was theorized, was striking for the Jerusalem Plank Road. Consequently, Russell had been told to rush two brigades to bolster Wright's left.

165 *Ibid.*, 356.

Wright (at 7:00 p.m.), in reply to Meade's latest telegram complained, "So far it has been as much as I could do to prevent my flank being turned and quite impossible to form a column of attack." The Confederates were undoubtedly present in force, but where they would strike remained uncertain. Till then, Wright was of the opinion that the correct role for his corps was defensive. In this stand, he was supported by two of his three division commanders.

Five minutes later, an increasingly jittery Wright warned Meade, "I imagine that all the disposable rebel force is moving round our left for a general flank attack." The sooner Meade called up and posted heavy reinforcements, extending beyond the Plank Road, the better. If Meade were unable to do this, the VI Corps should withdraw as soon as it was dark.

Meade, after reflecting on the information supplied by Colonel Lyman, suggested at 7:15 p.m. that if the Rebels were driving toward the Plank Road, Wright should cross Second Swamp and take them in the flank. The army commander feared that if Wright continued to procrastinate it would "prove disastrous," because the VI Corps could not extend its left, and the army commander had no reinforcements to send to the point of danger.

Growing more agitated by the minute, Meade (at 7:20 p.m.) wired Wright that as there was no time to form columns, he was to attack in line of battle. If the Confederates interposed between the VI Corps and the Plank Road, Meade fumed, he would hold Wright responsible.[166]

This note, as expected, served as a goad. At 7:30 p.m. Wright replied tersely, "I will attack shortly from what may be considered my present right. The left toward the Williams house must stand fast."

Meade (at 7:35 p.m.) notified Wright that from the time the Confederate threat had materialized, he had urged his corps commander "to decide promptly, either to attack or to withdraw your left to the position of last night, extending from the Christian house to Strong's." Focusing his ire on Wright, Meade wrote, "Your delay has been fatal." Meade would "not blindly order" Wright to attack, but the responsibility for not doing so must rest on the corps commander's shoulders.

Seventy-five minutes later Meade had his answer. Wright would withdraw his corps to the "position held last night, and shall commence the movement at once." When he redeployed his troops, two divisions would be in line, one in reserve, with the two V Corps brigades "still farther to the left extending over the plank road."

Wright had failed to give him any data on which to form a "judgment," either as to the strength or position of the foe, so Meade decided it would be unwise to

---

166 *Ibid.*, 357. Wright had not talked to his other division commander.

overrule his subordinate. Permission was therefore granted for the VI Corps to retire. Wright, however, must be prepared "to take the offensive tomorrow at early daylight." The corps' pickets were to be left as far out as possible, when the troops were pulled back, and extended on the left a considerable distance down the Plank Road. General Barlow was to be kept advised of the retreat of the VI Corps, so that he might "conform to it." [167]

Wright, when given the green light, lost no time. Orders were prepared for the officers' guidance. Russell's division on the right was to reoccupy the rifle pits "commencing from the Strong house, and connecting with the II Corps." Ricketts' troops were to move into the works on Russell's left. Wheaton's division was to take position on Ricketts' left, with at least one brigade between Second Swamp and the Plank Road. The two V Corps brigades were to occupy the "first open field on the other side of the Plank Road in rear of the prolongation of General Wheaton's line to the left."

When the corps took up its new positions, the pickets were to be kept at least one-half mile to the front. Outposts from Wheaton's division were to connect with those from V Corps. Chief of Artillery, Charles H. Tompkins was to have one battery report to Wheaton, and "whatever can be used" to the senior officer present with the V Corps brigades. Colonel Bryan was to advance his cavalry down the Jerusalem Plank Road at least three miles, and watch all the roads coming in from the west.[168]

Immediately after the overwhelming of Wheaton's picket line by Finegan's and Harris' brigades, Wright called on General Ricketts for help. Ricketts told the commander of his advance brigade, Col. Benjamin F. Smith, to detail three regiments to report to General Grant. Smith named the 6th Maryland, and the 110th and 122nd Ohio. Within a few minutes, orders arrived for Smith to recall the rest of his brigade and mass it to the rear of Wheaton's hard pressed division. Colonel William S. Truex's brigade moved up from the reserve to occupy the rifle pits vacated by Smith's bluecoats.

When the Maryland and two Buckeye regiments reported to Grant, he posted them alongside his Vermonters. The officers were instructed to hold their men ready to charge the Confederates, whom they could hear moving about in the pines and underbrush to their front. At first it seemed to the Federals as if the Rebels were massing for a frontal assault. Several light thrusts were made and parried by Wheaton's pickets. Then the sounds reaching the Yankees seemed to indicate that

167 *Ibid.*, 358-359.

168 *Ibid.*, 359.

the enemy had moved around their left and were striking out toward the Plank Road.[169]

Wright encountered no difficulty in breaking contact with the foe, because the Confederate leaders, several hours before, had determined to return to their lines. By midnight the VI Corps had retired and taken up the positions described in Wright's memorandum.[170]

Unknown to Wright and his generals, General Hill, who had spent most of the day with General Mahone, had determined late in the afternoon to recall the column. After telling Mahone to collect his troops and retire into the Petersburg lines, General Hill, accompanied by his staff, headed back up the Halifax Road. Reaching his headquarters at 9:00 p.m., Hill telegraphed General Lee a terse report of what had happened up till the hour that he had left Globe Tavern. According to the corps commander, "We did not accomplish anything; taking about 100 prisoners of the VI Corps. It was so hot, the undergrowth so thick, and the enemy retiring all the time, our men did not press forward. Indeed, could not sufficiently fast to get up with their main body."[171]

Sergeant Sale, along with the other pickets left to hold the works when the division moved out, was relieved at 5:00 p.m. The men of the 12th Virginia started looking for their brigade, Weisiger's. Sergeant Sale recalled that at first this appeared to be a hopeless task, "as no one knew anything about what direction they had taken. By some means they heard their direction and took" the Halifax Road. After proceeding about two miles, the soldiers encountered General Hill's party. Hill told them to halt and rest as the division would soon be "coming up."

Mahone and his brigade commanders at dark recalled their troops. As soon as all the brigade commanders had reported in with their units, Mahone put his column in motion up the Halifax Road.

Sergeant Sale and his comrades heard the division as it approached. Glancing at his watch, Sale noted the hour: it was 10:00 p.m. As Weisiger's brigade passed, Sale and his men fell in. Mahone and his troops, after re-entering the Petersburg perimeter, camped for the night near Battery No. 35. Before retiring, the butternuts were issued rations.[172]

Reporting to General Hill on his return, Mahone explained that shortly after the corps commander had left the front, Finegan's Floridians had enveloped a

169   OR 40, pt. 1, 495, 506, 508, 510, 511, 512.

170   Ibid., 493, 494, 495, 497, 503, 506.

171   OR 51, pt. 2, 1027.

172   Sale, Diary, n.d.

portion of the VI Corps picket line, forcing a large number of bluecoats to ground their arms. All told during the day's expedition, the division had captured 600 prisoners, including 28 officers.[173]

Wilcox's division, on the 23rd, had been redeployed. The Light Division was pulled out of the rifle pits near the Weldon Railroad and marched a mile to the left, where the brigades relieved the troops holding the works to the right and left of the Jerusalem Plank Road. As this movement was made during the daylight hours, with part of the route in "full view of the foe," McGowan's brigade came under fire from a Union battery as it approached its new position. Since these guns enfiladed this sector of the line, "a rapid plunge into the works behind the traverses saved the brigade from any casualties." Skirmishers were then advanced to occupy and hold the picket line, which at this point was about 400 yards in front of the main line of resistance.[174]

Along the II Corps' front on the night of the 22nd, Colonel Tidball had repositioned one of his batteries. The cannoneers of Battery F, 1st Pennsylvania Light Artillery were called up and emplaced their 3-inch rifles east of the Jerusalem Plank Road, and to the right of the 6th Maine's Napoleons. A company from the regular engineer battalion was called up to throw up emplacements to cover these guns. Colonel Tidball shortly after daybreak had the 4th New York Heavy Artillery report to General Gibbon, who placed the artillerists turned infantrymen in the rifle pits to the left of the Plank Road. The Confederates had the Plank Road under observation, and when their spotters reported the two V Corps brigades as they marched for the Williams' house, their guns opened fire. Before the Rebel gunners could seriously interfere with the column, three II Corps batteries (the 11th New York, 6th Maine, and Battery F) roared into action, quickly demonstrated a marked superiority, and silenced the grey clads' cannons.[175]

*   *   *

Before catching a few hours sleep on the night of the 23rd, General Wright issued orders for his division commanders to see that their picket lines were advanced at 6:00 a.m., "for the purpose of feeling the enemy (if they still remain in our front) . . . " The skirmishers were to push forward till they reached the ground

---

173 *OR* 51, pt. 2, 1028; McCabe, "Defense of Petersburg," 277.

174 Dunlop, *Lee's Sharpshooters*, 131; Caldwell, *History of a Brigade of South Carolinians*, 166.

175 *OR* 40, pt. 1, 397, 424, 427, 435, 438.

from which the corps had just retired. Colonel Bryan at the same time was to throw out mounted patrols to see if he could ascertain the Confederates' position.[176]

A change of officers along the picket line occasioned some delay, but by 6:30 a.m. the VI Corps' skirmish line had moved out. Within 75 minutes, one of the patrols organized by Colonel Bryan had advanced two and one-half miles to Dr. Gurley's without encountering any Rebels. Pushing on, the horse soldiers crossed the railroad at Globe Tavern.

In front of the VI Corps, the skirmishers, as they worked their way cautiously forward, saw few grey clads. Most of these had a good head start and were able to elude the Yanks. Fifteen butternuts, who had straggled when their brigades retired into the Petersburg perimeter, were captured by the VI Corps' picket line. None of these proved to be very "intelligent or communicative." About all the Union intelligence people could learn on questioning them was that while most belonged to Finegan's Florida brigade, several came from other brigades of Mahone's division, with one or two from Kirkland's brigade of Heth's division.[177]

Wright's skirmishers, by 10:15 a.m., had advanced to the position occupied by the picket line on the 23rd, which was two and one-half miles beyond the breastworks currently held by the corps. Notifying Meade of this development, Wright inquired, "Do you wish them to continue to go forward?"

At 10:30 a.m. Chief of Staff Humphreys replied for Meade. The pickets were to push on, and they were to be supported. As they did, they were to maintain contact with Birney's skirmishers, which had also been ordered forward. When his pickets had "secured sufficient ground," Wright was to advance his battle line, "connecting with General Birney's, whose left will be moved to correspond with your right." Wright was to leave the two V Corps brigades where they were, and post his left to give security to his main line of resistance.[178]

In response to this directive, Wright, at 11:45 a.m., alerted his division commanders to "be prepared to move as soon as orders to that effect are received by them." These instructions were to be sent as soon as notice from the corps' officer of the day was received that the picket line had reached the area held by the 23rd, and connection made with that of the II Corps.[179]

---

176 OR 40, pt. 2, 392. Colonel T. O. Seaver of the 3rd Vermont was named corps officer of the day, and would report to Wright's headquarters at 5:30 a.m.

177 *Ibid.*, 376, 386, 387.

178 *Ibid.*, 388.

179 *Ibid.*, 393.

Before this order could be implemented, General Grant visited Meade's Jerusalem Plank Road command post. After learning that the fight on the 22nd had resulted in a stampede by Hancock's II Corps, Grant determined to abandon for the time being his efforts to invest Petersburg. He ordered Meade to refuse his left flank, while the II Corps and VI Corps "strongly fortified" the ground west of the Plank Road.[180]

In view of this decision by Grant, Meade at 12:40 p.m. notified Wright and Birney that they need not advance beyond their present lines until directed to do so.[181] Wright, after conferring with Meade, notified his division commanders, as it was possible they could remain where they were for "a day or two" that they have their soldiers "strengthen the works already thrown up."[182]

Since there would be no attack, Wright had the corps officer of the day make several adjustments in the picket line. The outposts on the right were to maintain contact with Barlow's skirmishers, "to advance with them, and halt when they do." By nightfall the picket line was as far advanced as safety allowed. Depending on ground cover and terrain, it was from one mile and one-half to two miles in front of Wright's main line of resistance.[183]

Meade's headquarters had suggested at 9:00 a.m. that Wright see that a "small reconnoitering party of cavalry" was advanced down the "old Norfolk Road," which paralleled the Norfolk & Petersburg Railroad.[184]

General Wright saddled Colonel Bryan with the responsibility for seeing that this task was carried out. Marching orders were accordingly issued to the 18th Pennsylvania Cavalry.[185]

Chief of Staff Humphrey's, at 10:00 a.m., inquired of Wright, "Have the cavalry scouts . . . been as far down the Plank Road as its intersection with the road from Prince George Courthouse?"[186]

Wright replied to this dispatch immediately. A patrol from Bryan's command had been down the Plank Road at least five miles beyond the Second Swamp

180 *Ibid.*, 372, 373-374, 389, 393. Meade's command post was west of the Plank Road, just beyond Jones' house.

181 *Ibid.*, 381, 389.

182 *Ibid.*, 393.

183 *Ibid.*, 391.

184 *Ibid.*, 387.

185 *History of the Eighteenth Regiment of Cavalry*, 54.

186 OR 40, pt. 2, 387.

crossing. Scouts had examined all roads leading into the Plank Road from the west, without seeing any Confederates.[187]

The 18th Pennsylvania, guided by a local black man familiar with the area, rode down the old Norfolk Road about seven miles. Although no Rebels were seen, the horse soldiers were told by local blacks they questioned that there were about 2,000 Rebel cavalrymen operating in Sussex County.[188]

Grant, on learning that Meade had run into difficulty west of the Jerusalem Plank Road, got in touch with General Butler. At 4:00 p.m. on June 23, Grant directed Butler to give Baldy Smith as many reinforcements as he could spare. Smith was then to relieve as much of Burnside's IX Corps as possible, hopefully at least one full division, so that Meade could "extend and protect his left." If feasible, Grant wanted to see Burnside's division relieved by no later than "tomorrow morning."

At 4:35 p.m. Butler replied, "Dispatch in regard to reinforcing Smith received. It shall be done." Butler would pull Brig. Gen. John W. Turner's X Corps division out of the Bermuda Hundred Line and have it cross to the south bank of the Appomattox. With the departure of Turner's troops, it would cut the strength of the force holding that line to 4,000.[189]

Baldy Smith was notified that he would be reinforced during the night by Turner's division, described by Butler, as "one of the best divisions I have got." As soon as Turner's bluecoats arrived, Smith was to see that his XVIII Corps assumed responsibility for as much of Burnside's front as possible.[190]

At 6:00 p.m. Meade's headquarters advised General Burnside of what was coming. As soon as Baldy Smith's bluecoats had relieved his right flank division, Burnside was to have the troops thus freed march toward the left, where they were to replace Warren's right flank division in the rifle pits.[191] Simultaneously, a telegram was delivered to Warren notifying him that as soon as Burnside's IX Corps division had relieved one of his divisions, he was to replace Birney's right flank division.

Warren, at 9:00 p.m., inquired of Burnside, "When will the IX Corps replace my right division?"

187 *Ibid.*, 388.

188 *Ibid.*, 392.

189 *Ibid.*, 362.

190 *Ibid.*, 369.

191 *Ibid.*, 360.

"I will relieve your division just as soon as Smith relieves mine, which I hope will be very soon," Burnside countered. The IX Corps commander wanted to know the strength of the division he was to relieve, Crawford's.

"3,551 officers and men," Warren answered.[192]

General Turner, as soon as it was dark, pulled his troops out of the Bermuda Hundred Line. Soldiers belonging to Brig. Gen. Alfred H. Terry's X Corps division replaced Turner's. After the units had been formed and mustered, Turner passed the word to move out, the division crossing the river on the Point of Rocks pontoon bridges. While en route down the Point of Rocks Road, Turner was joined by several of Smith's and Burnside's staff officers. Guided by these men, Turner turned his division into Prince George Courthouse Road, and at 1:00 a.m. on June 24, his troops began relieving Willcox's IX Corps bluecoats.

The position now held by Turner's division was on the left of Martindale's XVIII Corps division. Turner's right center was dug in immediately in front of the Hare house, while his center and left, passing over Hare House Hill, extended down the slope and across a branch of Poor Creek, and connected with the IX Corps in "a piece of woods a short distance beyond."[193]

Willcox's troops, on being relieved by Turner's, marched rapidly to the left. Having fought and marched over much of this ground, Willcox was able to push his men hard. The rifle pits occupied by Crawford's V Corps division, which they were to relieve, were a short distance to the right of the sector where Willcox's men had attacked on June 18. Willcox's division by daybreak had replaced Crawford's behind the works.[194]

Crawford's division, as it crossed the Jerusalem Plank Road and prepared to relieve Gibbon's troops, came under a galling fire of artillery and small-arms. Crawford, at 11:40 a.m. June 24, notified Warren that his troops had replaced Gibbon's. On doing so, Crawford had been shocked to see that Gibbon's people were still in a "very bad state of demoralization," as a result of their stampede on the 22nd. Crawford had heard that four of Gibbon's regiments at that time had surrendered to one Confederate. When he examined the rifle pits into which his troops had just moved, Crawford shook his head, because he considered the line laid out by Gibbon to be "a bad one."[195]

---

192 *Ibid.*, 345-346.

193 OR 40, pt. 1, 696-697.

194 *Ibid.*, 197, 198; OR, 40, pt. 2, 397.

195 OR 40, pt. 1, 190; OR, 40, pt. 2, 381, 385.

Upon being relieved by Crawford, Gibbon assembled his four brigades and marched them down the Plank Road to Williams'. Two batteries (the 10th Massachusetts and Battery G, 1st New York) accompanied Gibbon's column. Near Williams', they relieved the two V Corps brigades that had been posted there since the previous evening's emergency.[196] Sweitzer's and Dushane's brigades then returned to their camps in rear of the fortifications held by the V Corps.[197]

Part IV
Hagood's Brigade Takes a Beating

General Beauregard, upon the arrival of the Army of Northern Virginia at Petersburg, remained in immediate charge of the Petersburg lines held by troops from his District of North Carolina and Southern Virginia.[198] The troops from Beauregard's command committed to the defense of Petersburg were organized into two infantry divisions (Maj. Gen. Bushrod R. Johnson's and Robert F. Hoke's) and one cavalry brigade (Brig. Gen. James Dearing's). Nightfall on June 18 found one of Beauregard's divisions, Hoke's, holding the earthworks from the Appomattox on the left to the area where the Norfolk & Petersburg Railroad passed through the defenses. Johnson's division, having been relieved by Kershaw's troops, was posted in reserve.

On the 19th Beauregard issued orders redeploying two of his brigades. Brigadier General Archibald Gracie's brigade of Johnson's division was to recross the Appomattox and resume its position at Fort Clifton, while Col. John S. Fulton's brigade was to join Maj. Gen. George Pickett, who was in charge of the force holding the Howlett Line. Dearing was to report to Maj. Gen. W. H. F. "Rooney" Lee on the Jerusalem Plank Road, where he would be assigned to protect the Weldon Railroad.[199]

Forty-eight hours later, on the 21st, Beauregard, having observed that the salient occupied by Brig. Gen. Alfred Colquitt's brigade was hammered

---

196 OR 40, pt. 2, 381.

197 OR 40, pt. 1, 459, 470.

198 Roman, *The Military Operations of General Beauregard*, vol. 2, 259.

199 OR 40, pt. 2, 668-669. At this time the 64th Georgia, which was posted on Swift Creek, was relieved by Gracie's troops and assigned to the brigade led by Brig. Gen. Alfred Colquitt.

unmercifully by Union artillery, determined to let another unit share the hazards. Orders were accordingly issued calling up from the reserve Brig. Gen. Matt W. Ransom's brigade of Johnson's division. Upon being relieved by Ransom's North Carolinians, Colquitt's Georgians were to report to General Johnson.[200]

The Confederate generals knew that with the II and VI Corps operating west of the Jerusalem Plank Road, the force holding the investment line between the Appomattox and Baxter Road would have been weakened. They also knew that the Union supply line linking the II and VI Corps with their base at City Point passed behind the works held by the IX and XVIII Corps and along the river. General Lee, in conjunction with General Beauregard, determined to seize the initiative, roll back the Union right, and cut Grant's supply line. Lee and his officers were also encouraged to note the low morale displayed by many Union units in the fighting west of the Jerusalem Plank Road.[201]

General Lee placed Beauregard in charge of the attacking force. Meeting with his staff on Dunn's Hill on June 23, Beauregard drafted his plan for a powerful thrust against the lines held by Baldy Smith's XVIII Corps. At daybreak on the 24th the batteries emplaced north of the Appomattox were to go into action, hammering the Union lines and emplacements in front of General Hoke's sector. This bombardment was to continue for one-half hour. The guns would then cease firing for five minutes, as a signal for Hoke to advance his infantry. The cannons would then roar back into action, concentrating "on batteries and distinct lines and masses of the enemy," such as can be fired upon without endangering Hoke's foot soldiers. As their fuses weren't too reliable, the Rebel cannoneers were to employ "mostly solid shot."

At the same time, Confederate troops posted near the Weldon Railroad were to feign an attack on the VI Corps, so the Federals would be pinned down and thus be unable to reinforce the XVIII Corps.

When Hoke assaulted, he was to maneuver his right, so as to take the Yankees' first and second lines in the flank, and move rapidly against the Union position near the Hare house. Having captured Hare House Hill, Hoke was to push on and retake the works abandoned on the 15th.

Field's division, which under the cover of darkness would be relieved by Johnson's, was to be positioned to support Hoke's attack and protect his left. As soon as practicable, Brig. Gen. George T. Anderson (who led Field's 1st Brigade) was to throw his Georgians into the rifle pits from which Hoke had driven the

200   *Ibid.*, 678.

201   Hagood, *Memoirs of the War of Secession*, 271.

bluecoats, on which rested Hoke's left. The Georgians were to follow Hoke, and Anderson would "fill up with other troops the gap between the river and Hoke's left until the whole line shall be occupied." Should he discover the opportunity, Anderson was to advance and assault the old Confederate line from Battery No. 2 to Battery No. 9. As soon as Hoke's right had uncovered his front, Kershaw's division was to advance, to be followed by Johnson's. Johnson's mission would be to retake the old line of works between Batteries No. 19 and 24.[202]

General Hoke, during the evening, told Brig. Gen. Johnson Hagood to be ready for a movement at daylight. No other officer in the division was told of Beauregard's plan, because Hoke wanted to be certain the foe was kept in the dark as to Confederate intentions. At this stage, as on the 18th, Hagood's South Carolinians held Hoke's left. The 27th, 21st, and 11th regiments held the rifle pits from the Appomattox to the City Point Road, and the 25th Regiment and 7th Battalion prolonged the brigade front south of the road. Four hundred yards to Hagood's front, and parallel to it, were the Union entrenchments. An open field with "a rank growth of oats" lay between. Each side had thrown up a line of slight rifle pits to shelter their pickets, a short distance in front of their main line of resistance.[203]

Following the fighting on the 18th, General Hagood, taking into consideration that most of his units were without field officers, had divided his brigade into wings. Lieutenant Colonel Patrick H. Nelson was placed in charge of the regiments north of the City Point Road.[204]

As soon as it was dark on the 23rd, Bushrod Johnson marched his division up from the reserve. Not wishing to alert the Federal outposts, the Confederates moved slowly and quietly. It was well after midnight before Johnson's grey clads had relieved the last of Field's division in the works between the Baxter and Jerusalem Plank Roads. After assembling their brigades well behind the lines, Field's brigade commanders put their columns in motion for the previously designated rendezvous—Iron Bridge on the City Point Road.[205]

202 OR 40, pt. 1, 804-805.

203 Ibid., 797, 802-803.

204 Hagood, Memoirs of the War of Secession, 278.

205 OR 40, pt. 1, 761, 766; C. W. Field, "Campaign of 1864 and 1865," in Southern Historical Society Papers, vol. 14, 549. Brigadier General John Bratton's South Carolina brigade of Field's division on the afternoon of the 18th had been posted in the works to the left and right of Battery No. 34. Bratton, at dark, had marched his troops to the left and relieved one of Kershaw's brigades in the works covering Baxter Road. Bratton's left now rested on Pegram's Salient. During the period, June 19-23, Bratton's men worked hard strengthening the works

Shortly before daybreak on the 24th, Hoke returned to Hagood's command post, and gave him detailed instructions as to the part the South Carolinians were to take in bringing on the battle. When the guns which were about to open fell silent, Hagood was to have his left wing (the 27th, 21st, and 11th South Carolina) take up the advance. When they left the shelter afforded by their works, the grey clads were to be formed into two heavy skirmish lines. Hagood's brigade was to be closely supported by General Anderson's Georgians. After Hagood's South Carolinians had driven the Yankees from their first line, Anderson was to occupy it until his supports arrived, when he was to press on against their second and third line. Meanwhile, Hagood was to pivot his left wing to the right, call up the right wing, and reform his men along the City Point Road, his brigade perpendicular to its initial position. He would then sweep forward, rolling up the Union line on the slope of the Hare House Hill and clear Ransom's front.

While Hoke and Hagood were discussing the situation, Lieutenant Andrews of Anderson's staff rode up and reported that the Georgia brigade had filed into position in rear of the earthworks held by Hagood's left, and were concealed from the Federals' view by a knoll. Close behind was another of Field's brigades, Col. Dudley M. DuBose's.[206]

The artillery (44 guns) opened as soon as the morning's mist had cleared, pounding the lines held by the XVIII Corps with "unusual severity." At 7:30 a.m. the cannons ceased fire. General Hagood at 7:20 a.m. had sent Lieutenant Andrews to tell General Anderson that the South Carolina brigade would advance in five minutes. After holding their fire for five minutes, the Rebels' big guns reopened, directing their attention upon the Yankee batteries. General Hoke recalled, "as far as I could see," this was the only service rendered by our guns. Indeed, he feared, "we were injured more than we gained by the use of our guns, as it notified the enemy of our intended attack."[207]

---

they occupied. On the night of the 23rd they were relieved by Brig. Gen. Stephen Elliott's brigade of Johnson's division.

206 *OR* 40, pt. 1, 797, 803.

207 *Ibid.*, 797, 803. The cannoneers of the four artillery battalions assigned to Beauregard's command had posted their pieces along the line and at commanding points in its rear to aid in the defense. Two of Beauregard's batteries, the Confederate Guards and Wright's, had unlimbered their guns north of the Appomattox. Most of the guns which shelled the XVIII Corps on the morning of the 24th were north of the river. These pieces were mounted in three sectors. Emplaced on the commanding bluff at Archer's house were the rifled guns of Battery A, Sumter South Carolina Artillery and Lewis' Virginia battery. One-half mile up the Appomattox from Archer's were the rifled guns of Clutter's and Thompson's Virginia Batteries. The cannoneers of Poague's Battalion had unlimbered their guns farther upstream,

Because of some unforeseen difficulties, it was 7:42 a.m. before Hagood's forward line of skirmishers, 400 picked officers and men, advanced. Close behind came the second line of skirmishers, about 550 strong. Colonel Nelson of the 7th Battalion led the first line, General Hagood the second.

Nelson had been standing beside Hagood, when Hoke's aide brought the order to advance. The men, who had been told to follow Nelson, were watching him, and when he was ordered to go, without speaking, he drew his handkerchief from his breast and raised it aloft. The South Carolinians sprang over the parapet with a yell and rushed out into the oat field. Nelson's skirmishers carried the Union picket line, capturing about 30 bewildered bluecoats. To General Hagood it appeared that the "enemy's whole line" was "seriously shaken." While awaiting the advance of Anderson's troops, the South Carolinians, in accordance with orders from Hagood, laid down in the oats. When the fresh brigade came up, they would go in with it.[208]

The picket line captured by the South Carolinians had been occupied during the night by troops from General Stannard's XVIII Corps division. When the Rebel artillery ceased firing at 7:30 a.m., Stannard, suspecting that an attack was impending, told Colonels Henry and Cullen to recall their outposts. As in all wars, some of the pickets didn't get the word and were overrun. The troops posted behind the Union main line of resistance waited until the outposts had retired and then opened with a "rapid and telling fire."[209]

General Hoke, seeing the Federal pickets scatter, waited impatiently for Anderson's battle line to come up. Realizing that a moment's delay would be fatal, Hoke asked General Field to order Anderson's brigade forward. A staff officer was sent galloping to the rear with an urgent message for Anderson to put his Georgians in motion. When Anderson failed to show up, Field repeated his order. This time,

---

alongside the three 20-pounder Parrotts manned by the Confederate Guards Artillery and the five field pieces served by Wright's Virginia battery. On the night of June 23, eight 24-pounder Coehorn mortars were emplaced in rear of Hagood's left. Two Napoleons were emplaced on Hagood's line, where it crossed the City Point Road. OR 40, pt. 1, 757; Hagood, *Memoirs of the War of Secession*, 281.

208 OR 40, pt. 1, 803; *Hagood, Memoirs of the War of Secession*, 278.

209 *OR 40, pt. 1, 716, 718; OR, 40, pt. 2, 401; OR 51, pt. 1, 1250-1252. Stannard's troops, since occupying the works between the river and City Point Road, had spent many hours "remodeling and rebuilding their lines." Two covered ways were started, linking the front and rear lines. On the 23rd, a black brigade led by Col. Nelson Ames had reported to General Stannard. The general placed the black troops in his rear line of works, thus freeing Burnham's brigade, which was sent a mile to the rear to rest. Colonel Cullen's brigade replaced Burnham's troops in the rifle pits on Stannard's right.

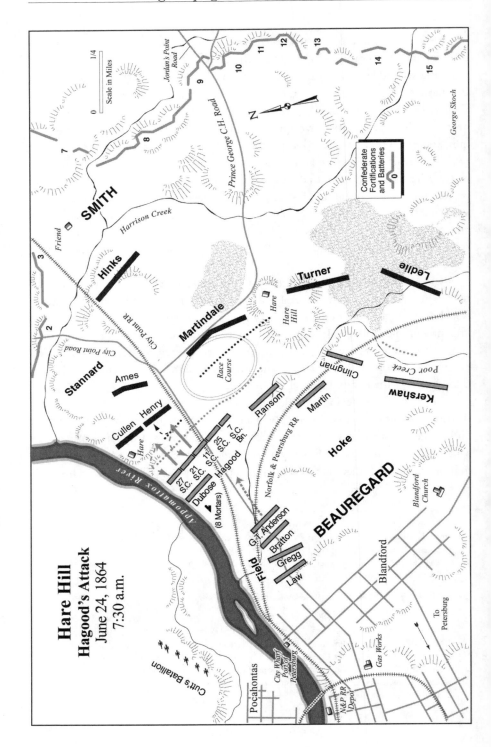

Hare Hill
Hagood's Attack
June 24, 1864
7:30 a.m.

Field received an answer. Anderson reported that the entrenchments to his front were occupied by Hagood's South Carolinians. Looking about, Hoke could see that in making this statement, Anderson was in error. The only troops in the trenches referred to were stragglers. Colonel DuBose's brigade, by this time, had marched up. After reaching the trenches, DuBose's troops moved down them by the left flank and occupied the position General Anderson was to have taken.[210]

Instead of advancing over the knoll to support the attack, Anderson, when compelled by repeated orders to move, went to the rear by file as far as Iron Bridge, nearly one-fourth mile. He then led his column up Poor Creek hollow, until he reached the shelter of the entrenchments near Colquitt's Salient, and then came "stumbling along them already crowded with men," until he reached the sector Hagood had left. Anderson was more than one hour getting to a position to which he had little more than 150 yards to march straight ahead, and with nothing in his way but "the usual hazards of hostile fire." Meanwhile, DuBose's brigade had come up three-quarters of an hour before the brigade that was to precede it.[211]

Long before DuBose's men put in their appearance, Stannard's troops had seen that Hagood's soldiers were unsupported. Volley after volley crashed into the Confederates. No soldiers in the world could have long withstood the terrible punishment to which the South Carolinians were subjected. The Rebels were trapped. Some of the men scrambled to their feet and retired into the rifle pits, out of which they had so confidently charged a few short minutes before. Colonel Nelson had to calm his men. Getting to his feet, he walked along his line through the oats. Shortly after reaching the left, he was cut down by a Union sniper. Seeing that their situation was hopeless, a number of the butternuts got to their feet and grounded their arms. A captain and 60 enlisted men surrendered to Henry's men, and 4 officers and 130 soldiers to Cullen's brigade.[212]

About one hour after the repulse of Hagood's three regiments, General Field put two brigades in the trenches on the left of the City Point Road with a view to resuming the attack. Hoke, however, advised against it, as the Federals had had ample time to prepare for "us." At this time orders were received for Hoke and Field to report to General Lee. After ascertaining the facts, Lee told Field to forget his projected attack.[213]

210 OR 40, pt. 1, 797, 803; Field, "Campaign of 1864-1865," 550.

211 Hagood, *Memoirs of the War of Secession*, 277.

212 *Ibid.*, 277; OR, 40, pt. 1, 716, 718, 803; OR 40, pt. 2, 401.

213 OR 40, pt. 1, 797-798.

After his officers had assembled and mustered their units, General Hagood found that this fiasco had cost his brigade 25 killed, 72 wounded, and 209 missing.[214] Union losses in this engagement were 72: 57 in Cullen's brigade and 15 in Henry's.[215]

It is not difficult to see why the Confederates' attack failed. Hagood's troops, who were to spearhead the thrust, and the supporting units looked to different division commanders for their orders. General Field was on the field, and no blame appears to have attached to him. If it were impracticable for the assault to be made and supported by the same division, a common superior should have been on the spot to coordinate the operations of the divisions. Generals Lee and Beauregard were near the batteries across the river in close view of the field, but without means of direct communication, and therefore unable to take tactical direction of the affair. Hagood was understandably incensed at Anderson. He was of the opinion that "Anderson should have been shot." For some reason, Lee failed to order a court of inquiry, "though the common sense of that portion of the army that knew anything of the affair kept afloat for two or three weeks the daily rumor that one had been ordered."[216]

* * *

The battle of the Jerusalem Plank Road ended on June 24 with the Army of the Potomac grimly digging in to hold the ground gained west of the road. Grant and Meade had extended their lines a considerable distance, but not to the west as they had hoped. The Federals' first attempt to invest Petersburg had failed.

On the 22nd the Confederates had sent the II Corps reeling. Mahone had followed up his initial success scored at Barlow's expense with "an enterprise, audacity and shrewdness rarely exhibited, even by their able commanders." The entire affair of that day had been short, swift, and decisive. Birney's II Corps had been "defeated almost without being engaged." There had been very little fighting, and comparatively small loss, except in prisoners. Of these, the II Corps had lost 1,700: more than it had on the Peninsula; more than it had at Antietam, Fredericksburg, and Chancellorsville combined. Four guns, the only ones taken from the corps by the foe till this stage of the conflict (except those abandoned,

---

214   *Ibid.*, 804.

215   OR 51, pt. 1, 1251. Twenty-four dead Confederates were found in front of the rifle pits held by the Spencer-armed 40th Massachusetts.

216   Hagood, *Memoirs of the War of Secession*, 276-277; Field, "Campaign of 1864 and 1865," 551.

disabled, on the banks of the Po) were carried as trophies by Mahone's terrible men. The entire operation had been like that of an expert mechanic who touches some critical point with a fine instrument, in exactly the right place, producing an effect seemingly altogether out of proportion to the force exerted.[217]

The performance of the VI Corps on the 23rd was almost as dismal. Once again, General Mahone and his officers were able to take advantage of their knowledge of this section of Prince George County to deal the Yankees another punishing blow. Indeed, the Confederate movements were conducted with such skill as to all but paralyze General Wright. For several hours, Wright was unable to make up his mind. Should he attack? Should he hold his ground? Should he retreat? This situation became so acute that an examination of the correspondence passing between Wright and Meade at this time leads one to believe that Meade was on the verge of relieving the commander of his VI Corps.

On June 24, the assault by the Confederates on the XVIII Corps was a fiasco, which partially nullified their successes of the previous 48 hours. The net advantage of the current operations depended on the outcome of the cavalry raid led by General Wilson against the Weldon, South Side, and Danville railroads. Wilson's horse soldiers had moved out simultaneously with the advance of Birney's infantry on the 21st.

Editor's Conclusion

When the fighting ended on the night of June 24, it was evident that Grant had failed to seize even the Weldon Railroad much less the vital South Side Railroad. However, Lee had also failed to dislodge the Union right in his attack of the 24th.

The Federal II Corps collapse on June 22 further demonstrated the decline of that splendid corps. The failure of Lee's offensive revealed that some of his subordinates could not mount a successful offensive, a disturbing fact that distressed Lee and boded ill for future Confederate operations.

The Federals lost 2,962 officers and men on June 22-23. The Confederate III Corps lost 700. On the 24th Hagood's South Carolinians lost

217 Walker, *History of the Second Corps*, 545-546.

25 killed, 73 wounded, 208 missing, a total of 306 while the Federals lost fewer than a dozen.[218]

On June 22, the same day the II Corps was routed at the Jerusalem Plank Road, a cavalry force of 5,000 troopers from the divisions of Generals August Kautz and James H. Wilson rode south to tear up the railroads supplying Petersburg. They destroyed 60 miles of track, but on their return to Union lines were intercepted by the cavalry divisions of Generals Wade Hampton and Fitzhugh Lee and roughed up. The Federals lost 12 cannon, 1,445 men, and hundreds of horses; Confederate losses amounted to only some 300.[219]

---

218   *The Petersburg Campaign*, 33 and 88, and Hagood, *Memoirs of the War of Secession*, 273.

219   *The Petersburg Campaign*, 95.

Chapter 4

The Crater

July 30, 1864

Editor's Introduction

U. S. Grant's first offensive against Petersburg ended on the night of June 18. The next day, Grant scouted the north bank of the James River in search of a location to create a bridgehead on the same side of the river as Richmond. His purpose was to provide Maj. Gen. Philip Sheridan a pontoon to cross to Bermuda Hundred when that cavalry general returned to the Richmond area after his Trevilian Station raid in Louisa County, Virginia.

The Sheridan-Hunter Expedition failed because Sheridan turned back east after his defeat at Trevilian Station (June 11-12) instead of following orders to proceed to Charlottesville, Virginia, to join with Maj. Gen. David Hunter's Army of the Shenandoah. Grant's orders to Hunter were rather loosely arranged, and when he did not hear from Sheridan, Hunter decided to march on Lynchburg to capture that important rail junction. Hunter was rebuffed at Lynchburg by Lt. Gen. Jubal Early on June 17-18 and withdrew into the mountains of West Virginia.

Grant, meanwhile, found the perfect location for a pontoon bridge at Deep Bottom, which drew its name because the flow of the James River had scooped out the bed to an unusual depth. High bluffs overlooked the site and, properly fortified, would protect the camp and the pontoon bridge. On the night of June 20, Brig. Gen. Robert Foster and 2,000 Federals crossed the river to Deep Bottom and fortified the site.

Sheridan was trying to reach Deep Bottom when Maj. Gen. Wade Hampton's cavalry defeated him at Samaria Church on June 24, which in turn forced Sheridan to cross the James downstream at Wilcox's Landing. Although Deep Bottom had not provided Sheridan with a crossing place, Grant maintained the valuable bridgehead. The fortified Deep Bottom site provided a ready means of shifting troops from Petersburg and Bermuda Hundred to north of the James to threaten and attack Richmond, and was later used in the First and Second Battles of Deep Bottom in July and August of 1864 and the attacks on Fort Harrison and New Market Heights that September.

Around Petersburg, meanwhile, operations continued as Grant launched his second offensive on June 21. This ambitious effort to extend his lines west of Petersburg and then northward to the Appomattox River was met on the 22nd and 23rd by Gen. Robert E. Lee, who attacked the Federals near the Jerusalem Plank Road and inflicted heavy losses, especially in prisoners. A secondary operation was also undertaken in the form of a large-scale cavalry raid under Brig. Gens. James H. Wilson and Augustus V. Kautz against the Danville and Weldon railroads. The Wilson-Kautz raid (June 22-July 1) also ended in a costly defeat and repulse, bringing Grant's second offensive to a close.

Grant issued orders several times to mount operations against Lee that July, but circumstances convinced him to cancel the proposed operations, including his belief that he needed more men before he risked another major battle. Jubal Early's repulse of Hunter's army left him free of Federal interference, and Early took advantage of that by marching his small Confederate force north to the gates of Washington on July 11. With Early threatening the city, Grant dispatched Maj. Gen. Horatio Wright's VI Corps to save the capital. He was waiting for that corps to return to Petersburg before undertaking another operation. Grant was also waiting for the XIX Corps, which was en route to join him from Louisiana. Another concern was a shortage of fresh horses, the direct result of the recent taxing cavalry raids.

By the third week of July, Grant realized there was no point in waiting any longer for Wright's VI Corps. Since Early had withdrawn from the capital without being defeated, the VI Corps would not be returning to the Army of the Potomac for the foreseeable future. However, the arrival of parts of the XIX Corps, together with cavalry remounts, convinced him he was ready to strike once more. The only question was where to attack Lee's powerful lines.

The mounting problems in the Shenandoah Valley increased the pressure on Grant to find a way to solve the deadlock at Petersburg. During the latter days of July, he believed he finally had the answer: a diversion, followed by a main attack. Maj. Gen. Winfield S. Hancock and his II Corps, together with two of Sheridan's cavalry divisions, would move north of the James River to threaten Richmond, compelling Lee to send reinforcements that would weaken his lines at Petersburg. Thereafter, he would detonate a large mine that Maj. Gen. Ambrose Burnside's men had been digging under the Confederate front east of Petersburg, to be followed by an infantry assault to unravel the Southern front and capture the city.

Hancock and Sheridan set out on July 26 and arrived on the north bank of the James River the following day. The Federal's plan was to force the Confederates into the outer defensive lines ringing Richmond so that Sheridan's cavalry could raid the Virginia Central Railroad. The Federals captured a line of works a couple of miles to the north, but strong fortifications blocked any additional penetration. The next day Sheridan tried to outflank these trenches and compel the Confederates to fall back to the outer defensive line, but was stopped in a drawn battle near Riddle's Shop. The heavy threat above the James River worked, however, and by July 29 Lee had stripped much of his army from the Petersburg trenches, leaving behind only three divisions to garrison the front. One of Hancock's divisions left its camp north of the James for Petersburg on the night of July 28, and the rest departed the following night.

The stage was set for the infamous assault of July 30, 1864.[1]

---

1   Unfortunately, Ed Bearss did not write a chapter on the Battle of the Crater when he originally prepared these essays. In order to maintain continuity of the Petersburg story, Patrick Brennan, author of *Secessionville: Assault on Charleston* (Savas Publishing, 1996), graciously agreed to work with Ed and research and write this chapter. He based his research on the Official *Records*, unit histories, quality secondary sources, and other pertinent documents.

Part I

Making a Mine

Petersburg, Virginia. Summer, 1864. The tough coal miners of the 48th Pennsylvania had finished carving out their new defenses from the Virginia soil and took stock of their surroundings. For six weeks they fought and bled across the blasted landscape from the Rappahannock River to the gates of Richmond. Now they hunkered down in a trench line some 500 yards from Blandford Church and the eastern environs of Petersburg. The historic colonial city now was the key to the survival of the Confederacy, its road and rail network the last connection between the capitol of Richmond thirty miles to the north and the rest of the South. However, Petersburg may as well have been Moscow as far as the Pennsylvanians were concerned. As they peered from their trenches, they could see no church steeples, no sturdy homes, no stately courthouses. They stood in a wide ravine running north and south coursed by Taylor Creek, and before them lay a bare plain rising to a ridgeline 500 feet away. Stretching north and south on the ridge yawned seemingly endless Rebel trenches, and crowning the ridge directly to their front was a frowning Rebel fort, its guns poised to sweep the area and make any assault across the barren ground a bloody defeat.

The 48th Pennsylvania, indeed the entire Army of the Potomac, had had their fill of attacking earthworks the previous forty days. Success was rare, and exploiting breached enemy lines proved nearly impossible. As a result, the grand flanking maneuver became the standard tactical tool of the Federal army. Perhaps only a miner could consider going under the ground instead of over it, but eventually the Keystoners recognized a possible alternative to the usual attack or flanking movement. "We could blow that damned fort out of existence," they bragged, "if we could run a mine shaft under it."

Colonel Henry Pleasants, the doughty leader of the 48th, heard the talk and liked it. Besides letting his men work at their craft, the colonel was convinced a mine could be built and the enemy lines destroyed by running chambers from the mine's end under the Reb trenches, packing the shafts with powder, and blowing the whole thing—fort and all—to Hell. He broached the idea to his superiors, and eventually his division commander, Brig. Gen. Robert Potter, brought the idea to Maj. Gen. Ambrose Burnside at IX Corps headquarters.

Burnside occupied an odd place in the Army of the Potomac. In late 1862 he had briefly commanded the Army, but the disaster at Fredericksburg literally forced him out. The War Department sent him and his IX Corps west, but when they

Major General Ambrose Burnside
Library of Congress

rejoined the eastern army in the spring of 1864 after their winter in Tennessee, Burnside ranked the titular head of the Army and the hero of Gettysburg, Maj. Gen. George Gordon Meade. Accommodations had to be made. Lieutenant General Ulysses S. Grant now ran the entire Federal war effort, but he accompanied the Army of the Potomac during the Overland Campaign. To solve the thorny problem of rank, Grant had Burnside report directly to him, not knowing he was creating more difficulties than he solved. Immediately communications suffered and Burnside had trouble coordinating his movements with the rest of the army, to say nothing of Meade's possibly bruised feelings on the matter. Recognizing the need for efficiency in an army already wracked with discord, Grant finally relented and ordered Burnside to take orders directly from Meade.

Everyone involved knew Burnside to be a genial man who understood his limitations well. On June 25, he let Meade know that the mining operation had commenced. As Meade in turn alerted Grant—who thought little of the operation or Burnside himself—the IX Corps commander could climb a hill 600 yards east of the Pennsylvanians. Before him stretched the stage for this drama: the 48th Pennsylvania's position, the bare plain, a stand of trees to the right, the Rebel fort and adjoining trenches, another piece of open land, and a hill crowned by the Blandford Church Cemetery. If Pleasants was correct, that Rebel fort could be obliterated and the IX Corps troops would rush through the blasted remains of the enemy line, take the hill with the church, and force the Confederates to abandon Petersburg. Where Meade and Grant saw an exercise to keep bored Union soldiers engaged as the war ground to a halt, Burnside saw a chance for victory, for glory.

On June 25, the same day Burnside informed Meade of the mine, Henry Pleasants and his Pennsylvanians put shovel to dirt. The mine was begun.

*   *   *

That the Army of Northern Virginia now faced down the Army of the Potomac at Petersburg was in itself something of a miracle. The deadly waltz between the two forces began May 3, 1864 in the Wilderness west of Fredericksburg and came to a temporary standstill one month later at Cold Harbor. There Gen. Robert E. Lee appeared to seal off the approaches to Richmond north of the James River, finally halting Grant's bloody mix of frontal assaults and flanking maneuvers. Grant however had a bulldog gene deep in his DNA. He determined to hold Lee in place while he marched most of his army south across the James River then capture the transportation hub of Petersburg before Lee could react. Thus isolated from the rest of the Confederacy, Richmond would fall.

The Federal high command had created a brilliant plan that contained one fatal flaw. The Army of the Potomac suffered from a fatigue brought on by a month of intense, brutal, and bloody campaigning. Never before had American soldiers faced this kind of trauma, and the toll would quickly tell.

Grant put the plan into action on the evening of June 12 when he ordered Gen. William F. Smith and the XVIII Corps to depart the trenches at Cold Harbor and march to the White House on the Pamunkey River where they boarded steamers to Bermuda Hundred. Smith had been part of Gen. Benjamin Butler's Army of the James and was on detached duty under Meade when the orders came. On the 14th Grant met Butler whose command had been bottled up on a peninsula called Bermuda Hundred and asked him to issue orders for Smith to march on Petersburg early the next morning. Grant also told Meade to send Hancock and the II Corps to a point halfway between Petersburg and City Point on the James River. Unfortunately, Grant neglected to reiterate the goal of these movements. As a result neither Hancock nor Meade realized that Grant intended to capture Petersburg.

Unaware that Hancock was moving to his support, Smith left Bermuda Hundred at 5:00 a.m. on the 15th, dividing his force into three separate columns. To the south, Brig. Gen. Augustus Kautz's cavalry brigade moved along the Jordan's Point Road, followed by Brig. Gen. Edward Hinks' division of black infantry. Kautz's objective was to threaten the Rebel works where they passed near the Norfolk & Petersburg railroad. Further north strode the division of Gen. W. T. H. Brooks supporting Kautz's right near the City Point Railroad. On the northern flank of Smith's corps near the Appomattox River marched Gen. John Martindale's division on the Spring Hill Road. In all Smith had somewhere between 10,000 and 14,000 Union soldiers moving toward Petersburg.[2]

By August of 1862, Confederate military planners recognized well Petersburg's strategic value and acted accordingly. When Smith's men pulled up before the city, a long line of earthworks and trenches east of Harrison's Creek ran from the Appomattox River to the Norfolk & Petersburg Railroad, some four miles of well constructed and well placed defensive works. However, with the Army of Northern Virginia still at Cold Harbor north of Richmond, Gen. Pierre Gustave Toutant Beauregard headquartered on the Howlett Line fronting Butler at Bermuda Hundred. The so-called Dimmock Line at Petersburg was defended by Gen. Henry Wise's brigade, part of Gen. James Dearing's cavalry brigade, and a motley assemblage of artillerymen and home guards. Only 2,700 Confederates faced down Smith's entire Corps, concentrating in the northernmost section of the defenses, and awaiting the worse.

2   Thomas J. Howe, *Wasted Valor* (Lynchburg, 1988), 19, 22.

Kautz's cavalry began the action before noon when they uncovered a Rebel outpost on the Baylor Farm. Hink's men soon joined the action and finally drove the determined Rebels back, capturing a cannon in the process. Smith however displayed undue caution and spent the entire day advancing on and examining the Rebel works. Around 4:00 p.m., as Smith continued his field examinations, Grant informed the general that Hancock was four miles in his rear. Smith immediately sent a message to Hancock to come up and assist him. The message reached Hancock at 5:30 p.m., just after the general had received orders from Grant to move his II Corps quickly to support Smith. The van of Hancock's corps under Birney arrived at 6:30 p.m. Almost as soon as they arrived, Smith's assault on the Dimmock Line began.

At 7:00 p.m. the Federals move out in a long sweeping line. The ground was broken and patches of trees interrupted the advance, but within minutes the crush of bluecoats swept up against the weakly held Confederate positions. Wise's men put up a heroic struggle, but by the time the fighting ceased two hours later, the Federals had captured redans Five through Ten, a mile and a half of the enemy lines, and the Confederates were in full retreat. A large part of the Dimmock Line was broken and Petersburg lay beyond for the taking.

With night fully fallen, Baldy Smith considered his successes of the day and concluded, "I thought it prudent to make no farther advance."

Hancock finally met with Smith at 9:30 p.m. Although Smith's earlier dispatch had asked for Hancock to take position on his left, Smith instead asked Hancock to relieve his troops in the captured works. The II Corps had been in the thick of the fighting over the previous six weeks and had been marching for nearly 36 hours. Hancock recognized the soul-crushing fatigue that had brutalized his troops and halted them a number of times on the march to conserve their energy. Although he ranked Smith, Hancock deferred to Smith's judgment and complied with his request.

The "might have been's" of June 15, 1864 easily match any day of the Civil War. Had Hancock marched hard and arrived on the field at noon, had Smith not spent a day reconnoitering unmanned trench lines, had either general known Grant's intentions and the opportunity presented, the war could have ended and the horrors of the next ten months avoided. As it was, Gen. Pierre Gustave Toutant Beauregard had made another grand entrance onto the stage, and, as was his wont, he played the hero perfectly.

*   *   *

During that day, as the Unionists slowly moved towards Petersburg, "Old Borey" recognized quickly the crisis east of Petersburg. He decided on a risky gamble. The Creole general eventually left a skeleton force on the Howlett Line to keep Butler corked at Bermuda Hundred and rushed Robert Hoke's and Bushrod Johnson's divisions to the Petersburg front. Hoke's people arrived as the Federal evening attacks ended, and Beauregard assumed that a Yankee night assault would crush his force and take the city. While peppering Robert E. Lee with requests for reinforcements, the general scratched out a second defensive line and awaited the Bluecoat attack. It never came.

On June 16, the Federals continued to mass east of the Cockade City. Ambrose Burnside rode in with his IX Corps accompanied by Ulysses Grant, swelling the Union numbers to 50,000 troops. Burnside formed south of the II Corps, and in preparation for a general assault, and a resulting probe along Hancock's front— blunted by the arrival of Bushrod Johnson's grayclad brigades—developed the Rebel lines. But a strangulating lethargy engulfed the Northerners for the remainder of the day. Burnside did little but move his Corps cautiously forward to locate the Confederate defenses, and while an evening attack along the II Corps front netted a bit more of the now untenable Dimmock Line, the XVIII Corps accomplished little as Rebel batteries north of the Appomattox swept the front.

George Meade already owned a reputation as a snapping turtle, and his patience was about to be tried. Knowing that his opponent Robert E. Lee remained near Richmond, Meade ordered Burnside's IX Corps to make a midnight assault on the Rebel right, but circumstances forced a delay until 3:00 a.m. The wait was well worth it. The Northerners of Brig. Gen. Robert Potter's Second division crushed Bushrod Johnson's Rebels at the Shand House north of the Baxter Road, creating a mile wide hole in the Rebel line and capturing over 600 prisoners. However, as Potter's attack ground down, neither of his supporting divisions joined the initial advance. Finally, early in the afternoon, Orlando Willcox pushed his division forward on Potter's left but could not press the advantage. James Ledlie enjoyed more success north of Potter with a late afternoon attack, but Confederate counterattacks drove that thrust back. Reportedly, an overserved Ledlie saw nothing of his division's efforts.

While Meade stewed over the day's results, Beauregard knew the game was up. Most of the Dimmock Line was now in the enemy's possession, and spotters saw that Maj. Gen. Gouvernor Warren's V Corps had arrived, further strengthening the Federal hand. Beauregard ordered his entire force back to a new defensive line west of Harrison's Creek, much closer to Petersburg but more compact and easier to defend. On the morning of the 18th, the battered but unbowed grey clads of Beauregard's command hunkered down in their new surroundings and awaited the Yankee response. Suddenly, marching out of Petersburg appeared a long gray line. Sometime after midnight, Robert E. Lee discovered that the enemy had bridged the James River and that Beauregard's high strung warnings were, in fact, correct.

Marse Robert immediately ordered Kershaw's and Field's divisions to march to Petersburg. Kershaw arrived first, forming south of Bushrod Johnson and Field arrived soon thereafter. Soon the entire Army of Northern Virginia was coming to Petersburg to take up the fight.

George Meade would experience many frustrating days during his command of the Army of the Potomac. Few would match June 18, 1864. The army commander had four corps lined up north to south from the Appomattox River, and he ordered his entire command forward to overrun the Rebels at dawn. A quick, no doubt brutal fight, and the Rebels would be destroyed and Petersburg captured. However, things had changed. Much to everyone's surprise, the Rebels were gone.

The rest of the morning was spent fitfully searching west for enemy, picking through choking creek beds and generally losing any cohesion the Federal attack force might have had. Around noon, elements of both the II Corps—now led by Maj. Gen. David Birney when Hancock's Gettysburg wound flared up the night before—and the XVIII Corps stumbled upon Beauregard's new line. The fight was indeed quick and brutal, and the Federals fell back before the storm of fire. Meade exploded and demanded his entire army renew the advance with no pause for communication or coordination. Warren offered unacceptable excuses for his own lack of action but finally launched a doomed effort around 3:00 p.m. An hour later, Birney made a final push. Typical of the II Corps' experience was the 1st Maine Heavy Artillery who lost 632 of their 850 attackers. At places along the line, Union veterans simply refused to quickstep to a sure death.

Sometime before 6:00 p.m., Burnside summoned one last push. Willcox and Potter managed to gain a position in a wide depression formed by Taylor Creek about 500 feet from the enemy lines. As the sun set, the Federals dug in across the front, conforming their new lines to the ground the IX Corps men had gained. The Confederates seemed content to let them be. It had been a day of bloody conclusions for the bluecoats, a day of angry frustration for the Army commander, a day of miraculous deliverance for the defenders of Petersburg. The Northern plan to take the Cockade City, as brilliant in design as it was awful in failure, had collapsed.

*   *   *

Within days, two massive lines wound south from the Appomattox River, built to take advantage of the hilly terrain and open fields of fire. Ironically, the point where the opposing lines came closest—the Taylor Creek depression— proved to be one of the safest. The geographic quirk that shielded the two forces from visual contact prevented either side from engaging in the usual sniper fire. That same quirk allowed the coalminers of the 48th Pennsylvania to dig their mine under a cloak of relative secrecy.

Although Burnside had great faith in the plan, the Rhode Islander gained little traction at army headquarters. Meade's chief engineer, Maj. James Duane, shared his commander's disdain for the project and did little to support the effort. Burnside had to locate a theodolite himself, an instrument that calculated distance as the mine moved forward; Duane had refused to issue one. The engineer also declined to obtain mining tools, timber, wheelbarrows or even sandbags. Instead the industrious miners modified standard picks and shovels to use in close quarters, scrounged wood for building mine supports (even tearing down a nearby bridge), used cracker boxes to carry out the diggings, and relied on Benjamin Butler to get sandbags.

The mine itself turned out to be a model of engineering. Five feet wide at the bottom, two and one-half feet wide at the top, and five feet in height, the chamber ran on an average about twenty feet under the ground. Pleasants devised a simple way to pump fresh air into the expanse. About 120 feet from the entrance (and still out of sight of the Confederates), the colonel sank a shaft into the galley. He constructed wooden ductwork, which ran along the corner base of the mine and was lengthened as the work progressed. Where the airshaft entered the galley, miners kept a small fire burning in a grate. The heated air escaped through the airshaft, pulling fresh air through the duct into the work area. The miners also made a cloth partition that isolated their work area, increasing the effectiveness for the flow and preventing the fresh air from escaping back into the mine. A simple yet brilliant solution to the difficulty of running long mine shafts without suffocating the miners, Pleasants' design was another idea demeaned by Duane.

The digging through the soft Virginia clay progressed well. On July 2, the mine measured 250 feet, not quite halfway to the Rebel lines. Coincidentally, the next day Grant asked Meade if the IX Corps could mount an assault on its front, so the army commander forwarded the request. Burnside replied that completion of the mine would assure greater success as long as he controlled the operation, to which Meade snapped that he, not Burnside, was the army commander. Meade then made a curious statement. Playing both sides of the coin, Meade told Burnside that the mine had neither been conceived nor sanctioned by headquarters but that the completion of the mine was perhaps a good idea if an attack were to be made. Burnside dutifully apologized for his perceived affront, as the politics in the highest offices of the Army of the Potomac raged unabated.

At the same time Meade and Burnside dueled with their pens, the miners hit a vein of quicksand, forcing them to shore up the support construction. Soon thereafter, the Pennsylvanians encountered a hard, clay-like marl that slowed the work considerably. Pleasants responded by angling the shaft further up—some thirteen feet higher over the next one hundred feet of length—until the marl was passed. When the miners again hit good ground, the work continued apace.

*   *   *

The Keystoners completed the 510 foot shaft on July 17, not quite a month after the IX Corps had occupied the area. The next day work began on the lateral tunnels, which were to extend north and south under the Rebel trenches. Within a week the miners finished both auxiliary galleries—37 feet to the south, 38 feet to the north—which included four pairs of evenly spaced passages facing opposite each other. Each gallery arced toward the rebel lines then curled back, the northern extension more so than the southern one. With that, Henry Pleasants announced the mine complete. Almost 600 feet of tunnel measuring over 18,000 cubic feet of dirt, the mine confounded various army engineers. No military man had ever attempted a work of such length, much less completed it in such a short time. Considering the almost total lack of support from the higher-ups, the Pennsylvanian's mine was indeed an engineering miracle.

The 48th Pennsylvania immediately took a well-deserved break. All that was left was to pack the mine with powder, blow the Rebels to kingdom come, march into Petersburg, and end the war.

Part II

Thunder on the Hill

The Confederate works overlooking the valley of Taylor Creek were manned by troops new to the Army of Northern Virginia. Stephen Elliott's brigade had been assigned to Bushrod Johnson's division in June after their arrival from the Charleston defenses in South Carolina. Johnson gave the South Carolinians their assignment almost immediately, so Elliott's five regiments had been hard at work strengthening their position since June 18th. The 26th South Carolina dug in on the left of the brigade, connecting with Robert Ransom's North Carolina brigade to the north. Also deployed north of the 26th South Carolina were the four guns of Wright's battery. The 17th South Carolina continued the brigade line south, their trenches rising up the hill to the fort. The earthwork which was now known as Elliott's Salient was manned by the 18th South Carolina and the four smoothbores of Pegram's battery. Continuing south down the hill were the 22nd and 23rd South

Major General Bushrod Johnson
Library of Congress

Carolina respectively, joining at the Baxter Road with Wise's Virginians. Drawn up behind Wise's men were the guns of Davidson's battery, well positioned to sweep Elliott's entire front.

The line possessed a number of distinct defensive advantages. A stand of trees covered the no man's land along the left front, making any enemy attack on that stretch unlikely. A tributary of Taylor's Creek burbled through these trees. It separated Elliott's men from Ransom's, but the water's depression formed a natural trench that ran vertically through the Confederate works then angled south behind the fort. Confederate engineers also constructed a secondary infantry trench—the gorge line—which gouged the ground west of the fort. A "trench cavalier" was constructed to support Davidson's and Wright's batteries, and a covered way ran from the Blandford Cemetery on the Jerusalem Plank Road 500 yards east to Ransom's position.

Not two weeks after the Confederate defenses were begun, E. Porter Alexander was exercising his role a Chief Artillerist for the 1st Corps when he noticed a distinct lack of action along Elliott's front. An engineer himself, he told the South Carolinian that he suspected a Yankee mining operation in the vicinity, but Alexander soon suffered a wound and his warnings went unheeded. Still, as July progressed and the mine got closer, the Confederates realized that something was up. Sappers and engineers began countermining operations, and although they got close, the Southerners never dug quite deep enough and failed to locate Pleasants' masterpiece.

Instead, they strengthened their own positions and waited.

*   *   *

Between July 5 and 9, Grant was forced to deal with the dangers posed by Jubal Early's raid through the Shenandoah Valley, which inexplicably made it into Maryland and threatened Washington DC. The raid forced Grant to order Gen. Horatio Wright and the IV Corps to relieve the capital's defenses and redirect the corps—originally intended to reinforce the Army of the Potomac—to continue to Washington. Early's raid did more than shift soldiers. Lincoln always feared these types of Rebel operations, and it seems as though some consideration was given to abandoning Petersburg. Even though Wright's eventual pursuit of Early proved inept, Grant stood firm. He was not about to let go of Petersburg and he quickly conceived his next move.

Early on the morning of the 25th Grant announced his plan to Meade. He would make a demonstration north of the James, the real object being the destruction of the railroads north of Richmond. Winfield Scott Hancock would command the Union forces, consisting of his II Corps, two of Sheridan's cavalry divisions under Sheridan himself, and Kautz's cavalry division from Benjamin Butler's Army of the James. The command would cross the James River at Deep Bottom and march to Chaffin's Bluff. From there Sheridan could ride up to the city, dismount, and enter the Confederate capital at the first available point. If Sheridan succeeded, Hancock would press the II Corps forward to expand the gains. However, if the cavalry failed, Hancock would take up a line to protect the cavalry's return. The task of the cavalry was to destroy the Virginia Central Railroad from the Chickahominy all the way to the South Anna.

Later on the 25th Grant ordered Meade to load Burnside's mine with gunpowder. Grant figured that Hancock's expedition might cause Lee to weaken his force defending Petersburg. If that were the case, Meade would detonate the mine while Burnside pressed the advantage. Unless it was found necessary to fire it earlier, Grant set the date for the explosion for the afternoon of Wednesday, July 27th.[3]

For all appearances, neither Grant nor Meade had much use for the mine, and both officers reluctantly accepted its use in the upcoming operation. Certainly Duane's ill consideration of its likely success weighed on the matter. True too was Meade and Grant's low opinion of Burnside. Grant himself had had two unfortunate experiences with military mines during the Vicksburg Campaign. Whichever factor weighed more makes little difference to the result. The mine now

---

3   Lt. Gen. U. S. Grant to Maj. Gen. George G. Meade, July 25, 1864, in OR Vol. 40, pt. 3, 438.

occupied a central position in Grant's next attempt to take Petersburg, and Burnside's pet was about to be tested under the most difficult of circumstances.

While the upper echelons of the War Department debated the finer points, Burnside spent a good deal of his time developing his plans for the operation. The IX Corps' Fourth (Colored) Division would lead the attack. These troops would pass on the far side of the area of the explosion, thus keeping the command intact. The two lead regiments would form themselves perpendicularly to the Rebel trench line and wheel to the right and left respectively to drive back any surviving Confederates. This would prevent the Rebels from firing from the flanks into the troops that followed. The rest of the division would deploy in column of regiments, push past the explosion and seize the crest of Cemetery Hill at the Jerusalem Plank Road. Their corps mates would follow them across the crest. Additionally, Burnside thought that the two corps on his flanks would need to cooperate in the attack. On July 26th, the IX Corps commander presented his plan to Meade.

*   *   *

When word arrived on July 27 that Grant and Meade had approved using the mine to blow up the Rebel lines, Henry Pleasants dove into action. As usual, little went according to plan. Although Burnside had requested 12,000 pounds of powder, only 8,000 pounds arrived. Worse yet, while Pleasants wanted 1,000 yards of safety fuse, he was given normal blasting fuse, which would have to be spliced together in the damp confines of the tunnel to cover the distance. Fuming at the poor fusing materials, the colonel damned the army's engineers and gamely forged ahead.

Starting at 4:00 p.m. and running for six hours, the Pennsylvanians carried the powder into the mine and deposited it into the four wooden magazines built in each lateral gallery. Small troughs connecting the magazines were also filled with explosives. The Unionists finished the dangerous operation around 10:00 p.m. Pleasants then ran three different fuses along the mine's floor. With so many splices due to the varied lengths of the blasting cord, the colonel felt tripling the ignition system would assure a proper explosion. The miners then spent twenty hours loading 1,000 cubic feet of sandbags into the mine to tamp the powder. Ten feet of each lateral gallery and thirty-four feet of the main tunnel were packed with the sandbags, placed in such a way as to allow oxygen access to the fuse system. Finally, on July 28, near 6:00 p.m., Col. Henry Pleasants of the 48th Pennsylvania announced the mine ready for detonation.

Earlier that day, almost the last moment before the IX Corps attack was to commence, Meade belatedly learned something he didn't know about and ordered Burnside to make a change in plans that would have severe repercussions. For the previous four weeks, General Ferrero's division of black troops of the IX Corps had been off the front lines training to lead the attack after the mine was detonated. Ignoring how well Hink's division had done on June 15, General Meade feared the division would fail with heavy casualties and he, the Army Commander, would attract the ire of the press for sacrificing the lives of black soldiers. He evidently had not reviewed how well Hink's division had done on the 15th day of June. He ordered Burnside to select another division to make the assault. Meade simply told Burnside this was unacceptable. He did not believe the black troops could be called upon to do the important work charged them.

Burnside protested that Ferrero's troops were the freshest he had. The divisions of Ledlie, Potter, and Willcox had been in the lines since June 17. Each division was losing some 30 to 60 men a day to sniper and artillery fire, and after three months of heavy campaigning in the field, the IX Corps men were simply exhausted. Meade evidently felt otherwise.

Earlier, Grant had provided guidance for all future attacks that included the ability to withdraw quickly if the attack failed and the determination to push to the front at all costs without worrying about the flanks. Based on these new principles, Meade did not approve of Burnside's idea of sending the lead regiments sweeping up the Confederate trenches. Instead, the troops would charge directly towards the crest of Cemetery Hill.

Ambrose Burnside protested vigorously, so much so that Meade said he would put the matter to Grant. However, the subsequent meeting between the army commander and his boss considered the political ramifications of the operation more than the military ones. According to Meade, if black troops led the assault and were slaughtered, the press would accuse Meade and Grant of using the troops as "cannon fodder." Meade was particularly testy as he and the media had a stormy relationship. Grant had also had his problems with the newspapers, so he agreed with Meade's concerns and overrode Burnside's decision.

On the morning of Friday, July 29th, Burnside met with General Willcox and General Potter, commanders of two of his white divisions, to talk over the attack now slated for next day. Burnside told them he had been very much upset the day before for fear Meade would replace the black division in the van of the assault, but that he was pretty well satisfied Meade had dropped his concerns as he had heard nothing further about it. However, in the midst of the conversation Meade arrived. He tersely informed Burnside that Grant too felt that white troops should lead the assault. The corps commander was visibly shocked. He asked if there was any possibility of the orders being changed. Meade told him the orders were final. Burnside angrily acquiesced and told his commander he would try to do the best he could.

Brigadier General James Ledlie
Library of Congress

Meade departed. Burnside then sent for the third commander of his white divisions, James Ledlie, who arrived soon thereafter. The four men discussed who should now take the lead in the upcoming attack. None felt particularly confident although Potter's division was arguably in the best shape. Then Burnside unwisely decided to choose the attacking division by having his commanders draw straws. Perhaps the worst division commander in the Union Army won the lottery.

James Ledlie, a New York lawyer, was by all evidence both a drunk and a coward. A high ranking acquaintance had somehow assured Burnside that Ledlie was capable for the post, and Burnside had even praised Ledlie to Grant for action on June 17. Burnside appeared unaware of Ledlie's pronounced shortcomings. It is probable that Ledlie's staff concealed their commanders's myriad problems. Whatever his standing, Ledlie's men had not been trained for the assault so Meade had to write out detailed directives for them.

Meanwhile, when Hancock's expedition launched on the 26th north of the James had produced few results, Meade decided to withdraw Hancock's forces and incorporate them into Burnside's assault. Meade's battle plan called for operations to begin at dusk. Burnside would withdraw Ledlie and Willcox from between the Norfolk and Jerusalem Plank Roads and place them in his front. General Warren would reduce the troops holding his front to a minimum and concentrate them on his right to support Burnside. General Mott of the II Corps would relieve Maj. Gen. E. O. C. Ord's XVIII Corps and form his troops behind the IX Corps and be ready to support Burnside. Hancock would move from Deep Bottom and form his men behind Mott and be prepared to follow up the attacking and supporting columns. Sheridan would likewise withdraw from Deep Bottom and be ready at daylight to move against the Rebel right. Major Duane would have the pontoon bridge ready to cross the Appomattox River. Despite having never visited the area of the attack, Meade insisted on commanding all the troops from the II and V Corps. If Burnside wanted their assistance, he would have to funnel all correspondence through Meade.

In preparation to move troops to the front, Burnside had built two covered ways. They began in the Taylor's Creek ravine and zig-zagged their way 1,000 yards to the Union front lines. They were deep enough to protect the men from enemy fire and wide enough for a regiment to pass forward in column of twos, perhaps even a column of fours.

Sometime after dark, Ledlie met with his brigade commanders and issued orders. The Second brigade was to secure the lines north of the fort while the First brigade captured those to the south. Engineers would then connect both lodgments back to the Federal works. The next two divisions would expand upon these gains and extend the battle lines west toward the Jerusalem Plank Road. The *coup de grace* would be applied by the United States Colored Troops (USCT) division. With both flanks secured, the colored troops would race through over Elliott's Salient and take Cemetery Hill.

Orders circulated that the mine would be detonated at 3:30 a.m. on the morning of July 30. The infantry attack would commence immediately thereafter.

*   *   *

Around 2:00 a.m. on July 30, Burnside moved one mile from his Dunn House headquarters to the Fourteen Gun battery, now christened Fort Morton. Roughly 600 yards from the entrance to the mine, the position provided an excellent view of the upcoming battle. A half hour later, Meade moved to the Dunn House— Burnside's unoccupied headquarters tent sat on a small rise—and reined up there about 3:15 a.m. Considering that Meade would have direct control of over half the forces on the field, his choice of location for his command post was unfortunate. Both places would be linked by telegraph, to each other and to the rest of the army, but Meade would be almost two miles from the operation.

As the Federal troops fumbled about in the oven-like darkness trying to locate their assigned positions, Henry Pleasants entered the mine around 3:15 a.m. and lit the fuse. Then, the Federals waited. Tensions grew to almost untenable levels as 3:30 a.m. came and went. Seconds ticked by as sweat dripped, hands tightened, stomachs knotted and feet tapped nervously. By 4:15 a.m., Pleasants knew that something had gone terribly wrong. Two men, Lt. Jacob Douty and Sgt. Henry Rees, volunteered to investigate. They felt their way into the vast darkness of the tunnel, hoping against hope that a sudden blast wouldn't bury or kill them. Only one hundred feet in, they discovered that the fuse had gone out at one of the splices. They repaired the fuse, lit it, and hustled out as fast as they could.

Meanwhile, a testy exchange raged across the telegraph wires connecting Burnside to Meade. For almost an hour, Meade demanded to know what was going on and badgered the corps commander with orders to begin an artillery barrage and launch the attack with or without the mine. For his part, Burnside thought the reason for the delay was obvious and didn't feel compelled to apprise Meade of the situation every five minutes. Meade, on occasion the snapping turtle, cursed a blue streak and continued his heated queries.

Finally, at 4:40 a.m., a strong concussion and muffled rumble shook the area. Some Rebels in a countermine tumbled as a tremor swept through the clay. Others above ground awoke with a start. Across the way, the Federals stared into the growing daylight goggle-eyed. For a moment, no one knew.

Then, in a sudden, fiery blast, the hill with the Rebel earthwork literally exploded. Huge chunks of earth catapulted through the air as a great geyser of smoke and dust lit by the explosion of 8,000 pounds of gunpowder ascended into the air. All seemed to rise in slow motion, practically hypnotizing the Yankees in the front trench. But, when the detritus of the explosion and the accompanying cloud of dust rolled at them like a demented prairie storm, the front line of bluecoats panicked and ran.

James Ledlie immediately told his two brigade commanders to open the attack, then he made his way to a nearby bombproof. He had no intention of seeing this one through. Instead he caressed a bottle of rum. However, his two brigade commanders, one-legged Brig. Gen. Frank Bartlett and Col. Elisha Marshall, went to work. For perhaps as many as fifteen minutes they coaxed their shocked commands back into their position behind the trenches then ordered them over the top. Immediately the attack went awry. Although Federal artillery opened on the entire Rebel line, with more than 12 cannon trained on the breakthrough sector alone, no provision had been made for the Northerners to scale their own six-foot high trench walls. Luckily, Yankee ingenuity came into play. Men started to boost their comrades over the trench face while others mimicked ladders by sticking their bayonets into the walls and climbing up the improvised rungs. Slowly, singly and in groups, Ledlie's troops started to make their way across the moonscape of no man's land, through a half-lit cloud of earthen—and human— debris.

Marshall's men of the 2nd Brigade moved first, four regiments in three ragged lines. Bartlett's 1st Brigade followed, two regiments in two lines. Navigating the trenches however had literally destroyed the deployments, and order was haphazard at best, non-existent at worst. With Federal ball and shell roaring overhead, the blinded, choking Northerners navigated the considerable abatis that had separated the two armies then started up the hill. Shockingly, the crown had been replaced by a serrated, jagged wall of fresh earth, like the lip of a volcano, running from 170 feet across their front. Some of the Federals climbed up closer and beheld a ghastly sight previously unseen. Before them yawned a crater, fifty feet wide, thirty feet deep at its greatest depth, a great gouge in the earth filled with massive blocks of clay, guns, broken gun carriages, projecting timbers, and Rebels

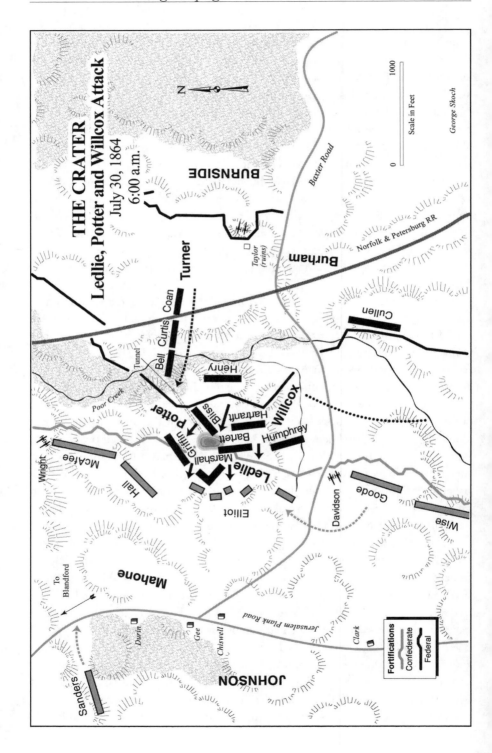

THE CRATER
Ledlie, Potter and Willcox Attack
July 30, 1864
6:00 a.m.

buried in various states. A vast pall of dust and smoke wafted over the area, and a few wounded Rebs cried for help. Some generous Northerners scrambled down to rescue the suffering Southerners, but as more Union troops arrived, many began to lower themselves into the pit, driven by curiosity more than anything else. No one seemed to know what to do next. The commands started to jumble together as more men pressed forward into the chaos, and any sense of order disappeared. Suddenly from just north of the shambles, rifle shots cut through the air.

The Battle of the Crater had begun.

*   *   *

Within seconds of the eruption of Henry Pleasants' bomb, Elliott's Salient ceased to exist. Pegram's battery was gone, the guns buried, 22 artillerists dead. Also in the fort at the time of the ignition, the 18th South Carolina practically disappeared with 82 men lost in the blast. Hardest hit with 170 casualties was the first regiment south of the explosion, the 22nd South Carolina. Some Rebel survivors were seen running in a panic toward Petersburg, wild-eyed and covered with dust and grime. However, either fearless or senseless, many Carolinians remained at their posts. Surrounded by an immense, orange-colored haze, their visibility was practically nonexistent, and they could only guess what had happened. Finally, after 15 minutes, when the air began to clear, they saw the Yanks literally yards from them, milling about the crater. The grey clads opened fire.

As the Rebel riflery began to pick up, Bartlett and Marshall tried to get their men moving. Bartlett pushed some of his men into the trenches to the south, while Marshall directed a portion of his troops to the west and north. Beyond the pit, Northerners ran into a cluster of men from the 18th South Carolina under Capt. John Floyd. A firefight broke out with hand-to-hand fighting punctuated by artillery blasts. Then, as if by mutual agreement, both sides fell back to safety, the battered Rebs to the nearby trench cavalier, the Yanks to the yawning pit.

By this time, most of the two Federal brigades had dissolved into milling crowd. Still, small knots from different regiments held together well enough to begin working their way north from the crater, Col. Steven Weld of the 56th Massachusetts among them. Three covered ways funneled this movement in varying degrees, but the further the soldiers penetrated the area beyond the crater's northern edge—some as many as 350 yards—the more aggressive the Rebel defense became. As counter fire erupted, Unionists would tumble from one parallel trench line to another to try to continue forward, but the advance soon ground down.

To the south of the pit, Maj. Charles Houghton helped some members of the 14th New York Heavy Artillery manhandle two buried Napoleons into position

Brigadier General Robert Ransom
Library of Congress

and raked the nearby Confederate trench line. Forty-five dazed Rebs immediately surrendered. But, in a sign of things to come, Davidson's guns from the 13th Battalion Virginia Light Artillery wheeled from their position behind Wise's Old Dominion division and opened on the improvised Federal battery.

From north to south, as if awakening from a haymaker, the Confederate artillery shook out the cobwebs and fired up. While Davidson's gunners dueled with the New York Heavies, Maj. James Coit rushed into action. He commanded an artillery battalion which included Pegram's now decimated battery and Wright's battery north of the crater. When he saw the destruction at Elliott's Salient, he ran to Wright's guns and immediately had them open with shell and canister on the bluecoats sweeping across no-man's land. When they recoiled from his fire, Coit took on the Yanks along the crater's northern flank. Well positioned and sheltered by the stand of trees, Wright's battery would perform its bloody work unimpeded for the rest of the day.

Stephen Elliott arrived on the scene resplendent in his full uniform and found his revived Carolinians grimly trying to seal all approaches northwest of the crater. After the explosion, the 26th South Carolina had resisted the first enemy attempts to move out of the crater. Elliott however had bigger ideas. He ordered his small command to attack the crater. The resulting assault barely dented the mass of bluecoats in the pit, and Elliott went down in the first wave of fire. Some of the Carolinians made it into the crater where they were captured, while others ducked into some nearby trenches, lifted their rifles over their heads, and fired into the teeming enemy. In the mayhem, Col. Fitz William McMaster took over the brigade. He re-deployed the 200 survivors of Elliott's assault into a creek depression west of the pit where comrades from their brigade rallied on them. They were now the only troops between the two Federal brigades and Cemetery Hill.

Around this time, the next Confederate brigade to the north, Robert Ransom's Tarheels, began to stream into the combat. The 25th North Carolina deployed first, linking the left of the 26th South Carolina back to the main Confederate trench line. Two more Tarheel regiments sidled down to connect with the 25th's left flank and support what was left of the 17th South Carolina just north of the crater. This line doused several Yankee forays and successfully locked down the sector.

To the south Wise's Virginians also moved to support Elliott's battered survivors. Lining a trench some thirty yards from the Unionists, elements of four regiments from the two brigades put down a withering fire and crushed a number of disjointed Federal thrusts. Artillery posted near the Griffith House near the intersection of the Baxter Road and the Jerusalem Plank Road also added to the Rebel steel. In the meantime, Confederates worked their way west along the trench trying to button with the 26th South Carolina.

As the game Southerners improvised their new defensive posture, a second wave of Yankees swept through the storm of no-man's-land and swarmed onto the scene. The battle hung in the balance.

Part III

Southern Clay, Soldiers' Blood

The explosion of the mine had barely occurred when the Confederate high command raced into action. From his headquarters north of the Appomattox River, Robert E. Lee quickly got word of the breakthrough and sent orders for Gen. William Mahone to move two of his brigades to the scene of the crisis. The eruption awakened Lt. Gen. A. P. Hill at his headquarters in Petersburg. With a mushroom cloud rising in the morning gloaming, the III Corps commander immediately started south on the same mission. Much of the Army of Northern Virginia had relocated north of the Appomattox to counter Hancock's operation, and Mahone's division—then four miles south of battle—represented the closest reinforcements.

Lee started for the front and stopped first at Hill's headquarters. Apprised that Hill was personally summoning Mahone, Lee then trotted to Bushrod Johnson's command post near Cemetery Hill. Near there he could see for himself the Crater and the mass of the bluecoated enemy pressed into the front. Beauregard reined up, and together the two generals made for the Gee House where they climbed to the second floor to monitor the action. Lee knew one of his best division commanders

Brigadier General Robert B. Potter
Library of Congress

would soon be marching for the front, but he also knew at least a division of Yankees was swarming around this great gash in his defenses. Time, as usual, would be critical.

*   *   *

Soon after Ledlie's men came to grief in the Crater, Burnside's Second division commander— Brig. Gen. Robert Potter— pushed his two brigades into the maelstrom. Brig. Gen. Simon Griffin went first, sending seven undersized regiments against the fortified Rebel line north of the explosion. However, the choking dust and the battle smoke trebled the confusion, and enemy fire scythed the Federals as they lurched toward the front. Blinded by the fog of battle, nearly half of Griffin's disorganized command unintentionally angled south and stumbled into the churning chasm, but some of the regiments forced their way through the crowd and took some trenches east and north of the breakthrough. Lieutenant Colonel Daniel White of the 31st Maine directed a foray north against Elliott's survivors and their Carolinian supports, but the thrust bogged down after 200 yards, forcing White's command to go to ground in a maze of trenches and traverses. Griffin meanwhile tried to organize the rest of his brigade to move west against the Jerusalem Plank Road. He requested and received three regiments from Col. Zenas Bliss's First brigade who tramped forward and formed between Daniel White's winnowed wing and the Crater. Griffin then ordered everyone within sound of his voice to attack.

The movement was as gallant as it was doomed. The ground between the Crater and the road betrayed a honeycomb of bombproofs, covered ways, and intricate trench works. The regiments lost all cohesion as they crashed into and scrambled out of the maze, while a ring of Confederate artillery and musketry took the Yankees under aim and raked them. One unit thought they got to within 100 yards of the Gee House—then occupied by Generals Lee, Beauregard, and

Bushrod Johnson—but most simply went as far as their courage took them. Then, in the murderous Rebel crossfire, the assault dissipated in a welter of blood, and the survivors tumbled back into the Crater.

While Potter's men made their ill-fated assault, Brig. Gen. Orlando Willcox threw Burnside's Third division into the maelstrom. Brigadier General John Hartranft's brigade was to expand the Federal breakthrough to the south, but the lead regiments were drawn almost hypnotically toward the Crater where they became entangled with the First division. Two of Hartranft's regiments simply stopped on the slope rising to the "horrid pit." With the First and Second divisions stymied in their breakout attempts, the Crater overflowed with confused, milling bluecoats, and there was no place for these final two regiments to go. Stunned by this development, Willcox cautioned Burnside to advance no more troops.

When word of the bottleneck reached Meade, the commander exploded. At 5:40 a.m., he ordered all troops to be pushed forward to the crest of Cemetery Hill regardless of their current dispositions. Willcox did his best to obey, throwing the 27th Michigan south along the Rebel trenchline and straight into the teeth of Wise's Virginians to make room for maneuver south of the Crater. The Virginians would have none of it and halted the Michigander thrust almost as soon as it began. Meanwhile Willcox's Second brigade led by Col. William Humphrey found their front blocked by Hartranft's stalled column. Eager to get to the front, Humphrey deployed his brigade in no-man's land and attacked the enemy trenches with three regiments in battle line. Michigan men all, they raced across the abatis-strewn field and crashed over the Rebel works, capturing prisoners and relieving for a moment the pressure on the southern flank of the Crater. But their success was fleeting as the Virginians rallied to seal the breach while those South Carolinians peppering the Crater turned their attention to this new threat. In this blast furnace, Humphrey's refused left suddenly gave way led by the jittery Germans of the 46th New York. In no time, the three Michigan units found themselves bitterly isolated in the Rebel lines and taking fire from three directions.

It was now around 6:00 a.m. As Burnside's three divisions squeezed into the now hellish front, the Virginia temperature rose with the blood red sun. Although the explosion had blasted a sixty-yard chasm in the enemy lines, the exploited breach never got beyond some four hundred yards. Many determined Yankees hunkered down in the maze of trenches that fanned out from the Crater and fought vicious little battles with equally determined Rebels, but most had simply crammed into the teeming pit. A line of bluecoats hugged the western edge of the oven-like abyss and lay down a steady rifle fire, while the rest of the Northerners had nothing to shoot at and less to do. Rebel mortar fire started to spin through the humid air and slam into the Federal mob, blood and severed limbs splattering the survivors. The Confederate artillery continued their work unabated. Casualties mounted by

Brigadier General Orlando B. Willcox (seated, second from right) and his staff.
Library of Congress

the minute, and Rebel riflery pinched closer and closer. Indeed, the Northerners were no longer capable of moving much beyond their bloody perimeter as Ambrose Burnside's ambitious plans to end the war dissolved in a jumble of incompetence and Confederate bravery. But even as the outcome of the battle was sealed, two divisions—one Union, the other Confederate—maneuvered toward the front and prepared to enter the fray.

*   *   *

As the Federal operation ground to a halt, George Gordon Meade approached apoplexy. He continued to shower Burnside with demands for the Northerners to simply rise up and take Cemetery Hill. For his part, Burnside took the word of his frontline officers that there was literally no room for more soldiers and that any reinforcement would be a simple waste of manpower, but Meade's word held sway. Sometime after 7:00 a.m., Brig. Gen. Edward Ferrero received orders to commit Burnside's Fourth Division—two brigades of nine black regiments—into the battle.

It had been a harrowing morning for the Colored troops lining the trenches leading to the front. A steady procession of broken bodies and dispirited soldiers moved past Ferrero's shaken men as the wounded made their way back to the field hospitals. They also knew that their role in the operation had radically changed. They were to lead this assault and had trained specifically for the maneuver. But the battle had now raged for over two and a half hours and they still had not made a move. Finally word passed down the lines that they were to join the fight. The watching and the waiting were over.

As his troops began to shuffle, Ferrero retreated to James Ledlie's bombproof and helped himself to the rum.

Lieutenant Colonel Joshua Sigfried ordered his brigade forward, but his men encountered the same problems as their corps mates. The trenches funneled the regiments toward the front, and as they scrambled out of the trench and pressed forward, Rebel fire scythed their lines. The intervening no-man's land seemed like a moonscape, the detritus of the explosion now compounded by dead and the dying Unionists, and in the maelstrom all cohesion was lost. Elements of the first two regiments forced their way through the milling mass in the Crater while others skirted the chasm to the north and disappeared into the honeycomb of trenches and bombproofs. In the confusion, the 30th USCT fired on the 9th New Hampshire and rendered it *hors du combat*. Despite the mistake, the blacks moved north along the Rebel entrenchments and slammed into the 17th South Carolina, killing with abandon as they went. More of Sigfried's brigade followed the lead and charged the cavalier trench west of the Crater held by Elliott's survivors, screaming, "No quarters, remember Fort Pillow." In a storm of blood, the black soldiers rounded up hundreds of prisoners and killed any who showed the slightest resistance. After hours of deadlock, the breach began to expand.

Ferrero's Second brigade led by Col. Henry Thomas attempted to follow up on Sigfried's success, but Thomas quickly lost control of his regiments as they either descended into the maze north of the Crater or stumbled into the pit. Thomas did get some of his men to form on Sigfried's left, but a hailstorm of bullets and shells blasted them back into the cavalier trench. McMaster's Confederates in the creek depression then redoubled their efforts and tore the van of Sigfried's advance apart. Staff officer Lt. Christopher Pennell attempted to rally his shaken troops by raising a downed flag and calling for a charge. The Carolinians took the brave officer under aim, and as the bullets found their mark, Pennell spun around again and again, a grotesquery that finally ended when he fell dead. For a moment, the Unionists tried to do his bidding, but in a hail of musketry the attack proved short-lived and Ferrero's crushed survivors fell back into the trench.

Under pressure from Meade and his own stark realization that the battle was nearly lost, Burnside thought his men had another charge in them. He ordered Sigfried and Thomas to attack Cemetery Hill again, this time with support from Marshall and Bartlett. Only three of the USCT regiments could be properly

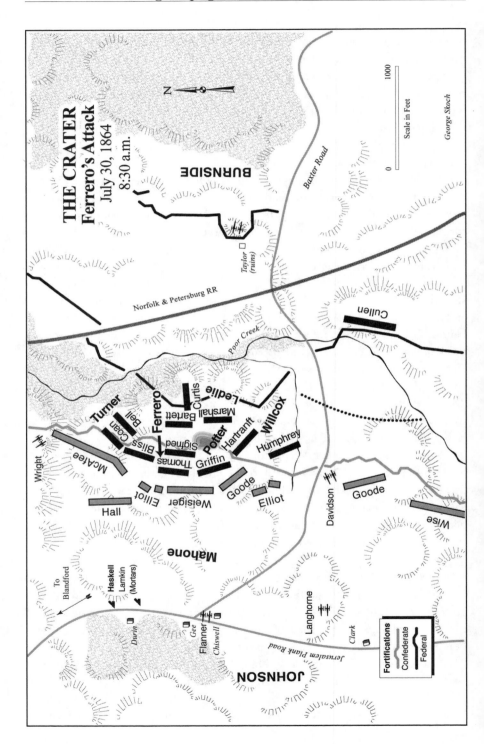

THE CRATER
Ferrero's Attack
July 30, 1864
8:30 a.m.

George Skoch

Colonel David Weisiger
Library of Congress

organized for the movement, and few of the white troops moved in concert. Lieutenant Colonel John Bross of the 29th USCT climbed out of the cavalier trench waving a flag and urging his men to join him. Displaying courage in the extreme, the remnants of the Fourth division shook out a ragged line and formed on the colors. Over the pandemonium, a command rang out. Eight hundred yards away lay the hill and the end of the war. So, they swept forward, into the hot summer morning, into their own valley of death.

*   *   *

Billy Mahone had his men on the move as soon as they received orders. He marched two of his brigades north along Lieutenant's Run until they arrived at the Jerusalem Plank Road near Cemetery Hill. The Virginians in the First brigade strode with special determination. Many were Petersburg natives and knew they would be fighting to defend their families and their homes. While his boys formed for battle, Mahone negotiated the covered way that led to the creek depression where McMaster's South Carolinians had made their remarkable stand. The General's clear view of the action revealed eleven flags fluttering over the Crater but the enemy appeared terribly disorganized. Still, the Yankee numbers concerned him, so he immediately sent for his third brigade to come up. He then scurried back to his command. It was a little past 8:00 a.m.

Colonel David Weisiger's five Virginia regiments of Mahone's brigade led the move, filing first into the covered way before filling into McMaster's natural trench. Mahone sent Wright's Georgia brigade, led by Lt. Col. Matthew Hall, to support Weisiger's right flank. As the Confederates jostled into place, word spread that

Major General Edward Ferrero
Library of Congress

black soldiers had made some of the last enemy attacks, that no quarter was given, and none was expected. This combination—the "cowardly" use of a mine, defense of the soldiers' very homes, and the employment of black troops—stuck in the craw of every Southerner preparing for battle. Mid-morning, July 30, 1864, just east of Petersburg, Virginia, the Civil War suddenly got a lot more personal. By 9:00 a.m. the two brigades were in place, locked and loaded, bayonets fixed.

*   *   *

Perhaps 200 black troops answered Lieutenant Colonel Bross' entreaties and started east. Their cheer caught the attention of Weisiger's Virginians. Some opened on the enemy, but Mahone quickly determined to answer fire with fire. He ordered his entire command to pitch into the attackers. In a line 200 yards wide and three lines deep, two North Carolina regiments joined McMasters' survivors, Mahone's Virginians, and elements of two Georgia regiments as they leapt out of the creek depression and roared toward the isolated USCT formation. A ferocious yell reverberated across the field as the Confederates ate up the intervening ground, even as the USCT attack floundered and then fell back. Mahone's gray wave then lapped up to the cavalier trench, where it was met with a sweeping Union volley. The fire gouged terrible gaps in the gray wall but offered bare resistance to the charge. Like a fearful flood, the Confederates covered the last yards and crashed into the trench.

Combat indescribable erupted along the entire line. Bayonets flashed and gun butts pounded. The gory violence at close quarters drove the soldiers on both sides into a frenzy, the Rebels particularly so. Visions of Confederates killing black soldiers begging for their lives haunted many memories long after the war, but this was the brutal reality of this most brutal encounter. Then, as they cleared out the cavalier trench, the Rebels bloodily worked their way toward the crowded maze north of the Crater, killing with abandon and taking few prisoners, white or black. Panic began to take hold. Mobs of bluecoated soldiers broke for the rear only to find no-man's-land a cauldron of deadly crossfire. Many overran elements of the XVIII Corps that had formed on the north to support Burnside's assault. Other wild-eyed Yankee survivors simply tumbled into the perceived safety of the Crater, with Mahone's demons hot in pursuit. There, demoralized white soldiers fearing reprisal from the Rebels bayonetted a number of the incoming USCT. The ghastly had turned surreal.

Approaching Confederates deployed coehorn mortars fifty feet from the pit and launched a steady stream of explosives into the depression. Mahone reached the front and shook out a line of sharpshooters to sweep the western edge of the pit before launching the rest of the Georgia brigade against its southern flank. The Georgians made two bloody assaults and managed to extend Weisiger's line south, but failed to retake the trenches south of the Crater. Wise's Virginians, who had been dueling with the Yanks since the explosion, continued driving out the last of the interlopers from the trenches in their front. By the time Mahone finished, the Crater and a small section of works to the south were the last Federal foothold in the Rebel line.

Mahone's attack had taken about 20 minutes. At 9:00 a.m., just before the attack began, Burnside had begged that the V Corps join the fight south of the Crater. By 9:30 a.m. Meade ordered Burnside to withdraw. The Corps commander sought out his superior, and in language "extremely insubordinate" Burnside demanded the operation continue with the launching of the V Corps. Grant was called in and calmly backed Meade. A disconsolate Ambrose Burnside returned to his field quarters at Fort Morton and prepared to pull his battered command back to safety.

The final act had begun.

*   *   *

The horrors of the Crater now played out in the extreme. Blood pooled everywhere and greased the already slick walls of clay. A ring of Rebel artillery blasted the serrated edges and mortar shells exploded in the milling, helpless crowd of Unionists. Wounded and dead alike were trampled underfoot, while the rising temperature and summer sun baked the humid chasm. Northerners used the bodies of their dead to buttress the Crater's battered edges. Brave men negotiated the maelstrom of no-man's-land trying to bring water and ammunition to the survivors. In one last desperate effort, a group of engineers attempted to carve out a

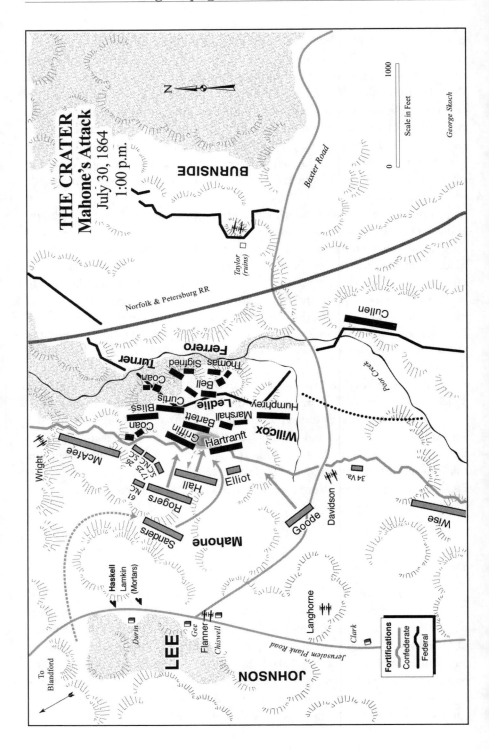

THE CRATER
Mahone's Attack
July 30, 1864
1:00 p.m.

N

Scale in Feet

0   1000

George Skoch

BURNSIDE

Baxter Road

Taylor
(ruins)

Norfolk & Petersburg RR

Cullen

Poor Creek

Ferrero

Turner

Thomas Sigfried

Coan

Bell

Curtis

Ledlie

Bliss

Marshall

Bartlett

Humphrey

Coan

Griffin

Hartranft

Willcox

Wright

McAfee

17th SC
26th SC
NC

Hall

Elliot

34 Va.

Rogers

61st NC

Sanders

Mahone

Goode

Davidson

Wise

Haskell
Lamkin (Mortars)

Durin

Langhorne

Clark

LEE

To
Blandford

Gee

Flanner

Chiswell

Jerusalem Plank Road

JOHNSON

Fortifications
Confederate
Federal

trench from the pit back to Union lines. Still, the Federals succeeded in keeping the Confederates at bay, throwing back a series of limited Rebel thrusts despite the abject confusion and brutal conditions.

More and more knots of bluecoats sprang out of the trap and raced back to their lines, enduring a horrific crossfire that brought many of them down. Those who stayed moved about looking for a familiar face and dodging the constant mortar fire. Many of their officers were dead, wounded, or just plain lost. A sense of doom engulfed the scene, while thirst and hunger maddened the throng. In the southern section of the pit, Chippewa riflemen from the 1st Michigan Sharpshooters covered their heads and sang their death songs over the deafening cacophony.

As noon passed, the remaining Federal officers huddled to sort out their rapidly diminishing options. Hartranft, Bartlett, Marshall, and Griffin still believed an effort to the north might produce results, but they also realized that any retreat must be covered by nightfall. None of these officers knew how much longer their men could hold out under such trying c ombat circumstances. At 12:30 p.m., word arrived that Burnside had thrown in the towel and ordered a retreat. The method and timing would rest with the discretion of the frontline officers. With no-man's-land a torrent of Rebel musketry and artillery fire, the officers grimly realized there was little to do but wait.

A few hundred yards to the west, Billy Mahone knew there was no time to pause. He guided General Wilcox's Alabama brigade—under the command of Col. John C. C. Sanders—down the covered way and into the creek depression. Mahone ordered these five tough Alabama regiments to circle the Georgia brigade's right flank and attack the Crater from the southwest. Their goal was simple: expel the Yankees—who counted black troops among them—from the lines. The method was even simpler: one shot, then the bayonet. An artillery barrage would precede the assault, and at 2:00 p.m. the men would jump off. One last thing: Robert E. Lee would watch the charge from the Gee House.

* * *

Everyone noticed it. Around 1:30 p.m., a lull fell over the field. Knots of Federals continued to flee to the rear, but others took up post on the western face and peered into the bloody field. Most knew it to be the calm before the storm, so there was little surprise when the Rebel artillery broke the ominous calm and opened with a will. After a short barrage, the Alabamians supported by Carolinians North and South stepped off.

For about one hundred yards the assault wave moved undetected; the brow of the hill prevented the Yankees from seeing the charge. However, after they passed

Brigadier General Stephen Elliott
Library of Congress

the cavalier trench, the Rebels started to take rifle fire from the Crater. Closer they ran, raising the yip-yip-yip of the Rebel yell, alerting the bluecoats to exactly what was coming. The last few yards proved to be the hardest. As the ground evened out, the Confederates were momentarily exposed to Union artillery. Great gaps were torn in the gray wall, but the Rebs closed the ranks and came on, reaching the very edge of the Crater before more harm could be done.

The horror of these last minutes is near unimaginable. The Yankees clinging to the western edge of the pit were quickly suppressed. Rifles with their bayonets still attached seem to lie everywhere, so Confederates picked them up and launched them like javelins into the teeming crowd. Then groups of Alabamians began to boil over the crest and slash their way into the southwest quadrant of the pit. The dense mass of humanity presented little room for loading weaponry, so bayonets and knives ruled the combat and rifles became clubs. Survivors recalled the slaughter here as a hell on earth, and the USCT troops seemed destined for the worst of it. The Confederates simply did not accept the surrender of any USCT and killed them with a horrific brutality. Again fearing Rebel reprisal, many white troops also dispatched their black comrades. Some of the USCT died demoralized, but others fought with a frenzy that surprised even their enemies.

As the Alabamians butchered their way north through the grim chasm, Virginians and Carolinians swept up to the Crater's perimeter and plastered the area with rifle fire. The rupture destroyed any hope for an orderly withdrawal; with the Rebels pouring over the top, John Hartranft and Simon Griffin ordered any Northerner within range of their voices to retreat. It would be every man for himself. Frank Bartlett however wasn't so lucky. His cork leg had been destroyed and he wished to stay and surrender. Despite taking a scalp wound toward the end of the shooting, he managed to survive those final, brutal minutes and got his wish.

The vicious last act of the Crater continued to play out in bloody array. The Federal perimeter disappeared as Rebels poured into the pit and hacked away. A veritable flood of Yankees now braved the run through no-man's land, and with rebel metal scouring the area, more Unionists were killed in the retreat than in the morning attack. Those at the back of the shrinking pack still in the Crater turned to fight the delirious Rebs, the battle as savage as any in the war. Finally, a few white flags rose from the bedlam, and a few surrenders became many. Still, the Confederates executed black Federals on the spot until Billy Mahone himself arrived and ordered mercy for the captured.

Near the very southern edge of the Crater, some Michiganders from Willcox's division fired off a last few rounds then humped it to safety. Except for some mop-up operations, it was over.

The sublime defense of Elliott's Salient came with a cost. Mahone's division lost nearly 600 men, and Elliott's brigade of Bushrod Johnson's division suffered 700 casualties, including 351 missing. After all the reports came in, total casualties for the Army of Northern Virginia stood over 1,600 for the day. Considering the odds of 5 to 1, it seems a miracle that the Confederates were able to hold the line. Considering the litany of heroic actions that marked the last nine months of Robert E. Lee's army, the Battle of the Crater stands simply as one of many, one more honor on the road to Appomattox.

*   *   *

Lines of Yankee prisoners began to trudge west to Petersburg to begin their incarceration. Occasionally a USCT soldier would be pulled from the line and summarily executed, but many of the USCT were detached for fatigue duty back at the Crater. Relief parties removed the wounded and the Rebel dead while burial squads tossed the Yankee corpses into the bottom of the pit and covered them with clay. Pioneers and engineers worked all night, and by the morning of July 31, the chasm of the Crater was reincorporated into the Rebel defenses.

Ambrose Burnside sat truly alone as casualty figures came in. Potter reported near 2:30 p.m. that his division was "annihilated." Full regiments had been captured whole, and the field officers across the board were decimated. The other division commanders reported similar losses, and stories of the treatment of his Fourth division—by Reb and Yank alike—deepened his horror. While a profound depression swept the survivors, Burnside struggled to make sense of the tragedy. In all, he had committed some 13,000 troops from his corps to the operation. In six hours, he lost nearly 35% of them.

One source claimed that of the 150 USCT who were captured that day, only seven survived the Southern prison pens.

Amazingly, despite inquiries from his commander, Burnside failed to report officially to Meade on the matter until 6:40 p.m. the next day. He admitted to a loss of 4,500 men and implied most occurred because of lack of support by the adjoining corps. As Meade and Burnside continued to trade barbed messages, a four-hour truce was arranged for August 1. Finally the dead and wounded littering no-man's land were brought into Union lines, and the putrefying stench that had permeated the area began to dissipate. However, the repercussions of the failure were just beginning.

The same day the truce brought an element of peace to the sector, Ulysses Grant suggested an official inquiry be held to judge the matter. President Lincoln supported the investigation that proceeded on August 6. Not surprisingly, the officers chosen for the board were all friendly toward George Meade, and all displayed some disquiet with Burnside and his IX Corps. Burnside testified for three days then left the army on leave. Thirty-one other witnesses also provided testimony, most of it injurious to the IX Corps chieftain. Finally, on September 9, the board found five main reasons for the failure of the operation. All of them devolved upon Ambrose Burnside.

He never returned to active service.

Burnside did have connections in Washington DC, and his pull prompted the Joint Committee on the Conduct of the War to hold their own investigation of the disaster. Their findings—issued in February of 1865—placed much of the blame for the failure on George Meade and even found Grant to be somewhat wanting in his role. Despite the results, Burnside's military career was over, and the Crater would stand as a final exclamation point on a career honorably served but justly notable for its many failures and few successes.

*   *   *

Henry Pleasants applied for a leave of absence immediately after the battle. Before he left, he made two calls. The first was with his corps commander who effusively praised the miner's efforts yet admitted his own shortcomings in the operation. The second was with George Meade. As the army commander offered his own praise, Pleasants could not help but recall all the roadblocks Meade and his staff threw in his way: the lack of tools and equipment, the gunpowder shortage, the improper fuses. Pleasants left the meeting slightly disgusted.

When he returned to the army, he was given command of the Second brigade in Robert Potter's Second division. He could still visit the Pennsylvanians of his former command, and if he so desired he could make his way to Fort Morton and look out at the scene of his handy work.

Henry Pleasants had built the longest military mine of its time. He had conquered the Virginia clay and provided his army with an unprecedented opportunity. He would be brevetted Brigadier General for his efforts. It was a peak moment in a life of accomplishment.

As for the ensuing battle, U. S. Grant described it perfectly: a stupendous failure.

Editor's Conclusion

Even today, nearly 150 years after the battle, historians disagree about the causes of the Union defeat at the Crater. A military court of inquiry held shortly after the battle laid the blame on Burnside and Ledlie. Several months later the Joint Committee on the Conduct of the War held its own hearing and blamed Meade for the defeat, pointing out that the division of IX Corps USCT troops had been specifically trained for the assault and replaced at the last minute by Meade. The Committee concluded that the black troops would probably have won the battle had Meade not interfered. There is a third viewpoint that the Confederate position was so strong and the Union troops so demoralized that the attack was doomed to fail.

The Battle of the Crater stands alone because it was the only action during the Siege of Petersburg in which Grant directly assaulted Confederate fortifications. All of his other offensives were attempts to flank the earthworks and cut logistical lifelines.

The Federals lost 3,798 officers and men in this battle and the Confederates about 1,500.[4]

---

4   Horn, *The Petersburg Campaign*, 33.

Chapter 5

The Battle of the
Weldon Railroad

August 18 – 21, 1864

Editor's Introduction

A few days after his Third Offensive ended in defeat at the Battle of the Crater (July 30, 1864), General Grant met with President Abraham Lincoln at Fort Monroe, Virginia. The President made it clear to Grant that the threat to Washington posed by Jubal Early's Confederate army operating in the Shenandoah Valley had to eliminated. Grant told the president that he would appoint Maj. Gen. Philip Sheridan to command a coalition of forces against Early. In order to make sure Sheridan understood his mission, Grant spent several days conferring with him at Monocacy Junction before returning to his headquarters at City Point on August 8.

Once back at the Petersburg front, Grant reviewed the latest intelligence reports on the whereabouts of Gen. Robert E. Lee's various units. These reports indicated to Grant that Lee had heavily reinforced Early's command with Maj. Gen. Joseph Kershaw's infantry division, Maj. Wilfred Cutshaw's artillery battalion, and Maj. Gen. Fitzhugh Lee's cavalry division. About the same time, Lee redeployed Maj. Gen. Charles Field's infantry division and Maj. Gen. Cadmus M. Wilcox's III Corps infantry divisions and Maj. Gen. Wade Hampton's cavalry division from south of the Appomattox River to north of the James. In an effort to force Lee to recall these reinforcements, Grant sent a second expedition north of the James River to threaten Richmond. He also hoped the presence of these Union troops on Richmond's doorstep would compel Lee to strip his Petersburg lines to meet the threat, which might in turn offer Grant an opportunity to capture Petersburg or at least destroy the Weldon Railroad running southwest out of the city. Finally, Grant wanted to send cavalry north of Richmond to tear up the Virginia Central Railroad, which linked Richmond to the Shenandoah Valley.

Grant selected Maj. Gen. Winfield S. Hancock to lead the expedition against the Weldon Railroad. His command would consist of his own II Corps, two divisions from the X Corps under Maj. Gen. David Birney, and Brig. Gen. David M. Gregg's cavalry division.

On August 14, Hancock's II Corps attempted to outflank the Confederate left flank while Birney's X Corps divisions pinned down the main Confederate force north of Deep Bottom with heavy skirmishing. The II Corps attacks failed with heavy losses. After transferring the X Corps to his right flank above Fussell's Mill, Hancock attacked again on August 16. Despite temporarily breaching the Confederate line, the Federals were ejected with heavy losses. Union Cavalry operations on the right flank also ended in defeat. This was the bloodiest day of what became known as the Second Battle of Deep Bottom. Union losses for the battle, which lasted from August 14-20, were 2,901 from all causes, while Confederate losses totaled about 1,500.

Hancock's sharp attacks at Deep Bottom north of the James River alarmed General Lee, who had sent a large portion of his army below the James. Only the infantry divisions of Robert Hoke, Bushrod Johnson, and William Mahone remained to defend the city. Hancock sent one of his divisions back to Petersburg on the night of August 18. Its return to the front lines permitted Maj. Gen. Gouverneur K. Warren to set out for the Weldon Railroad. The rest of Hancock's II Corps and Gregg's cavalry returned to Petersburg on August 21.

Part I

The V Corps Affects a Lodgment on the Weldon Railroad

The summer of 1864 in eastern Virginia had been oppressively hot. No rain fell in the Petersburg area from June 3 to July 19. When it did start to rain, life in the trenches became worse, the high temperatures continued, and the atmosphere became damp and humid. Men of both armies hoped that they could get out of the earthworks. Therefore, when orders came for the IX Corps of the Army of the Potomac to relieve the V Corps from the entrenchments, it was hailed with joy by the men who fought under the Maltese Cross.[1]

Major General Gouverneur K. Warren's soldiers of the V Corps were accordingly withdrawn from the Petersburg investment line on the night of August 14.[2] Before another 36 hours had elapsed, the commander of the Army of the Potomac, Maj. Gen. George G. Meade, had received a number of interesting reports from Maj. Gen. Winfield S. Hancock, the signal officer in charge of the observation stations, and other intelligence sources. These reports indicated that Gen. Robert E. Lee had cut his force south of the James to three divisions.

Meade, on the evening of August 16, alerted General Warren to have his corps formed and ready to march at 3:00 a.m. The V Corps was to move by way of Strong's house and strike the Weldon Railroad near the Vaughan Road crossing (about two miles southeast of Petersburg). If the entrenchments in that area were "weakly" held, Warren was to "endeavor to carry them and occupy the crest in rear of their first line of works opposite the fronts held" by the II and XVIII Corps.

---

1 Powell, *The Fifth Army Corps*, 710; Survivors' Association, *History of the Corn Exchange Regiment 118th Pennsylvania Volunteers, From their First Engagement at Antietam to Appomattox* (Philadelphia, 1888), 497.

2 Humphreys, *The Virginia Campaign of '64 and '65*, 272-273. After the failure of the Petersburg Mine, Lt. Gen. Ulysses S. Grant planned to cut the Weldon Railroad. Hancock's II Corps, with the cavalry and a portion of the X Corps, was sent across the James. Going ashore at Deep Bottom, the Federals advanced on Richmond. This offensive had a second objective—to prevent Gen. Robert E. Lee from sending reinforcements to assist Lieutenant General Jubal Early in the Valley. The Deep Bottom offensive was commenced on August 13 and pushed with great determination. Skirmishers were boldly thrown forward, troops moved up to the advanced lines, and demonstrations of great strength made. The deception was excellent. Lee hastened to the north side of the James, to give his personal attention to checking the Union thrust. Charles H. Porter, "Operations against the Weldon Railroad, August 18, 19, 21, 1864," in *Papers of the Military Historical Society of Massachusetts*, vol. 5, 246.

Major General Gouverneur K. Warren
Library of Congress

Brigadier General August V. Kautz was to mass his cavalry division near the Jerusalem Plank Road to keep W. H. F. "Rooney" Lee's cavalry division from assailing the V Corps's rear.[3]

Lieutenant General Ulysses S. Grant wasn't altogether satisfied as to the disposition of the Confederate troops. Since he preferred to await further developments, Meade's order was suspended.[4]

Union officers closely grilled all prisoners captured in General Hancock's offensive in the Deep Bottom sector north of the James. Two hundred and sixty-seven Rebels had been sent to City Point on the evening of August 16 for questioning. From these men, the intelligence people were able to ascertain that two and possibly three Confederate brigades had crossed the James on Sunday (the 14th) to reinforce the units opposing Hancock's thrust. Troopers from both brigades of Maj. Gen. W. H. F. "Rooney" Lee's cavalry division had been bagged by the Federals. These men were in agreement that all Rebel cavalry had been withdrawn from the Weldon Railroad area. The other Confederate cavalry divisions, they said, were with Lt. Gen. Jubal Early up in the Shenandoah Valley.[5]

General Grant determined to capitalize on this situation. A telegram, on the morning of the 17th, was sent to General Meade. Grant wanted Meade to send General Warren with his V Corps and "a little cavalry" to destroy as much of the Weldon Railroad as practicable, but under no circumstances was Warren "to fight any unequal battles nor to assault fortifications." Warren's movement was to be a reconnaissance in force "to take advantage of any weakness of the enemy he may

---

3   *OR* 42, pt. 2, 226.

4   *Ibid.*, 226; Humphreys, *Virginia Campaign of '64 and '65*, 273.

5   *OR* 42, pt. 2, 245-246.

discover." Three or four days rations were to be carried by the troops of the V Corps. If Warren were unable to reach the Weldon Railroad near the Petersburg defenses, he was to "strike or feel farther south." General Grant's dispatch concluded, "I want, if possible, to make such demonstrations as will force Lee to withdraw a portion of his troops from the valley, so that [Maj. Gen. Philip H.] Sheridan can strike a blow against the balance."[6]

Accordingly, Warren was instructed by Meade on the afternoon of August 17 to take his corps at 4:00 a.m. in the morning and "endeavor to make a lodgment upon the Weldon Railroad, in the vicinity of the Gurley house, or as much nearer to the enemy's line of entrenchments as practicable." Warren was to have his troops destroy the railroad as far south as possible. In addition to the destruction of the railroad, Warren was to consider his movement "a reconnaissance in force," and be prepared to take advantage of any weakness the Rebels might betray. It was not expected at headquarters that Warren "would fight under serious disadvantages or assault fortifications." If the V Corps found the Confederates dug in along the railroad, Warren was to pin them in position.

When the V Corps took the field, Warren was to see that his troops carried four days rations on their persons. All the corps artillery, as well as part of the ambulances and medical wagons, were to accompany the expedition. The corps train was to be parked at "convenient and secure points in rear of the army."

General Kautz would be instructed to have one of his brigades report to General Warren. The horsemen were to be used to picket the ground between the corps' left and Blackwater Swamp.

Meade notified his corps commander that, according to Confederate prisoners captured in the Deep Bottom operations, nearly all the Rebel cavalry had been withdrawn from the south side, and that General Lee had "considerably less than four infantry divisions" south of the Appomattox. Warren was warned that Meade would be unable to send him any reinforcements if he got into trouble, consequently, he "must depend entirely" upon his own resources. The only help Warren could expect from the troops holding the Petersburg investment lines was that of "obliging the enemy to maintain his line."[7]

Upon the receipt of his marching orders, Warren addressed a circular to his division commanders and staff officers. When the corps took the field, Griffin's division was to have the lead, to be followed by Ayres', Crawford's, and Cutler's. Batteries were to accompany the divisions to which they had been previously

---

6   *Ibid.*, 244; Humphreys, *Virginia Campaign of '64 and '65*, 273.

7   *OR* 42, pt. 2, 251.

assigned. The reserve artillery, one-half the ambulances, and one medicine wagon per division were to fall in behind Cutler's division. Since Warren planned to move light and fast, he announced that the ordnance train, the battery wagons, traveling forges, and all baggage wagons, except the spring wagons, would be left. A staff officer would be sent to each division command post to guide the division commander.[8]

As soon as they received their copies of the circular, the division commanders called staff meetings. The officers in charge of the brigades were told to have their units formed and ready to march at the designated hour.

Long lines were soon formed in front of the ordnance and commissary tents as the troops drew ammunition and rations. Inspections were held by the regimental commanders to see that the men had the stipulated four days rations in their knapsacks and 40 rounds of ammunition in their cartridge boxes.

Warren's chief quartermaster informed the general that if the corps were to wreck a railroad more tools would be required. A request was forwarded to City Point for picks, bars, and shovels. By 6:00 p.m. several wagons had rolled out of the big City Point quartermaster depot with "440 sets of implements for destroying railroad."[9]

During the day, Union officers had gleaned additional information through their interrogation of Rebel prisoners. It was revealed that Maj. Gen. William Mahone's division and one brigade belonging to Maj. Gen. Bushrod R. Johnson's division had crossed the James to oppose the Deep Bottom thrust. Grant was delighted by this news. When he relayed it to Meade's headquarters at 10:00 p.m., Grant observed, "This leaves the force at Petersburg reduced to what it was when the mine was sprung. Warren may find an opportunity to do more than I had expected."[10]

Meade forwarded this news to General Warren.[11]

Meanwhile, Meade's headquarters had contacted General Kautz. The cavalry leader was advised of the impending expedition, and that he was to assist Warren by assigning one of his brigades (two regiments) to screen the infantry's left. Kautz was

---

8 *Ibid.*, 252. Battery E, 1st Massachusetts Light Artillery and Battery D, 1st New York Light Artillery were to march in rear of Griffin's division; Battery C, 1st Massachusetts Light Artillery, Battery B, 1st New York Light Artillery, and Battery D, 5th U.S. Light Artillery would follow Ayres' division; the 9th Battery, Massachusetts Light Artillery and Battery B, 1st Pennsylvania Light Artillery were to follow Crawford's division. OR 42, pt. 1, 540.

9 OR 42, pt. 2, 251.

10 *Ibid.*, 245.

11 *Ibid.*, 251.

to see that this force was provided "with the full amount of rations" and all the forage the troopers could carry.[12]

Kautz lost no time in getting in touch with General Warren. Warren was notified that the two regiments currently picketing the army's left would be the units designated to operate with the V Corps. At the moment, the two regiments mustered between 800 and 900 effectives. Warren would find Col. George W. Lewis, who would command the two regiments, at McCann's house near the Jerusalem Plank Road. Lewis had been alerted to hold his men ready to ride at 4 a.m.[13]

* * *

General Warren was in good spirits when he awakened early on August 18. Headquarters was a scene of feverish activity. Staff officers were going and coming. Warren was delighted to learn that his four division commanders had completed preparations and were ready to move out as scheduled. Before mounting his horse and riding off to join Brig. Gen. Charles Griffin's column, Warren telegraphed Meade that he "was exceedingly pleased" that his corps had been selected to undertake the expedition against the Weldon Railroad. The division commanders had voiced a similar feeling. Warren promised to keep in contact with army headquarters through the use of hourly messengers. Should anything "interesting" develop, a courier would be immediately dispatched.[14]

A slight hitch developed; it was 5:00 a.m. before General Griffin's division left its camp near the Chieves house. The 1st Brigade commanded by Col. William S. Tilton took the lead as the column moved out and turned into the Jerusalem Plank Road. A three mile march brought the vanguard to Second Swamp. A short distance beyond this watercourse at Temple's, a staff officer turned the head of Tilton's brigade into the Vaughan Road. Up until this moment, it had seemed to many of the soldiers that they were marching away from Petersburg. Now that the column had changed directions, they knew that they were striking for the Weldon Railroad.[15]

---

12 *Ibid.*, 260.

13 *Ibid.*, 260. The two cavalry regiments assigned to cooperate with the V Corps were the 3rd New York Cavalry and 1st District of Columbia Cavalry.

14 *Ibid.*, 271.

15 *OR* 42, pt. 1, 458, 460, 464; Mary G. G. Brainard, *Campaigns of The 146th Regiment New York State Volunteers* (New York, 1915), 237.

Major General Charles Griffin
Library of Congress

The Vaughan Road ran almost due west and crossed the Weldon Railroad at Globe Tavern. As the bluecoats tramped along the sandy road, they began to suffer from the heat. One of the soldiers recalled, "The day was one of those exceedingly close, sultry, August dog days, well known to every one who has served in Virginia, extremely debilitating and exhausting to both man and beast."[16]

Near Gurley's house (a large, square, white house, with very red brick chimneys at each gable), General Griffin called a halt and told Colonel Tilton to form his brigade. Tilton deployed his unit into double line of battle, while one regiment (the 150th Pennsylvania) was thrown forward as skirmishers.[17] Colonel Edgar M. Gregory's brigade marched up and was formed into double line of battle on Tilton's left. Gregory covered his front with skirmishers from the 32nd Massachusetts. The Vaughan Road separated the two brigades.[18]

While waiting for Griffin's Third brigade (Col. James Gwyn's) to take post in support of Gregory's bluecoats, General Warren (at 7:00 a.m.) addressed a message to General Meade's headquarters. Upon reaching Gurley's house, Warren had questioned several of Kautz's pickets—troopers from the 3rd New York Cavalry. The horse soldiers told the general that Rebel outposts had told them that they were

---

16 Porter, "Operations against the Weldon Railroad, August 18, 19, 21, 1864," 247-248. Globe Tavern was also known as Six Mile House and Yellow Tavern.

17 *Ibid.*, 248; OR 42, pt. 1, 458, 460. Tilton's first line was composed of the 149th and 187th Pennsylvania, while the 121st, 142nd, and 143rd Pennsylvania constituted his second.

18 OR 42, pt. 1, 458, 460, 466, 467.

to be relieved at any minute. As soon as Griffin had completed his dispositions and Brig. Gen. Romeyn B. Ayres' division had closed up, Warren wrote, the advance would be resumed.[19]

It was a little after 8:00 a.m. when General Griffin notified Warren that his division was ready to resume the advance. Warren told Griffin to go ahead. Covered by a strong skirmish line, Tilton's and Gregory's brigades drove toward the Weldon Railroad, a mile to their front. On the right, skirmishers of the 150th Pennsylvania encountered vedettes from the 7th Confederate Cavalry. The Rebs retired rapidly toward the railroad, losing a score of men as they did. By the time the Yank skirmishers approached the track, the grey clads had vanished.

At 9:00 a.m. Griffin's battle line crossed the railroad at Globe Tavern. Before doing anything else, several men snipped the telegraph wire. The skirmishers (the 150th Pennsylvania and the 32nd Massachusetts) advanced another 500 yards, halted, and took post parallel to the track. Colonel Tilton stopped the 149th and 187th Pennsylvania at Globe Tavern. As soon as tools could be broken out by the quartermaster people and passed out, the Pennsylvanians were turned to tearing up the rails, stacking the ties with the rails on top, and setting them on fire. Three of Tilton's regiments (the 121st, 142nd, and 143rd Pennsylvania) were wheeled to the right. A battle line was formed across the railroad. The three Pennsylvania regiments advanced toward Petersburg. After proceeding about one-third of a mile, the troops were halted and put to work digging rifle pits and slashing timber.[20]

Except for the 32nd Massachusetts deployed as skirmishers west of the railroad, Gregory's troops were given dual tasks of wreaking havoc on the Weldon Railroad and erecting breastworks.[21] Gwyn's brigade was held in reserve near Globe Tavern.[22]

Globe Tavern was situated near the center of "a large and beautiful area of cleared ground of several hundred acres, extending east and west of the railroad and north along" the Halifax road for about one-half mile. The belt of pines which bounded the clearing on the north was about 500 yards in depth. These woods extended eastward to the open fields adjacent to the Aiken house. From Aiken's to Fort Davis, on the Jerusalem Plank Road, the countryside was densely forested. Besides Globe Tavern, there were three houses in the large clearing—Dunlop's to

---

19 OR 42, pt. 2, 272.

20 OR 42, pt. 1, 458, 460-461, 462, 463, 464, 465, 466.

21 *Ibid.*, 466-467.

22 *Ibid.*, 467, 469.

Major General Romeyn B. Ayres
Library of Congress

the east, Lennear's to the south, and Blick's west of the railroad. Corn was the money crop on these farms, and the stalks were beginning to turn brown.

The Halifax Road paralleled the railroad. Beyond it, to the westward, about a mile was the Vaughan Road. This road entered the Halifax Road about one and one-half miles north of Globe Tavern. Between the Vaughan and Halifax Roads timber and cultivated lands alternated. Numerous cart ways and paths well known to the Confederates cut through the woods and swamps surrounding the fields about Globe Tavern.[23]

The day was very hot; it was 10:00 a.m. before General Ayres' division reached Globe Tavern, where Warren had established his command post. Warren, when he discussed the situation with Ayres, was disappointed to learn that the surgeons, although the day was still young, were reporting "a great many cases of sunstroke." Upon relaying this information to Meade's headquarters, Warren complained, "Marching today is very slow." Patrols had been thrown out, Warren wrote, and as soon as he had completed his dispositions, he would "move up the railroad."[24]

In accordance with Warren's instructions, Ayres deployed his division near the Blick house. Brig. Gen. Joseph Hayes formed his brigade in double line of battle across the railroad. The 12th U.S. Infantry, 146th New York, and a battalion of the 140th New York were thrown out as skirmishers.[25] The Maryland brigade, Col. Nathan T. Dushane commanding, was posted in line of battle to the left and rear of

---

23 *Ibid.*, 503; Survivors, *History of the Corn Exchange Regiment*, 498; Porter, "Operations Against the Weldon Railroad, August 18, 19, 21, 1864," 248-249.

24 *OR* 42, pt. 2, 272.

25 *OR* 42, pt. 1, 474.

Hayes' bluecoats. Lieutenant Colonel Michael Wiedrich's 3rd Brigade would support the advance.[26] Cannoneers of Battery C, 1st Massachusetts Light Artillery threw their four Napoleons into battery near the Blick house.[27]

Before Ayres had completed his deployment, the Confederates succeeded in bringing up a two-gun battery. Unlimbering their pieces about three-quarters of a mile north of Blick's, the Rebel cannoneers shelled the Federals. Gunners of Battery C replied with two of their Napoleons.[28]

Reports reached Warren's command post from Colonel Tilton on the railroad north of the Blick house that the foe's guns were covered by a small force of cavalry. Shortly before 11:00 a.m., Warren told Ayres to drive up the Weldon Railroad toward Petersburg. As soon as Ayres' bluecoats passed through his line, Colonel Tilton recalled the 121st, 142nd, and 143rd Pennsylvania and put them to work turning over track.[29]

Ayres' battle line advanced slowly. About 1,100 yards north of Blick's house, Ayres' skirmishers engaged Confederate sharpshooters. Confederate artillerists at the same time employed their guns to delay the Union thrust. Much of the ground across which the Yanks worked was covered by a dense "undergrowth of pine and oaks."

Hayes' skirmishers (comprised of the 12th U.S., and the 140th and 146th New York regiments) drove Southern sharpshooters from Davis' house and compelled the Confederate artillerists to hurriedly limber their two pieces and retire to a less exposed position. The cannoneers of Battery C, 1st Massachusetts had pulled their Napoleons out of battery and drove them up the Halifax Road. Hardly had the butternuts given up Davis' house before the Yankee cannoneers thundered up, threw their four guns into battery, and resumed their duel with the Confederate artillerists. It was almost 2:00 p.m. by the time Hayes' battle line approached the edge of the dense belt of timber that bounded Davis' cornfield on the south. Screened by the tall green corn stalks beyond, Union skirmishers and Confederate sharpshooters engaged in a deadly game of hide and seek. When a detachment of the 146th New York led by Capt. James Stewart passed through a gap in the Confederate skirmish line, enemy soldiers surrounded and captured it. The main body of the 146th New York continued crawling about the cornfield, ducking as

26 *Ibid.*, 480; Brainard, *Campaigns of The 146th Regiment New York State Volunteers*, 238.

27 *OR* 42, pt. 1, 540.

28 *Ibid.*, 540; *OR* 42, pt. 2, 273.

29 *OR* 42, pt. 1, 461, 463; *OR* 42, pt. 2, 273.

Brigadier General Lysander Cutler
Library of Congress

the whizzing minie balls sang over their heads and clipped off the tops of the grain stalks.[30]

Brigadier General Lysander Cutler's division, bringing up the V Corps' rear, had reached the railroad at 11:00 a.m. From General Cutler, Warren received some discouraging news. Like the other division commanders, Cutler complained of the oppressive heat and its effects on the men. Addressing a note to Meade's headquarters at this time, Warren reported, "The men give out fearfully in the sun and compel us to move slowly to keep them in the ranks. Several officers have been sun struck . . ."[31]

To establish contact with Burnside's IX Corps on his right, and to outflank the Confederates disputing Ayres' drive up the railroad, General Warren called for Brig. Gen. Samuel W. Crawford. Upon reaching Globe Tavern, Crawford had massed his division, about 3,000 strong, east of the railroad and awaited orders. Warren told his division commander of Ayres' activities: Crawford was to advance his troops and take position on the left of Ayres' battle line. The division moved out promptly— Col. Peter Lyle's brigade on the left, Col. Richard Coulter's in the center, and Col. William R. Hartshorne's brigade to the right and rear of Coulter's unit.[32]

---

30 OR 42, pt. 1, 471, 474, 540; Porter, "Operations Against the Weldon Railroad, August 18, 19, 21, 1864," 249; Brainard, *Campaigns of the 146th Regiment*, 238.

31 OR 42, pt. 2, 273; A. P. Smith, *History of the Seventy-Sixth Regiment New York Volunteers* (Cortland, 1867), 307-308.

32 *Ibid.*, 307-308. OR 42, pt. 1, 491.

As the troops advanced across the clearing toward the woods, it started to rain very hard. After about 15 minutes, the downpour ceased, but by this time the bluecoats had been drenched.[33]

Before reaching the thicket which bounded the clearing on the north, Crawford sent word for Colonel Lyle to deploy one of his regiments as skirmishers. Colonel Lyle halted his brigade, while he threw forward the 107th Pennsylvania. Advancing into the woods about 20 yards, the skirmishers halted. Meanwhile, the Rebel battery posted north of Davis' had turned its attention on Crawford's battle line. Within a matter of moments, the Confederates found the range. Crawford sought to get his men out of the open and under cover.

A staff officer was sent with instructions for the skirmishers of the 107th Pennsylvania to extend to the right to screen the other brigades of the division as they drew abreast of Lyle's. Crawford at the same time sent another aide into the pines to the left front to pinpoint the right flank of Ayres' division; he was to guide Lyle's brigade into position so that there would be no gap between the two divisions.

The officer soon returned with the desired information—Ayres' right flank extended a short distance east of the railroad. At this, Lyle's brigade advanced into the woods with orders to connect with the right of Ayres' command. Since the underbrush was very thick, Lyle determined to advance his brigade by successive regiments. The 16th Maine on the left moved first and established contact with Ayres' troops on its left. While Colonel Lyle was "exerting himself" to guide the rest of his units through the "thick and tangled wood and underbrush," the Confederates launched a furious counterattack.[34]

Confederate Brigadier General James Dearing had notified Gen. P. G. T. Beauregard, who (with Lee supervising operations north of the James) had been left in charge at Petersburg, that the Yanks had driven in his pickets and reserve east of Globe Tavern. According to Col. V. H. Taliaferro of the 7th Confederate Cavalry, the Federals were out "in force with infantry and cavalry." Dearing, after handing the message to a courier, had headed for the point of danger at the head of one of his regiments.

Beauregard (at 10:15 a.m.) forwarded Dearing's communication to General Lee. Since he didn't have any cavalry, Beauregard inquired, "Can any cavalry reinforcements be sent Dearing?"

33 *OR* 42, pt. 2, 273.

34 *OR* 42, pt. 1, 491, 503, 508.

Brigadier General Samuel W. Crawford
Library of Congress

Shortly before noon, Beauregard received further news from Dearing. The cavalryman tersely reported, "Enemy is advancing in force both upon railroad and Vaughan Road." Beauregard, in view of this development, determined to act. Orders were sent through Lt. Gen. Ambrose P. Hill for Maj. Gen. Henry Heth to support Dearing's cavalry with two infantry brigades. The force holding the Petersburg earthworks had been cut to a minimum, so Beauregard cautioned Heth that the foot soldiers must be returned to their positions in the rifle pits by nightfall.[35]

Heth quickly organized a striking force consisting of the infantry brigades led by Brig. Gen. Joseph R. Davis and Col. Robert M. Mayo, and the Letcher Virginia Artillery. As soon as the unit commanders had formed their commands, Heth's column marched out of the Petersburg defenses via the Vaughan Road.[36]

Shortly after Heth's column had moved out, Brig. Gen. Alfred H. Colquitt received orders to put his Georgia brigade into motion for the Weldon Railroad. Washington L. Dunn of the 27th Georgia recorded in his diary, "We are out near Petersburg. It rained today and about ____ o'clock p.m. we received orders that the Yankees were on the Weldon Railroad, about 4 miles from the City and we received

---

35 *OR* 42, pt. 2, 1186.

36 Humphreys, *Virginia Campaign of '64 and '65*, 274; *OR* 42, pt. 1, 857, 858; Joseph P. Bashaw, "My Experiences in the War," Tennessee State Library and Archives. Archer's and Walker's brigades had been consolidated. Colonel Mayo led the consolidated brigade in the battle of the Weldon Railroad. *OR* 42, pt. 2, 1273-1274.

orders to go down there and we started some thing after one and marched down on the road . . ."

Meanwhile, General Dearing reported that his cavalry had checked the Union advance at Davis' house. Although the Federals were exhibiting a strong line of battle, Dearing felt they were bluffing. He notified Beauregard that he doubted if the Yanks had "more than a few regiments of infantry and one or two of cavalry."[37]

* * *

General Ayres, taking cognizance of the increasing tempo of the skirmishing to his front, sent instructions for Colonel Dushane to form his brigade into line of battle on the left of Hayes' command. Dushane massed his Marylanders near the edge of the wood, about 100 yards south of Davis' cornfield. The left flank of the Maryland brigade was guarded by a few skirmishers.

Screened by the tall corn stalks and Dearing's cavalry, General Heth quickly completed his dispositions. As soon as Davis and Mayo had formed their brigades into double line of battle, Heth passed the word to attack. The Federals first sighted the grey clad infantrymen as they stormed out of the woods beyond Davis' house. Sweeping the blue clad skirmishers before them, the butternuts struck Hayes' line "in front and flank."[38] As soon as he sighted the onrushing Rebs, Colonel Dushane called for his Marylanders to fire. Several crashing volleys caused the Confederates to the Maryland brigade's front to seek shelter.[39] East of the Weldon Railroad, the Southerners overlapped Hayes' battle line and assailed the 16th Maine.[40]

Hayes' brigade quickly gave way. Taking their walking wounded with them, the Unionists retired through the woods.[41] The retreat of Hayes' troops left the Federal units to the left and to the right in embarrassing situations. General Heth, to exploit the breakthrough, hurled Davis' fierce Mississippians and North Carolinians against Dushane's right flank. Dushane shouted for his Marylanders to retreat.[42] As the brigade started to pull back, a number of men panicked. The thick underbrush and the pursuing Confederates didn't help the situation. The Maryland brigade

---

37 *OR* 42, pt. 2, 1187; Dunn, Diary. n.d.

38 *OR* 42, pt. 1, 474; Bashaw, "My Experiences in the War."

39 *OR* 42, pt. 1, 480.

40 *Ibid.*, 503.

41 *Ibid.*, 474; Brainard, *Campaigns of the 146th Regiment,* 238.

42 *OR* 42, pt. 1, 480.

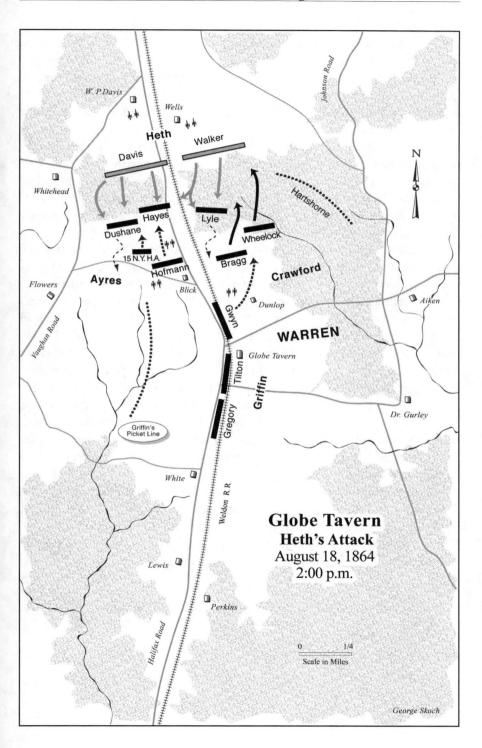

W. P. Davis

Wells

Heth

Walker

Davis

Whitehead

Hartshorne

N

Hayes

Lyle

Dushane

Wheelock

15 N.Y. H.A.

Bragg

Hofmann

Flowers

Ayres

Blick

Dunlop

Crawford

Aiken

Gwyn

WARREN

Tilton

Globe Tavern

Griffin

Gregory

Dr. Gurley

Griffin's
Picket Line

White

Weldon R R

Globe Tavern
Heth's Attack
August 18, 1864
2:00 p.m.

Lewis

Vaughan Road

Halifax Road

Perkins

0   1/4
Scale in Miles

George Skoch

retired in confusion. After the soldiers had "disentangled" themselves from the woods, the officers succeeded in rallying and reforming them.

Colonel Charles W. Tilden of the 16th Maine was angered and at the same time distressed by the retreat of Ayres' troops to his left. He bellowed for his men to stand fast to allow Colonel Lyle to bring up the rest of the brigade. As the Maine men traded volleys with Mayo's butternuts, the 39th Massachusetts, followed by the 90th Pennsylvania, drew abreast of the Maine regiment's right. After several minutes of bitter, close range combat, Colonel Tilden saw that the Rebs were infiltrating the woods to his left and rear. To avoid having his unit captured en masse, Tilden called "retreat!" The regiment fell back and was rallied on the left of the 104th New York. Upon the retreat of the 16th Maine, the rest of Lyle's brigade retired and reformed at the southern edge of the woods.[43]

About this time, General Crawford learned that the 107th Pennsylvania was so understrength that it was unable to cover properly the division front. Recalling the regiment, Crawford replaced it with skirmishers from the 119th Pennsylvania.[44]

As they retreated through the pines, Lyle's bluecoats encountered Coulter's brigade. Not having fully recovered from the effect of his wounds, Colonel Coulter turned over command of his brigade to the next senior officer, Col. Charles Wheelock of the 97th New York. Wheelock moved promptly to stabilize the situation. Three companies of the 97th New York, the lead regiment, were pushed out as skirmishers. While these men delayed Mayo's Rebels, Wheelock formed the brigade into battle line. Since his right flank overlapped the grey clads' line, Wheelock threw forward his right regiment, the 88th Pennsylvania. The badly outnumbered Confederates halted when confronted by the fresh brigade. While the Southerners and Wheelock's troops banged away, Colonel Lyle redeployed his brigade on Wheelock's left.[45]

To help stem the Confederate tide that had punched a hole in the Union line, General Ayres called up his reserve brigade. Colonel Wiedrich formed his artillerists turned into infantrymen on either side of the railroad. Hayes' and Dushane's troops, as they retreated from the woods, rallied on Wiedrich's command.[46]

43 *Ibid.*, 503, 508. In this fighting, Lyle's brigade lost a number of officers and men. Lt. William T. Spear of the 39th Massachusetts was killed, while Lt. Col. Charles L. Peirson and Lt. John D. Read were wounded.

44 *Ibid.*, 491.

45 *Ibid.*, 509.

46 *Ibid.*, 471.

Major General Henry Heth
Library of Congress

Ayres had called for help. Warren accordingly told General Cutler to reinforce the Second division with one of his two brigades. Cutler decided to send the brigade led by Col. J. William Hofmann.

On the morning's march, Hofmann's column had brought up the rear; fully one-half the men had straggled. By 3:00 p.m., when the orders to move to the front arrived, many of these people had rejoined their units. When Hofmann gave the word, the troops fell in on their colors and took arms. The brigade tramped northward from Globe Tavern toward the sound of the guns. Reaching the woods one-half mile north of the tavern, Hofmann formed his regiments into line of battle, the left flank resting on the railroad. Soldiers of the 147th New York were deployed and advanced as skirmishers. The New Yorkers beat their way through the timber for several hundred yards, before encountering any Rebs. When they did, both sides blazed away.

At 4:00 p.m. Hofmann was directed to report to General Ayres. The general had Hofmann shift his troops west of the railroad and relieve Colonel Dushane's Marylanders. Hardly had Hofmann's troops taken position and allowed Dushane's badly shaken foot soldiers to pass through their lines, before they found themselves engaged with Davis' Mississippians and North Carolinians.[47]

Upon being notified that Hofmann's brigade was being sent west of the track, General Cutler had Brig. Gen. Edward S. Bragg form his brigade. Bragg's troops

---

47 *Ibid.*, 483-484, 485, 486, 488, 490; Smith, *History of the Seventy-Sixth Regiment*, 308. Hofmann's troops advanced to the front in heavy marching order. Captain Thomas E. Carter of the 157th Pennsylvania reported that while his troops were lying in line of battle "a solid shot from the enemy struck in the left company tearing off the knapsack and scattering the contents of the haversack of one man.. . ." 490.

would be used to plug the gap which the Confederates had opened between Ayres' division on the left and Crawford's on the right. Arriving on the ground at the edge of the woods where Hofmann had first deployed, Bragg halted his troops. The 6th Wisconsin was thrown forward as skirmishers. Hardly had the boys from Wisconsin disappeared into the thick undergrowth, before Bragg had formed his other units into line of battle and put the soldiers to work throwing up breastworks.[48]

Skirmishers from the 6th Wisconsin filed into line on the right of the 147th New York. For the next several hours, the two Union regiments battled the Johnnies to their front.[49]

As soon as it was known that the Confederates were counterattacking, Col. Charles S. Wainwright called up his artillery. Six batteries galloped up and emplaced their guns along a line running from west to east across the Weldon Railroad. The cannoneers of the left flank battery (the 15th New York) unlimbered their four Napoleons a short distance west of Blick's house. When Ayres' troops retired out of the pines to their front, the gun captains put their pieces into action. The ground seemed to tremble as the 24 pieces hammered away with shot and shell at the Rebs and their supporting artillery. Within a few minutes, the Yankee cannoneers had silenced the Confederate guns (the Letcher Virginia Artillery). This enabled them to give the grey clad foot soldiers their undivided attention. Fortunately for the Southerners, they were screened by the trees and dense undergrowth.[50]

General Warren (at 4:00 p.m.) dispatched a message to army headquarters. He reported that the forced withdrawal of Ayres' division had "deranged" his plans considerably. At the moment, the corps commander wrote, he was "getting things in order again." The Confederates, Warren believed, had lost heavily and had been compelled to yield some of their gains. Headquarters was advised that Ayres and Crawford, supported by Cutler, had been ordered to counterattack. Having to rely on his own resources, Warren had been compelled to hold Griffin in reserve in case the Rebels assailed his flanks. Warren didn't feel the Confederates were strong enough to drive the V Corps from the Weldon Railroad, and if practicable, he would endeavor to push his lines closer to the Petersburg perimeter.[51]

48 Ibid., 534, 535.

49 Ibid., 488. The 147th New York belonged to Hofmann's brigade.

50 Ibid., 540. From left to right the guns were emplaced: the 15th New York Battery; Battery B, 1st New York Light Artillery; Battery H, 1st New York Light Artillery; Battery D, 5th U.S. Light Artillery; 9th Massachusetts Battery; Battery B, 1st Pennsylvania Light Artillery.

51 OR 42, pt. 2, 274.

Heth's attack had been checked by the arrival of reinforcements from Cutler's division and the bombardment by Wainwright's massed artillery. While Ayres' troops, bolstered by Hofmann's brigade, held their ground, Warren planned to employ Crawford's division, supported by Bragg's soldiers, to turn Heth's left. Following the receipt of orders to throw his right forward, Crawford ordered his skirmish line strengthened. The Feds slowly forged ahead. So dense was the tangled undergrowth that it was impossible to see more than 20 or 30 feet. The fighting in this jungle was nasty. Men were struck down without warning, victims of hidden marksmen. On the right and center of Crawford's line, the bluecoats drove Mayo's butternuts from "two chains of hastily constructed rifle pits."

Lyle's troops on the left recovered most of the ground from which they had been driven. Wheelock's brigade in the center pressed forward and reached the edge of Davis' cornfield. Here, they found themselves within 100 yards of a strong force of Confederates posted behind earthworks on the opposite side of the rows of corn stalks. As his bluecoats emerged from the woods, Wheelock spotted the fortifications and shouted, "Lie down!" It was fortunate for the Federals that the colonel was quick-witted, because as they hit the ground, a crashing volley ripped through the undergrowth just above them.[52]

General Warren (at 5:30 p.m.) reported to army headquarters on the progress of his counterthrust. East of the railroad, Crawford's troops were gaining ground, but the dense timber made the advance "slow and difficult," as the officers found it all but impossible to control their units. As the Federals pushed ahead, Confederate wounded fell into their hands. General Warren notified Chief of Staff Humphreys that General Hayes had lost his horse, and that the 15th New York Heavy Artillery "behaved remarkably well."[53]

Since it was beginning to get dark, Crawford sent orders for his brigade commanders to halt their commands and be prepared to defend the ground gained.

At the same time, a message was addressed to General Warren. Crawford notified his corps commander that his right flank could carry Davis' cornfield in the morning should Warren deem it desirable. The Confederates, Crawford warned, were already toiling away strengthening their position. If his right were covered, a section of artillery could be employed with advantage to support a thrust against the Confederates in the cornfield.

"You have done very well indeed in getting forward through that difficult country," Warren (at 8:00 p.m.) wrote Crawford. Warren wanted Crawford to

52 OR 42, pt. 1, 492, 503, 510, 517; Bashaw, "My Experiences in the War."

53 OR 42, pt. 2, 274-275.

strengthen his position and hold on. In the morning, Warren would try to reinforce Crawford's division with Bragg's brigade, and establish contact on the right with the IX Corps' picket line. In closing, the corps commander observed, "We are going to hold on here."[54]

Upon receipt of Warren's 8:00 p.m. dispatch, Crawford issued instructions for his troops to start entrenching. On the left, the soldiers of Lyle's brigade exchanged shots with the Rebels to their front as they dug in. Along toward midnight, the firing ceased and the bluecoats, except those detailed to keep watch, were able to get a few hours sleep. Wheelock's brigade on the right had an easier time. They were harassed only slightly as they erected breastworks.[55]

General Ayres' troops, unlike Crawford's, were unable to regain the ground from which they had been dislodged by Heth's grey clads. Seeing that the sun was about to set, Ayres had his men dig in. To protect the soldiers as they threw up barricades, the unit commanders advanced skirmishers. Ayres on inspecting his line, found the brigades, posted from left to right: Dushane's, Hofmann's, Wiedrich's, and Hayes'. The Weldon Railroad separated Wiedrich's and Hayes' units, while Dushane's left flank veered around to the left.[56]

To the right and rear of Ayres' division, General Cutler saw that the troops of Bragg's brigade dug rifle pits. Skirmishers from the 6th Wisconsin of Bragg's brigade and the 147th New York of Hofmann's command held their position near the Confederate main line of resistance until shortly before dark, when they were relieved by Lyle's bluecoats.[57]

General Warren approved Ayres' and Cutler's actions. Not knowing that Lyle had relieved the 6th Wisconsin, Warren directed Ayres to see that the Wisconsin soldiers were replaced at daylight by the 12th U.S. Warren proposed to employ Bragg's brigade to bolster Crawford's division on the right.

Ayres, along with the other three division commanders, was to put his men to work slashing timber. All trees and underbrush between the railroad and the Vaughan Road, as well as other obstructions (such as houses, fences, etc.) were to be destroyed or thrown down.

Ayres acknowledged Warren's dispatch at 8:30 p.m. When he did, he observed that he could dispense with Bragg's brigade. He had anticipated Warren, he continued, and orders had already been issued for "entrenching and slashing." Men

54 *Ibid.*, 278.

55 OR 42, pt. 1, 492, 502, 510, 515, 517, 522.

56 *Ibid.*, 471, 474, 480, 483, 484; Brainard, *Campaigns of the 146th Regiment*, 239.

57 OR 42, pt. 1, 488, 535.

had also been detailed and were hard at work cutting a deep ditch across the railroad embankment and the Halifax Road. Ayres was confident of holding his position in the morning, should the Southerners renew the attack.[58]

Toward dusk, Colonel Wainwright redeployed several of his batteries. The gunners of the 15th New York Battery shifted their Napoleons about 100 yards farther to the west of the Blick house, while the gunners of Battery H, 1st New York Light Artillery moved their four Napoleons up from the reserve and emplaced them west of the Halifax Road. Both these batteries were pointed so that they could fire to the north or to the west. Battery C, 1st New York Light Artillery was also called up from the reserve, and unlimbered its four 3-inch rifles to the right and rear of the four pieces manned by Battery B, 1st Pennsylvania Light Artillery. Battery E, 1st Massachusetts Light Artillery, and Batteries D and L, 1st New York Light Artillery were posted along the Halifax Road facing east.[59]

The soldiers of Griffin's division, during the late afternoon, who were destroying the railroad north and south of Globe Tavern, were subjected to a "severe" shelling by the Letcher Virginia Artillery. Many of the bluecoats ceased work and took cover. An enlisted man in the 118th Pennsylvania, standing alongside Capt. James B. Wilson, stepped aside to avoid a mud hole. The captain took the mud; a solid shot which came bounding down the line struck and killed the soldier. Wilson, except for getting his uniform dirty, was unharmed.[60]

General Griffin now received instructions to use one of his brigades to reinforce Crawford's division. Marching orders were issued to Colonel Gwyn. Within a few minutes, Gwyn had assembled his brigade. Deploying into line of battle on the double, Gwyn's troops moved from the area behind Globe Tavern to Crawford's assistance. By the time they had reached the point of danger, the tide had turned.[61]

General Warren shortly before dark directed General Griffin to employ his division to protect the corps' left flank. Griffin recalled Gwyn's brigade. The troops of the First division crossed the railroad and took position about 100 yards from the tracks, facing west. Tilton's brigade on the right anchored its flank on the Maryland brigade. One regiment, the 150th Pennsylvania, was sent out as pickets. Gregory's brigade took position on Tilton's left; Gwyn's was on the corps extreme left. As

58 OR 42, pt. 2, 277.

59 OR 42, pt. 1, 540-541.

60 *Ibid.*, 461, 466, 467; Survivors, *History of the Corn Exchange Regiment*, 500.

61 OR 42, pt. 1, 461, 466, 467.

soon as the men had taken posts parallel to the railroad, the soldiers were put to work throwing up breastworks.[62]

Chief of Staff Humphreys (at 5:15 p.m.) handed a message to Capt. Campbell D. Emory for delivery to General Warren. General Meade, upon receiving Warren's dispatches telling of the Confederate counterattack, had determined to alter Warren's instructions. If the V Corps were unable to feel the Petersburg defenses, it was to entrench as near to the Rebel works as it could penetrate. On doing so, Warren was to extend his left "well" to the west of the Weldon Railroad. Under no circumstances was Warren to construe this communication as preventing him from taking advantage of any weaknesses displayed by the Confederates or of withdrawing his corps if in his judgment it became necessary.[63]

It took Captain Emory 105 minutes to reach the Blick house. Warren, after studying the dispatch, drafted his reply. Headquarters was advised that the V Corps had already pushed its lines as close to the foe as it could and was entrenching. Warren's pickets on the right were in contact with the outposts of the IX Corps near the Strong house. According to the latest reports from the front, the grey clads were erecting breastworks between the V Corps and Petersburg. Warren felt he could hold his ground astride the Weldon Railroad in face of further Rebel attacks, provided contact with the IX Corps could be maintained.

After tersely describing the day's fighting, Warren observed, "It has been a hard day on the men and the fight today was severe on both sides." When the advance had been suspended, Crawford's troops on the right had penetrated to within sight of the main Petersburg defenses, a mile and three-quarters to their front. If all went according to schedule, the signal corps people had told Warren, they would have a telegraph line in operation linking his command post with army headquarters before morning.

Warren complained that the wet weather had interfered with the destruction of the railroad. The afternoon's thunderstorm had put out the fires which Griffin's troops had kindled to bend the rails.

Warren informed Chief of Staff Humphreys:

The enemy's proximity to his fortified line enabled him to act with boldness, and I do not now think he considered us strong and made his effort to drive us from the

---

62 *Ibid.*, 461, 463, 465, 467. The left flank of Gwyn's brigade rested near where Fort Dushane was subsequently erected.

63 *OR* 42, pt. 2, 274.

Major General John G. Parke
Library of Congress

railroad. He has taken some prisoners from us today and now knows our strength. If he tries again, it will have to be with a very large force to succeed.[64]

At 8:30 p.m. General Warren forwarded a sketch of his position to General Meade's headquarters. At the same time, he notified Meade that the prisoners captured by the V Corps during the day's fighting belonged to the 7th Confederate Cavalry, Heth's division, and Hoke's brigade. When questioned, the Rebels had proved very uncooperative. Several had indicated, however, that General Beauregard had a strategic reserve within the Petersburg lines.[65]

Meanwhile, one of Maj. Gen. John G. Parke's staff officers, Capt. George W. Gowan, had called on General Warren. Gowan learned, while at Warren's command post, that the gap between the left of the IX Corps and the right of the V Corps was too big to be sealed unless Parke's IX Corps was reinforced. To reduce the size of the interval, General Parke ordered the leader of his First division, Brig. Gen. Julius White to readjust his lines. The left flank brigade, which had heretofore been refused, was advanced. This enabled the Yanks to shorten the interval to about one and one-half miles. Troopers from the 3rd New York Cavalry were detailed to patrol this gap.[66]

News of the limited successes scored by the Confederates on Warren's front caused General Meade (at 8:00 p.m.) to act. Parke would reinforce Warren. A division from the II Corps was to be rushed from Deep Bottom to replace the

64 *Ibid.*, 275.

65 *Ibid.*, 275-276.

66 *Ibid.*, 281, 282. General Parke on August 14 had relieved General Burnside as commander of the IX Corps.

troops Parke was to dispatch to Warren's assistance. Parke would have one of his divisions ready to march as soon as the replacements arrived. Meade believed the II Corps troops should reach the Petersburg lines shortly after daybreak on the 19th. The soldiers ordered to Warren's assistance were to carry four days rations on their persons and entrenching tools. Some ambulances and ordnance wagons would accompany the column.

Forty-five minutes later, Parke was notified that the division of the II Corps ordered to relieve his troops would be led by Brig. Gen. Gershom Mott. According to the latest returns, Mott's division mustered about 5,000 effectives. A staff officer would be sent to guide Mott to the sector where his troops were to take position.[67]

At 9:20 p.m. Meade fired a terse inquiry to General Parke, "How many men will you be able to relieve with Mott's division and send to Warren?"

Parke replied (at 10:00 p.m.) that he proposed to have Mott's bluecoats replace the divisions commanded by Brig. Gen. Robert B. Potter and Orlando B. Willcox in the Petersburg investment line. These two divisions had about 4,000 men in the rifle pits. In addition, if Meade were agreeable, Parke proposed to relieve the fatigue party that was being employed to strengthen the earthworks.[68]

Meanwhile, Meade had notified Parke that General Ord of the XVIII Corps had 1,500 men in reserve that could be utilized. Meade had telegraphed Ord to dispatch these men to Parke. This, in the army commander's opinion, would enable Parke to increase materially the strength of the contingents sent to bolster Warren. Parke was to advise Ord where he was to send the strategic reserve.[69]

Meade (at 10:00 p.m.) handed one of his staff officers a letter addressed to General Warren. Warren was notified that as soon as Mott's troops arrived from Deep Bottom, the V Corps would be reinforced by 5,000 to 6,000 of the IX Corps. Fifteen hundred troops from the IX Corps, who were to be released upon the arrival of Ord's reserve, should report to Warren during the night or early in the morning, Meade added.[70]

After discussing the situation with his staff, Meade learned that it would be 3:00 a.m. before Ord's soldiers would replace Parke's men in the investment line. When the reinforcing column started for Globe Tavern, Parke was to see that it

67 *Ibid.*, 281.

68 *Ibid.*, 282.

69 *Ibid.*, 282, 289.

70 *Ibid.*, 276.

Brigadier General Julius White
Library of Congress

took the shortest route.[71] A courier galloped off to notify General Warren of this development.[72]

Parke (at 10:30 p.m.) advised General Ord that the XVIII Corps soldiers were to relieve Willcox's division. Willcox had from 1,000 to 1,200 troops in the earthworks adjoining Ord's corps on the left. Already, Willcox had been alerted to dispatch an aide to show Ord's officers the rifle pits they were to occupy.[73]

General Warren (at 10:00 p.m.) had written Parke in regard to the route the reinforcing column was to follow. The IX Corps soldiers were to turn off at the Williams house. If it were possible, Warren in the morning proposed to establish and man a picket line linking his right with Parke's left.

Within the hour, Warren's message was in Parke's hands. Replying, Parke announced that he would rush Warren "at least 1,500 men in the morning." At the same time, he would notify General White of Warren's intentions in regard to the picket line. White was also alerted to have his division ready to march to Warren's assistance as soon as relieved by Mott's bluecoats.[74]

Seven hours before, General Meade had moved to increase the strength of the mounted force assigned to cooperate with the V Corps. General Kautz (at 4:00 a.m.) was directed to give Warren a third regiment. Kautz was perplexed by this order. On checking with Col. Samuel P. Spear, one of his brigade commanders, he learned that Warren as yet had only availed himself of a portion of one of the two

71 *Ibid.*, 283.

72 *Ibid.*, 276.

73 *Ibid.*, 290.

74 *Ibid.*, 283-284.

cavalry regiments previously directed to report to him. The 1st District of Columbia had not moved from its camp, while only part of the 3rd New York Cavalry had gone with the V Corps. Nevertheless, orders were orders. Kautz issued instructions placing the 11th Pennsylvania Cavalry at Warren's disposal.[75]

General Beauregard was encouraged by the successes registered by Davis' and Mayo's brigades in the fighting north of Globe Tavern. Upon questioning Union prisoners, Gen. A. P. Hill had been able to identify two divisions of the V Corps. Beauregard, on relaying this information to General Lee, inquired, "Has the V Corps left your front?"[76]

Up to this hour, Heth had not committed Colquitt's troops. Colquitt's Georgians had taken position at Davis'. A diarist reported that as the brigade formed lines of battle, "the Yankees raised a yell and charged some troops [Davis' and Mayo's] in front of ours, but they were repulsed."

About dusk, General Heth, who was in tactical command at the front, reported to Beauregard that his troops had rolled back the Federals for a considerable distance beyond Davis' house. Over 150 prisoners had been taken. When examined, troops belonging to Ayres', Crawford's, and Cutler's divisions were identified. If he could be reinforced, Heth believed, he could continue his sweep. Since he already had all the infantry (three brigades) Beauregard could spare, orders were sent for Heth to disengage his command and retire into the Petersburg earthworks.[77]

Upon pulling back, Heth's troops took cover behind the trenches near the Lead Works, about two and one-half miles north of Warren's position. Part of Heth's troops were held in reserve ready to resist an attack the Confederate generals feared the Federals were about to mount on the eastern approaches to Petersburg. Along toward morning one of Colquitt's Georgians, who had spent the night near the "Iron Bridge," observed, "We did not get to rest much tonight."[78]

Beauregard (at 7:00 p.m.) telegraphed this news to General Lee's headquarters. General Lee upon receipt of this message ordered General "Rooney" Lee's cavalry division to proceed to the south side at once.[79]

---

75 *Ibid.*, 290-291.

76 *Ibid.*, 1187.

77 *Ibid.*, 1187; Dunn, Diary. n.d.

78 Porter, "Operations against the Weldon Railroad, August 18, 19, 21, 1864, 254; Dunn, Diary. n.d.

79 Freeman, *Lee*, vol. 3, 485.

Part II

The Confederates Hammer the V Corps

General Warren, before retiring for the night on August 18, issued instructions that Bragg's brigade be employed to establish and man a picket line connecting his V Corps with Hancock's II Corps. The staff officer entrusted with the delivery of this dispatch reached Bragg's command post at 2:00 a.m. Inside of an hour Bragg had aroused, mustered, formed his brigade, and reported to General Crawford. Crawford directed Bragg to take his command, about 760 strong, and assume a position on the right flank of the Third division and once there await further orders. Crawford sent one of his staff officers, Capt. Walter T. Chester, to guide Bragg's column.[80]

It was daylight before Bragg's brigade reached the extreme right flank of Crawford's division. Before doing anything else, Bragg called for the 1st New York Sharpshooters and a battalion of the 7th Indiana. These troops were sent forward to relieve the 88th Pennsylvania, which had spent a long and miserable night on picket. The left flank of Bragg's line of outposts connected with Hartshorne's brigade, while the right, which rested in the air, was "slightly refused." The remainder of the brigade dug in at a crossroad about 100 yards in rear of the picket line.[81]

Captain Emmor B. Cope of Warren's staff rode up to Crawford's command post about this time. Calling to Crawford, Cope said that Warren wanted Bragg to extend his brigade to the right until contact was established with the IX Corps. Crawford dispatched Captain Chester, who had returned after successfully discharging his previous mission, to assist Cope.[82]

Cope and Chester reached Bragg's headquarters at 7:00 a.m. Bragg was told that beginning at Crawford's picket line, he was to advance skirmishers by the flank toward the northeast until they engaged the foe. The skirmishers would then retire a short distance and "push on by the flank as close [to] the enemy as could be and join the picket of the Ninth Corps."[83]

80 *Ibid.*, 461, 475.

81 *Ibid.*, 535.

82 *Ibid.*, 492, 536, 538. Cope and Chester were accompanied by Lieutenant James P. Mead.

83 *Ibid.*, 536.

Bragg shook his head. He told Cope that it would be very hazardous to "push out" a skirmish line, "not knowing where they were going and what was in their front."

Pointing to the road on which they were standing, Cope asked where the road led.

Bragg replied that he "thought from the general direction it would lead to the Gurley House Road."

"I think from the orders we have," Captain Chester interrupted, "General Warren desires that we shall make our picket-line across the shortest line to connect with the Ninth Corps pickets."

At this, Cope pulled out a map and said he thought the direction ought to be northeast, but he wasn't certain.

Captain Chester, reaching into his pocket, took out another map, and remarked that the connection should be made nearer the Jones' house.

"Well, we will do it." Bragg retorted.

Stepping aside, Bragg called for his regimental commanders to deploy their men as skirmishers and get ready to move. A staff officer was dispatched to see if he could locate the IX Corps' picket line.

While the officers were breakfasting, it was determined that the IX Corps' picket line was posted on a road near Aiken's house, about a mile and one-half to the southeast.

Bragg instructed his troops to move out. Advancing down the road, Bragg's soldiers struck the IX Corps' outposts about 80 rods northeast of Aiken's house. The men of the brigade were deployed along the road to cover a "long train of ambulances."[84]

Accompanied by Captain Chester, General Bragg rode along the IX Corps line as far as the Strong house. Bragg wished to see where he could "make the shortest and most feasible line" if unchecked by the foe. What he saw satisfied Bragg that he would be able to advance the right side of his line to a point nearly opposite the Strong house.

Returning to his command, Bragg gave orders for his brigade, which was deployed as skirmishers, to execute "a left half-wheel." As the troops advanced, those on the left were to maintain contact with Hartshorne's pickets; those on the right were to remain in touch with the IX Corps. As the soldiers of Bragg's brigade prepared to carry out this order, Captain Chester saluted, wheeled his horse about,

84 *Ibid.*, 535, 536, 538-539.

and reported back to Crawford's command post. As Chester rode off, one of the officers noted the time. It was 8:00 a.m.[85]

Bragg's bluecoats had a difficult time beating their way through the dense undergrowth. To make matters worse, a driving rain set in.

General Crawford, about 8:00 a.m., had reconnoitered the area as far as the Strong house. The general, although he didn't see Bragg, expressed satisfaction with the steps taken by the brigade commander to secure a connection with the IX Corps.[86]

Before leaving his command post, Crawford had studied the reports sent in by his three brigade commanders. As soon as it was light enough to see, patrols had been sent forward to feel for the Confederates. On the left, Colonel Lyle's scouts found that during the night the Rebel outposts to their front had pulled back about 300 yards to the center of Davis' cornfield. In advancing to the edge of the woods, the bluecoats passed several dead Rebs and a number of small-arms. The slain were buried, and the small-arms collected and sent to the rear.[87] Wheelock's position on Lyle's right remained unchanged. The pickets were about 150 yards in front of the battle line, and about the same distance from the Confederates' works.[88] Colonel Hartshorne's brigade on the division right had held its ground, within 200 yards of the Rebel outposts.[89] A memorandum containing this information was forwarded to General Warren's headquarters.[90]

Crawford's troops spent the morning of August 19 strengthening their breastworks and slashing timber.

Like Crawford's bluecoats on their right, Ayres' worked to improve their fortifications. To the left of the Weldon Railroad, General Hayes advanced his picket line. The Yanks, as they pressed ahead, reached the southern edge of Davis' cornfield, in advance of the ground secured by Lyle's skirmishers on their right. In doing so, they counted about 50 Confederate dead. A number of Union casualties (dead and wounded) from the previous afternoon's fighting were recovered and

---

85 *Ibid.*, 535, 536, 538-539. This road ran from a point on the Halifax Road, about three-quarters of a mile north of Davis', in a southeasterly direction toward the Aiken house, and entered the Johnson Road, one-half mile north of Aiken's dwelling.

86 *Ibid.*, 492.

87 *Ibid.*, 504; OR, 42, pt. 2, 313-314.

88 *OR* 42, pt. 2, 314.

89 *Ibid.*, 313.

90 *Ibid.*, 314.

removed. The injured Yanks reported that the Johnnies were feeling their way toward the Union left.[91]

General Warren reasonably interpreted the intelligence regarding the Confederates leaving their dead on the field as evidence that the enemy was withdrawing into the Petersburg defenses. To check out this theory, Warren issued instructions for Ayres and Crawford to make a forced reconnaissance to their fronts.[92]

The men of General Griffin's division, except those manning the picket line, were kept busy erecting breastworks on the 19th. Fatigue parties were sent forward by the brigade commanders to fell timber.[93]

Colonel Spear, who had arrived on the railroad during the night, had moved out about daybreak. Advancing southward down the Weldon Railroad, Spear's cavalrymen compelled the Confederate vedettes to retire to within a mile or so of Ream's Station. After establishing a strong roadblock at Crowder's, Spear received instructions to deploy his Federal troopers in a way to guard the left and rear of Warren's V Corps. Spear discharged this mission by employing the remainder of his brigade to patrol the roads west of the Weldon Railroad from White's to Crowder's.[94]

*   *   *

It was after 2:00 a.m. when the troops from the XVIII Corps reached the sector in front of the Crater and began relieving Willcox's division of Burnside's IX Corps. Several of Willcox's units were exposed to a severe fire from Confederate artillery and sharpshooters while they assembled behind the line. By 3:30 a.m. Willcox was notified by his brigade commanders that the soldiers had been supplied with the stipulated rations and units of fire. So informed, Willcox gave the word and the column moved out. Marching by way of Gurley's house, the division reached Globe Tavern about 7:30 a.m., where Willcox reported to Warren. In accordance with instructions from Warren, Willcox camped his men in the field east of Globe Tavern.[95]

91 Ibid., 313.

92 Ibid., 311-312, 313.

93 OR 42, pt. 1, 461, 463, 464, 465, 467.

94 OR 42, pt. 2, 305.

95 Ibid., 305; OR 42, pt. 1, 589, 593, 595, 596.

Meanwhile, General Mott had arrived at Parke's headquarters. General Meade, upon being notified that Mott had showed up, telegraphed General Parke, "How many men will you be able to relieve with Mott's division and send to Warren?"[96]

Parke, after studying his returns, concluded that he would be able to relieve Potter's and White's divisions, about 4,000 bayonets. He would be able to replace White's troops at once, Parke informed Meade, but he might encounter difficulty in pulling Potter's division out of the works, because of deep puddles of water in the covered way which compelled the troops to expose themselves in passing to and fro.[97]

It was 2:00 p.m. before the last of General White's troops had been relieved in the rifle pits by Colonel John Pulford's brigade of Mott's division. Prior to starting for Globe Tavern, General White marshaled his division near Jones' house.[98]

Soldiers in White's division, as they waited in ranks, recalled August 19 as "a day of drizzle, with mud deep and slippery in the fields."[99]

General Warren (at 11:00 a.m.) had written Parke that Bragg's picket line had established contact with outposts of the IX Corps at the Strong house. At the moment, Warren added, Bragg's troops were being advanced so as to connect with the IX Corps at the "most western point."[100]

Seventy-five minutes elapsed before Parke received Warren's message. Upon doing so, he relayed the communication to General White. In a covering memorandum, Parke pointed out that the Strong house was a short distance southwest of Jones' dwelling. This being the case, it would enable White or his replacement materially to contract his line. White or his replacement was to advance his left flank in conjunction with General Bragg, preserving the alignment and connection with the right. Parke cautioned, "Please be on the lookout for any movement of the enemy."[101]

96 OR 42, pt. 2, 315.

97 Ibid., 215-216.

98 OR 42, pt. 1, 557. At 10:30 Parke had inquired of army headquarters, "Shall I order . . . [Potter's and White's divisions] to move to Warren as soon as relieved without further orders." OR, 42, pt. 2, 316. Acknowledging Parke's telegram at 10:50, Chief of Staff Humphreys observed, "Potter and White should move to Warren as soon as relieved, without waiting the one for the other or for further orders." Ibid., 316.

99 Committee of the Regiment, History of the Thirty-Fifth Regiment Massachusetts Volunteers, 1862-1865 (Boston, 1884), 285.

100 OR 42, pt. 2, 319.

101 Ibid., 319.

Prior to General White giving the command to move out, one of Warren's aides galloped up to Jones' and handed White a slip of paper. Glancing at the order, White found that he was to march his division to Globe Tavern "by the most direct route, and camp for the present near General Willcox . . ."[102]

When the division hit the road at 3:00 p.m., the 1st brigade (Lt. Colonel Joseph H. Barnes commanding) took the lead. The division artillery was left to support Pulford's II Corps troops. White's column tramped along the Jerusalem Plank Road, turned to the left near Williams' house, and took the "right-hand" road. Because of the rain, the secondary roads of Prince George County were very bad; progress was agonizingly slow. It was 5:00 p.m. before the head of the column reached Aiken's house. Shortly thereafter, the rattle of musketry was heard to the right and front. Reining up his horse, White sent an aide galloping ahead to see where Warren wanted him to deploy his division. At the same time, the brigade commanders were ordered to move their units at the double-quick toward the sound of the guns.[103]

General Grant, at 8:50 a.m., from his City Point headquarters, telegraphed Meade that Hancock "by detaining a large force north of the James, makes our force at Petersburg relatively as strong as it would be if he was with it." It seemed to Grant that the Confederates were very sensitive to any thrust toward Chaffin's Bluff. Since Grant was anxious to compel the Rebels to withdraw from the valley the troops recently sent to bolster General Early, he believed it best if the Federals continued "to threaten as long a line as possible."[104]

At 10:45 a.m. General Meade's headquarters forwarded a copy of Grant's 8:50 a.m. dispatch to Warren. In a covering letter, Chief of Staff Humphreys pointed out that in addition to Willcox's 2,000 men, another 4,000 soldiers from the IX Corps would reach the V Corps during the day. Meade wanted to know if Warren considered these reinforcements sufficient to maintain his grip on the Weldon Railroad, and if practicable to extend his right flank to connect with the IX Corps. If possible, Warren, to shorten his lines, was to push back the Southerners toward the Lead Works.[105]

Warren (at 11:00 a.m.) telegraphed Chief of Staff Humphreys that with the additional 4,000 troops, he would be able to maintain his hold on the railroad.

---

102 *Ibid.*, 320.

103 OR 42, pt. 1, 550, 557; Committee, *History of the Thirty-fifth regiment Massachusetts Volunteers*, 285.

104 *OR* 42, pt. 2, 293.

105 *Ibid.*, 305-306.

Warren advised headquarters of his successful effort to establish contact with the IX Corps. Except for the denseness of the woods, Bragg's skirmishers had encountered no difficulty in beating their way ahead.

The reports brought in by his scouts, Warren observed, indicated that the Confederates had withdrawn their main force inside the Petersburg perimeter, "leaving a thin line in his entrenchments here." Because of the wet weather, Griffin's fatigue parties were having trouble burning the ties to heat and bend the rails. For the time being at least, the destruction of the railroad looked unpromising, Warren added.

Since Humphreys was out of the office, General Meade replied to Warren's telegram. As the decision had been made to maintain a grip on the railroad, its destruction had now become a matter of secondary importance. Because of the flooded covered ways, there would be "some delay in relieving" Potter's division of Parke's corps. "I am now on my way to visit you," Meade observed.[106]

*   *   *

Upon being notified by General Beauregard that the V Corps was astride the Weldon Railroad at Globe Tavern, General Lee returned Maj. Gen. William Mahone and the units of his division, which had accompanied him north of the James to Petersburg.[107]

By 8:00 a.m. on the 19th, Beauregard had learned from his scouts that the "three divisions of the enemy" that had been "repulsed" at Davis' farm were digging in on the railroad. Contacting General Lee, Beauregard announced that he would endeavor to dislodge these Federals with the four brigades of infantry and division of cavalry which Lee had promised to send him. The result would be more certain, Beauregard observed, if he had more infantry. To make matters worse, men manning one of the Confederate signal stations had spotted one of Mott's brigades as it marched southward on the military road in rear of Battery No. 5.[108]

A Union captain, captured in the fighting at Davis' farm, was questioned closely by the Confederates. The Yank told the Rebels that Warren's objective was to break the Weldon Railroad and compel the Southerners to disperse their strength. As soon as the Confederates rushed troops to cope with the lodgment on the railroad, the Federal generals would launch a blow at some other point. This

---

106 *Ibid.*, 306.

107 Humphreys, *Virginia Campaign of '64 and '65*, 275.

108 *OR* 42, pt. 1, 858.

placed Beauregard in a quandary. If he guessed wrong and stripped the Petersburg defenses of manpower to assail Warren and the bluecoats struck at some other point, disaster could result.[109]

Despite the dangers, Beauregard decided to gamble. General A. P. Hill was called in and placed in charge of the attacking force—five infantry brigades. Hill quickly organized his striking force into two divisions. General Heth would have Davis' and Mayo's brigades; Mahone would employ the brigades led by Brig. Gen. Alfred H. Colquitt and Thomas L. Clingman, and Col. David A. Weisiger. Lieutenant Colonel William Pegram was assigned three batteries to support Hill's infantry.

About noon, Col. David A. Weisiger received instructions from General Mahone to pull his brigade out of the lines. The brigades posted to the right and left of Weisiger's Virginians extended their flanks to close the gap. To conceal their departure from the people manning the Union lookout stations, the unit commanders led their men back through a ravine which debouched into Lieutenant Run. Passing by Mahone's headquarters, the column marched to the Johnson Road, where Weisiger reported to General Mahone.[110]

Moving out of the Petersburg defenses, Heth's column marched down the Halifax Road to the Vaughan Road intersection. According to Hill's battle plan, Heth's division was to launch a frontal attack on Ayres. The cannoneers who accompanied Heth's troops unlimbered six of their guns west of the Halifax Road near Davis' house, and two pieces west of the railroad. General Mahone's column tramped down the Johnson Road. Mahone, who was familiar with the area, planned to advance through the pines, breakthrough Bragg's skirmish line, wheel to the right, and roll up Crawford's division.[111]

It was shortly after 10:00 a.m., when General Warren learned that Crawford's command had established contact with the IX Corps pickets, one-fourth mile northeast of Aiken's house.[112] Warren, on studying his maps and discussing the situation with Maj. Washington A. Roebling, was disturbed to learn that the connection wasn't where he wanted it. Writing Crawford, Warren (at 10:15 a.m.) explained that Bragg's skirmish line should extend in a northeast not a southeast direction from the right flank of Hartshorne's brigade. Such a shift, in Warren's

---

109   *OR* 42, pt. 2, 1190.

110   *OR* 42, pt. 1, 858, 940; Sale, Diary. n.d.

111   Humphreys, *Virginia Campaign of '64 and '65*, 275; Porter, "Operations Against the Weldon Railroad, August 18, 19, 21, 1864," 254-255; Sale, Diary. n.d.

112   *OR* 42, pt. 2, 314.

opinion, would enable Bragg's bluecoats to watch the Petersburg defenses, while at the same time it wouldn't require half as many soldiers to hold. In rectifying his line, Bragg was to supervise its movements personally.[113]

Meanwhile, General Crawford had left his command post and had ridden over to inspect Bragg's right flank to satisfy himself that "it was properly established." About the time that Crawford reached Col. James Carle's command post (Carle commanded Hartshorne's right flank regiment [the 191st Pennsylvania] which connected with Bragg's skirmish line), he was hailed by Major Roebling. The major handed Crawford a copy of Warren's 10:15 a.m. message. Accompanied by Roebling, Crawford advanced to the vicinity of Davis' cornfield. Two trees were pointed out to Crawford by Roebling. He told the general that Bragg's skirmishers were to be pushed forward to the edge of the cornfield, and from the trees indicated the picket line was to run due east.

From what he saw, Crawford was satisfied that Bragg was endeavoring to advance his line as ordered. Nevertheless, Crawford decided it might be wise to confer with Bragg. As he rode eastward, the division commander passed along the front. Crawford was distressed on reaching Strong's house at not finding any of Bragg's soldiers.

A glance at the badge worn by the soldiers posted in the rifle pits in front of the Strong house told Crawford that they belonged to the II Corps. When he asked to whose unit they belonged, one of the officers replied, Pulford's brigade, Mott's division. The II Corps officer explained to Crawford that soldiers from Pulford's brigade had relieved White's division a short time before. Captain Chester was sent racing off to find the officer in charge of Bragg's skirmishers and tell him to advance his men.

Crawford now prepared to return to his command post. On doing so, he decided not to retrace his steps. He took the road along which White's division of the IX Corps was marching to Globe Tavern. As the general and his staff jogged along, they passed White's mud-spattered columns.[114]

It was about 2:00 p.m. when Captain Chester located Bragg's right flank unit—the 7th Wisconsin—in the woods west of the Strong house.[115]

General Bragg, in the meantime, had encountered Major Roebling. The major, who had left General Crawford at the Strong house, told Bragg to advance his skirmish line across Davis' cornfield to the two trees. Bragg was aghast. He told

113 *Ibid.*, 314-315.

114 *OR* 42, pt. 1, 492-493, 538.

115 *Ibid.*, 538.

Roebling that he feared if his troops carried out such a movement, they would goad the Rebels into attacking. After having registered his protest, Bragg relayed Roebling's instructions to his regimental commanders.

Bragg's skirmishers found the going difficult as they beat their way toward the cornfield. As if the thick underbrush wasn't bad enough, the rain continued to beat down. While his soldiers were moving through the pines, Bragg, accompanied by Lt. James P. Mead and two other staff officers, rode to the left of the brigade to see "if any change in the point of connection with the line of Colonel Hartshorne was desirable."[116]

While Bragg and his companions were talking with Colonel Hartshorne, several shots were heard off to the east. The firing increased rapidly in intensity and soon became very heavy. After listening a moment, Bragg put his spurs to his horse and hastened toward the apparent point of danger—the left center of his brigade. As he did, he issued orders for his reserve regiment, the 6th Wisconsin, to march to the sound of the guns. The 6th Wisconsin, 74 men in all, followed the general as he rode to the right.[117]

General Mahone's division had advanced to the attack in column of fours, left in front. The hard-driving Confederates struck and overran the section of Bragg's skirmish line held by the 19th Indiana. Mahone's cheering grey clads had reached the open field near the old mill by the time Bragg arrived at the head of the panting soldiers of the 6th Wisconsin. At a word from Bragg, the bluecoats from Wisconsin took cover in the woods fronting the field and sniped at the oncoming Southerners. Assisted by the staff officers, Bragg sought to rally the panic-stricken Indianans.

Bragg within a few minutes received additional bad news. After crashing through Bragg's skirmishers, Mahone wheeled most of his troops to the right. As they pressed westward along Bragg's line, the Confederates cut off and captured the 1st Battalion New York Sharpshooters and a detachment of the 7th Indiana. One of Bragg's regimental commanders, Lt. Col. Albert M. Edwards of the 24th Michigan, succeeded in extricating his men. Abandoning their position, the Michiganders retreated toward the Aiken house, capturing 12 prisoners en route.

The unit to the right of Mahone's breakthrough (the 7th Wisconsin) was joined by a number of stragglers from the 19th Indiana. Captain Chester galloped up at this time. Lieutenant Colonel Mark Finnicum of the 7th Wisconsin told Chester that Bragg's line to his left had been broken, and that he expected an attack at any moment. Chester informed Finnicum of the location of the breastworks occupied

116 *Ibid.,* 539.

117 *Ibid.,* 535, 539-540.

by Pulford's brigade. Moreover, he suggested that if the 7th Wisconsin were pressed too hard or flanked, Finnicum had better withdraw his command behind the fortifications. Finnicum took Chester's advice. His regiment, accompanied by a number of the Indianans, joined Pulford's II Corps troops behind the Strong house earthworks.[118]

The badly outnumbered 6th Wisconsin was unable to hold its ground in the face of Mahone's onslaught. Fighting a delaying action, the regiment pulled back. The soldiers from Wisconsin were deployed into line by General Bragg several times during the retreat. Although overpowered, they twice compelled the Confederates to halt and reform.[119]

Before General Crawford reached his headquarters, he encountered several badly frightened men from the 19th Indiana. Crawford demanded to know why they had left the front. The Hoosiers replied that they had been driven back by the Rebels, and wondered why the general had not heard the firing. Calling to a lieutenant who seemed to be in charge, the general directed him to regroup his troops and return to the front. Not knowing that Bragg had already attended to the matter, Crawford sent an aide galloping with instructions for the brigade commander to use his reserve (the 6th Wisconsin) to recapture the ground that had been lost by the 19th Indiana.

Continuing on his way, Crawford observed that the roar of battle was rapidly extending westward along the front of his division. By the time Crawford reached his command post, he learned that the Confederates had engulfed Bragg's brigade, stormed across the road leading from his headquarters to Aiken's, and were changing front preparatory to moving against his right flank. Now, to make matters even worse, another Confederate force, Harry Heth's division, launched a frontal assault.[120]

*   *   *

Several hours before William Mahone's troops overpowered the 19th Indiana, a strong force of Rebel skirmishers advanced across Davis' cornfield and into the pines beyond. These grey clads assailed the line of outposts held by the 190th and

---

118 *Ibid.*, 536, 538. As the afternoon progressed, a number of Confederate stragglers (two officers and 25 enlisted men) were captured by Pulford's pickets. OR 42, pt. 2, 317; Dunn, Diary. n.d.

119 OR 42, pt. 1, 536, 540. In this fighting, the 6th Wisconsin lost one-third of its men.

120 *Ibid.*, 493.

191st Pennsylvania of Hartshorne's brigade. After a brisk exchange, the Rebs retired.[121]

General Ayres heard this "picket-firing" to his right. It had ceased at 1:10 p.m., when Ayres wrote General Warren. Not knowing that the butternuts were getting ready to mount an attack, Ayres notified corps headquarters that the "picket-firing" had been suspended to allow time for both sides to bury their dead from the previous afternoon's fighting. According to the latest information brought back by his scouts, Ayres reported, the Southerners' battle line was in the pines north of Davis' cornfield.[122]

About the time that Mahone's troops struck Bragg's skirmishers, General Hayes, who commanded Ayres' right flank unit, received a report from his pickets that a strong Confederate column had crossed to the west side of the Weldon Railroad. Colonel Lyle's brigade of Crawford's division at the same time had shifted to the right.[123] This movement to the east on Lyle's part had been occasioned when Colonel Hartshorne had recalled his pickets, contracted his line to the right, and put his Pennsylvanians to work entrenching. With Hartshorne's brigade holding a reduced sector, Crawford's center brigade (Wheelock's) closed to the right several hundred yards. As soon as they had adjusted their lines, the officers turned their men to throwing up breastworks.[124]

It was about 2:00 p.m. when Lyle's bluecoats moved off by the right flank and occupied the rifle pits vacated by Wheelock's troops.[125] To hold the fortifications abandoned by Lyle's brigade, General Hayes called up the 12th and 14th U.S. Infantry. The 12th U.S. on the right anchored its flank on Lyle's unit, while the 14th U.S. Infantry rested its left on the railroad.[126]

General Heth's battle lines (Mayo's brigade on the left and Davis' on the right) were sighted by Ayres' scouts as they crossed Davis' cornfield. Driving the Federal outposts before them, the butternuts pressed into the woods beyond. West of the railroad, Davis' Mississippians and North Carolinians engaged the 4th Delaware, which had been deployed as skirmishers and pushed forward by Colonel Hofmann. The bluecoats retired slowly, making three stands behind crude field works. Unable

121 *Ibid.*, 492.

122 *OR* 42, pt. 2, 312.

123 *Ibid.*, 313.

124 *OR* 42, pt. 1, 510, 515, 517, 518, 522.

125 *Ibid.*, 504.

126 *Ibid.*, 479; *OR* 42, pt. 2, 313.

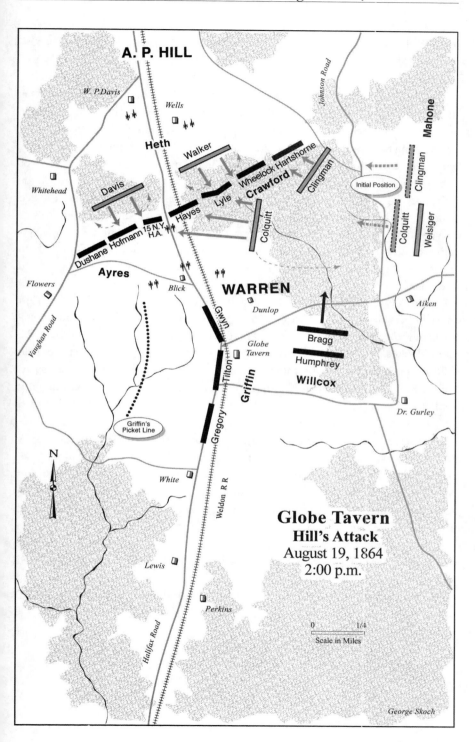

Globe Tavern
Hill's Attack
August 19, 1864
2:00 p.m.

0   1/4
Scale in Miles

George Skoch

to check Davis' grim fighters, the Delaware regiment rejoined the brigade behind the breastworks.[127] East of the railroad, Mayo's grey clads drove back Hayes' pickets.

On General Hayes' right, the soldiers of Lyle's brigade had been warned by their scouts that a strong force of Johnnies (Heth's division) was being marshaled in line of battle to their front. Whereupon, the men ceased talking, snatched up their entrenching tools, and started strengthening their rifle pits. Although it was raining very hard, the rattle of musketry came rolling in from the right as Mahone's troops overpowered Bragg's skirmish line. As the minutes passed, the roar of battle on the right grew in volume and seemed to be coming closer. Lyle's troops crouched behind their breastworks. The pickets to their front now began to pepper away as Mayo's battle line rolled forward. After getting off a few rounds, the pickets retreated and took refuge alongside their comrades in the rifle pits. Close behind the retreating bluecoats came Mayo's cheering Alabamans, Tennesseans, and Virginians.

Heth's Confederate division assailed the sector of the Union line held from left to right by Hofmann's, Hayes', and Lyle's brigades. The Confederate attack appeared to center on Lyle's troops. Three times Lyle's bluecoats hurled back the Confederates. Taking cover, within 30 yards of the rifle pits, the butternuts held their ground. Undaunted by the rain, the men in blue and in grey blazed away. Although Heth's outnumbered command had failed to score a breakthrough, it kept the Federals pinned in their rifle pits, while Mahone's division rolled over Bragg's bluecoats and wheeled to the right.[128]

General Crawford reached his command post in rear of Lyle's brigade, just as Heth's troops charged across Davis' cornfield. By this time, Mahone had completed his dispositions. Confederate sharpshooters infiltrated the cornfield and woods in front of Wheelock's and Hartshorne's brigades. These daring marksmen kept the Yanks ducking. Suddenly, without warning, Mahone's troops burst through the dark and dismal woods to the right and rear of Hartshorne's brigade. Within a matter of minutes, the 190th and 191st Pennsylvania had been surrounded. After a "short but determined fight," the Pennsylvanians destroyed their repeating rifles which had been issued to them several days before by breaking their stocks against trees and surrendered. General Mahone detached a small detail

---

127 *OR* 42, pt. 1, 484, 485; OR, 42, pt. 2, 313; Porter, "Operations Against the Weldon Railroad, August 18, 19, 21, 1864," 256. The 190th and 191st Pennsylvania consisted of men from the Pennsylvania Reserves who had reenlisted, when their original terms of service had expired.

128 *OR* 42, pt. 1, 471, 474, 484, 504; Brainard, *Campaigns of the 146th Regiment*, 239.

to roundup the prisoners and hurled his troops against the next Federal unit, Wheelock's brigade.[129] The first intimation that Wheelock's people had of the enemy being in their rear was the unexpected appearance of a squad of Confederates, led by a hatless and excited officer, coming directly through the woods from a direction that every man in the 88th [Pennsylvania] was fully convinced was the rear. They were immediately halted and ordered to surrender, but decidedly objected, explaining that we were the ones to surrender, as they had us surrounded; this story was not credited and, taking the officer's sword, Sgt. John Wallace, with an escort, proceeded with the prisoners back through the woods, when they ran into a moving column of the enemy and were in turn captured and run Dixie-ward without further ceremony.[130]

The pines in which Hartshorne's brigade had been overpowered were so dense that the Union troops marshaled near Globe Tavern were unable to see what was happening. A short time before the Rebels struck, the V Corps butchers had been slaughtering cattle at the edge of the woods. General Warren and Colonel Wainwright had ridden out to the Dunlop house and looked for the Confederate advance, but nothing was discernable. After a short time, the sounds from the woods and the appearance of a column of troops, convinced Colonel Wainwright that the Rebels were sending a force through the woods to fall upon Crawford's Third division. The Union artillery now roared into action. Throughout the morning and well into the afternoon, the Federals' guns, which were unlimbered in a line about 600 yards behind Warren's main line of resistance, had remained silent. From his vantage point at Globe Tavern, Colonel Wainwright saw Heth's battle lines as they advanced across Davis' cornfield. Confederate cannoneers supported this attack with a sharp bombardment from the two batteries they had emplaced in the opening at Davis' house. Wainwright's spotters correctly reported that the Rebels had eight guns. Word now reached Wainwright that Mahone's troops had broken through Bragg's skirmish line. Wainwright called for his battery captains to commence firing. At first, the Yanks concentrated on the Reb artillerists. A slow, deliberate fire was maintained. Within a short time, the Confederates ceased firing.

Wainwright now sighted the left flank brigade (Colquitt's) of Mahone's battle line as it debouched from the woods. The Johnnies, showing one battle flag, moved across the open ground in front of the Union batteries toward the railroad. Up to this moment, only a few of Crawford's bluecoats had come out of the woods.

129 OR 42, pt. 1, 493-494; Porter, "Operations Against the Weldon Railroad, August 18, 19, 21, 1864," 256-257, 259-260.

130 John D. Vautier, *History of the 88th Pennsylvania Volunteers in the War for the Union, 1861-1865* (Philadelphia, 1894), 197.

Wainwright recalled that on the previous evening, General Warren had told him that in case of emergency, the Union infantry would retire by the flanks, thereby unmasking the fire of the batteries. Since the foe was within 400 yards of his guns, Wainwright, after studying the situation, decided that Crawford's division was retreating westward across the railroad. Wainwright ordered his captains to turn their guns on the woods east of the railroad.[131]

The shells crashed into the timber and exploded, causing consternation to friend and foe. Projectiles smashed into the breastworks behind which Lyle's and Wheelock's troops crouched "killing some officers and men and wounding many others." As if this weren't bad enough, Mahone's sharpshooters had infiltrated the woods between the rifle pits and the field in which Wainwright's artillery was emplaced. The cry, "The enemy is in our rear!" was raised. Troops on the left of Lyle's brigade began to melt away; they were quickly joined by the rest of the unit. A number of men panicked. Several of the regimental commanders, such as hard-bitten Colonel Tilden of the 16th Maine, kept a tight rein on their men. As they fell back, a number of men were cut down by shot and shell from Wainwright's artillery which continued to hammer the woods.

Before the Federals reached the field, Mahone's battle line was encountered. Striking swiftly, the Rebs had cut off Lyle's line of retreat. Seeing that they were all but surrounded, most of the officers and men of Lyle's brigade grounded their arms. Before giving up, Colonel Tilden saw that the national colors carried by his regiment were destroyed. In the confusion which accompanied the capture of his brigade, Colonel Lyle, although compelled to abandon his horse, escaped.[132]

Upon reaching Globe Tavern, Colonel Lyle rallied and reformed the remnant of his brigade.[133]

The retreat of Lyle's brigade had left Wheelock's troops in an embarrassing situation. All the while, Wainwright's artillery continued to pound the woods "with great accuracy," many of the projectiles crashing into the works. To add to Wheelock's problems, one of Crawford's staff officers galloped up and excitedly directed his left flank regiment, the 97th New York, to follow Lyle's troops.

---

131 Porter, "Operations Against the Weldon Railroad, August 18, 19, 21, 1864," 256; OR 42, pt. 1, 541.

132 *Ibid.*, 504, 508-509. Altogether the Confederates captured 33 officers and 721 enlisted men of Lyle's brigade. Among the field officers captured and taken to Petersburg were Col. G. G. Prey of the 104th New York, Col. C. W. Tilden of the 16th Maine, Lt. Col. J. R. Strang of the 104th New York, Lt. Colonel William A. Leach and Maj. Jacob M. Davis of the 90th Pennsylvania. The "State colors" of the 16th Maine fall into Confederate hands.

133 *Ibid.*, 505.

Wheelock observing what was happening, rode to the left, and succeeded in preventing any other units from following the 97th.[134]

Realizing that the artillery was playing havoc with his command, Wheelock shouted for the troops to leap the breastworks and take cover on the opposite side. Hardly had the men taken position before a strong force of Mahone's grey clads appeared to their front. The officer in charge called for the Yanks to surrender. Wheelock refused. Instead, he bellowed for his men to fire. Several volleys proved sufficient to turn the tide in this sector.

The Confederates now found themselves in a ticklish situation. Besides being exposed to the small-arms' fire of Wheelock's troops, they were harassed by the projectiles from Wainwright's artillery. The grey clads soon gave way. Many of them, along with 13 Yanks whom they had captured, took cover alongside Wheelock's troops in the rifle pits. After the Rebels had been disarmed, Wheelock ordered out his right flank units in an effort to cut off the Johnnies' retreat. His men were too slow. The Yanks soon returned to the works with several prisoners and a stand of colors. Wheelock, realizing that he was surrounded, cautioned his men to remain where they were.[135]

Wheelock and his men stayed where they were until the Confederates had disappeared. All was now quiet in the area except for the explosion of the shells from Wainwright's artillery. To avoid these projectiles, Wheelock decided to pull his men out of the rifle pits. Moving cautiously through the pines, the brigade gained the open field north of Globe Tavern without further adventure. As soon as he saw Wheelock, General Crawford had him reform his brigade. Having reorganized Lyle's shattered command, the general ordered Lyle to take post on Wheelock's left.[136]

The collapse of Lyle's command and the retreat of Wheelock's exposed the right flank of Hayes' brigade. Up to this time, Hayes' bluecoats had been more than holding their own against the slashing frontal attacks delivered by Heth's grey clads. Earlier, Hayes had sent orders for his two regiments, the 12th and 14th U.S., posted east of the railroad to hold their ground at all hazards. After smashing Lyle's brigade, Mahone's troops, spearheaded by Colquitt's Georgians, drove against the rifle pits held by the Regulars. Observing that their commands were all but

---

134 *Ibid.*, 510, 517. The 97th New York succeeded in reaching the open field in which Wainwright had emplaced his guns "with but little confusion, though with a considerable loss." *Ibid.*, 571.

135 *Ibid.*, 493, 510, 515, 518, 520-521, 522; Powell, *History of the Fifth Corps*, 714.

136 *OR* 42, pt. 1, 494, 510.

encircled, the regimental commanders shouted for their men to withdraw. Before they had gone very far, the Regulars discovered, much to their dismay, that a strong force of Southerners had driven across their line of retreat. The Regulars sought to cut their way through. Some succeeded, but a large number were taken prisoner.

General Hayes was shocked to learn that his two regiments posted east of the railroad were encircled. Accompanied by his assistant adjutant general, Lt. George K. Brady, the general tried to reach the isolated units. Hayes and his aide found themselves engulfed in a surging Rebel tide. Seeing that escape was impossible, Hayes and Brady surrendered themselves, their swords, side-arms, and horses to Sgt. Richard H. Powell of Company C, 6th Georgia. Powell proudly escorted the two officers to General Colquitt's command post.

Meanwhile, Maj. James M. Culpepper of the 6th Georgia had placed himself at the head of 50 men. Culpepper and his Georgians dashed forward and captured a large number of Hayes' troops. The Yanks soon saw how few their captors there were. Taking advantage of the fluid nature of the fighting, the bluecoats endeavored to turn the scales by capturing Culpepper. The major, however, succeeded in escaping with most of his men and a few prisoners.[137]

To keep the remaining regiments of Hayes' brigade from being enveloped and destroyed, General Ayres ordered a retreat. Accompanied by soldiers of the 15th New York Heavy Artillery, the 5th, 140th, and 146th New York, and the 10th, 11th, and 17th U.S. Infantry abandoned the breastworks and fell back about 700 yards. General Ayres, upon being notified that Hayes was missing, placed Col. Frederick Winthrop of the 5th New York in charge of the brigade. Winthrop, aided by Ayres and the regimental commanders, reformed the brigade on the rising ground behind Wainwright's Artillery.[138]

Colonel Hofmann's troops, posted in the rifle pits to the left of the 15th New York Heavy Artillery, were able to hold their own. Undoubtedly, they (like the troops to their right) would have been enveloped but for the presence of General Willcox's division of the IX Corps. General Mahone, on sighting a battle line in the field near Globe Tavern, sent word for his heretofore victorious troops not to cross the railroad.

Meanwhile, Colonel Wainwright had watched with deep interest as his batteries shelled the woods east of the Weldon Railroad. Soon after the guns had growled into action, the Confederates (Colquitt's Georgians) who were sweeping

---

137 *Ibid.*, 472, 474, 479; Wendell D. Croom, *The War History of Company "C", (Beauregard Volunteers) Sixth Georgia Regiment, (Infantry)* (Fort Valley, 1879), 25-26; Dunn, Diary. n.d.

138 OR 42, pt. 1, 472, 474; Powell, *History of the Fifth Corps*, 714; Brainard, *Campaigns of the 146th Regiment*, 239.

across the fields south of the pines and parallel to the batteries took to their heels. The retreating Confederate soldiers were followed by several hundred Federals. Shortly thereafter, Wainwright learned that the attacking Confederate columns were between his artillery and Crawford's main line of resistance. Although the damage had already been done, Wainwright called for his gun captains to hold their fire.[139]

*   *   *

General Willcox had had the "long roll" beaten as the firing to his front and right increased in intensity. The troops fell out under arms on the double. The division was formed in double line of battle about 800 yards in rear of Crawford's earthworks. The left flank of Brig. Gen. John F. Hartranft's brigade rested about 400 yards east of the railroad. Before very long it was evident to Willcox and his bluecoats that the V Corps was getting the worst of the fighting. Large numbers of stragglers began to make their way to the rear.

Willcox soon learned that Crawford's division was in full retreat before the victorious Confederates. At this, Willcox ordered Hartranft's brigade (1,100 strong) forward to Crawford's succor. With a loud cheer for the Union, Hartranft's soldiers stormed forward. Confederate officers saw the fresh battle line approaching out of the gloom and mist. Recalling his men, Mahone massed them in line of battle in the cornfield at the southern edge of the pines from which they had driven Crawford's soldiers.[140]

The left four regiments of Hartranft's Federal battle line charged across an open field, while the three right regiments were screened by a copse of woods east of the cornfield. After the four regiments on the left were engaged, the right of the brigade drove deeper into the woods, where they were soon counterattacked. The Yankees more than held their own, and the Rebels were hurled back, leaving between 50 and 60 prisoners in the Federals' hands. At the same time, Hartranft's left flank units (the 27th Michigan, 109th New York, 51st Pennsylvania, and 8th Michigan) had cleared the grey clads from the cornfield. Hartranft's left wing sought to follow the retreating Southerners into the pines. Before the Yanks reached the timber, the Johnnies rallied and charged. Halting, the bluecoats sent several well-aimed volleys at a range of 75 yards crashing into the onrushing battle

139   OR 42, pt. 1, 541.

140   *Ibid.*, 589, 593. From right to left Hartranft's battle line was formed: the 37th and 38th Wisconsin, 13th Ohio Cavalry (dismounted), 27th Michigan, 109th New York, 51st Pennsylvania, and 8th Michigan.

line. This blunted the counterthrust. Mahone's fighters retired back into the woods.[141]

Colonel William Humphrey's brigade of Willcox's division had marched in support of Hartranft's battle line. Following the repulse of William Mahone's second Confederate counterstroke, one of General Warren's aides hailed Willcox. Warren, the staff officer crisply announced, wanted Willcox to rush Humphrey's brigade to the left to recapture the rifle pits flanking the Weldon Railroad from which General Ayres' division had just been routed. When he relayed these orders to Colonel Humphrey, Willcox directed him to make his attack in double line of battle.[142]

Humphrey accordingly faced his brigade to the west. As soon as his right flank had passed beyond Hartranft's left, Humphrey halted his troops, faced them to the right, and formed his brigade as directed.[143]

By this time, General White's division of the IX Corps had arrived on the field. White, taking account of the firing which seemed to be getting steadily nearer, formed his division into line of battle, the right flank of his lead brigade (Barnes') rested on a country road.[144] The staff officer sent racing ahead to contact Warren returned with instructions: White was to connect his left with the right flank of Willcox's division. To accomplish this, White marched his division by the left flank.[145]

As the regimental historians of the 35th Massachusetts recalled:

> We came out into wide cornfields with woods to the north-west and south-east, and, hearing musketry, the double-quick step was taken, and a series of hurried but well executed field movements ensued. We came by flank, into line of battle and went forward over fences toward the western woods, the regiments keeping their lines remarkably well, then halted and wheeled about in retreat a few rods, then fronting moved more to the left and again forward, all in accordance with orders from General White, who appeared on horseback in front of the regiment, waving his light felt hat

---

141   *Ibid.*, 593.

142   *Ibid.*, 590, 595.

143   *Ibid.*, 590, 593, 595.

144   *Ibid.*, pp, 550, 557. From left to right Barnes' brigade was formed as follows: the 59th and 57th Massachusetts, the 100th Pennsylvania, and the 21st, 35th, 56th, and 29th Massachusetts regiments.

145   *Ibid.*, 550, 557.

and calling upon the men to remember Campbell's Station and Knoxville, at which the boys cheered vociferously. It was the most inspiring scene for many a day.[146]

Before White's division came up, however, Hartranft was directed to close to his left and seal the gap which had opened between his brigade and Humphrey's. Skirting the pines to their front, Hartranft's bluecoats shifted about a brigade front to the left. Before Hartranft's troops could get into position, Humphrey's had disappeared into the timber on either side of the Weldon Railroad. The troops, fearing an ambush, worked their way cautiously ahead, until they were within sight of the breastworks formerly held by the Regulars, but now defended by Mayo's Virginians and Tennesseans. Humphrey had the charge beaten by regimental drummers. The brigade stormed ahead. At least one regiment, the 1st Michigan Sharpshooters, gained the rifle pits without firing a shot. Humphrey's cheering troops rolled back the Johnnies, capturing about 100 prisoners and the colors of the 47th Virginia.[147]

General White's troops, in the meantime, had moved into the sector formerly occupied by Hartranft's command. Orders to advance were received from Warren's headquarters. The division marched toward the woods. The left flank of Barnes' battle line encountered Colquitt's Georgians in the cornfield, while his right flank regiments and Lieutenant Colonel Gilbert P. Robinson's brigade engaged them in the pines.[148]

Soldiers of the 35th Massachusetts reported that the Confederates, led by Alfred Colquitt's brigade,

were coming through the woods upon the charge. Kneeling in the mud, the word was, "Fire, and give them hell!" and at it we went, firing and loading as rapidly as nimble fingers could. The only command of the officers was, "Fire low, men, fire low!" and the carnage was deadly.

As soon as our line of fire became distinct, the artillery in rear opened, throwing the shells so closely to our heads that the boys asserted they cut the tops of the corn stalks.

---

146 Committee, *History of the Thirty-Fifth Regiment Massachusetts Volunteers*, 285. The division had been heavily engaged during the fall of 1863 at Campbell's Station and Knoxville in East Tennessee.

147 OR 42, pt. 1, 595, 596-597, 598.

148 *Ibid.*, 550, 557. One of Robinson's organizations, the 3rd Maryland Battalion, did not reach the sector in time to participate in the fighting.

A steady fire was maintained for over half an hour, officers taking the guns of the wounded and adding their shots to the storm of bullets.[149]

Warren, hearing the clash of arms from his right, sent word for Hartranft to march to White's assistance. Hartranft's brigade retraced its steps, moving along the edge of the pines until its right was within 75 yards of White's left. At the same time, Crawford, having reformed Wheelock's and Lyle's brigades, moved forward. Crawford's battle line took position on Hartranft's left.[150]

By the time Hartranft's and Crawford's troops were in position, White's bluecoats, after 30 minutes sharp fighting, had broken the back of Confederate resistance to their front. When they retreated, Colquitt's Georgians left their dead, a number of wounded, and many small-arms behind. White's soldiers in mopping up the area rounded up about 60 Confederates, and collected 516 stand of small-arms, about one-half of which were of the type issued to the Rebels.[151]

As soon as the fighting in front of White's division ceased, Crawford's and Hartranft's battle lines pushed into the pines. Since it was starting to get dark, the woods were unusually gloomy. An advance of 200 yards brought the Federals to the breastworks from which Crawford's troops had been dislodged earlier in the day. Since the Confederates had withdrawn from this area, the Yanks encountered no resistance. Crawford's troops on the left moved more rapidly.

Before Hartranft's brigade entered the earthworks, Crawford dashed off a note to General Warren reporting that his troops had "retaken the entrenchments but there is no connection with my right." Crawford begged Warren to order Burnside's IX Corps forward. Long before this message reached V Corps headquarters, Hartranft's soldiers filed into the earthworks on Crawford's right. After occupying the rifle pits, the Union officers covered their fronts with a strong line of pickets.[152]

White's division had failed to advance in conjunction with the battle line to its left. A possibly dangerous gap was opened between Hartranft's and White's commands.

Darkness closed in almost before the smoke "had lifted through the misty air." Since White and his officers anticipated a renewal of the fight, the division closed to

149   Committee, *History of the Thirty-Fifth Regiment Massachusetts Volunteers*, 285-286.

150   *OR* 42, pt. 1, 494, 593.

151   *Ibid.*, 550, 557; Committee, *History of the Thirty-Fifth Regiment Massachusetts Volunteers*, 286.

152   *OR* 42, pt. 1, 494, 594; *OR* 42, pt. 2, 315.

the left into "a bow in the woods, where, upon cornstalk beds, the man got such sleep as the care of watching and the dripping rain allowed."[153]

Because of the thick undergrowth and the pockets of Union resistance, Colquitt and Clingman had lost control of their units. They were accordingly in no condition to offer effective resistance, when Warren brought the IX Corps divisions into action. Taking cognizance of this situation, General Hill ordered the regimental commanders to collect their men and return to their camps. Weisiger's Virginians were detailed to cover the withdrawal of Colquitt's Georgians and Clingman's North Carolinians.

John F. Sale of the 12th Virginia, Weisiger's brigade recorded in his diary:

> The order to move forward was soon given and . . . [we] went forward driving the enemy until [we] came to their first line of works when they made a stand and from the confused state of our brigade we were forced to retire with considerable loss. After retiring the brigade was brought to and occupied their old position in the line of works.[154]

General Heth remained on the field with Mayo's and Davis' grey clads.

Meanwhile, General Ayres had led Colonel Winthrop's brigade back into action. Winthrop's troops reoccupied the rifle pits west of the Weldon Railroad from which they had been driven. As the troops took position behind the barricades, several wounded Confederates fell into their hands.

General Heth now launched a thrust to cover the withdrawal of Mahone's division. Davis' and Mayo's brigades stormed ahead. On the Union left, Hofmann's Yanks repulsed Davis' Mississippians and North Carolinians. Private T. J. Jennings of Company K, 56th Pennsylvania, captured the colors of the 55th North Carolina.[155] Simultaneously, Winthrop's and Humphrey's bluecoats repulsed several attacks by Mayo's Virginians and Tennesseans. Although they stood fast in the face of the slashing Confederate thrusts, Winthrop saw that his men were fought out. A runner was sent to ask Ayres for reinforcements.[156]

About the time that Crawford's and Ayres' troops fell back in confusion before the Rebel onset, General Warren had sent word for General Griffin to pull two of

153   OR 42, pt. 1, 594; Committee, *History of the Thirty-Fifth Regiment Massachusetts Volunteers*, 287.

154   OR 42, pt. 1, 940; Sale, Diary. n.d.

155   OR 42, pt. 1, 472, 475, 585; Powell, *History of the Fifth Corps*, 714.

156   OR 42, pt. 1, 475, 590, 596; Brainard, *Campaigns of the 146th Regiment*, 239.

his brigades out of the breastworks west of the railroad. Griffin responded to the emergency with his characteristic alacrity. Marching orders were issued to Tilton's and Gwyn's brigades. While these units were being formed and mustered, Gregory's troops extended to the right and to the left to occupy the vacated rifle pits. Tilton's and Gwyn's brigades marched up the Halifax Road and were massed in line of battle in support of Ayres' battered division. At 7:00 p.m., the tide of battle having shifted, Gwyn's troops were returned to their former position. Tilton's battle line, with its left flank anchored on the railroad, advanced into the pine thickets.[157]

Just at this moment, Ayres called for help. Colonel Tilton rushed him the 187th Pennsylvania. The Pennsylvanians took cover in the rifle pits to the right of the 5th New York.

Shortly after the reinforcements arrived, Heth made a night attack on the sector of the Union line to either side of the railroad. This thrust was easily repulsed. At 8:30 p.m. the Confederates fell back and "quiet reigned" in the woods.[158]

Ninety minutes later, General Ayres called up the rest of Tilton's brigade. He used the fresh troops to relieve Winthrop's command. Upon being replaced, Winthrop's brigade was posted in the second line of works.[159]

About dark, there was a flurry of activity on the railroad south of Globe Tavern. A company of Dearing's Rebel cavalry charged the center of Spear's picket line and was "handsomely repulsed." Two Confederates were unhorsed and captured by the blue clad troopers. When he questioned these men, Colonel Spear learned that there were three regiments of Southern cavalry on the Vaughan Road to his front. Spear, to be on the safe side, strengthened his outposts. When he reported this affair to Warren, Spear promised to make a forced reconnaissance at daylight and seek to verify this report.[160]

*   *   *

During the fighting, General Warren kept Meade's headquarters posted as to the fluid situation. At 4:15 p.m. Meade was notified that William Mahone's

---

157   OR 42, pt. 1, 458, 461, 467; Survivors, *History of the Corn Exchange Regiment*, 500-501.

158   OR 42, pt. 1, 472, 475.

159   *Ibid.*, 461, 475.

160   OR 42, pt. 2, 325-326.

Confederate troops had overrun Bragg's skirmish line.[161] The crisis had passed before Meade replied to this message. When he did, Meade wanted to know if Warren had re-established his picket line.

A little before 8:00 p.m. headquarters was shocked to receive a communication from Warren dated 6:50 p.m., reporting that Crawford's and Ayres' divisions had been outflanked and rolled back. Headquarters felt better to learn that Warren's troops had counterattacked and had regained the lost ground, taking many Confederates. Union losses had been heavy, Warren reported, especially in prisoners.

Acknowledging this telegram, Chief of Staff Humphreys informed Warren that Meade felt that he should utilize the reinforcements from the IX Corps to establish a connection with the entrenchments at the Jerusalem Plank Road "tonight" and dig in.[162]

Meanwhile, Warren had received good news. The day was well along before the last of Potter's troops had been relieved by Mott's II Corps people. As Potter's men were leaving the trenches, they were exposed to a sharp fire. The route taken by Potter's column was circuitous, and the soldiers marched nearly six miles over a road turned into a ribbon of mud. Potter's vanguard reached Aiken's about the time that Mahone's Confederates were withdrawing. While at Aiken's, Potter was given instructions by a staff officer to use his division to close the gap which the Rebels had punched in the Union line.

Potter's brigade commanders formed their men in a clearing and pushed forward into the woods about a quarter mile, and took position across a wood road. Inside of ten minutes, the troops had thrown up "a good protection of logs." Colonel Zenas R. Bliss' 1st Brigade wasn't allowed to enjoy the protection afforded by the barricades, as orders were received to deploy as skirmishers. Considerable time was squandered as the regimental commanders maneuvered their men in the woods to establish contact with White's division on their left.[163]

Warren promptly notified Meade's headquarters that Potter's division was on the field. Arrangements had been made, the corps commander reported, "to connect my picket-line tonight along the road by Aiken's."[164]

---

161   *Ibid.*, 307.

162   *Ibid.*, 308.

163   OR 42, pt. 1, 76; OR 42, pt. 2, 310; Committee of the Regiment, *History of the Thirty-Sixth Regiment Massachusetts Volunteers* (Boston, 1884), 248-249.

164   OR 42, pt. 2, 308.

At 8:15 p.m. Warren telegraphed Chief of Staff Humphreys additional details of the afternoon's fighting. On checking rolls, it had been ascertained that "nearly all the Pennsylvania Reserves" were missing, while losses in Crawford's two other brigades had been heavy. Ayres' division had been hard hit; General Hayes was among the missing. His counterattack had been successful, Warren reported. The troops had regained "all ground fought over," besides capturing numerous prisoners, and two stand of colors.

Warren advised army headquarters that he didn't think it would be "possible to establish the line across" to the Jerusalem Plank Road, as suggested by Meade, before daybreak. With the arrival of reinforcements from the IX Corps, two divisions of which had been employed in driving back the foe, Warren felt he would be prepared to continue the engagement if the Rebels resumed their attacks in the morning. In any case, Warren didn't believe it would be wise for the Federals to reoccupy the picket line from which Bragg's troops had been expelled.[165]

Meade replied personally to Warren's 8:15 p.m. communication, and announced that he was "delighted to hear the good news . . . , and most heartily congratulate you [and] your brave officers and men on your success." Meade felt that the successes scored by the Federals in the day's fighting would "serve greatly to inspirit the whole army, and proves that we only want a fair chance to show our capacity to defeat the enemy." Meade hoped the Confederates would attack again. If possible, Meade informed Warren, he would try to get the IX Corps "to prepare a line and slash it well, so as to secure the connection with the Plank Road."[166]

General Meade at 10:30 p.m. forwarded to Warren a copy of a message which he had just received from General Grant. The lieutenant general commanding had wished to know if Meade could spare Mott's division to reinforce the V Corps. Reports reaching Grant's City Point headquarters from the front had led him to believe that the Rebels would employ all their reserves in an effort to dislodge Warren from the Weldon Railroad.[167]

In a covering letter, Meade informed Warren that it would be impossible to withdraw Mott's troops as Grant had suggested, because it would seriously weaken the investment line. Upon evaluating the stories told by Confederate prisoners and deserters, Meade concluded, correctly, that Warren was probably confronted by "a division and a half, say 10,000 men." In view of this intelligence, Meade inquired

165   *Ibid.*, 308-309.

166   *Ibid.*, 309.

167   *Ibid.*, 295.

into the possibility of Warren attacking the Rebels in the morning, before they could draw reinforcements from north of the James.[168]

Warren, when he acknowledged Meade's communication, announced that he had "given orders to advance at daylight in every direction." He promised to govern his movements according to Meade's instructions.[169]

When they mustered their commands and checked their rolls, the Union officers found that in the day's fighting, they had lost 94 killed, 457 wounded, and 2,596 missing and presumed prisoners.[170]

A. P. Hill's columns retired within the Petersburg perimeter during the evening. The Confederates made no report of their casualties in the fighting on August 19, although General Beauregard wrote Secretary of War James A. Seddon early on the 20th that they were not believed great. A soldier in Colquitt's brigade agreed with the general, "We did but little fighting: we got badly scattered. I do not think there were many killed on either side." General Warren claimed in his after-action report that the Rebels' losses in killed and wounded must have been heavy. At the same time, Gen. A. P. Hill reported that he had captured about 2,700 prisoners, including one brigadier general—Hayes. One Confederate general, Clingman, had been badly wounded in the leg in the day's fighting.[171]

"All was joy" in Petersburg on the night of August 19. While the Federals still held on to the Weldon Railroad, two Union divisions had been terribly mauled. In the morning, the Confederate generals planned to resume the attack and drive the bluecoats from their position astride the vital railroad.[172]

168   *Ibid.*, 309-310.

169   *Ibid.*, 310.

170   *OR* 42, pt. 1, pp. 430, 595, 596.

171   *Ibid.*, 858, 940; F. H. MacRae to Sister, August 22, 1864 in Thomas Strayhorn Papers, Civil War Collections, North Carolina Department of Archives and History; Dunn, Diary. n.d.

172   Porter, "Operations Against the Weldon Railroad, August 18, 19, 21, 1864," 260.

Part III

The Confederates Abandon Their Attempt To Dislodge the Federals From The Weldon Railroad

The night of August 19 was "cheerless and dismal"—the rain beat down in torrents, and the ground was soaked with water. During the night, all was still "except the groans and cries of the Confederate wounded in the dark forest, who had to wait until daylight before they could be moved."[173]

At the "first glimmer of daylight," the Union officers turned out their commands. General Potter, whose division was posted at Aiken's, advanced his skirmish line. After pushing forward one-half mile without encountering any Confederates, the officer in charge began to worry. A runner was sent to the rear to acquaint General Potter with the situation. If the troops to the left (White's) would advance, the skirmishers could continue to feel their way ahead. In addition, the skirmishers as yet had been unable to establish contact with Mott's men of Hancock's II Corps on their right.[174] Potter relayed this information to Warren's headquarters.

Within a short time, Potter received a reply. He was directed to hold his skirmishers in check until Major Roebling had established a picket line.[175] By this time, Potter's skirmishers had established a connection on the right with the 7th Wisconsin and the detachment of the 19th Indiana that had been cut off from the V Corps by Mahone's previous afternoon's breakthrough. Colonel Finnicum of the 7th Wisconsin told Potter's men that his troops were in contact with Mott's division. Upon receipt of this news, Warren breathed a sigh of relief because the gap punched through the Union line by Mahone's Confederates had finally been sealed.[176]

The 36th Massachusetts of Bliss' brigade spent a busy morning:

---

173   Committee, *History of the Thirty-Fifth Regiment Massachusett Volunteers*, 287; Committee, *History of the Thirty-Sixth Massachusetts Volunteers*, 249; William P. Hopkins, *The Seventh Regiment Rhode Island Volunteers in the Civil War, 1862-1865* (Providence, 1903), 212.

174   *OR* 42, pt. 2, 347.

175   *Ibid.*, 347-348.

176   *Ibid.*, 348. During their advance, Potter's skirmishers had picked up a few stragglers. Potter at this time moved his command post to the center of the large field near Gurley's house.

At half-past eight o'clock the order was given "Forward! Guide Left!" The dense undergrowth rendered it very difficult to maintain a good line as the regiment covered considerable ground. After advancing about three hundred yards we reached a cornfield about one hundred yards wide, with woods beyond. We moved across this field and halted in the edge of the forest, and connected out left with the right of . . . [White's] division. We were then ordered to build a line of breastworks. We had just completed a fine line of works, and were eating our dinner of roasted corn, gathered from the cornfield, when we were ordered to the left to reinforce that portion of the line, as an attack was anticipated. We accordingly moved a distance of about a hundred yards to the left, to that portion of the line which had been held by the Second New York Rifles, which had moved further down. Although they had occupied the position two hours, not a tree had been cut and no protection whatever had been secured. Our men went to work with a will and soon had a good Line of breastworks. We had just nicely settled down for the second time when the Adjutant-General came up at a gallop to order the regiment to extend to the right, as the enemy was threatening in that direction. We moved back to the first line of breastworks we had built, not a little angry at being obliged to build entrenchments for the Second New York.[177]

Meanwhile, General White had advanced his division and had established contact with General Hartranft's troops on his left, thus closing a possibly dangerous opening in Warren's front which the Confederates might have exploited. As soon as his troops were in position, White put them to work throwing up breastworks and slashing timber.[178]

On White's left, General Hartranft threw forward a "thin line" of skirmishers', supported by a strong "battle line." After advancing about 200 yards, the bluecoats sighted Rebel outposts. The Federals stopped, and as if by mutual consent both sides held their fire.[179]

Colonel Humphrey, as his first order of business following an early reveille, dispatched a detail to gather the arms and accouterments that were strewn along the breastworks occupied by his brigade and through the woods. Five hundred and thirteen stand of arms were collected. Most of the rifle muskets were found standing along the rifle pits, with the accouterments hanging across the muzzles of the pieces, or in a line of stacks some distance in the rear of the breastworks. This

---

177   Committee, *History of the Thirty-Sixth Massachusetts*, 250. The sector of the front occupied by Bliss' brigade, Potter's division, had been the scene of a fearful struggle on the previous day. *Ibid.*, 250-251.

178   OR 42, pt. 1, 551, 552; Committee, *History of the Thirty-Fifth Regiment Massachusetts*, 287.

179   OR 42, pt. 1, 594.

evidence indicated that Warren's V Corps soldiers posted in this area had been taken by almost complete surprise.[180]

Along Ayres' front west of the railroad, Yank and Reb pickets sniped at one another. An inspection showed Ayres that his front was "about as strong as it can be as a single line."[181] Talking to several cavalrymen who had just returned from patrol, General Ayres learned that the Rebels were felling timber beyond the Vaughan Road. Shortly thereafter, an excited scout dashed up and told Ayres that he had spotted grey clad infantry marching out the Vaughan Road.

When General Warren was notified of this development, he advised Ayres that it was his opinion the Confederates planned to emplace artillery to shell the Union headquarters area about Blick's house. If this were correct, the artillery wouldn't constitute a threat to Ayres' position, as the projectiles would be unable to reach the Second division's line.[182]

Chief of Staff Humphreys (at 9:10 a.m.) telegraphed Warren that Meade was desirous of learning the state of affairs in the Globe Tavern sector. Specifically, Meade wanted to know if Warren had attacked, and if he had the results.[183]

General Warren being absent on a tour of inspection, Lt. Col. Frederick T. Locke replied for his chief that "all was quiet at daybreak this morning." Since then there had been some banging away on the picket line. Patrols had pinpointed the Confederates, and they occupied the same ground as they had when fighting had ceased on the 19th.[184]

Warren returned to his command post by 10:00 a.m. On doing so, he notified Meade that he was redeploying his troops in case the Rebels resumed their efforts to dislodge the Federals from their stranglehold on the Weldon Railroad. Unless he was reinforced, Warren didn't believe he could hold a line across the area where Mahone had overran Bragg's skirmish line. At the moment, the picket line ran east and west by the Strong house. His visit to the front had satisfied Warren that the Confederates, except for their outposts, had retired into the Petersburg perimeter.[185]

---

180   Ibid., 596.

181   OR 42, pt. 2, 344.

182   Ibid., 344.

183   Ibid., 338.

184   Ibid., 338. Colonel Locke was Warren's assistant adjutant general.

185   Ibid., 338.

A brigade from Brig. Gen. David McMurtrie Gregg's cavalry division at this time reported to General Warren. The officer in charge, Col. William Stedman, told Warren that his troopers had left Deep Bottom late the previous afternoon, and they had been in the saddle much of the time since then. When he informed Meade of Stedman's arrival, Warren wanted to know if he should send the cavalrymen to Ream's Station. If he were reinforced by Stedman's brigade, Spear, in Warren's opinion, would have enough troopers to drive the butternuts away from the station.[186]

General Humphreys replied at 11:30 a.m. to Warren's communication. Army headquarters was in agreement that Stedman's brigade, plus Spear's troopers, would be sufficient to clear the Confederate horsemen from Ream's Station. In addition, Humphreys wanted to know if a 200-man working party from the Quartermaster's Department at City Point had reached Warren's command post. These people were being sent to assist in wrecking the railroad, and Humphreys wanted them to accompany the cavalry to Ream's Station.

About the same hour, Warren telegraphed Humphreys the latest news from Colonel Spear. Scouts ordered out by Spear were convinced that the Confederates only had a small brigade of cavalry on the Union left. According to the best information, the Rebels had evacuated Ream's Station. Spear had advised Warren that he was eager to start for Ream's with his 700 men. Stedman's troopers, although tired from their long ride, were also to march.[187]

General Humphreys (at 1:30 p.m.) notified Warren that as soon as the railroad wreckers arrived, they would be put to work twisting rails and burning ties. The pioneers were to work their way southward, while Colonel Stedman employed his brigade to cover them from Confederate raiders. Spear's troopers were to be used to feel toward the west.[188]

It was late in the afternoon, when the pioneers reached Globe Tavern and reported to General Warren. The general lost no time in turning them to tearing up the Weldon Railroad.[189]

Warren took advantage of the lull in the fighting to redeploy his troops and readjust his lines. West of the railroad, Colonel Tilton's brigade was relieved of duty on Ayres' line and reported back to General Griffin. Tilton's troops reoccupied the

186   *Ibid.*, 338-339.

187   *Ibid.*, 339.

188   *Ibid.*, 340.

189   *Ibid.*, 342.

rifle pits which they had previously held. Upon the return of Tilton's brigade, Gregory's troops closed to the left.[190]

Early on the 20th, General Ayres issued a special order assigning the 15th New York Heavy Artillery to Winthrop's brigade.[191]

There was a brief flurry of excitement during the day along Dushane's picket line. Lieutenant Colonel John W. Wilson, who was in charge of Dushane's skirmishers, led a charge which compelled the Rebel pickets to retire. The blue clads of the Maryland brigade recovered the outposts from which they had been driven on the afternoon of the 19th, capturing one Confederate officer and 13 enlisted men.[192]

Shortly after 2:00 p.m., General Warren received an interesting communication from army headquarters. According to Chief of Staff Humphreys, the signal officer at Gibbon's house had sighted a column of Rebel infantry, about 2,000 strong, marching southward from Petersburg.[193] Meanwhile, General Willcox's troops had captured a talkative member of Company A, 22nd Virginia Infantry Battalion, Pvt. James Crowley. When questioned by Union officers, Crowley announced that the Confederates to Warren's front had been reinforced by Brig. Gen. Montgomery D. Corse's division and would before dark renew the fight.

After talking with Crowley, Warren (at 2:40 p.m.) telegraphed Chief of Staff Humphreys that he felt certain the Rebels would attack. But he added, "I think we ought to be able to hold against everything." At the moment, he observed, he was preparing to resist an attack from any direction and to contract his main line of resistance.[194]

At 5:20 p.m. Humphreys advised Warren that the signal officer at Gibbon's house had spotted three Confederate infantry regiments, as they tramped out of Petersburg by way of the Halifax Road.[195]

Warren, upon evaluating this data, alerted General Ayres to be on the lookout for a thrust against his left—Dushane's brigade. If the Confederates didn't attack,

190   OR 42, pt. 1, 458, 461, 467.

191   OR 42, pt. 2, 345.

192   OR 42, pt. 1, 481. In this attack, the Maryland brigade lost 14 men, all wounded.

193   OR 42, pt. 2, 341.

194   Ibid., 340, 341. Humphreys informed Warren at 2:15 that Corse commanded a brigade in Pickett's division which had been operating in front of Bermuda Hundred. The chief of staff was of the opinion that this was the column sighted by the officer.

195   Ibid., 341.

the troop movements reported by Humphreys and Crowley could mean that the foe was extending his fortifications to the west to prevent the Federals from tightening their investment of Petersburg.[196]

Grant and his generals knew that the Confederates had no choice but to do everything in their power to drive Warren's V Corps from its position astride the vital Weldon Railroad. Unless they were able to dislodge the Federals, the Southerners would be compelled to unload their supplies formerly shipped into Petersburg via the Weldon Railroad well to the south at Stony Creek Station. A 30-mile haul in wagons by way of Dinwiddie Courthouse would then be necessary for these supplies that before had reached the Petersburg defenders over the Weldon Railroad.

Expecting another attack, General Warren determined to draw in his northern and northwestern defenses to adjust them better to insure artillery support. While the sun struggled to pierce the overcast, Warren and his engineers marked out a new line in the fields south of the woods. This line was to follow a slight crest from near the Dunlop and Lennear houses to the pines, where disaster had befallen the troops of the V Corps the previous day. Griffin's division on the left would continue to hold the breastworks covering the approaches to Globe Tavern from the west.[197]

East of the Weldon Railroad, General Willcox regrouped and redeployed the units of the IX Corps, which had reinforced Warren. Both brigades of the Third division (Hartranft's and Humphrey's) were recalled from the pines. General Hartranft, before retiring from the woods, detailed the 51st Pennsylvania, supported by the 27th Michigan, to remain behind and hold the picket line. Willcox posted his division in the field northeast of Globe Tavern; the left flank of Hartranft's brigade rested about 400 yards east of the railroad.[198] After detailing soldiers to man the picket line in the woods, White's division pulled back and entrenched in the open field on Willcox's right.[199] On their right, White's bluecoats maintained contact with Potter's division.[200]

---

196   *Ibid.*, 345.

197   *Porter*, "Operations Against the Weldon Railroad, August 18, 19, and 21, 1864," 261; Survivors, *History of the Corn Exchange Regiment*, 502; Brainard, *Campaigns of the 146th Regiment*, 240.

198   OR 42, pt. 1, 590, 594, 596, 597.

199   *Ibid.*, 552, 590; Committee, *History of the Thirty-Fifth Regiment Massachusetts Volunteers*, 287.

200   OR 42, pt. 1, 72.

General Crawford's battered division was pulled out of the pines east of the railroad. The troops were reformed and posted in support of Wainwright's artillery—Lyle's brigade on the right and Wheelock's troops on the left.[201]

As soon as it was dark, General Ayres put his soldiers to work throwing down their breastworks west of the railroad and slashing timber. By midnight, this work had been completed. Covered by a strong skirmish line, Ayres withdrew his division from the pines. The troops retired about 700 yards. Ayres' division (Winthrop's brigade on the right and Dushane's on the left) occupied the crest of a gentle slope in the large open field north of Globe Tavern.

Large details were turned to throwing up earthworks. Abatis were hurriedly erected in front of these trenches, and trip wires stretched just above the ground. Although the men were badly jaded by the past 72 hours of fighting and building fortifications, a call was made for pickets. Very reluctantly the men detailed for this task filed slowly out "to fight fatigue and keep a watchful vigil over the camps of their sleeping comrades."[202]

General Cutler was delighted to learn that his two brigades were being returned to him. With his division, Cutler was to take position on Ayres' left, refusing his left "so as to form a line nearly parallel with the railroad."

Bragg's brigade reported to Cutler during the afternoon and went into position west of the Weldon Railroad, fronting the Vaughan Road. As soon as they put in an appearance, Cutler saw that Bragg's soldiers were turned to throwing up rifle pits to the left of the batteries. It was after dark when Hofmann's brigade showed up. The brigade filed into position on Bragg's left along a crest extending south from the Blick house, and paralleling the railroad at a distance of one-fourth mile. Hofmann's troops spent the night, which was cold and rainy, entrenching.[203]

On the evening of August 19, a staff officer rode up to Brig. Gen. Johnson Hagood's command post. The aide told General Hagood to turn over command of his brigade in "the trenches" to the senior officer present and report to Gen. A. P. Hill. On doing so, Hagood was to take charge of a brigade from Maj. Gen. Bushrod R. Johnson's division and be prepared to reinforce the troops striving to dislodge the Yankees from the Weldon Railroad. Since Bushrod Johnson was in the habit of

---

201   *Ibid.*, 505, 510, 518, 521. Lyle's troops were posted in support of the 9th Massachusetts Battery.

202   *Ibid.*, 475; Porter, "Operations Against the Weldon Railroad, August 18, 19, and 21, 1864," 261.

203   OR 42, pt. 1, 484, 486, 488, 534, 536; OR 42, pt. 1, 536; Smith, *History of the Seventy-Sixth Regiment New York*, 308.

holding a regiment from each of his four brigades in reserve, he ordered these units to the designated rendezvous near the Lead Works.

The first of the units from Johnson's command reported to Hagood at 11:30 p.m. By 3:00 a.m. Hagood had effected a brigade organization, "appointing haphazardly an acting staff" and jotting down "their names and those of his regimental commanders, for it was too dark to see their faces." Hagood then reported to General Hill, who was asleep in his ambulance which was parked nearby. When Hill learned of the "heterogeneous character" of Hagood's "brigade," he declined to receive it. Orders were issued for the regiments to report back to General Johnson.[204]

This faux pas played hob with Confederate plans to renew on the 20th the battle for the Weldon Railroad.

Beauregard, at 8:15 a.m. on August 20, telegraphed General Lee that the latest news from A. P. Hill was that the Federals were maintaining their grip on the Weldon Railroad. To make matters worse, the bluecoats were continuing to dig in. If it were practicable, Beauregard promised to make another attempt during the day to dislodge them.[205]

It was apparent to General Lee, however, that if the Yankees were to be driven from the railroad, General Beauregard would have to act promptly. Lee urged Beauregard to throw in additional troops to accomplish the task. Upon receipt of these instructions, Beauregard advised Lee that from Union prisoners, he had ascertained that troops from Hancock's II Corps (Mott's division) had relieved the IX Corps in the Petersburg trenches. Information sent in by officers in the signal stations seemed to confirm this intelligence. Beauregard assured Lee that every man that could be spared from the trenches had already been withdrawn and concentrated for another attempt to drive the Federals from the Weldon Railroad. The attack was scheduled to take place in the morning. Beauregard, as authorized, promised to call on Maj. Gen. Cadmus M. Wilcox for a brigade to strengthen Hill's attacking column.[206]

Along toward dusk, Beauregard telegraphed Lee that he expected "to attack early in the morning." To increase Hill's striking force, Beauregard had called on Maj. Gen. Robert F. Hoke for two brigades (Hagood's and Kirkland's) and Bushrod R. Johnson for one (Ransom's). To replace these units in the Petersburg

---

204 Hagood, *Memoirs of the War of Secession*, 288-289.

205 *OR* 42, pt. 2, 1191.

206 *Ibid.*, 1192; Freeman, *Lee*, vol. 3, 485-486.

trenches, the brigades to their right and left extended their lines to the "utmost." When Hill moved out to attack, no reserves would be left.[207] General A. P. Hill spent the afternoon and evening of the 20th organizing his striking force.

Weisiger's brigade relieved Brig. Gen. Joseph Finegan's Floridians in the trenches on the 20th. During the day, General Mahone marched all of his division, except Weisiger's Virginians, to Battery No. 42. To enable Hill to assemble a powerful striking force, the Virginia Reserves, clerks, musicians, "in fact every man who could be gathered up by any means were put into the breastworks."

During the afternoon, General Hagood's South Carolina brigade was pulled out of the trenches. To fill its place, the units on either side extended to the left and right. As the brigade marched through Petersburg and went into camp near Battery No. 45, Hagood checked the returns and found that he had but 59 officers and 681 men left to command. When Hagood reported to Hill, he told the corps commander that more than two months of days and nights in the rifle pits had cut the effective strength of his brigade by two-thirds, while the remainder were so enfeebled that "they tired badly in the short evening march." Consequently, Hagood asked and received a promise from Hill that if it could be avoided, the South Carolinians would "not be used in the next day's work."[208]

The change from "the cramped and noisome trenches to the freedom of the bivouac, and the call for action, instead of endurance," bolstered the men's morale. Although it rained throughout the night, the camp fires "crackled merrily, and there was once more heard the light laugh, the ready joke, and the busy hum of voices as the men prepared their suppers or smoked their pipes stretched at length before the exhilarating blaze."[209]

The brigades which had participated in the fighting on August 18 and 19 had suffered heavy casualties. Beauregard accordingly determined to have them replace units in the trenches. As soon as it was dark, these combat weary commands moved into the Petersburg perimeter and relieved MacRae's, Ransom's, Kirkland's, and Cooke's brigades.[210]

Generals Beauregard and A. P. Hill spent much of the night organizing their attacking force. Once again, the brigades were arranged into "Provisional divisions." General Heth was given four infantry brigades (Cooke's, Ransom's,

---

207 *OR* 42, pt. 2, 1192.

208 Hagood, *Memoirs of the War of Secession*, 289.

209 *Ibid.*, 289-290.

210 Strayhorn to Sister, Aug. 22, 1864.

MacRae's, and Kirkland's) and two four-gun batteries from Pegram's Artillery Battalion. General William Mahone's "Provisional division" included Wright's, Sanders', Jayne's, and Hagood's brigades, supported by a dozen guns from Pegram's Battalion.[211]

Roger A. Pryor, who had resigned his brigadier general's commission in the Confederate Army the previous August, was still eager to help the cause. Being familiar with the area, Pryor spent considerable time reconnoitering the woods in front of Warren's left. Pryor climbed a tall tree and studied Ayres' line. Satisfied that Ayres' left flank was unsupported, Pryor returned from his scout and relayed this information to A. P. Hill.[212]

When they made their plans for their attack on the 21st, the confederate generals relied heavily on the information gleaned by Pryor. They didn't know, however, that under the cover of darkness, Ayres had retired to a new and stronger position. Once again, General Heth was to advance down the Halifax Road and make a frontal attack, while Mahone was to swing to the west and fall upon the Union left.[213]

General Heth put his column into motion at daylight. Passing through the Petersburg earthworks, Heth's brigades tramped down the Halifax Road. The troops halted at Davis' house to allow the cannoneers to throw their eight guns into battery. While the artillerists were unlimbering their pieces, the brigade commanders formed their commands into line of battle, with Kirkland's on the right, Ransom's in the center, MacRae's on the left, and Cooke's in reserve. After the brigade commanders completed their dispositions, Heth instructed them to have their men take it easy while waiting for Mahone's division to get into position.[214]

At 2:00 a.m. on August 21, Mahone's brigade commanders held reveille. After wolfing down a hurried breakfast, the troops moved out at half-past three. Hagood's brigade brought up the rear as the long column turned into the Squirrel Level Road. The rain which had fallen throughout the night and continued to beat down made the march especially "toilsome."

211 Porter, "Operations Against the Weldon Railroad, August 18, 19, and 21, 1864," 262; OR 42, pt. 2, 359. Sanders', Jayne's, and Wright's Confederate brigades had been recalled from the north side of the James River. These three brigades had reached Petersburg at 8:00 a.m. on June 20.

212 Porter, "Operations Against the Weldon Railroad, August 18, 19, and 21, 1864," 261-262.

213 Ibid., 262.

214 Ibid., 262; Strayhorn to Sister, Aug. 22, 1864.

General Mahone halted his division near Poplar Spring Church. All the brigades, except Hagood's, were formed into battle line facing east. Hagood was directed to halt his South Carolinians by the roadside and remain in reserve.[215]

The rain delayed the Confederates. When the precipitation ceased shortly after daybreak, the rain was succeeded by fog. It was 8:30 a.m. before the mist gave way to sunshine. Within the next half hour, Mahone had completed his preparations. Meanwhile, the three batteries, which had accompanied Mahone, unlimbered their 12 guns in a field near Flowers' house. Upon learning that Mahone's infantry was ready, Col. William J. Pegram had his 20 guns open fire on the Federals.[216]

Rooney Lee's cavalry division had reached Petersburg on the previous day. As Mahone was jockeying his division into attack formation west of the Weldon Railroad, Lee's troopers took position to cover the foot soldiers' right.[217]

* * *

Shortly after daybreak on August 21, General Warren notified army headquarters that he had "disposed" his "command on three sides of a parallelogram with a view to prevent the possibility of being turned, and the whole command is about here in the space of little over a square mile." Until such time as the Federals gained a better understanding of the local terrain on which to establish an entrenched line, Warren suggested that the II Corps be massed at some point between Globe Tavern and the Jerusalem Plank Road. The corps would then extend their lines until they joined. The country, in Warren's opinion, was so heavily timbered that it would "take some time to select the proper line," and while the engineers were reconnoitering, the troops could be resting. Warren reminded Chief of Staff Humphreys that "long lines in the woods" could be easily broken. Moreover, it was "impossible for the commander to provide against it if done while the line is being established, unless it is securely entrenched . . . "[218]

About 8:00 a.m. several excited scouts dashed in and reported to General Warren that a strong column of Confederates had been sighted on the Vaughan Road. A few scattered shots were heard. Moments later, blue coated skirmishers

215   Hagood, *Memoirs of the War of Secession*, 290; Porter, "Operations Against the Weldon Railroad, August 18, 19, and 21, 1864," 262.

216   Porter, "Operations Against the Weldon Railroad, August 18, 19, and 21, 1864," 262-263.

217   R. L. T. Beale, *History of the Ninth Virginia Cavalry in the War Between the States* (Richmond, 1899), 141.

218   *OR* 42, pt. 2, 366-367.

were sighted as they retired out of the woods to the north and west of Globe Tavern.[219]

The trip wires strung by Ayres' troops proved very embarrassing. Shots on the picket line had alerted the soldiers posted behind the breastworks. Soldiers in the 146th New York:

> could see the pickets running towards [sic] us and recognized several of our comrades among them. Suddenly a number of the men fell flat on their faces and we thought that they had been hit by the enemy's fire. To our surprise, they hurriedly scrambled to their feet again and continued toward us. A few steps more and again they plunged to the ground. It dawned upon us then what was the cause of their strange behavior. They had tripped over the telegraph wires stretched about a foot high along the ground. The men, too, realized what was the matter and they carefully picked their way the rest of the distance, being greeted with laughter as they approached. They, however, were in no mood to enjoy the merriment.

When the Rebel skirmishers debouched from the pines, Winthrop called for the 5th and 140th New York to pepper away at them. On Winthrop's left, the soldiers of the Purnell Legion, who manned Dushane's picket line, were heavily engaged.[220]

On the 20th, Colonel Wainwright had seen that his artillerists improved their emplacements—parapets were thrown up, embrasures cut, and platforms laid. Wainwright, at the first alarm, sent his gunners scrambling to their battle stations. The cannoneers took their positions not a moment too soon. Twenty Rebel field pieces manned by the cannoneers of Pegram's Battalion roared forth. By watching the flashes and smoke, Wainwright placed eight of the Confederate guns at Davis' house firing south, and twelve near the Vaughan Road, shooting east. The Federal gunners found themselves caught in "a very ugly cross-fire." Wainwright's cannons hammered back at the Southerners. Pegram's artillerists were at a disadvantage, because the Union guns were protected by parapets.[221]

The projectiles from the massed Confederate artillery passed over the rifle pits held by Ayres' division. Colonel Winthrop recalled that his brigade was "subjected to a most deadly cross-fire of artillery, but, as usual, fully sustained its old reputation for calmness and steadiness." A shot from one of Pegram's guns took off the head

219   *Ibid.*, 367.

220   Brainard, *History of the 146th New York*, 241; OR 42, pt. 1, 472, 475, 481.

221   OR 42, pt. 2, 367-368; OR, 42, pt. 1, 541.

of Colonel Dushane. Upon Dushane's death, the senior Colonel, Samuel A. Graham of the Purnell Legion, took charge of the Maryland brigade.[222]

A soldier in the 36th Massachusetts of White's division reported that the Rebel guns posted west of the railroad enfiladed their earthworks, and the Confederates:

> commenced pitching over round shot in the most lively manner. The men of . . . [Willcox's] division, to our left, were obliged to get over on the outside of their entrenchments for cover. Had the enemy thrown shell their bombardment would have been murderous; as it was, it proved a game of long bowling in a style which was quite amusing to the regiment. The shot would strike the ground once, usually, before reaching us, then rebound, skim our line, or rebound again, before or behind us, sometimes in the midst of us. One of the peculiarities was that the ball could be seen before it reached us, its line of flight calculated with accuracy, and by stepping forward or back the missile avoided, as one would a wild baseball or football. Some remarkable dodging was done, and more than one roar of laughter rose at some quick movement on the part of officer or man to escape the cold iron. We had two or three hit and badly bruised.[223]

Mahone, satisfied that Pegram's cannoneers had shaken the Federals, waved his battle line forward. The cheering Confederate infantry swept past the Flowers house.

At this time, the house was occupied by Mrs. Flowers and her teenage son. A Confederate officer, instead of joining his men as they pressed ahead, sought safety along with the mother and son in the cellar. The Union artillery played mercilessly on the house, one shot ripping through the walls. Mrs. Flowers had stood the ordeal up to this moment with stoicism, but at this shot she began weeping. The officer, in a very unmanly manner, "chided her tears and taxed her with her weakness." At this, the son spoke up and told the officer to remember that if he was where duty called he would have had no opportunity to see "his mother's tears." This cut silenced the shirker, and "the mother, nerved by her son's manly speech, soon recovered" her poise.[224]

Union gun spotters sighted Mahone's battle line as it emerged from the pines near Flowers' house. Men of Battery H, 1st New York and the 15th New York

---

222   *OR* 42, pt. 1, 472, 475, 481.

223   Committee, *History of the Thirty-Fifth Regiment Massachusetts Volunteers*, 287-288.

224   Survivors, *History of the Corn Exchange Regiment*, 505. The cellar walls of the Flowers dwelling extended two or three feet above the ground; the rest of the building was frame.

Battery wheeled their eight Napoleons to the left, and with a "well-directed fire" scattered the Confederates. When the Rebel officers sought to rally and reform their lines, the gunners of Battery L, 1st New York and Battery E, 1st Massachusetts brought their eight 3-inch rifles into play. A storm of shot and shell proved too much for flesh and blood. Colonel Pegram rushed one of his batteries to the hard-pressed infantry's assistance. The butternuts, however, were unable to put their guns into action.

A Confederate combat patrol infiltrated the pines west of Blick's house. Suddenly, the Johnnies debouched from the woods within 150 yards of the 15th New York Battery. Switching to canister, the Yanks sent the butternuts reeling back into the woods.[225]

Meanwhile, Colonel Wainwright had given Lt. George W. Dresser a special assignment. The lieutenant was to gallop to the right, get Battery C, 1st New York, and "post it toward the left of our line" so it would be able to deliver an enfilading fire upon the guns which Colonel Pegram had massed in the Vaughan Road sector. Dresser discharged his mission successfully. Unlimbering their four 3-inch rifles, the New Yorkers, in conjunction with several other batteries, compelled the Rebels (with whom they were dueling) to shift their guns.

Not having any batteries south of Globe Tavern, Wainwright feared that the Confederate officers, as soon as they realized this omission would push for the Union left, called for Lt. William J. Canfield. Canfield raced off to see General Potter; he was to ask for the two batteries Potter had previously placed at Wainwright's disposal. A section from the 11th Massachusetts Battery sent in response to Wainwright's call rumbled across the road, just as Griffin's skirmishers on the left were being driven in.[226]

Warren was satisfied with the way the fight was developing. At 9:30 a.m. he notified Chief of Staff Humphreys that he didn't think he could be "whipped if dispositions will save me, for my line extends well around, with considerable reserves." Should the Confederates penetrate the area where they had broken through on the 19th, Warren would like to see their rear harassed. Warren considered the day's action up to this point as a demonstration designed to obtain information as to his position.[227]

Mahone's initial thrust was directed against the sector held by Griffin's Union division. Pressing forward, the Rebels drove in the pickets covering Tilton's and

225   OR 42, pt. 1, 541-542; OR 42, pt. 2, 368.

226   OR 42, pt. 1, 542.

227   OR 42, pt. 2, 368.

Gregory's brigades. The Yanks retired, falling back slowly. An officer and 16 enlisted men from the 143rd Pennsylvania were cut off and captured by the butternuts as they drove toward the breastworks held by Tilton's brigade.

A soldier in the 118th Pennsylvania recalled: "Lines of gray three and four deep emerged from . . . [the woods], and with flaunting battle-flags bore down on the pickets." Batteries were run out on commanding eminences and thundered away effectively with an oblique fire. The pickets that were not captured fell back slowly, fighting.

The Confederates came up through the standing corn in four lines of battle. Six times the flag of the first line of Confederates fell, and six times a color corporal picked it up and was killed. After that it laid on the ground until it was captured. The cornstalks were cut off by the bullets as if with a knife.[228]

It quickly became apparent to Mahone's soldiers that it would be suicidal to attempt to storm the breastworks behind which Tilton's bluecoats crouched and blazed away at them. The Southerners veered to the right in an effort to turn Tilton's unsupported flank. Tilton, to cope with this threat, pulled the 121st, 143rd, and 187th Pennsylvania out of the works and sent them dashing to the left. Here, the Pennsylvanians were joined by two guns of the 11th Massachusetts Battery. The cannoneers threw their two 3-inch rifles into battery west of the White house. Between them, the Yank artillerists and foot soldiers blunted and then repulsed Mahone's drive to turn the Union left. As the sullen Confederates pulled back, they were followed for a short distance by the Federals. The Massachusetts artillerists were able to get off a few rounds from their rifled guns, before the grey clads regained the cover of the pines. Tilton's blue clads, in repelling this thrust, had inflicted telling losses on the Rebels, while losing very few men themselves.[229]

At 5:00 a.m. Hartranft's brigade, except the 51st Pennsylvania and the 27th Michigan, which continued to occupy the picket line, had moved up from its camp and took position across the railroad. The brigade's left rested on the 9th Massachusetts Battery in front of Blick's house and to its right on Battery D, 5th U.S. Light Artillery. Hartranft put his men to work throwing up breastworks. By the time the Confederate artillery opened, the fortifications were nearly completed. Soon after the Rebel attempt to turn Griffin's left had failed, Heth's division drove

---

228   OR 42, pt. 1, 461, 464, 465, 466, 467, 542, 600; Survivors, *History of the Corn Exchange Regiment*, 502.

229   OR 42, pt. 1, 461, 464, 465, 466, 467, 542, 600. The second section of the 11th Massachusetts battery, which had bogged down, reached the Union left after the fighting had died down. Confederate General Sanders was shot through the thighs in this attack, the ball severing both femoral arteries. In a few minutes he bled to death.

in the Union pickets (men from Willcox's and Ayres' divisions) posted in the pines north of the clearing, where Warren had massed his troops. As they forged ahead, the butternuts overran the outposts, capturing a number of skirmishers.[230]

Everything seemed to be working against the Confederates on the morning of the 21st. Heth had ordered his troops forward, as soon as he learned that Mahone's battle lines were in motion. But by the time they reached Davis' cornfield, north of Globe Tavern, Mahone's attack had been smashed. Heth called a halt. A soldier in the 11th North Carolina remembered, "We lay between our batteries . . . and theirs during the [artillery] duel which opened the ball, and came in for some pretty severe shelling." Heth's North Carolinians were surprised at the ease with which they swept across Davis' cornfield and into the woods beyond, where they had been led to understand they would encounter the Federals' main line of resistance. Overrunning the picket line, the Confederates were chagrined to discover that they had been hoodwinked—the Federals had abandoned their breastworks in the pines in favor of a strong position in the fields beyond.

Captain Thomas Strayhorn of the 47th North Carolina reported, we "soon came upon the enemy's works which the most of them had left very hurriedly and in bad order, leaving their tent-flies, blankets, meat and even their cooked breakfast for our men, with some three hundred prisoners."[231]

Pushing on, Heth's battle lines reached the edge of the clearing. Wainwright, observing this new Confederate threat, decided that he needed to replace Battery C, 1st New York which had been rushed to the left. Just at this minute, another of Potter's batteries (the 19th New York) rumbled up the road leading from the Gurley house. Wainwright ordered the IX Corps battery to occupy the emplacement vacated by Battery C. As soon as the first of Heth's grey clads (the Rebels were advancing in three waves) emerged from the pines, the cannons to their front opened with canister and case shot. Except for the sharpshooters, Hartranft's and Winthrop's troops held their fire.[232]

According to Captain Strayhorn, Ransom's brigade, which was on MacRae's right, debouched into the clearing first. Upon leaving the pines, the North Carolinians found themselves within "two or three hundred yards" of the Union fortifications. The Yankees, the captain wrote:

---

230 Ibid., 590, 594, 596.

231 Strayhorn to Sister, Aug. 22, 1864; Porter, "Operations Against the Weldon Railroad, August 18, 19, and 21, 1864," 263; W. J. Martin, "History of the 11th North Carolina Regiment," in Southern Historical Society Papers, vol. 23, 52-53.

232 OR 42, pt. 1, 542, 594, 596, 597, 598.

turned such a hot fire of . . . canister into . . . [Ransom's troops], they were compelled to retire which they did in no very good order. Our brigade [William MacRae's] suffered more I expect from . . . canister than Ransom's—it passing over their heads and striking in our portion of the line which then had been thrown in their rear. Our brigade, learning that Ransom's had been ordered to fall back to the first line of the enemy's works, also fell back to the same line which was only a few feet in our rear. While crossing over the works I lost just one half of the man I carried into action.

I hope that I may never be called on to go through just such another fiery ordeal while I live. Just the same, on the top of the works on right and left front and rear were lying the dead and dying which had been struck down in the twinkling of an eye, and only a few minutes before were the very pictures of health.[233]

Within a few minutes, Heth's thrust had been smashed by a fearful hammering from 26 Union guns.

Colonel William J. Martin of the 11th North Carolina, MacRae's brigade, recalled, "We lost some men killed and a number wounded, and if Warren had known how few we were in front and had sent out an adequate force, he might have captured the most of these two brigades, isolated as we were."

Patrols thrown forward to reestablish the picket line captured a number of Confederate prisoners. When questioned, the North Carolinians swore "the attack was formed in three lines of battle, but that the first line was broken by the fire of . . . [the Union] batteries before it emerged from the woods," while the second didn't get within 300 yards of the Yankee breastworks before it was shattered.[234]

*   *   *

On the morning of the 21st, General Lee directed Maj. Gen. Wade Hampton to move Brig. Gen. Matthew C. Butler's cavalry division south of the Appomattox. Orders were also issued for Maj. Gen. Charles W. Field to send two of his five brigades to Petersburg, provided the Federals had reduced their strength in the Deep Bottom sector. The superintendent of the Richmond & Petersburg Railroad

---

233 Strayhorn to Sister, Aug. 22, 1864. Captain Strayhorn reported that the regiment, the 47th North Carolina, "lost some twenty five or thirty killed and wounded." Out of that number, his company lost five. Strayhorn's company had carried only "ten guns" into action. Two of his men had been detailed as skirmishers, one as color guard, while the rest were on sick report.

234 *OR* 42, pt. 1, 542; Martin, "History of the 11th North Carolina Regiment," 52-53.

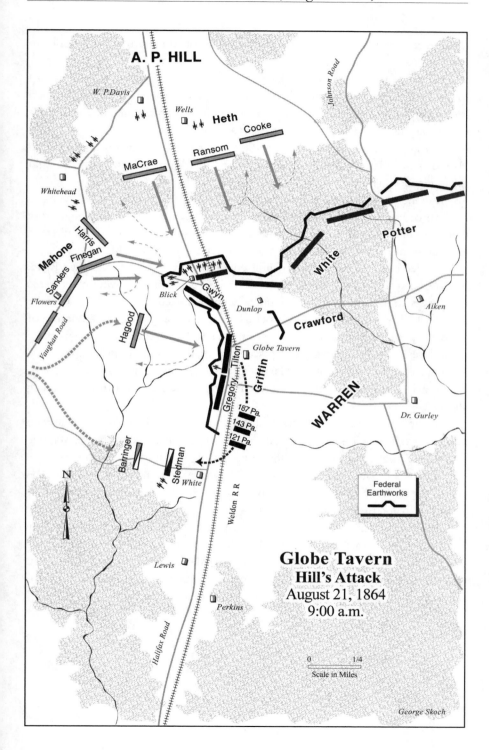

A. P. HILL

W. P. Davis

Wells

Heth

Cooke

Ransom

MaCrae

Whitehead

Johnson Road

Potter

Harris

Mahone

Finegan

White

Sanders

Flowers

Blick

Gwyn

Dunlop

Aiken

Vaughan Road

Hagood

Crawford

Globe Tavern

Gregory

Tilton

Griffin

WARREN

187 Pa.

143 Pa.

121 Pa.

Dr. Gurley

Barringer

Stedman

White

Weldon R R

Federal
Earthworks

N

Lewis

Globe Tavern
Hill's Attack
August 21, 1864
9:00 a.m.

Perkins

Halifax Road

0   1/4
Scale in Miles

George Skoch

was directed to have enough cars at Rice's Turnout to shuttle two brigades to Petersburg.[235]

Lee now determined to leave his temporary command post at Chaffin's Bluff to go to Petersburg and see for himself what was happening on the Weldon Railroad. The general arrived on "an excessively hot" morning, in time to witness a gallant but futile attack by Mahone west of Globe Tavern.

Through a misunderstanding on the part of Hill and Mahone, Jayne's and Hagood's brigades assailed the works held by Cutler's division and Griffin's right flank brigade—Tilton's.[236]

Hagood's South Carolinians were resting alongside the road and listening to the roar of battle as it rolled in from the east, when an aide with a message from General Hill galloped up on a sweat-lathered horse. The staff officer directed Hagood to move his brigade to the front and report to General Mahone.

Guided by the courier, Hagood utilized a short cut to gain the Vaughan Road. The brigade followed the Vaughan Road toward Petersburg until within 600 yards of Flowers' house, when it turned to the right and marched across a field toward the Weldon Railroad. As the South Carolinians hurried along, they saw a number of Pegram's guns. The cannoneers, many of them stripped to the waist, were working their pieces. Unseen Union guns emplaced beyond the woods to the Confederates' front were replying vigorously. Hagood's brigade, moving in column of fours, passed across this field on the double, suffering some casualties from exploding shells.

As the head of the brigade reached the woods east of the field, a general rode up and introduced himself to Hagood as General Mahone. Taking charge, Mahone formed the brigade into line of battle along the edge of the pines, facing east.

"Now," Mahone remarked to Hagood, "you are upon the flank and rear of the enemy. I have five brigades fighting them in front and they are driving them. I want you to go in and press them all you can."

About 50 yards to the brigade front within the woods was a small, swampy branch; beyond nothing was visible. All this time, the roar of artillery and the rattle of small-arms could be heard. Before riding off, Mahone told Hagood, "when you have crossed the branch swamp you will come upon a clearing in which some 300 yards further is the enemy's line, and they are not entrenched."[237]

235   Freeman, *Lee*, vol. 3, 486-487; OR 42, pt. 2, 1192-1193.

236   Freeman, *Lee*, vol. 3, 487.

237   Hagood, *Memoirs of the War of Secession*, 290.

Colonel Joseph M. Jayne's Mississippi brigade had formed some distance to Hagood's left. Just as Hagood was completing his dispositions, Jayne's Mississippians surged out of the pines about 400 yards to the front of the breastworks held by Bragg's and Hofmann's bluecoats. Letting go a wild "Rebel Yell," the grim Mississippians swept back the Union outposts. The grey clads moved steadily through a cornfield to within 50 feet of the works held by Cutler's division. All the while, the butternuts were exposed to the crashing volleys of Federal infantry. Repulsed, the Mississippians fell back, losing heavily in killed, wounded, and prisoners. Captain Charles P. Hyatt, who was in temporary command of the 6th Wisconsin, accepted the surrender of Col. E. C. Councill of the 16th Mississippi. Moments later, Hyatt was struck in the left leg by a fragment from an exploding shell. The limb was so badly mangled that it had to be amputated. When he filed his after-action report, General Bragg claimed that his brigade captured "6 field officers, 15 line officers and 101 enlisted men, 2 stand of colors (one of which belonged to the 16th Mississippi), a number of wounded, and a quantity of small-arms."[238]

Hagood's brigade advanced to the right of the Mississippians. When the general gave the order to attack, the South Carolinians' battle line made its way across the swamp. Upon arriving on the opposite side, Hagood's troops found themselves in the clearing, but they were unable to see the foe. What had happened was at this point, the Confederates were under a hill and the Yankees were on a plateau "sufficiently far above" to be out of sight. Hagood's advance had not gone unnoticed by the Federals, however.

The brigade's line had been "much broken" in wading the swamp. Hagood now halted his troops, while he pushed skirmishers up the hill to his front. A member of the general's staff accompanied the skirmishers. At the same time, Hagood and his adjutant, Capt. P. K. Maloney, reformed the battle line.

Within a few minutes, the brigade was again formed. Word now came back from the skirmishers that the Yanks had been spotted a short distance to the front, and they were in rifle pits. Hagood, "cautioning his men to move only at a quick step till he himself gave the order to charge," advanced his South Carolinians. The general dismounted from his bay horse, and, placing himself in front of the center to study the troops and repress excitement, "moved backward in front of the line for a short distance as if on a drill." Before reaching the crest, Hagood halted, the

238   OR 42, pt. 1, 484, 486, 534, 536, 939; Rowland, *The Official and Statistical Register of the State of Mississippi 1908*, 450, 466, 514. Brigadier General Nathaniel H. Harris being sick, Colonel Jayne led the Mississippi brigade on the 21st. Out of the 450 men carried into action, Jayne's brigade lost 254 killed, wounded, and missing.

line passed, and he followed with his staff behind the right of the 21st South Carolina. The 25th South Carolina was on the left of the 21st, and the three other units on its right.

As soon as the brigade topped the rise, a rapid fire was opened on it. Holding their fire, the South Carolinians marched forward steadily at quick time with arms at "right shoulder shift." The bluecoats holding the rifle pits took to their heels as the Rebels approached. At this, the Confederates gave out with a "Rebel Yell," and the men, as if by command, broke into "double quick." General Hagood now made a shocking discovery. The line to his front had only been an entrenched skirmish line, and 250 yards beyond were the main breastworks, "crowded with men and artillery, extending right and left as far as he could see." To make matters worse, the five attacking Confederate brigades were "nowhere visible."[239]

The South Carolina brigade had advanced against a "re-entrant" in the Union line to the left of Hofmann's brigade and to the right of the breastworks held by Tilton's troops. Hofmann's right flank regiments, the 3rd Delaware and the 76th New York, banged away at the advancing grey clads until they reached "a point a little in our rear."[240]

Colonel Wainwright saw that the guns emplaced west of the Weldon Railroad were turned on Hagood's South Carolinians as they charged. Hardly had the Johnnies emerged from the pines to the left and rear of Hofmann's line, before they found themselves exposed "to a cross-fire of musketry" from the 3rd Delaware and the 76th New York to the left and Tilton's troops to their right. As if this weren't bad enough, Battery E, 1st Massachusetts, and Batteries D and L, 1st New York Light Artillery hammered them with canister, while Battery C, 1st New York shelled the woods from which they had charged.[241]

Observing at a glance the hopelessness of an assault under such conditions, General Hagood halted. Again and again he shouted for his men to stop. But the crash and rattle of 16 guns and 2,500 rifle-muskets drowned his voice, and the fury of the battle was upon his men. "Moving forward with the steady tramp of the double quick, and dressing upon their colors," the South Carolinians, "intent only on carrying the position before them, neither broke their alignment until it was

239   Hagood, *Memoirs of the War of Secession*, 290-292.

240   OR 42, pt. 1, 483, 484, 486, 488-489. The breastworks held by the 3rd Delaware, Hofmann's left flank unit, were refused at a 45 degree angle to those occupied by the rest of the brigade.

241   *Ibid.*, 542.

broken by the irregular impact upon the enemy's works, nor stopped to fire their guns until their rush to obtain the parapet was repelled."

When General Hagood saw his soldiers rushing into what seemed certain destruction, "he felt that if they were to perish he should share their fate." Accompanied by three members of his staff (Captain Maloney, Lt. Benjamin Martin, and orderly Dwight Stoney), Hagood followed the advancing line. Before they had gone 50 yards, Lieutenant Martin fell, shot in the knee; a few steps farther Captain Maloney was cut down, a minie ball through the head. Hagood and Stoney, the orderly having been hit in the shoulder but not disabled, reached the works.

Meanwhile, the 25th and 21st South Carolina, being on the left from the oblique direction of the advance, had struck the works held by the 3rd Delaware and 76th New York of Hofmann's brigade. While these two regiments struggled to force an entry, the three other units of the brigade swept on. When these commands reached the ditch fronting the trenches held by Tilton's troops, there was a gap of about 100 yards separating the two wings into which the brigade had broken.[242]

General Hagood joined the commander of the 21st South Carolina, Maj. S. H. Wilds. The major, realizing that success was the key to safety, exhorted his men to make another assault. Hagood, glancing to his right, saw to his horror that about 200 of his soldiers had entered the "reentering angle," between the breastworks held by Hofmann's and Tilton's brigades. Exposed as they were to a deadly crossfire, these troops panicked. "Some ran into the low ground and held up their hands and the butts of their guns in token of surrender, while some made a rush backward and got away."[243]

Suddenly, a Union officer, Capt. Dennis Dailey, galloped out of "a sally-port" and seized the colors of the 27th South Carolina from the bearer. The Yank called on the South Carolinians to lay down their arms. Several officers and men complied with the Federal's orders. General Hagood was dismayed by what he saw. At this moment, the fight still raged to Hagood's right and left; except for the knot of soldiers gathered about Captain Dailey, the men in blue and in grey seemed disposed to continue the fight.

General Hagood called for his men to shoot the Union captain and retreat. Either they did not hear their General, or bewildered by the surrender of a number of their comrades, failed to obey. It was a critical moment and demanded instant and decisive action. Within a few moments, the disposition to surrender would

242   Hagood, *Memoirs of the War of Secession*, 292, 294.

243   Survivors, *History of the Corn Exchange Regiment*, 507.

spread and the entire brigade would be lost. Although exposed to a regular fire by file from the enemy's line, scarce thirty yards off, Hagood dashed toward the spot where the Union officer was brandishing the colors. As he ran up to Captain Dailey, Hagood demanded the return of the colors, and warned the bluecoat to return to his lines. The Yank argued with Hagood, pointing out that the South Carolinians were in a desperate plight. Hagood cut Dailey short, and demanded a categorical reply—yes or no.

Dailey was a man of "fine presence and sat with loosened rein upon a noble-looking bay that stood with head and tail erect and flashing eye and distended nostrils, quivering in every limb with excitement, but not moving in his tracks." Answering this abrupt demand, Captain Dailey raised his head and said, "No!" Hagood shot him through the body. As Dailey reeled from the saddle, Hagood sprang into it from the other side. Orderly Stoney snatched the colors of the 27th South Carolina from Dailey's falling hands.[244]

While Hagood and Dailey argued, Colonel Wainwright, acting under the impression that the Confederates had surrendered, called for his gunners to cease fire.[245]

There was no thought of surrender now. The shout from the brigade told Hagood that his troops were once more in hand and would go wherever ordered. Calling for them to face about, Hagood led them back across the ground over which they had advanced. Stoney held aloft the recaptured colors of the 27th South Carolina, which he had torn from its staff.

Before he had gone very far, a scrap of iron from a bursting shell tore open the loin of Hagood's bay. As the steed fell, the general jumped clear. In struggling to rise, the horse kicked Lt. William Taylor of the 7th South Carolina Battalion in the head. The lieutenant was stunned and had to be led from the field by one of his men.[246]

Union Colonel Hofmann saw that a number of the South Carolinians had thrown away their arms, and, "as they still moved forward," he concluded that they intended to surrender. Like Colonel Wainwright, Hofmann had called for his soldiers to stop shooting.[247]

As soon as Hofmann saw that the Rebels were attempting to escape, he shouted for his men to blaze away. Adjutant Manuel Eyre of the 3rd Delaware led a

---

244   Hagood, *Memoirs of the War of Secession*, 294-295; *OR* 42, pt. 2, 1196.

245   *OR* 42, pt. 1, 542.

246   Hagood, *Memoirs of the War of Secession*, 295.

247   *OR* 42, pt. 1, 484.

sortie. Leaping out from behind the barricades, Eyre's combat patrol raced after the retreating South Carolinians. Two stand of colors were captured by the men from Delaware, one by Eyre and the other by 1st Sgt. John Shilling of Company H. To the right of the 3rd Delaware, Capt. J. C. Hatch of Company G, 76th New York jumped over the works as the Johnnies retired and brought off the colors of the 25th South Carolina. All told, Hofmann's brigade claimed the capture of two lieutenant colonels, a number of line officers, and nearly 300 men.[248]

Troops from Gwyn's left flank unit, the 18th Massachusetts, likewise followed and harassed the South Carolinians. Besides capturing 60 prisoners, the soldiers from the Bay State brought back the colors of the 27th South Carolina.[249]

Upon reforming his brigade near Poplar Spring Church and checking the rolls, Hagood discovered that out of 681 officers and men carried into action, only 292 answered when their names were called.[250]

As soon as Hagood's troops had reached the shelter of the pines, Pegram's Artillery went back into action. The gunners' fire was very erratic. After a few minutes, the Confederate guns fell silent.[251]

General Mahone, following this repulse, rode out and reconnoitered the Federals' position. Returning, he encountered General Lee near Davis'. Notwithstanding the ease with which the Federals had repulsed his attacks, Mahone lost his head and told Lee that if he were given two fresh brigades, he would guarantee to drive the Yankees from the Weldon Railroad. Lee assented and sent for the reinforcements, but when they failed to arrive in the stipulated time, the commanding general concluded that the bluecoats had too firm a grip on the railroad to be shaken loose.[252]

General Warren and his officers were delighted with the way the fighting on the 21st had gone. Mustering their commands, the officers reporting to Warren listed their casualties as 41 killed, 263 wounded, and 232 missing.[253]

---

248   *Ibid.*, 483, 484, 486-487; Smith, *History of the Seventy-Sixth Regiment New York Volunteers*, 308-309. On the 22nd, 300 stands of arms were collected and 50 Confederates buried in front of the works held by Hofmann's brigade. *Ibid.*, 484.

249   OR 42, pt. 1, 467, 468.

250   *Ibid.*, 936.

251   *Ibid.*, 542.

252   OR 42, pt. 2, 1194; Freeman, *Lee*, vol. 3, 487; Porter, "Operations Against the Weldon Railroad, August 18, 19, and 21, 1864," 265.

253   OR 42, pt. 1, 431, 595, 596.

For the first time since the beginning of the 1864 campaign, Colonel Wainwright was satisfied that his guns had played a prominent part in winning a victory. As the artillery chief observed:

> Our lines being formed entirely in open ground, though within short range of the surrounding woods, afforded the very best opportunity possible for an effective artillery fire, which was so well employed that the infantry had comparatively little opportunity to take part in the fight. Particular instructions had been given the day before that in firing into the woods only solid shot should be used, and fired at so low an elevation as to strike the ground at the edge of the woods and enter on the ricochet. The appearance of the woods and enemy's dead left there gave ample testimony to the excellence of this practice.[254]

Shortly before 10:30 a.m., Warren telegraphed Chief of Staff Humphreys that his troops had just repulsed an attack by "Mahone's division from the west of the railroad."

"Whipped it easily," he added.

Warren (by 10:50 a.m.) had spoken with his provost marshal. That officer told the general that the V Corps had captured several hundred prisoners. Men belonging to Mahone's and Hoke's divisions had been identified.[255]

Meanwhile, the division commanders had advanced a strong force of skirmishers and reoccupied the line of outpost from which their pickets had been driven earlier by the Confederates.

At 11:10 a.m. Chief of Staff Humphreys forwarded to Warren a dispatch General Meade had just received from Grant's City Point headquarters. Grant observed that without being on the field it was difficult to say what ought to be done. It seemed to Grant that when the Rebels came out of their works to attack and were repulsed, they should be "followed vigorously to the last minute with every man."

"Holding a line," Grant wrote, "is of no importance whilst troops are operating in front of it."[256]

Humphreys in a covering memorandum noted that the First and Second divisions of the II Corps, having recrossed the James on the evening of the 20th, were en route to the Strong house. The II Corps soldiers were to fortify the sector

---

254   *Ibid.*, 542-543.

255   OR 42, pt. 2, 368.

256   *Ibid.*, 355.

between the Strong house and the IX Corps' right flank. If an emergency developed, Hancock was to march to Warren's assistance. At the same time, General Parke had been directed to reinforce Warren with Brig. Gen. Edward Ferrero's division.[257]

It was 3:00 p.m. before Warren acknowledged the receipt of Humphreys' message. When he did, Warren assured headquarters that if the Rebels attacked him so as to get "a crushing repulse," he would take advantage of the situation. Warren expected the Confederates to make one more push to dislodge his troops from the railroad, and he had alerted his officers to be on the lookout for such a move. To his front, Warren explained, the Southerners had retired into their entrenchments. But, if he marched west with his corps, Warren explained, he would have to make a detour to keep the grey clads from following on his flank. Moreover, if he moved he would "lose all the advantage" of his artillery and "get the effect" of the Rebels. Taking a pot shot at Grant, Warren observed, "I believe I have fought against the army opposed to me [enough] to know pretty well what to do here on the field."[258]

General Parke reached the Glove Tavern sector during the afternoon. The general had been accompanied as far as Strong's house by Ferrero's division. Halting, Ferrero put his troops to work entrenching and slashing timber. Parke, upon his arrival, resumed command of the three divisions of his corps which had been reporting to Warren since the 19th.[259]

*   *

South of Globe Tavern, all had been quiet on the night of the 20th along the line of outposts manned by Colonel Spear's troopers. Late the previous afternoon, Spear had made a forced reconnaissance west of Ream's Station. A 100-man Confederate detachment, which had been encountered at Ream's Station, was scattered by the hard-riding bluecoats. Before returning to his camp, Spear satisfied himself that Confederate horsemen were patrolling the Vaughan Road. The best available intelligence indicated that General Dearing's three-regiment brigade was camped three miles west of the Weldon Railroad.

Colonel Spear on the morning of August 21 moved out with three regiments. The Union horsemen gained the Vaughan Road without difficulty, the Confederates having pulled in their pickets. Pushing on, the bluecoats reached

257   Ibid., 368-369.

258   Ibid., 369.

259   Ibid., 369, 374; OR 42, pt. 1, 80, 590.

Colonel Wyatt's house. Here, they encountered a Confederate outpost. The Yanks attacked and drove in the Johnnies. From several prisoners, Spear learned that General Rooney Lee's cavalry division had reinforced Dearing's brigade. The shoe was on the other foot; the Federal cavalry in the Globe Tavern sector was now outnumbered. All the roads in the area had been barricaded by the grey clads, and if Spear advanced farther it would cost him many men.[260]

Leaving a strong force of vedettes on the Vaughan Road to watch the Confederates, Spear doubled back and headed for Ream's Station. Thundering into Ream's Station, the Yanks routed a 70-man Confederate detachment. While most of the Unionists pursued the fleeing Rebs several miles down the railroad, Spear had his demolition teams destroy two large water tanks, pumps, and burn a large storehouse. Before returning to their base at Perkins' house, the horsemen cut and rolled up several miles of telegraph wire. At the same time, Lieutenant Euphronous P. Ring, with a raiding party, had attacked and routed a Rebel detachment on the Brent Road.[261]

Spear's scouts, about dark, discovered that the Confederate force which had assailed Warren's left had disappeared. The ground northwest of Flowers' house was found "'vacant.'" The cavalrymen were unable to discover where the grey clads had gone.[262]

Stedman's cavalry spent the day guarding the pioneers as they wrecked the railroad south of Globe Tavern. By nightfall, the working party had demolished a mile and one-half of track.[263]

General Gregg, accompanied by Col. Charles H. Smith's brigade, had recrossed the James and Appomattox rivers on the night of the 20th and marched to Prince George Courthouse. The troopers reached the courthouse early on the 21st and camped. At 10:15 a.m. Chief of Staff Humphreys notified Gregg that Warren held the Weldon Railroad at Blick's. Spear's brigade of Kautz's division and Stedman's troopers were picketing Warren's left flank and covering the pioneers engaged in destroying the railroad. Meade wanted Gregg to march out to the Weldon Railroad and cooperate with Warren. If in Gregg's judgment part of

260   *OR* 42, pt. 2, 389.

261   *Ibid.*, 389; *OR* 42, pt. 1, 833.

262   *OR* 42, pt. 1, 833.

263   *OR* 42, pt. 2, 369-370, 375.

Spear's command should return to the left bank of the Blackwater River, he was to give the necessary instructions.[264]

Upon receipt of this directive, Gregg turned out Smith troopers. The column proceeded by way of Sturdivant's Mill to the Jerusalem Plank Road. Halting early, Gregg notified Humphreys that he had established his command post on the Plank Road below McCann's.[265]

General Meade and his staff, during the day, visited Warren's headquarters. They were there when they learned that Gregg had gone into camp at McCann's. Meade told Humphreys to have Gregg immediately march Smith's brigade to Globe Tavern, and assume the responsibility of guarding the army's left with his division. Kautz's troopers in the future were to cover the area from the Jerusalem Plank Road to the James. Since the roads in the Globe Tavern area were hub-deep in mud, Humphreys warned Gregg to leave his artillery and train behind.[266]

*   *   *

During the four days of fighting, the Federals had lost 251 killed, 1,149 wounded, and 2,879 missing; but they had maintained their grip on the Weldon Railroad.[267]

The contingency General Lee had anticipated from the time he moved into the Petersburg defenses was at hand. The northern section of the Weldon Railroad from Ream's Station to Petersburg was lost. The defense of Richmond and the subsistence of the Army of Northern Virginia from now on depended on the full employment of the South Side and of the Richmond and Danville Railroads. There were rumblings in Richmond that the Weldon line need not have been lost if Beauregard had met Warren's initial advance with a larger column,[268] but Lee knew both the limitations under which Beauregard fought and the inevitability of the breaking of the railroad by the Federals. With the simple assertion that "the smallness of the attacking force prevented if from dislodging" the foe,[269] Lee devoted himself to making the most of the lines of supply left him.

264   *Ibid.*, 374-375.

265   *Ibid.*, 375; OR 42, pt. 1, 617.

266   OR 42, pt. 2, 375.

267   OR 42, pt. 1, 128.

268   OR 42, pt. 2, 1198.

269   *Ibid.*, 1194.

The loss of the Weldon Railroad came, unfortunately for the Confederates, at a time when there was no corn either in Richmond or at the army depots around Petersburg. Lee at once set wagon trains to hauling supplies over the 30 miles of road that lay between Petersburg and Stony Creek, which was a station on the Weldon Railroad below the point where it had been wrecked by the Federals. He believed that by a wise use of these trains, and of the remaining railroads, with perhaps some importation of grain by way of Wilmington, it would be possible to subsist the troops until the Virginia corn crop was harvested. In a broader view, with an eye to the approaching Presidential campaign in the North, Lee believed the failure of the Yankees to drive the Confederates from Petersburg, after so much sacrifice, would have a dispiriting effect on the people of the United States.[270]

Editor's Conclusion

Warren's V Corps had been badly shattered by Grant's incessant attacks during the Overland Campaign. The Weldon Railroad revealed the extent of the corps' demoralization. Describing the rout of August 19, John Horn writes, "Attacked by Confederates on their front and flank, subjected to friendly artillery fire from the rear, Warren's soldiers cracked and surrendered in droves . . . when it was over 2,700 Federals filed into captivity."[271]

The Federals lost 4,279 officers and men at the Weldon Railroad, the Confederates 1,300.[272]

270 Ibid., 1195.

271 The Petersburg Campaign, 137.

272 The Petersburg Campaign, 33.

Chapter 6

The Second Battle of Ream's Station

August 25, 1864

Editor's Introduction

Despite heavy losses, Maj. Gen. Gouverneur K. Warren, the commander of the Federal V Corps, still held a portion of the Weldon Railroad on the night of August 21, 1864. Although Maj. Gen. Winfield Scott Hancock's II Corps was exhausted and seriously weakened after seven days of fighting (August 14-20) at the Second Battle of Deep Bottom (Fussell's Mill), Gen. U. S. Grant dispatched the battered corps south, well beyond Warren's position, to tear up more of the Weldon-Wilmington line. Grant's decision exposed Hancock's men to a potentially crippling Confederate counterattack.

Like the South Side Railroad feeding Petersburg and Richmond farther west, the Weldon artery played a critical role supplying Gen. Robert E. Lee's Army of Northern Virginia with food, ammunition, and other vital supplies. Its loss would make it that much more difficult for the Confederates to maintain their position.

Part I

Hancock's Troops Occupy Ream's Station— Lee Prepares to Strike

General Winfield S. Hancock, accompanied by the First and Second division of the II Corps, left their Deep Bottom encampments, shortly after dark on August 20, 1864. The troops took the road to Jones' Neck, Maj. Gen. John Gibbon's Second division in the lead. Hancock's blue clads commenced crossing the pontoon bridges at 7:00 p.m.—the infantry on the upper bridge, Brig. Gen. David McMurtrie Gregg's cavalry on the lower. General Hancock and most of his staff remained on the north side of the James until the last of the soldiers had crossed. Rain beat down throughout the night, and the corps pressed on over roads turned into ribbons of mud. Hancock recalled the night's march as "one of the most fatiguing and difficult performed by the troops during the campaign." Day was starting to break, when the exhausted corps halted and went into camp near the "Deserted House," east of Petersburg.[1]

The soldiers were soon turned to preparing breakfast. Hardly had the bluecoats finished eating, before Hancock received orders to put his corps into position near the Strong house.

By 11:30 a.m. on August 21, the officers had formed and mustered their units. Hancock gave the word and the column moved out. Marching via the Jerusalem Plank and farm roads, the two divisions reached the Strong house early in the afternoon. Short as was the distance, hundreds dropped out along the roadside, overcome by the heat and the exhausting efforts of the previous ten days, and particularly of the night before.

Within a short time, Hancock received additional orders; the II Corps was to march to Gurley's house and take up a position in support of Maj. Gen. Gouverneur K. Warren's V Corps, which had secured a stranglehold on the Weldon Railroad at Globe Tavern. Hancock's bone-weary Federal troops fell into ranks once again, and the mud-spattered column started its fitful march for

---

1   OR 42, pt. 1, 222, 244. For more information on these matters, see F. A. Walker, "Reams' Station," in *Papers of the Military Historical Society of Massachusetts*, vol. 5, 271; Walker, *History of the Second Army Corps*, 580-581.

Major General Winfield Scott Hancock
Library of Congress

Gurley's. When Hancock's men reached Gurley's house, the two divisions were allowed to go into camp to get some rest.[2]

Because of the terrible Virginia mud, Maj. Gen. George G. Meade had decided that for the time being it would be unwise for Hancock to take his artillery and trains west of the Jerusalem Plank Road.[3] Hancock had accordingly issued orders that the only wagons which were to accompany his column to Gurley's would be those hauling entrenching tools. The quartermaster, commissary, and ordnance people were to keep the rations, ammunition, and forage packed and be ready to forward these items when called upon.[4] The artillery brigade, in view of Hancock's orders, camped near Jones' house, a short distance west of the Plank Road.[5]

General Meade had left his headquarters about noon to visit the scene of the fighting at Globe Tavern. While en route to the Weldon Railroad, Meade passed Hancock's divisions. At 2:30 p.m. Meade telegraphed Lt. Gen. Ulysses S. Grant, "As soon as I get on the field and Hancock is up I will assume the offensive—before if practicable." Meade had been distressed to see how "weary" Hancock's troops were. As he informed General Grant, they "will not be fit for much today and will not much more than get into position."

---

2   OR 42, pt. 1, 222, 244; Walker, "Ream's Station," 271. General Hancock and his division commands slept on the ground alongside with their men in a pouring rain.

3   OR 42, pt. 2, 363.

4   *Ibid.*, 364.

5   OR 42, pt. 1, 406.

After examining Warren's position astride the Weldon Railroad, Meade (at 5:25 p.m.) wired Grant, "Hancock's men are so exhausted with their long march that nothing can be expected of them this afternoon." Having concentrated two divisions of Hancock's II Corps at Gurley's, Meade had shifted Maj. Gen. John G. Parke's IX Corps to the right. At the moment, Parke's soldiers were extending to the east to link up with Brig. Gen. Gershom Mott's division of the II Corps at Strong's house.[6]

By 9:20 p.m. Meade was back at his headquarters. Reporting to Grant, Meade announced that he had "found it impracticable to arrange any offensive movement for tomorrow." While Warren was confident of holding his grip on the Weldon Railroad, he had advised Meade against attacking. Hancock's men at the same time were fagged out by their forced march from Deep Bottom. Nearly one-third of the troops had straggled.

Grant, at 10:00 p.m., acknowledged Meade's latest dispatch. The commanding general assured Meade that he didn't expect any offensive operations on the 22nd, unless Maj. Gen. Benjamin Butler's Army of the James scored a success in its projected attack between the Appomattox and Bake-House Creek. If Warren's V Corps could retain its grip on the Weldon Railroad, Grant observed, it would be "a great advantage."

Grant inquired, "Has much of the railroad been destroyed?" After Hancock's men had rested, Grant felt that it would be wise to support the cavalry with a division of infantry and wreck as much of the Weldon Railroad as possible.

At 11:00 p.m. Meade replied that he would be prepared to act on the 22nd, "according to developments." During the day, the pioneers had been burning ties and twisting rails, but as yet no reports of their progress had reached his headquarters. If necessary, Meade promised to reinforce with infantry the force of cavalry covering the pioneers.[7]

Chief of Staff Andrew A. Humphreys, before retiring for the night, telegraphed Hancock and Warren to alert them that "circumstances may render it necessary to assume the offensive tomorrow." Consequently, Meade wanted the two corps commanders to have their men turned out and under way at an early hour.[8]

*   *   *

6   *OR* 42, pt. 2, 357.

7   *Ibid.*, 358.

8   *Ibid.*, 363.

Grant, on the morning of August 22, notified Meade that Butler's attack north of the Appomattox had been cancelled. As to the Weldon Railroad, Grant wanted Warren to maintain his hold at Globe Tavern, while the tracks were being ripped up as far to the south as possible. Grant assured Meade that he didn't plan to assail the Confederates behind their fortifications, unless Gen. Robert E. Lee pulled a large number of troops out of the Petersburg defenses. There was therefore no need for Warren to shift his corps, unless he could gain a better position by doing so. In case the Rebels resumed their attacks on Warren's troops during the next 48 hours, Grant had directed Butler to hold the X Corps ready to assault the Confederate line north of the Appomattox.[9]

General Meade paid a second visit to Warren's command post at Globe Tavern on the morning of the 22nd. While en route from army headquarters to the Weldon Railroad, Meade had been delighted to see that soldiers of the II Corps were rapidly entrenching the line from the railroad to Strong's house. Meade was elated to learn from Warren that the Confederates had disappeared from the V Corps' left flank, west of the railroad.

Touring the front with Warren, Meade was impressed. He was satisfied that the V Corps was "occupying the most favorable point in case a permanent lodgment on the railroad" was determined upon. Meade told Warren to hold his ground, and push forward skirmishers to feel the Rebels' position.

Hancock's troops at daybreak had fallen out under arms. When no Confederate attack came, the men were organized into fatigue parties and put to work repairing roads. When Meade had stopped at Gurley's house, while en route to see Warren, he had told Hancock to send one of his divisions "to assist in destroying the railroad and covering the working party." Reports reaching Meade's headquarters had indicated that many of the pioneers charged with wrecking the railroad had been alarmed at the stepped up activities of the Rebel cavalry and had deserted their work. Hancock's other division for the time being would be held in reserve at Gurley's.[10]

Early in the afternoon, Warren's scouts reported that as they pushed northward, they had established contact with Confederate outposts about one mile north of Globe Tavern. This was about 1,300 yards south of the Petersburg fortifications. The V Corps skirmishers, however, had been unable to pinpoint any Confederate troop concentrations; notwithstanding the reports that Warren had

9   *Ibid.*, 391.

10   *Ibid.*, 391-392; OR 42, pt. 1, 222, 269. A battalion of the 4th New York Heavy Artillery drew the assignment of building a corduroy road from Gurley's house to Globe Tavern.

been receiving from personnel in the signal towers telling that the Southerners were massing troops about the "lead-works."

When Meade relayed this news to Grant's headquarters, he reported that the pioneers worked very indifferently at tearing up the railroad.[11]

At the time that General Meade told Hancock to send a division to assist in wreaking havoc on the Weldon Railroad, the commander of his First division, Brig. Gen. Francis C. Barlow, was sick. With Barlow absent, the ranking brigade commander, Brig. Gen. Nelson A. Miles, led the division. Chief of Staff Charles H. Morgan (at 12:00 p.m.) called at Miles' command post and told him "to move the division to a point on the Weldon Railroad near the Perkins' house, to the left of the position occupied by the Fifth Corps, and to destroy the railroad, keeping half... [his] force at work, the remainder being held in reserve and covering the working party." One of Gregg's cavalry regiments, the 13th Pennsylvania, would report to Miles and be assigned the task of screening the infantry's left flank.[12]

At a word from Miles, the division was formed in column of fours. Before giving the word to move out, Miles sent a staff officer to draw from the V Corps implements needed to tear up the track. According to the latest information, the 200 men sent by the Quartermaster's Department to do this work had all returned to City Point.[13]

Miles' troops were cheered and jeered by their comrades as they left Gurley's. The division halted in the vicinity of the Perkins' house, where Miles and his brigade commanders deployed their troops into line of battle east of, and parallel to the Weldon Railroad. Skirmishers were advanced well to the west of the tracks, and the remainder of the Yanks were turned to wrecking the railroad. Teams of burley soldiers were put to work tearing loose rails; others collected and piled the ties in heaps. The torch was applied to the ties. As soon as they were blazing fiercely, several men laid the rails across the ties. After the middle of the rail had been heated to a cherry red, soldiers seized the ends and wrapped them around trees. If the rails were to be used again, they would have to be sent to a rolling mill.

By nightfall, Miles' division had destroyed two miles of track. Miles now recalled his brigades. Except for the units assigned to outpost duty, the soldiers bivouacked near Perkins' house.[14]

---

11   *Ibid.*, pt. 2, 392.

12   *Ibid.*, pt. 1, 222, 250-251.

13   *Ibid.*, pt. 2, 399.

14   *Ibid.*, pt. 1, 251, 261, 269, 277, 278, 279, 282, 285. Lieutenant Colonel Oskar K. Broady's 4th Brigade spent the night on the picket line.

Brigadier General David McM. Gregg
Library of Congress

*   *   *

Chief of Staff Humphreys, early on August 22, had advised cavalry General Gregg that the Rebels had retired from Warren's front. Meade wanted Gregg to see that the country west of the railroad was thoroughly reconnoitered. If the information gleaned from Rebel prisoners was true, Humphreys warned Gregg, a formidable Rebel mounted force, Maj. Gen. William H. F. "Rooney" Lee's division and Brig. Gen. James Dearing's brigade, were operating west of the Weldon Railroad.[15]

Meanwhile, Col. Samuel P. Spear, whose brigade had been cooperating with the V Corps since August 18, was preparing to report back to Brig. Gen. August V. Kautz. Preparatory to being relieved by Gregg's horsemen, Spear had sent a staff officer to tell the quartermaster and commissary people not to send any more rations and forage for his command to the Weldon Railroad. As soon as Gregg showed up, Spear would recall his pickets and start for the Blackwater.[16]

Pending Gregg's arrival, Spear led a reconnaissance to the area where the Confederate right had rested the previous evening. Spear found the Rebels. Notifying Warren of this situation, Spear theorized that if the grey clads had disappeared from the Vaughan Road as reported by the V Corps scouts, then the foe had either "swung around or divided." The Reb cavalry, Spear found, were becoming very cautious, and were constantly shifting their picket posts.

At the time (10:00 a.m.) that Spear addressed this note to Warren's headquarters, two of Gregg's regiments had arrived and were relieving his outposts.

---

15 *OR* 42, pt. 2, 407.

16 *Ibid.*, pt. 1, 833.

Major General W. H. F. "Rooney" Lee
Library of Congress

As soon as all his troopers had reported, Spear proceeded to Globe Tavern. There, he found several senior officers—Meade, Warren, Humphreys, and Parke. After listening to Spear's report of the situation in the Ream's Station sector, Meade determined to hold Spears' brigade for several more days. Instead of rejoining Kautz, Spear was to "report to General Gregg for duty."[17]

The addition of Spear's command gave Gregg a mounted striking force of three brigades. Gregg determined to employ Col. William Stedman's and Charles H. Smith's brigades to picket the expanse of countryside from the Jerusalem Plank Road on the east to the left flank of the V Corps on the west. Spear's troopers were sent on a forced reconnaissance west of the railroad with instructions to "proceed and attack Lee's cavalry."[18]

Spear's column marched as directed, taking a country road. At Wyatt's, the Federals encountered several hundred Confederates. The bluecoats attacked the Johnnies. A sharp three-quarters of an hour clash ensued. Overpowered, the grey clads fell back cross-country toward Petersburg. Spear's cheering troopers followed until stopped by a bridge the butternuts had destroyed. Before rejoining Gregg on the railroad, Spear was told by several blacks that the Confederate infantry had retired into the Petersburg defenses on the night of the 21st via the Squirrel Level Road.[19]

---

17 *Ibid.*, 834; OR 42, pt. 2, 417-418.

18 OR 42, pt. 1, 606, 834.

19 *Ibid.*, 834. In the clash at Wyatt's, Spear reported the loss of six men, one dead and the rest wounded. The Confederates made no report of their casualties, although Spear claimed the capture of several prisoners.

Late in the afternoon, Chief of Staff Humphreys notified Gregg that if the Confederates still held Ream's Station, they should be driven out. If need be, Gregg was authorized to call on General Miles for assistance. The railroad wrecking operation would be continued for another "day or two."

Accompanied by the 1st Maine Cavalry, General Gregg proceeded to find out if there were any Rebels at Ream's Station. Entering Ream's Station, the bluecoats found no grey clads. Questioning several of the inhabitants, Gregg was told that a Rebel cavalry brigade (Col. J. Lucius Davis') was camped behind Rowanty Creek, three miles away.[20]

*   *   *

General Meade, on the morning of August 22, got in touch with Grant. He wanted Grant's opinion on how far Miles' division "should go down the railroad destroying it." To assist Grant in making his decision, Meade reported that the division in question was "small, less than 4,000 effectives." A cavalry brigade of about 1,000 troopers had been attached to Miles' division.

From the stories told by Confederate deserters, Meade's staff had reason to believe that the Rebels had sent infantry to defend the Weldon Railroad on the night of the 21st. In addition, Union intelligence officers knew that "two divisions" of Confederate cavalry were in the area, besides the troops rushed up from North Carolina to oppose Miles' advance. Meade was of the opinion that Miles ought not to go beyond Rowanty Creek.

To make matters worse, Miles, because of muddy roads, hadn't taken his artillery or his trains with him. If Warren were satisfied that his position at Globe Tavern was secure, Gibbon's division and a second brigade of cavalry could reinforce Miles. But, Meade warned, "This is extending very far and leaves no means of repairing any casualties should the enemy, by a successful movement, penetrate our line at any point."[21]

Not having received a reply to his dispatch to Grant, Meade at noon sent another. Since his last, Meade reported, Warren had assured him that he had so strengthened his position at Globe Tavern that he felt "secure against any attack without the aid of the Second Corps."

---

20 *Ibid.*, 87, 606, 617; *OR* 42, pt. 2, 408. Col. J. Lucius Davis' brigade of Brig. Gen. Rufus Barringer's division, was encamped at Tabernacle Church. Beale, *History of the Ninth Virginia Cavalry*, 142.

21 *OR* 42, pt. 2, 418-419.

Major General Francis C. Barlow
Library of Congress

In determining future movements of the II Corps, Grant would have to take into consideration the condition of the roads on the south side. Except for the principal roads, all the others were "impassable for artillery and wagons." The rain which had beaten down on the evening of the 22nd would, Meade feared, keep them so for some days, unless there was an improvement in the weather—"a warm sun and drying winds." The question of supplying a large detached force had thus become very important. With pack mules, the Quartermaster's Department could keep supplies moving to the troops, provided they weren't too far removed from the trains.[22]

At 2:15 p.m., Grant wired Meade that "it would be imprudent to send General Miles with his small force beyond the support of the main army to destroy the Weldon Railroad." If the Federals could just hold their ground till the muddy roads dried, Grant would send Maj. Gen. Edward O. C. Ord with the XVIII Corps and cavalry to wreak havoc on the railroad as far south as Hicksford.[23]

Chief of Staff Humphreys (at 9:50 a.m.) had telegraphed General Hancock that Miles' division might be required to remain at its work of destroying the Weldon Railroad longer than had been originally anticipated. Consequently, arrangements would have to be made to see that additional supplies were forwarded to Miles' soldiers. Meade's headquarters, not Hancock's, would determine when the division would be recalled. Miles, upon reaching Ream's Station, was to leave a force to hold that point, but under no circumstances were his troops to go beyond Rowanty Creek.

---

22 *Ibid.*, 419.

23 *Ibid.*, 420. Major General Edward O. C. Ord assumed command of XVIII Corps on July 22, 1864, replacing Maj. Gen. William F. "Baldy" Smith.

Hancock saw that this dispatch was forwarded to General Miles for his guidance.[24]

Miles put his soldiers back to work early on the 23rd tearing up the railroad. During the morning, Colonel Spear reported as directed to Miles' Perkins' house command post. Miles told Spear to take his two regiments and make a forced reconnaissance down Vaughan Road to Stony Creek. Spear's troopers were to return via the railroad. While executing this sweep, Spear was "to ascertain the strength and location of the enemy's picket-line, their reserves, etc." As soon as Spear had reported, Miles released the 13th Pennsylvania Cavalry to allow it to rejoin Gregg's division.[25]

By 11:00 a.m. Miles' troops had destroyed the railroad to within one mile of Ream's Station. At that hour General Barlow returned from the hospital and resumed charge of the division. As soon as Barlow had taken over, Miles took command of his old unit, the 1st Brigade.

Upon questioning Miles, Barlow was disturbed to learn that Ream's Station hadn't been occupied. Barlow told Miles to rush a force to the station. Within a few moments, Miles had organized a special task force to occupy Ream's Station led by Col. James C. Lynch.

Placing himself at the head of the 81st and 183rd Pennsylvania, Lynch started southward, down the Halifax Road. No opposition was encountered as the Federals moved into the village on the double quick. Miles reached Ream's Station with the rest of his brigade at 1:00 p.m. After stacking arms near the abandoned rifle pits, Miles turned his troops to tearing up and twisting the track north and south of the station.[26]

The consolidated brigade had fallen out at an early hour. Colonel Levin Crandell led his troops down the railroad. Near Church Road, a halt was called; the soldiers stacked arms and began tearing up track. After the rails were wrenched loose from the ties, they were heated, and twisted. Pickets took position west of the road to protect the working parties against dashes by Rebel cavalry.[27]

Most of the troops of the 4th Brigade remained on outpost duty till early in the afternoon. At 2:00 p.m. Lt. Col. K. Oscar Broady assembled his troops and

---

24 *Ibid.*, 425.

25 *Ibid.*, 427; OR 42, pt. 1, 251, 269, 834, 835. Two companies (A and H) of the 4th New York Heavy Artillery were mounted and ordered to report to Colonel Spear.

26 OR 42, pt. 1, 251, 261, 269; OR 42, pt. 2, 428.

27 OR 42, pt. 1, 287-288. The 2nd and 3rd Brigades of the First division, II Army Corps were consolidated on June 27, 1864.

Brigadier General Nelson A. Miles
Library of Congress

marched them to within a mile of Ream's Station. Broady's troops as they tramped southward passed Crandell's bluecoats. Here, Broady's troops discovered a section of track still in operating order. A halt was called, while fatigue parties were organized and put to work wrecking the railroad.[28]

* * *

General Gregg (at 8:30 a.m.) notified Chief of Staff Humphreys that Miles was working his way down the Weldon Railroad toward Ream's Station. The cavalry leader wanted to know if he ought to send additional units to cooperate with Miles, or should he keep his troopers concentrated to patrol the ever increasing gap between the left of the V Corps at Globe Tavern and Miles' division. Currently, Gregg reported, he had one brigade posted at Crowder's, a mile north of Ream's Station, where the road to Monk's Neck Bridge and Dinwiddie Courthouse veered off to the southwest. Moreover, a number of his mounted units were becoming embarrassed because of a shortage of forage.[29]

A "change of circumstances," Humphreys replied, made it "desirable that a brigade of cavalry" should accompany Miles' division. Meade had suggested to Humphreys that Gregg detail Spear's troopers to assist with the destruction of the railroad. The cavalry leader was to see that this was done. Gregg was to employ the remainder of his troopers to cover the army's left. The animals of the cavalry

28   *Ibid.*, 278, 279, 283.

29   *OR* 42, pt. 2, 435.

division's supply train would have to be employed to pack forage from the depots to the front.[30]

At 11:00 a.m. Meade determined to alter slightly Gregg's mission. The cavalryman was to concentrate his troopers at Ream's Station, and picket from there to Warren's left. In case it was decided to send out another infantry division, Gregg was to hold his horsemen ready to cross Rowanty Creek and destroy the railroad.[31]

Thirty minutes later, Humphreys notified Hancock that an examination of the ground between Globe Tavern and the Confederate entrenchments had satisfied Meade that Warren's troops could hold their position. Since a farther advance up the railroad toward Petersburg had been vetoed, Meade wanted Hancock to send Gibbon's division to assist the First division in the destruction of the Weldon Railroad.[32]

Humphreys shortly thereafter advised Hancock of the decision to have Gregg concentrate his division at Ream's Station. Consequently, General Barlow wouldn't have to leave any of his troops at the station, as he pushed southward toward Rowanty Creek.

Hancock (at 12:10 p.m.) acknowledged the receipt of Humphreys' communications. On doing so, he announced that marching orders had been issued to General Gibbon.[33]

It was a number of hours before Gibbon's troops could get their gear squared away and finally break camp. The sun was setting when Gibbon's troops, with Col. Thomas A. Smyth's brigade in the lead, moved out. Four batteries of artillery (the 12th New York, Batteries A and B, 1st Rhode Island, the 3rd New Jersey, and the 10th Massachusetts Battery) accompanied the division.[34]

The 3rd New Jersey Battery, one of the artillerists recalled, was commanded by Capt. Christian Woerner, and was known in the corps as the "Dutch Battery." This battery was well officered and well disciplined, and did good and effective service. The captain, however, was a little peculiar sometimes in his ideas of military duty. One day the batteries of the corps, being in great part in service in the forts, a

---

30   *Ibid.*, 435.

31   *Ibid.*, 436.

32   *Ibid.*, 425-426.

33   *Ibid.*, 426.

34   OR 42, pt. 1, 222, 244, 302, 322, 331, 406. Two of the batteries (the 10th Massachusetts and Batteries A and B, 1st Rhode Island) were to report to the First division upon reaching Ream's Station.

Brigadier General John Gibbon
Library of Congress

vigorous cannonade broke out, putting all the other batteries and headquarters as well, on the alert for fear of a sudden attack on some point. Aides and orderlies were hurriedly sent to every battery of the corps to find out the cause of the sudden outburst. The aides sent to the other batteries found them all aroused and ready for action, but not firing. The one sent to Captain Woerner found him firing case-shot along the line of the enemy's pickets, on a portion of which his position had an enfilading fire. In response to an inquiry as to the cause of his firing, the foreign-born officer replied: "Oh, I was firing at those pickets; I likes to make them jump."[35]

Because of the terrible condition of the secondary roads, Hancock determined to move the long column to Ream's Station via the Jerusalem Plank Road. To reach the Plank Road from Gurley's, the division tramped eastward past Williams' house. Turning into the Jerusalem Plank Road, the head of the blue column pushed on about two miles. Because by this time it was beginning to get dark, General Hancock, who rode with John Gibbon, spied a large open field on the right of the road. Hancock called a halt. The division was moved into the field, and the troops were allowed to camp.[36]

The troops were going into bivouac when the clouds opened with a hard shower. After it ended, large numbers of soldiers collected under trees, "and woke the evening echoes in their attempts to drive away discomfort by singing with

35   George K. Dauchy, "The Battle of Ream's Station," in *Military Essays and Recollections. Papers Read before the Commandery of the State of Illinois, Military Order of the Loyal Legion of the United States,* (Chicago, 1899), vol. 3, 128-129.

36   *OR* 42, pt. 1, 222, 244, 302, 406; Dauchy, "The Battle of Ream's Station," 129.

unusual unction, 'John Brown's Body,' 'Marching Along,' 'Rally 'round the Flag,' and every other song of kindred character generally familiar."[37]

Meanwhile, Colonel Spear and his troopers had moved out to make a reconnaissance down the Vaughan Road to Stony Creek. Four miles northwest of Ream's Station, Spear's troopers encountered a Confederate roadblock manned by hard-nosed cavalrymen from Brig. Gen. Matthew C. Butler's division.

Major General Wade Hampton on the previous day had assembled Butler's troopers, who were guarding the roads leading eastward from Richmond. Accompanied by Butler's people, Hampton moved to the south side. On the morning of the 23rd, Butler's troopers relieved Rooney Lee's outposts on the picket line west of the Weldon Railroad.[38]

A hard fight ensued between Spear's and Butler's troopers. Satisfied that he was outnumbered, Spear sent an aide galloping off to contact General Gregg with an appeal for help. Long before the courier returned with word that Gregg could do nothing to help him, Spear had been compelled to fall back, leaving eight dead and wounded on the field. Spear now dispatched a plea to General Miles for reinforcements. When this man returned, he reported that Miles could send only 100 men.[39]

After retiring to the railroad, Colonel Spear addressed a note to Warren's headquarters. Besides describing what had occurred and his difficulties with Gregg and Miles, Spear reported that he had encountered the Confederates in force. Spear believed that if he were reinforced by one or two regiments of infantry, he could rout the Johnnies. Could Warren send his hard-pressed fighters any help? Spear inquired. His troopers were exhausted, Spear reported, but they would continue at all hazards to protect the V Corps' left. Spear was satisfied that where Miles and Gregg had gone, there were no Rebels.[40]

---

37 John D. Billings, *The History of the Tenth Massachusetts Battery of Light Artillery in the War of the Rebellion 1862-1865* (Boston, 1909), 301-302.

38 OR 42, pt. 1, 269, 835; OR 42, pt. 2, 427; Frank M. Myers, *The Comanches: A History of White's Battalion, Virginia Cavalry, Laurel Brig., Hampton Div., A.N.V., C.S.A.* (Baltimore, 1871), 322; Edward L. Wells, *Hampton and His Cavalry in '64* (Richmond, 1899), 227.

39 OR 42, pt. 2, 427; pt. 1, 269, 835. In the fighting, the two companies of the 4th New York Heavy Artillery serving with Spear's brigade lost 9 men: 3 killed, 4 wounded, and 2 missing.

40 OR 42, pt. 2, 427. During the afternoon, the two companies (A and H) of the 4th New York Heavy Artillery which were serving with Spear's brigade were replaced by Companies G and M of the same regiment. At first, Spear held the heavy artillerists in reserve. Late in the afternoon, Companies G and M were engaged against a Rebel cavalry patrol. In the fighting, the New Yorkers lost three men, one killed, and two wounded. OR 42, pt. 1, 269-270.

Brigadier General Thomas A. Smyth
Library of Congress

Upon receipt of Spear's dispatch, Warren replied that the cavalrymen were so far out that he would be unable to send any V Corps units.[41]

General Hancock was completely surprised by Spear's communication. When Hancock forwarded it to army headquarters, he pointed out that he had asked General Barlow, if Spear still held the field, to have the Rebel dead counted. In his report of the engagement, Spear had claimed that his men had counted 184 dead Confederates.[42]

Meade fairly boiled when he saw a copy of Spear's report. He dashed off a message for Hancock "to call on Generals Gregg and Miles for an explanation of the charge" against them lodged by Colonel Spear.[43] Hancock in turn asked Barlow to submit a report covering the accusations made by Spear against Miles and Gregg.[44]

Gregg, in accordance with Hancock's instructions, had marched his division early on the afternoon of August 23 down the railroad from Perkins' to Ream's Station. Shortly after his arrival at the station, Gregg was told by his scouts that Spear's troopers had encountered the Rebs about four miles out on the Dinwiddie Stage Road. To ascertain if there were any grey clads on the road linking Ream's Station with the Dinwiddie Stage Road, Gregg ordered out two regiments from Colonel Smyth's brigade. Should the Southerners be encountered within "reasonable distance" of Ream's Station, the combat patrol was to be prepared to

41 *OR* 42, pt. 2, 427.

42 *Ibid.*, 426.

43 *Ibid.*, 427.

44 *Ibid.*, 429.

engage them. The rest of the division would then be marched to the patrol's support.

Gregg accompanied the two regiments (the 2nd and 16th Pennsylvania) as they rode westward. About one and one-half miles from the station, Gregg spotted a large force of dismounted cavalry massed in the open field ahead. Gregg estimated that the Rebel force to his front totaled "more than a division." As Gregg formed his command and dispatched aides to the rear to bring up the rest of his command, the butternuts advanced toward his position.[45]

When the shout "Yanks were coming" was raised by Confederate pickets, General Butler called out his division. Troopers of the 35th Virginia Cavalry Battalion were quickly mustered. Captain F. M. Myers with the first squadron reported to General Butler on the right of the road, while Lt. Col. Elijah White with the remainder of the battalion joined Brig. Gen. Thomas L. Rosser's brigade on the left.

Butler's first order to Myers was to "find the Yankees in his front and tell him how many there were." Accompanied by five men, Captain Myers moved out. Deploying at the edge of a wood, the butternut scouts rode out into a field "covered with tall sedge grass and small pine bushes." The scouts hadn't advanced very far before they were fired upon. Wheeling their horses about, the Johnnies galloped back to where General Butler was impatiently waiting. Calling to Butler, Myers exclaimed that he had found about 1,200 Yankees on the left of the road.

"Very well," General Butler replied, "I know what's on the right." Calling to Brig. Gen. John Dunovant, Butler told him to dismount and advance his brigade. As soon as horse holders had been detailed, the officers formed the South Carolina brigade into line of battle. One of the men recalled, "this wooden-legged General [Butler] led them in a furious attack upon the enemy, galloping along full fifty yards in front of his line, and exposed to the fire of both friends and foes."

Gregg's combat patrol retired in the face of the South Carolinians' slashing onslaught. Butler and his cheering grey clads pursued the blue clads for about one-half mile. Here, Butler's advance was checked by the arrival of Union reinforcements.[46]

Each reinforcing Federal regiment as it reached the field was dismounted and brought to the front. By 5:00 p.m. "the action had fairly begun." Rosser's Confederate brigade now moved up and took position on Dunovant's left. Recalling the 35th Virginia Cavalry Battalion, Butler had Colonel White mass his

---

45   *Ibid.*, 436; *OR* 42, pt. 1, 606-607, 617.

46   Myers, *The Comanches*, 322-323; Wells, *Hampton and His Cavalry*, 277.

Brigadier General Matthew C. Butler
Library of Congress

"Comanches" on a hill in the road. White was told to hold his men ready to charge should the Federals attempt to advance.[47]

Butler maneuvered his troopers skillfully. Testing the bluecoats' strength, he jabbed "successively" at different points in Gregg's line. Gregg (by 7:00 p.m.) had all nine of his regiments on the field. Of this force, eight regiments were dismounted and engaged with the Rebs; the other command remained mounted to protect Gregg's flanks and be ready to move to the point of danger in case Butler sent a mounted column surging toward the Yanks' main line of resistance.[48]

The roar of battle on the western approaches to Ream's Station caused General Barlow to have the "long roll" beaten. As soon as the alarm was raised, the infantrymen ceased twisting rails and assembled on the double. Barlow dispatched his staff officers to see that the brigade commanders posted their units in the rifle pits covering the approaches to Ream's Station from the west. These earthworks had been thrown up in June by the VI Corps.

General Miles' 1st Brigade filed behind the breastworks, "its right extending across the railroad and facing north and west."[49] Colonel Broady's 4th Brigade took position behind the fortifications on Miles' left.[50] At the time that the alert reached him, Colonel Crandell of the consolidated brigade called for his troops to stop what

---

47   Myers, *The Comanches*, 323; OR 42, pt. 1, 606-607, 617. The 35th Virginia Cavalry Battalion was known as the "The Comanches."

48   OR 42, pt. 1, 606-607, 617.

49   *Ibid.*, 261.

50   *Ibid.*, 277, 278, 279, 282, 285, 286.

they were doing and fall in. After the pickets had been recalled, Crandell's brigade guided by Capt. Silas Marlin started down the railroad. The column reached Ream's Station at dusk. Crandell placed his men in the works on Broady's left.[51]

General Butler misinterpreted Barlow's actions. He feared the Union Infantry was en route to join in the fight. As the general sat his horse under a "very hot fire," he called for a courier to go to his line of dismounted troopers and tell them to retire. The messenger was shaken by the storm of minie balls that whistled around him. Seeing this, General Butler remarked, "Young man, you're scared; go back to Captain Myers and tell him to send me a courier!"

At this, the fellow lost no time in getting in touch with the captain, who detailed Sgt. George F. Everhart to carry out the mission. When Everhart reported to Butler, the general asked if he would carry a dispatch to the dismounted men. The sergeant replied, "By God! I'll start! Don't know so much about going."

"You'll do," Butler snapped.

Everhart turned his horse about and relayed Butler's instructions to the brigade commanders. Securing their horses the Confederates pulled back.[52]

The action had lasted till 8:00 p.m. By that hour Gen. Wade Hampton had satisfied himself that the Federals were demolishing the railroad in the Ream's Station sector. Hampton had taken advantage of the fighting to reconnoiter the ground. Returning to his camp, Hampton notified General Lee that the Federals were not "well placed." If Lee could see fit to send infantry reinforcements, Hampton felt that the Ream's Station Yankees could be isolated and overwhelmed.[53]

Following the withdrawal of the butternuts, Gregg's bluecoats held their ground. Gregg, notifying army headquarters of what had transpired, pointed out that although the Southerners were armed with "muskets," he didn't think that any of Lee's infantry was present. A hasty check had indicated that Union losses in the engagement wouldn't exceed 75.[54]

While the fighting was in progress west of Ream's Station, Union surgeons established a field hospital in the village church. Within a short time, ambulances began to arrive from the front. Asstistant Surgeon Elias J. Marsh of Gregg's

---

51 *Ibid.*, 287-288.

52 Myers, *The Comanches*, 323-324.

53 OR 42, pt. 2, 436; Freeman, *Lee*, vol. 3, 488; Wells, *Hampton and His Cavalry*, 277.

54 OR 42, pt. 2, 436; Wells, *Hampton and His Cavalry*, 277. In the fighting, the Confederates lost 21 killed, 103 wounded, and 12 missing.

Major General Wade Hampton
Library of Congress

division reported, "Many of the cases were severe and required operations, and all were dressed and made comfortable for the night."[55]

* * *

General Hancock (at 7:30 p.m.) on August 23, notified Chief of Staff Humphreys that the heavy rain that had been falling throughout the day had hindered the First division's working parties. The soldiers had had a difficult time keeping the fires used to heat and bend the rails going.[56] Thirty minutes earlier, Hancock addressed a note to General Barlow. Barlow was informed that Hancock, along with Gibbon's division, was en route to Ream's Station by way of the Jerusalem Plank Road. If all went well, Gibbon's troops would join Barlow in the morning. Gibbon's command and the artillery were slated to occupy Ream's Station, thus freeing Barlow's troops, reinforced by Spear's cavalry, to wreck the Weldon Railroad to Rowanty Creek, and, if possible, as far as Stony Creek. Should Barlow be hard-pressed during the night, he was to call on Gibbon for help.[57]

At 8:08 p.m. Barlow replied. The general proudly reported that the First division had destroyed the railroad to Ream's Station. At the moment, his troops were posted in the rifle pits covering the Western approaches to Ream's Station.

Barlow reported that Gregg's cavalry had been heavily engaged. The Yankee troopers had held their ground, and the firing had ceased. According to the information which reached him from the front, Gregg's entire division had been

55   *OR* 42, pt. 1, 617-618.

56   *OR* 42, pt. 2, 428.

57   *Ibid.*, 429.

engaged. Gregg had notified Barlow that he considered the position taken up by his troopers as "a desirable one," but he was afraid that an ammunition shortage might compel him to abandon it. The cavalryman had intimated to Barlow that it would be appreciated, if he would send his foot soldiers to relieve the horsemen if they were withdrawn. Barlow, however, opposed such a move, because it would require him to march his troops a mile west of Ream's Station and place them in a position which could be easily turned. Furthermore, as he understood his instructions, they were to destroy the railroad. In the morning, if things were quiet, Barlow wrote, he would put his men to work wrecking the railroad south of Ream's Station.

There was one question raised by Hancock that Barlow failed to answer. While Barlow informed his chief that Spear's cavalry, reinforced by a detachment of the 4th New York Heavy Artillery, had been in contact with Rebel cavalry throughout the day, he failed to mention the charges lodged against Miles and Gregg by Colonel Spear.

Hancock acknowledged Barlow's communication at 10:30 p.m. On doing so, he announced that Barlow's view of his primary mission was correct. But, should the Rebels press Gregg as hard as to prevent the infantry from destroying the railroad, Barlow was to march to the cavalry's aid and await the arrival of Gibbon's division. Hancock assured his division commander that "it is not supposed that the railroad can be destroyed before the enemy is driven off." Barlow was advised to send back for ammunition in case he was "likely to need more."[58]

*   *   *

Reveille sounded well before daybreak on August 24 in General Gibbon's camp. By 3:15 a.m., the troops had wolfed down their breakfasts, gulped their coffee, and had taken their position in the ranks. General Smyth's brigade took the lead as the division moved out. The long blue column left the Jerusalem Plank Road, soon after the troops had crossed Warwick Swamp, and turned into a road leading westward toward the railroad. Smyth's brigade reached Ream's Station at 7:00 a.m. In accordance with instructions from General Gibbon, Smyth had his troops file into position behind the breastworks on the left of Barlow's division.[59]

Gibbon's two other brigades (Rugg's and Murphy's), along with the artillery, reached Ream's Station by 9:00 a.m. Lt. Col. Horace P. Rugg posted the men of his 1st Brigade in the rifle pits north of the station, while Col. Mathew Murphy's

58   *Ibid.*, 430.

59   *OR* 42, pt. 1, 322, 328, 331.

bluecoats were kept standing in ranks.[60] The cannoneers massed and parked their artillery pieces in an open field on the left of Oak Grove Church, east of the railroad.[61]

One of the cannoneers recalled. "By daylight we found ourselves in the midst of a country which had not been much desolated by the march of war. Through this we passed cheerily along amid apple trees laden with fruit, and cornfields whose ears were just ready for roasting."[62]

The works at Ream's Station had been thrown up in the latter part of June by troops of the VI Corps, at the time they had been ordered out to cover Brig. Gen. James H. Wilson's Federal cavalrymen on their return from the raid on the South Side Railroad. They had been hurriedly thrown up, badly constructed, and poorly positioned. Instead of utilizing the railroad dump for a base, the rifle pits, facing west, were located about 20 to 40 yards west of the railroad. From 70 to 80 yards in front of the rifle pits were thick pine woods. The rifle pits paralleling the railroad extended about one-half mile and were not more than three feet in height, and "of frail structure, being built of fence-rails within," and "slightly banked with sods and loose earth." There were openings in the center for the Dinwiddie Stage Road and at each end for the Weldon Railroad and Halifax Road to pass through.

After crossing the railroad, there was a "return" extending in a northeasterly direction for about 1,000 yards, forming an obtuse angle at the right. The section of the railroad inside the fortifications passed through a cut on the right and along a fill on the left. On the left, the ground behind the breastworks rose slightly. In case of attack, troops posted there would be for practical purposes in an enclosed work, making "it impossible for ammunition or reserves to be brought up, except at the greatest disadvantage, from the rear, or for the troops thus enclosed to retire without exposure to observation and to fire."

South of the site of the depot, the Dinwiddie Stage Road (an important route linking Dinwiddie Courthouse with the Jerusalem Plank Road) crossed the Halifax Road and the railroad and disappeared in the pines to the west. A second road also connected Ream's Station with the Jerusalem Plank Road. This road, which had been followed by Gibbon's troops on their march, passed to the north of the Dinwiddie Stage Road.[63]

60   *Ibid.*, 308, 317.

61   *Ibid.*, 414.

62   Billings, *History of the Tenth Massachusetts Battery*, 308.

63   Walker, *History of the Second Corps*, 582-583; "Ream's Station," 272-274; Billings, *History of the Tenth Massachusetts Battery*, 308, 311; Dauchy, "Battle of Ream's Station," 129-130.

*   *   *

Early on the 24th General Barlow succeeded in obtaining, on the presentation of a "surgeon's certificate of disability," a 20 days' leave of absence. As soon as he could turn over command of the First division to General Miles, Barlow left for City Point, where he planned to catch a boat to Washington.[64]

Upon his arrival at Ream's Station from the Gurley house, Hancock called for General Miles. Hancock told Miles that his troops were to be relieved from duty in the rifle pits by Gibbon's. After this had taken place, Miles' division, accompanied by Spear's cavalry brigade, was to move southward destroying the railroad as it advanced.[65]

After recalling their pickets, Miles' brigade commanders formed and mustered their units. Exchanging good-natured cheers and jeers with Gibbon's troops, Miles' men marched down the Weldon Railroad about a mile and one-half. Colonel Lynch, who had resumed command of the 1st Brigade, halted his soldiers. After pickets had been thrown out, Lynch put his men to work wrecking the railroad. The consolidated brigade and the 4th New York Heavy Artillery were likewise put to work tearing up, heating, and twisting rails. Miles' other brigade, Broady's, was deployed into line of battle to cover the working parties. With skirmishers thrown forward, Broady advanced his battle line and took position in a cornfield west of the railroad.[66]

Colonel Spear with his two cavalry regiments had preceded Miles' infantry and had taken post at Malone's Crossing. Before very long, Spear's pickets on the Stony Creek and Malone's roads were attacked by Rebel patrols from Rooney Lee's mounted division. Spear called for help. Miles sent the cavalryman two of Broady's regiments—the 145th and 148th Pennsylvania. Reinforced by the sturdy infantrymen, Spear's horsemen made a forced reconnaissance down the railroad to within a short distance of Rowanty Creek. Roadblocks were established and manned by Spear's bluecoats on all roads leading from Rowanty Creek toward the area where Miles' foot soldiers were burning ties and twisting rails.[67]

Meanwhile, General Gibbon had organized a large number of his soldiers into fatigue parties to breakup the railroad between Ream's Station and the sector where Miles' troops were working. Colonel Rugg put 500 men of the 1st Brigade to work

64 OR 42, pt. 2, 447.

65 OR 42, pt. 1, 222, 251.

66 *Ibid.*, 261, 270, 278, 280, 282.

67 *Ibid.*, 222, 251, 285, 286, 835.

"destroying in a more complete manner railroad property, etc., which had been partially damaged."[68] One of Rugg's regiments, the 19th Massachusetts, was sent out as skirmishers to cover the approaches to the rifle pits held by the brigade west of the railroad. Rugg's bluecoats had occupied these breastworks at the time that Miles' division had marched south.[69]

Upon the withdrawal of Miles' troops, General Smyth, in compliance with orders from Gibbon, had shifted his brigade to the right. Smyth anchored his left flank on the Halifax Road. The 1st Delaware, reinforced by a pair of companies from the 2nd Delaware, was thrown forward and picketed the front to the left of the outposts manned by the 19th Massachusetts. The 69th and 106th Pennsylvania picketed the area east of the earthworks manned by Smyth's brigade. Once they moved into position, the Pennsylvanians relieved the 4th New York Heavy Artillery.

Throughout the remainder of the day, fatigue parties from three of Smyth's units worked to complete the destruction of the Weldon Railroad in rear of the rifle pits held by the brigade.[70]

As soon as Miles' command was out of the way, Colonel Murphy's brigade occupied the "return" east of the railroad and to the right of Rugg's troops.[71]

Shortly before noon, Capt. J. Henry Sleeper of the 10th Battery, Massachusetts Light Artillery had his gunners unlimber their four 3-inch rifles west of the railroad in the interval between Rugg's and Smyth's brigades. The rifles were emplaced behind a low line of breastworks, and the gun captains were told to "register their pieces on the Dinwiddie Stage Road."[72]

Between the cannoneers and the railroad embankment, a distance of not more than eight rods, the ground rose slightly. In this open space the limbers were parked, while the caissons were posted just across the Halifax Road. Having taken the station assigned them, Sleeper's artillerists had nothing to do but enjoy themselves as they chose, "for fatigue duty did not usually pertain to the lot of light artillery men." One of the men recalled:

---

68   *Ibid.*, 302, 308.

69   *Ibid.*, 302, 305, 311.

70   *Ibid.*, 322-323, 328, 331. From right to left, Smyth's troops were posted: the 14th Connecticut, the 4th Ohio (Battalion), the 10th New York (Battalion), the 12th New Jersey, the 7th West Virginia (Battalion), and the 108th New York.

71   *Ibid.*, 322-323, 328, 331.

72   *Ibid.*, 322, 414.

A cornfield not far off furnished us a liberal quantity of roasting ears during the day, and some good early apples were brought into camp by the more enterprising foragers. We remember the day as an extremely pleasant one, both in respect of the weather and our enjoyment of the surroundings. It seemed very holiday-like to us as we lounged about the guns . . .[73]

The right section of Batteries A and B, 1st Rhode Island Light Artillery manhandled its guns into position behind the breastworks on the left of Sleeper's rifles. Soon thereafter, the left section joined the right section. Batteries A and B were separated from the Massachusetts cannoneers by a traverse, and they had "stronger and better constructed works with embrasures." Lieutenant Walter S. Perrin, who was in charge of the battery, to be ready in case of an emergency issued instructions for his cannoneers to keep the teams harnessed.[74]

Lieutenant George K. Dauchy had the men of the 12th Battery, New York Light Artillery emplace their four 3-inch rifles about 300 yards west of Oak Grove Church, near the angle made by the right "return" with the railroad. Here, the works were "quite high and strong, with embrasures for artillery." Captain Woerner's unit, the 3rd New Jersey Battery, unlimbered its four guns behind the barricades to the right of the 12th New York Battery.[75]

To free Spear's brigade to cooperate with Miles, General Gregg early in the day called for Colonel Stedman. Stedman's troopers had relieved Spear's and took position west of Ream's Station on the Dinwiddie Stage Road. The regiments of Gregg's 2nd Brigade (Smith's) were given the task of picketing the country between the Dinwiddie Stage Road and the left flank of the V Corps, and from the Weldon Railroad to Gary's Church on the Jerusalem Plank Road.[76]

General Hancock at 10:30 a.m. notified Meade that Gibbon's division was occupying the entrenchments covering the western approaches to Ream's Station, while Miles' division was "pushing on with the destruction of the railroad." According to the reports reaching Hancock's command post from the front, the Confederates had shown no force. Their outposts retired as the Federals advanced. Hampton's Cavalry, which had been present in heavy force west of Ream's Station

---

73 Billings, *History of the Tenth Massachusetts Battery*, 311-312.

74 OR 42, pt. 1, 407, 423; Billings, *History of the Tenth Massachusetts Battery*, 311; Dauchy, "Battle of Ream's Station," 130.

75 OR 42, pt. 1, 420; Billings, *History of the Tenth Massachusetts Battery*, 311; Dauchy, "Battle of Ream's Station," 130.

76 OR 42, pt. 1, 222, 607.

the previous evening, had disappeared. The Rebels, however, continued to hold the junction of the Stage and the Dinwiddie-Ream's Station Roads.[77]

Late in the afternoon, Colonels Lynch, Broady, and Crandell reassembled their brigades. After the soldiers had fallen into ranks, the troops were put in motion for Malone's Crossing. Upon reaching the crossing, the bluecoats resumed wreaking havoc on the railroad.

About 5:30 p.m. Colonel Crandell received instructions from General Miles to withdraw his pickets, march his brigade back to Ream's Station, and bivouac for the night. Before reaching the rifle pits, Crandell was told by Miles to take charge of the picket line covering the western approaches to Ream's Station. It was starting to get dark before Lynch's and Broady's troops stopped work and started back up the railroad. The 145th and 148th Pennsylvania rejoined their parent unit—Broady's command—before it marched from Malone's Crossing. Spear's troopers remained behind to hold the crossing.[78]

Upon the return of Miles' division at 8:00 p.m., Gibbon redeployed his troops. Colonel Rugg, after recalling his fatigue parties and the 19th Massachusetts, shifted his brigade to the right about one-half mile. His troops now occupied the earthworks on the extreme right of the Ream's Station perimeter.[79] General Smyth moved his brigade east of the railroad, and occupied the breastworks "in two lines" on the left of Rugg's troops. Soldiers from Colonel Murphy's brigade held the rifle pits on Gibbon's left. After the officers had been alerted to have their units ready to march at 5:30 a.m. in the morning, Gibbon's bluecoats retired for the night.[80]

Miles saw that his division took position behind the earthworks on Gibbon's left. From left to right Miles posted his brigades: Lynch's, the consolidated, and Broady's. Lynch's brigade was west of the railroad, with its right flank anchored on the cut.[81]

Upon the return of Miles' division, Hancock at 8:00 p.m. notified Chief of Staff Humphreys of the day's happenings. The railroad, he reported, had been destroyed for "about three and a half miles beyond Ream's." Miles' troops had returned from their work and were safely behind the breastworks. In the morning, Miles' command was to be rested, and Gibbon's given the tasks of ripping up the railroad

77   *OR* 42, pt. 2, 448.

78   *OR* 42, pt. 1, 222, 261, 282, 288.

79   *Ibid.*, 302, 308, 311.

80   *Ibid.*, 323, 331.

81   *Ibid.*, 261, 278, 282, 288.

from Malone's to the Rowanty. The Rebel cavalry had been very quiet throughout the day. According to General Gregg, the grey clads still occupied the junction of the stage and the Dinwiddie-Ream's Station Roads.

Hancock warned Humphreys that his troops were "much fatigued." That very day, Miles had warned his corps commander that his men "were fagged out." Hancock was satisfied that the men hadn't "recovered from the fatigue of their late marches." When General Gibbon moved out in the morning, Hancock observed, he would be separated from Miles' division by three or four miles. In case the Rebels cut between Gibbon and Ream's, he could fall back via the Jerusalem Plank Road.

According to a local black man who had come into the Union lines that day, the Rebels were expecting the Federals to push on to Dinwiddie Courthouse.[82]

*   *   *

It was apparent to Hampton and his principal subordinates that the Federals were in too heavy force at Ream's Station to be dislodged by cavalry. Hampton accordingly addressed a note to General Lee proposing the dispatch of a strong infantry force from Petersburg to attack and, if possible, destroy Hancock's isolated command.

To this communication General Lee replied, pointing out that he deemed it inadvisable to send any portion of the infantry so far from the Petersburg lines.[83]

But on mature consideration of the high stakes involved, Lee determined to do something about the Yankees Hampton had pinpointed at Ream's Station. If the Federals were allowed to destroy the tracks from Ream's Station to Rowanty Creek, it would compel the Southerners to haul supplies being brought in from North Carolina over the Weldon Railroad by wagon from Stony Creek Depot to Dinwidddie Courthouse, and then over the Boydton Plank Road to Petersburg, a distance of 30 miles. It was desirable therefore that the Federals not be left free to destroy the railroad indefinitely to the southward, for this would increase the distance between Petersburg and that section of the railroad still in Confederate hands. In the political arena, also, every defeat inflicted on Union armies would tend to discredit the war party in the North. With these considerations in mind, Lee read Hampton's proposals for an attack on the Union force operating out of Ream's Station sympathetically and determined to adopt it. But the mistake made at

82   OR 42, pt. 2, 448.

83   Walker, "Ream's Station," 278-279.

Lieutenant General Ambrose P. Hill
Library of Congress

Globe Tavern of attacking piecemeal with an insufficient force would not be repeated.[84]

Two brigades of Heth's division, two of Mahone's, one of Field's, and three of Wilcox's were alerted to march for Ream's Station. Two divisions of Hampton's cavalry corps (Butler's and Barringer's) were to cooperate in the attack. As plans developed, Lee decided to increase the force that Maj. Gen. Charles W. Field had been directed to bring to Petersburg from north of the James. In addition to the two brigades already sent, Field was alerted to hold a third in readiness to join the others.[85]

The experiences of John F. Sale of Col. David A. Weisiger's brigade were typical of those of the soldiers assigned to march against the Ream's Station Federals. Sale wrote in his diary that the command was turned out at 1:00 p.m. Upon being formed and mustered, the troops were told to "prepare to move & leave your baggage." Major General William Mahone put his column into motion at 4:00 p.m., and the troops marched along behind the breastworks as far as Battery No. 41.

Early in the afternoon, Hampton, not knowing that Lee had changed his mind, started for army headquarters. While en route, he encountered an orderly bearing a dispatch from Lee, stating that Lt. Gen. Ambrose P. Hill had been ordered into the field with a strong force of infantry. Later a second messenger arrived with information that Maj. Gen. Henry Heth's combat-ready division was to accompany Hill. Hampton was to report to Hill, and do all in his "power to punish the enemy." Lee wanted Hampton to send his scouts to ascertain the Northerners' "position and the best point to attack them."[86]

General Hill had quietly marshaled his infantry brigades in the area west of the "lead-works." Major General Cadmus M. Wilcox's Light division—less Thomas' brigade— took the lead as the column marched out. Close behind came MacRae's and Cooke's brigades of Heth's division and Anderson's brigade of Field's division, which had been organized into a "provisional division" led by General Heth. Accompanied by Lt. Col. William J. Pegram's Artillery Battalion, the long column tramped down the Squirrel Level Road. General Mahone with his two brigades (Weisiger's and King's) brought up the rear.[87]

84 Freeman, *Lee*, vol. 3, 488; Humphreys, *Virginia Campaign of '64 and '65*, 278, 279.

85 Freeman, *Lee*, vol. 3, 488-489; OR 42, pt. 2, 1193.

86 OR 42, pt. 2, 1202; Walker, "Ream's Station," 279; Sale, Diary. n.d.

87 Freeman, *Lee*, vol. 3, 489; OR 42, pt. 2, 445-446; Caldwell, *The History of a Brigade of South Carolinians*, 180; Dunlop, *Lee's Sharpshooters*, 189-190; Sale, Diary. n.d.; Pegram was

Major General Cadmus M. Wilcox
Library of Congress

Hill's army, turning into the Vaughan Road, crossed Hatcher Run near Armstrong's Mill. It was starting to get dark when the division commanders halted their men near Holy Point Church. After preparing their rations, the troops bedded down for the night.

Hill and Hampton spent the night of the 24th at Monk's Neck Bridge.[88]

While he was waiting for reinforcements, Hampton had told his division commanders to keep their men well in hand and to be ready to take the offensive in a moment's notice.

Except for the half-hearted resistance offered by Brig. Gen. Rufus Barringer's (Barringer was in temporary command of Rooney Lee's division) outposts to the advance of Spear's Union horsemen beyond Malone's Crossing, the Rebel cavalry displayed little activity. General Barringer reported (at 10:00 a.m.) that the Yanks didn't seem disposed to advance beyond Malone's Crossing. A Union deserter had turned himself into Barringer's pickets, and, upon being questioned, had identified the troops at Malone's as belonging to Miles' division of the II Corps. To check on the Yankees' movements Barringer dispatched scouts to Stony Creek.[89]

Since his command was short of forage, Butler determined to send his train to Stony Creek. The wagons were rolling early on the 24th. It was 11:00 a.m. when the vehicles reached Stony Creek Depot. One of the troopers detailed to escort the

accompanied by the Letcher Virginia Artillery, the Purcell Virginia Artillery, Battery A, Sumter Artillery, and sections of Hurt's Alabama Battery and Clutter's Virginia Battery. *OR* 42, pt. 1, 858.

88 Walker, "Ream's Station," 279; Caldwell, *The History of a Brigade of South Carolinians*, 180; Sale, *Diary.* n.d.

89 *OR* 42, pt. 2, 1037.

wagons recalled, "Here they found big, luscious watermelons from North Carolina by the car load, which they enjoyed to their utmost until late in the evening."

By 2:00 p.m. the wagons had been loaded with forage and had started back to Butler's camp. After enjoying their watermelon feast, the troopers of the escort put their spurs to their mounts, and soon overtook the lumbering wagons. It was midnight before the train returned to its base, and the escort disbanded.[90]

*   *   *

Men manning Union observation posts along the Petersburg lines kept track of the Confederate troop movements. At noon, 700 grey clad foot soldiers with knapsacks on their backs appeared from the woods in front of the Federal earthworks and moved off in the direction of the Weldon Railroad. Two and one-half hours later, a column of infantry, estimated to number from 3,000 to 4,000 soldiers, emerged from the woods near the "lead-works" and marched southward along the Squirrel Level Road. A four-gun battery headed this column. At the same time, a 3,000-man column crossed the railroad and took position near a large fort east of the tracks. After remaining there one-half hour, the Rebels returned in the same direction (westward) from which they had come. About 40 wagons and 25 ambulances were sighted rolling southwestward along the Vaughan Road.[91]

At 5:30 p.m. Chief Signal Officer B. F. Fisher notified Chief of Staff Humphreys that a "column of infantry, extending a mile and a quarter in length, four files deep and well closed up" had moved out of Petersburg along the Squirrel Level Road. When last seen, the Confederate foot soldiers had disappeared into the woods a mile southwest of the "lead-works." Fifteen minutes later, another column, numbering about 2,000, came out of Petersburg and took the road pioneered by the first. Sixty-six wagons and 17 ambulances had preceded the first column.[92]

Several hours later, Major Fisher notified army headquarters that a third infantry column, three-quarters of a mile in length, had appeared in the vicinity of the "lead-works." Like the others, this one was marching via the Squirrel Level Road and was accompanied by ambulances and wagons.[93]

90   Myers, *The Comanches*, 324.

91   *OR* 42, pt. 2, 445.

92   *Ibid.*, 445.

93   *Ibid.*, 446.

General Humphreys, on the receipt of these reports from Major Fisher, studied the battle maps of the area. After doing so, he decided to alert Generals Hancock and Warren. Humphreys (at 8:20 p.m.) dispatched identical messages to the two corps commanders. They were warned that the signal people had sighted "large bodies" of Rebel "infantry passing south from their entrenchments" by the Vaughan and Squirrel Level Roads. Hancock was cautioned that these troops were "probably destined to operate against General Warren" or his troops. Humphreys felt that the II Corps was probably in the greater danger of being assailed. It was 11:00 p.m. before the courier with Humphreys' message reached Hancock's command post. Hancock, on acknowledging the receipt of the Chief of Staff's communication, pointed out that nothing was said about the Confederates' strength or the time they were observed. If the Rebels had ordered out a "considerable force to operate" against the II Corps, Hancock questioned the wisdom of sending his force so far from any supporting elements of the Army of the Potomac.[94]

Humphreys was in receipt of Hancock's message by 1:00 a.m. Replying immediately, he noted that the Rebel troops reportedly moving southward out of the Petersburg defenses numbered 8,000 to 10,000. The time that they had been seen last "was a little before sunset."[95]

A copy of a 9:00 p.m. message Chief of Staff Humphreys had received from General Warren was also handed to the staff officer for delivery to Hancock. Warren, after having read Humphreys' 8:20 p.m. dispatch, had advised headquarters that the butternuts observed marching out the Vaughan and Squirrel Level Roads might be working parties. All prisoners questioned during the day at V Corps headquarters had said that the Confederates were throwing up new earthworks. If the Rebels did plan to attack, Warren wrote, it would be Hancock's Corps, as his position at Globe Tavern was impregnable.[96]

Here is a severe indictment of strategic thinking at Union headquarters. The destruction of the Weldon Railroad between Malone's Crossing and the Rowanty cannot be cited to have been a matter of such vital consequence at that time as to justify any considerable loss, much less to run the risk of a serious disaster. Moreover, it was becoming evident that in the face of stiffening Confederate opposition that not much further progress in wrecking the railroad could be anticipated. If General Hancock were to fight, he should have his troops

94   *Ibid.*, 449.

95   *Ibid.*, 481.

96   *Ibid.*, 452; OR 42, pt. 1, 223.

concentrated and well in hand. This would be inconsistent with the continued destruction of the track. It seems that the alternative should have presented itself to Meade—either withdraw Hancock or reinforce him immediately.

General Meade had frequently expressed the desire that the Rebels might come out of their works, so the Army of the Potomac could fight them in the open. The movement of Hill's columns offered to Meade and his army the long-desired opportunity.

Hancock had at Ream's Station 7,000 infantry, with perhaps 2,000 cavalry. Meade could have rushed 25,000 men to Ream's more easily than Lee could send 13,000. The fresh divisions, which might have been deployed at Ream's on the morning of August 25, would have been in far better fighting trim than the jaded troops of the II Corps.

If Meade did not intend to fight, Hancock should have been recalled. If he intended to give battle, Hancock should have been heavily reinforced. Even conceding that Hancock might be able to repulse the Confederates, what was the use of putting anything in jeopardy when everything might be made entirely secure? But more than this: if Hancock were really to be assailed, where was the justification of losing the long sought for opportunity of encountering the foe in the open, with advantage of numbers corresponding to the excess of Meade's army over the Army of Northern Virginia.[97]

Part II

The Confederates Drive the II Corps from Ream's Station

At daylight on August 25, 1864, General Miles, as previously directed, relieved Gibbon's pickets. Gibbon, at the same time, was told by Hancock to have his troops remain where they were. The destruction of the railroad would be postponed pending the recall of Gregg's cavalry.[98]

Hancock (at 6:15 a.m.) issued instructions for General Gregg to have a combat patrol visit the junction of the Dinwiddie Stage and Vaughan roads to ascertain whether there was any Rebel infantry west of the Weldon Railroad. If possible, Gregg's troopers were to drive the Confederate horsemen from that strategic point

---

97   Walker, *History of the Second Corps*, 584-585; "Ream's Station," 275-276.

98   OR 42, pt. 1, 223. Seven hundred men from Miles' division were used to man the line of outposts.

to insure that the Federals would have timely warning "should any considerable force advance." Hancock promised to give Gregg "a good brigade of infantry" to bolster his cavalry division.[99]

Army headquarters was notified by Hancock that in view of the reported Rebel threat to his corps, he had decided not to send Gibbon's division to continue the destruction of the Weldon Railroad, until he had satisfied himself that no large enemy force was lurking in the neighborhood. Hancock informed Chief of Staff Humphreys that Gregg's horsemen were being dispatched to "clear the roads" to his right and front. In closing, Hancock warned, "I consider my force too small to separate such a distance until sure that the enemy's infantry is not in my front."[100]

Gregg's cavalry advanced westward and reached the Vaughan Road at two different points. The troopers in the course of their forced reconnaissance saw no Confederate infantry.

After studying the reports sent in by Gregg, Hancock determined that there was no immediate threat to his corps. Orders were drafted for General Gibbon to assemble his troops, march southward, and proceed with the wrecking of the railroad as far as Rowanty Creek.[101]

Gibbon pulled his division out from behind the breastworks covering the approaches to Ream's Station by 7:00 a.m. The troops were massed in a sorghum field in rear of the railroad, facing west. At 9:00 a.m., Gibbon was notified by Hancock "to move down the railroad and continue its destruction." When the column left the sorghum field and started down the Halifax Road, Smyth's brigade had the lead.[102]

As soon as Gibbon's troops had been pulled out of the rifle pits east of the track, facing north, Colonel Lynch was directed to occupy them. Lynch's men promptly carried out this assignment. When he inspected the brigade in its new position, Lynch found that its left flank was anchored on the railroad.[103]

---

99   *OR* 42, pt. 2, 497.

100 *Ibid.*, 481.

101 *Ibid.*, 481. *OR* 42, pt. 1, 223.

102 *OR* 42, pt. 1, 302, 308, 317, 323, 328, 337. During the night, troops from Miles' division had relieved the 1st Delaware and the battalion from the 2nd Delaware on the picket line. The 69th and 106th Pennsylvania of Smyth's brigade didn't rejoin the unit until after the brigade had reached the sorghum field.

103 *Ibid.*, 216. From left to right Lynch's brigade was posted: the 81st Pennsylvania, 28th Massachusetts, 28th Michigan, 5th New Hampshire, 183rd Pennsylvania, 120th New York, 2nd New York Heavy Artillery, 61st New York, and 140th Pennsylvania.

The consolidated brigade held the breastworks west of the railroad. Major John W. Byron, with Colonel Crandell absent in charge of the picket line, inspected the sector held by the consolidated brigade. He found that the brigade's right rested near the gap in the works through which the railroad passed through a cut. A heavy growth of pine and underbrush fronted the consolidated brigade's right and center. The timber had been slashed to a depth of about 30 feet. On the left of the brigade, there was an open field, and a ten-yard opening in the works to allow for the passage of the Dinwiddie Stage Road between Byron's unit and the right of Broady's brigade.[104]

Colonel Broady's bluecoats and the 4th New York Heavy Artillery—the ex-artillerists on the left—held the rifle pits to the left of the consolidated brigade.[105]

Upon occupying the works, Miles put all his pioneers, reinforced by 50 axmen, to work slashing timber in front of the division and cutting roads behind the line to facilitate the movement of troops and artillery.[106]

Colonel Spear's cavalry brigade had spent the night at Malone's Crossing. Strong outposts watched the roads leading from the Crossing to Rowanty Creek.[107]

*   *   *

Over at Holy Point Church, Confederate Generals Heth and Wilcox had rousted out their combat-ready foot soldiers at an early hour. By 8:00 a.m. the brigade commanders reported that their troops were formed and anxiously awaiting the word to move against the foe.[108]

Several hours earlier, Generals Hill and Hampton had had an important meeting at Monk's Neck Bridge. Hill told Hampton to divide his cavalry corps. The cavalry leader was to hit the Yankees east of the Weldon Railroad with his main force, while the remainder of his corps was to screen the advance of Hill's infantry toward Ream's Station. Hampton made his plans accordingly. General Barringer with Col. William H. Cheek's North Carolina brigade was to advance up the Halifax Road toward Malone's Crossing; Col. J. Lucius Davis' brigade was to march via

104 *Ibid.*, 288.

105 *Ibid.*, 270. Three companies of the 4th New York Heavy Artillery were assigned to picket duty—Companies I and K watched the division right and Company K the left.

106 *Ibid.*, 250.

107 *Ibid.*, 834, 835.

108 Caldwell, *History of a Brigade of South Carolinians*, 180; Dunlop, *Lee's Sharpshooters*, 190.

Malone's Road. General Butler with two of his three brigades (Rosser's and Young's) was to follow Davis' brigade as it drove for Malone's Crossing. Dunovant's brigade would be left to protect the rear and flank of Hill's infantry.[109] Word that something big was in the mill leaked out. The camps occupied by Hampton's troopers were alive on the night of the 24th "with preparation for something lively in the near future." Rations and ammunition were issued. "Boots and Saddles" sounded about midnight. After the brigade commanders had mustered their units, the columns moved out.[110]

An hour before daylight, Colonel White of the 35th Virginia Cavalry called to Captain Myers:

> A. P. Hill was coming down during the day to drive the Yankees away from Ream's; that Hampton was going to draw their attention and amuse them until Hill could get his position; that the colonel was going on a scout for Hampton, and would be gone all day, and that Myers was to take charge of the battalion . . . [111]

General Rosser soon rode up at the head of the Laurel brigade. Spotting Captain Myers, Rosser told him that he wanted "his people" for duty as the advance guard.

Myers replied that he didn't "mind the hanging half as much as he did the being told of it so long beforehand."

Taking post at the head of the Laurel brigade, the Comanches headed for the Malone's bridge rendezvous.[112]

After seeing that all his men were in the saddle, Hampton (at 5:00 a.m.) said goodbye to General Hill. Hampton crossed the Rowanty at Malone's bridge with his advance brigade (Davis'). A short distance beyond the stream, troopers of the 9th Virginia Cavalry surprised two of Colonel Spear's bluecoated cavalrymen "busily engaged in skinning a cow." Dropping their knives, the Yankees took to their heels.[113]

Before they had gone another hundred yards, the Virginians encountered several of Spear's pickets. Scattered shots were exchanged; the Federals fell back on

---

109 OR 42, pt. 1, 942-943. With Barringer in command of Rooney Lee's division, Colonel Cheek led Barringer's brigade.

110 W. B. Brooks, *Butler and His Cavalry in the War of Secession 1861-1865* (Columbia, 1909), 303.

111 Myers, *The Comanches*, 324-325.

112 *Ibid.*, 325.

113 Beale, *History of the Ninth Virginia Cavalry*, 142; OR 42, pt. 1, 834, 835, 943.

their supports. The Union officer in charge posted his men in a strong position and sent a messenger racing to alert Colonel Spear. It was 8:00 a.m. when the courier reached Malone's Crossing. Mounting his horse, Spear headed for the point of danger. By the time the colonel had reached the roadblock, Davis' Virginians had arrived in force.[114]

Impressed by the strength of the Union position, Colonel Davis dismounted a portion of his brigade. After a sharp fight, the Federals gave way, retiring up the road to Malone's Crossing. As soon as they had remounted, the Confederates pounded off after the Yanks. Spear's rear guard and the Rebel vanguard were in constant contact as the Northerners pulled back, leaving a number of dead and wounded sprawled in the road.[115]

Meanwhile, Colonel Spear had sent one of his aides, Lt. John W. Ford, to warn General Hancock that Hampton's cavalry had crossed the Rowanty in force, and that his cavalrymen were unable to check the Rebel advance.[116]

When he received this intelligence, Hancock sent orders for General Gibbon to forget about wrecking the railroad and drive the Rebel horsemen back across Rowanty Creek. Relaying this information to army headquarters, Hancock observed that the Confederates "show a pretty strong front," but he felt it was "only cavalry."[117]

The head of Gibbon's division had reached a point on the Halifax Road about three-quarters of a mile south of Ream's Station, when a staff officer galloped up to inform Gibbon that he was to march to Spear's assistance. Gibbon halted his troops while making necessary dispositions to carry out his new mission. General Smyth was directed to deploy one of his best regiments to act as skirmishers to the right side of the railroad. These skirmishers were to be supported by a second regiment. Covered by this force, Smyth's brigade was then to push forward to Malone's Crossing, drive back the Confederates in his front, and procure the entrenching tools that had been left there on the previous afternoon by Miles' bluecoats.

In compliance with Gibbon's instructions, Smyth threw the 1st Delaware forward as skirmishers. One hundred yards behind the Delaware regiment, also deployed as skirmishers, came the 12th New Jersey. Smyth's brigade, spearheaded

114 *OR* 42, pt. 1, 834, 835, 943.

115 *Ibid.*, 834, 835, 943.

116 *Ibid.*, 835.

117 *OR* 42, pt. 2, 482.

by these two units, resumed its march down the Halifax Road. Gibbon's other two brigades followed Smyth's column.[118]

Colonel Spear, learning that Gibbon's division was en route to his assistance, urged his troopers to hold on. After falling back to Malone's Crossing, the Federal horsemen had dismounted and taken up a position with their left flank resting on a railroad cut and their right flank on an old brick kiln. As the dismounted grey clads of the 9th Virginia Cavalry beat their way ahead, they discovered that the Yankees' left overlapped their right for a considerable distance. Colonel Richard L. T. Beale of the 9th called for his men to lie down, while Colonel Davis called up the 10th Virginia.[119]

When Major Clemens of the 10th Virginia rode up, Colonel Davis ordered him to move his troopers along the base of a hill and form them on the right flank of the 9th Virginia. Meanwhile, General Hampton had called for artillery support. A section of guns manned by McGregor's Virginia Battery rumbled up the road from Malone's bridge. The cannoneers threw their pieces into battery. Almost as soon as the trails struck the ground, the horse artillerists had their pieces in action. A storm of iron shot and shell from these guns helped unnerve Spear's outnumbered command.

Troopers of the 9th Virginia were delighted to hear the cannons and see the reinforcements. Letting go a "Rebel Yell," they charged the Federals (men of the 1st District of Columbia Cavalry) holding the kiln. Not wanting to meet the butternuts in hand-to-hand combat, the 1st District of Columbia fled in "dismay," receiving as it did an enfilading fire from the left. Many of the bluecoats, finding that they were a hindrance, dropped "their fine rifles and ammunition in the road." Spear succeeded in rallying and reforming his battered command on the high ground behind Smart's house.[120]

Before pushing on, the Confederate officers mustered their units and learned that they had suffered about 15 casualties in the engagement. A short distance beyond the crossing, the scouts sighted "a large body of cavalry and led-horses" in a field about one-half mile to their front. As Colonel Beale recalled it, "The opportunity for a charge was the rarest we had seen, and Ball's Squadron, which was kept always mounted, and which carried only pistols and sabres, was up and ready for the fray."

118 OR 42, pt. 1, 323, 328, 332.

119 Beale, History of the Ninth Virginia Cavalry, 142.

120 Ibid.; OR 42, pt. 1, 223, 245, 835, 943.

Hampton, who was with Colonel Davis, told his brigade commander to hold up, pending the arrival of one of Butler's regiments. Long before the reinforcing column arrived, Spear's bluecoated horsemen had disappeared into the woods.[121]

Colonel Cheek's North Carolinians in the mean time, had crossed Rowanty Creek and were advancing up the Halifax Road. As he approached Malone's Crossing, General Barringer, who was riding with Cheek, saw that Davis' Virginians had already reached that point. Barringer accordingly had Cheek's troopers cross to the east of the railroad.[122]

Davis' troopers hadn't advanced very far beyond Malone's Crossing, before the cry, "Yankee infantry!" rang out. A strong body of Union foot soldiers could be seen coming down the Halifax Road on the double. These troops belonged to General Smyth's brigade.

General Smyth's infantry brigade on approaching Malone's Crossing found Spear's cavalry in full retreat. As the Union skirmishers closed in on Davis' grey clads, Smyth called for his skirmish line to make a left half-wheel. In the face of this Union threat, Hampton shouted for Davis to have his men dismount. There was a crackle of small arms, as the men in blue and in grey blazed away. Smyth, seeing that both his flanks were exposed, sent two companies of the 12th New Jersey scampering to the left, while he called up the 108th New York. The New Yorkers were formed to the right, their battle line nearly perpendicular to the skirmish line. About this time, two of McGregor's guns began to hammer away at the Yanks.[123]

Observing that Smyth was in contact with the Rebels, Colonel Rugg called a halt. Two regiments (the 7th Michigan and the 59th New York) were advanced to the left to feel for Confederates. Deployed as skirmishers, these two regiments kept pace with Smyth's troops west of the railroad. Rugg formed the remainder of his brigade into line of battle east of the railroad, but instead of advancing these troops held their ground.[124]

When McGregor's gunners opened fire, several projectiles from their rifled pieces exploded in the Ream's Station earthworks. Captain Sleeper of the 10th Massachusetts Battery called for Lt. H. H. Granger. The lieutenant was told to take a section of the guns and report to General Gibbon. Orders were given for the right section to limber up its pieces. The artillerists drove their guns down the Halifax

---

121 Beale, *History of the Ninth Virginia Cavalry*, 142-143.

122 OR 42, pt. 1, 223, 943; OR 42, pt. 2, 482.

123 OR 42, pt. 1, 323, 943; Beale, *History of the Ninth Virginia Cavalry*, 143.

124 OR 42, pt. 1, 302, 311. The 59th New York was deployed to the right and the 7th Michigan to the left.

Road about one mile. There, they were hailed by General Gibbon. The general told Granger to emplace his guns in a burned-over field about 70 yards east of the railroad. Supported by Rugg's battle line, the Massachusetts cannoneers engaged McGregor's rifles. After expending 48 rounds of ammunition, Granger's men forced the grey clads to cease firing and shift their pieces. During the artillery duel, a fragment from a bursting Rebel shell cut the lieutenant's bridle reins.[125]

Daring the cannonade, Generals Rosser and Butler had sat their horses near McGregor's guns. As the shells from the 10th Massachusetts Battery whistled low overhead, some of the men were seen to duck. General Butler remarked to Rosser, "They are disposed to be rather familiar this morning."

Rosser answered, "Yes, politeness is in order this morning, but don't bow too low boys, it isn't becoming."

One of the troopers in the 35th Virginia Cavalry Battalion, Henry Simpson, overheard the general and exclaimed, "Yes it is; it's becoming a little too darned hot here, if that's what you mean."

Most of the boys agreed with Simpson.[126]

Smyth's Federal skirmishers west of the railroad drove in the Confederate vedettes. After advancing about one-half mile, the blue-uniformed troops were checked by stiffening resistance. To get his stalled attack moving, Smyth shouted for Lt. Col. Richard S. Thompson of the 12th New Jersey to redeploy his right battalion in close support of the 1st Delaware's skirmishers and charge. A staff officer at the same time was sent to bring up the remainder of the brigade, which had halted when McGregor's guns had opened. As soon as the column filed into position behind the skirmish line, the skirmishers charged and drove Davis' dismounted Virginians through a cornfield, across an open field, and into the pines beyond.

Hampton, seeing that Davis' troopers were in trouble, called up two of Butler's brigades—Rosser's and Young's. Dismounting and deploying into line of battle on the run, the Rebs posted themselves behind a rail fence and anxiously awaited the Union advance.

Smyth's skirmishers, upon driving Davis' pickets through the woods, sighted a formidable battle line moving toward them. The bluecoats retreated to the crest of the rise occupied prior to their advance. Hampton's dismounted troopers followed the Yanks part way across the open field, and then retired into the pines out of

---

125 Billings, *History of the Tenth Massachusetts Battery*, 313; *OR* 42, pt. 1, 407, 414.

126 Myers, *The Comanches*, 325-326.

which they had advanced. All the while, McGregor's cannoneers continued to hammer the Federals.[127]

General Smyth dispatched an aide to report what had happened to Gibbon. Within a few minutes, the staff officer returned and said that Gibbon wanted the brigade to press the foe, "and ascertain, if possible, his force and position." To discharge this mission, Smyth redeployed his brigade: the 7th West Virginia Battalion, 4th Ohio Battalion, and left battalion of the 14th Connecticut were called up and massed in double line of battle. The right battalion of the 12th New Jersey was posted *en echelon* to the left of the battle line, while the right battalion of the 14th Connecticut was deployed as skirmishers and positioned to the right and rear of the 7th West Virginia. The 69th and 106th Pennsylvania were to support the forced reconnaissance.

Smyth, as soon as his officers had completed their dispositions, waved his troops forward. Screened by the skirmishers of the 1st Delaware, the brigade advanced in line of battle parallel to, and, west of the railroad. Once again, Hampton's pickets gave way. Although the Yanks were exposed to artillery and small-arms fire, casualties were slight. After forging ahead about one-half mile, Smyth saw that a swamp lay across the line of march of his right wing. A number of Rebs could be seen filing into position on the opposite side of the morass. Confederate resistance at the same time stiffened all along the brigade front. Taking cognizance of the physical obstacle and the formidable force Hampton had massed to his front, Smyth called a halt.[128]

Hampton's butternuts in opposing the thrust by Smyth's soldiers instinctively followed the directions General Butler had given to one of his colonels, who had requested reinforcements because he was being outflanked, "Well! Flank them back then!"[129]

Hampton at the time of Smyth's initial thrust had notified Gen. A. P. Hill that the bluecoats had rushed up their infantry and had recalled their cavalry. In reporting this information to Hill, Hampton suggested that since the Federals had sent a strong infantry column against his cavalrymen, the Confederate foot soldiers should promptly attack Ream's Station.

Generals Hampton, Butler, and Rosser were sitting in the yard of a farm house, when a courier rode up with Hill's reply. Glancing at the scrap of paper handed him by the messenger, Hampton learned that Hill was marshaling his troops,

---

127 OR 42, pt. 1, 323, 332, 943.

128 *Ibid.*, 323, 328, 332.

129 Wells, *Hampton and His Cavalry*, 279.

preparatory to attacking. Meanwhile, he wanted Hampton to draw the Unionists farther down the railroad, so the infantry could take then in the rear.[130]

These were the tactics Hampton had employed in coping with Smyth's forced reconnaissance. After falling back about 400 yards, Hampton dispatched a strong column to bluff an assault on Smyth's right. Smyth spotted this force and decided it would be unwise to launch a frontal attack on Hampton's dismounted troopers. To meet the danger to his right, Smyth called up and deployed the battalion of the 10th New York. Bypassing the New Yorkers, the grey clads sought to reach the Halifax Road. If successful, they would be able to isolate and perhaps smash Smyth's brigade. Smyth was alerted to this danger in the nick of time. Two regiments, the 108th New York and 1st Delaware, came up on the double, took position to the left of the 10th New York, and succeeded in keeping the butternuts from sweeping around Smyth's right and gaining the Halifax Road.[131]

Meanwhile, Cheek's North Carolina brigade charged the picket line held by the 13th Pennsylvania Cavalry. Union General Gregg had given the Pennsylvanians the task of watching the countryside between Ream's Station and the Jerusalem Plank Road. The Rebel horsemen broke through and reached Jones Hole Swamp, east of the railroad. Learning of this threat to his communications, General Hancock sent word for Miles to be on the lookout. Miles told Colonel Broady to rush the 116th and 145th Pennsylvania to the cavalry's assistance. Accompanied by the 4th Pennsylvania Cavalry, the foot soldiers hastened eastward. Near Jones Hole Swamp, the bluecoats encountered Cheek and his North Carolinians. The Federals bested the Confederates, and the butternuts retired on Malone's Crossing.

Upon being advised that Cheek's men had run into difficulty, Hampton sent word for General Barringer, who had ridden with Cheek, to picket strongly the Emmons' Mill Road. After establishing the roadblock, Barringer reported to Hampton at Malone's Crossing. Barringer and Cheek showed up at Hampton's command post just as Davis' and Butler's troopers were retiring in face of Smyth's advance. Hampton hailed Barringer and had him dismount one of Cheek's regiments—the 2nd North Carolina Cavalry. This regiment double-timed into position east of the railroad, ready to turn Smyth's left should the opportunity present itself.[132]

General Hancock, satisfied that the slashing attacks mounted by the Rebel cavalry spelled trouble, resolved to recall Gibbon's division. As soon as the aide

---

130   Brooks, *Butler and His Cavalry*, 303; OR 42, pt. 1, 943.

131   OR 42, pt. 1, 324, 328, 332.

132   *Ibid.*, 223, 251, 607, 943.

with this message reached his command post, Gibbon issued orders for Rugg's and Murphy's brigades to retire into the Ream's Station entrenchments. Smyth's blue coats for the time being were to hold their ground and keep the Confederate horsemen from harassing their comrades as they tramped northward.[133]

Murphy's brigade took the lead as the division pulled back. Reaching Ream's Station, Murphy's bluecoats filed into the newly constructed "light" breastworks east of the railroad, facing southeast. The railroad dump separated Murphy's left from the right of the 4th New York Heavy Artillery. Rugg's soldiers, accompanied by Granger's guns, reached the Ream's Station perimeter hard on Murphy's heels. The 7th Michigan and 59th New York, which had been deployed as skirmishers, had advanced in conjunction with Smyth's brigade and were in contact with dismounted troopers of the 2nd North Carolina east of the railroad. The North Carolinians hounded the Union skirmishers as they retired.

Before reaching Ream's Station, Colonel Rugg sent orders for the 7th Michigan and 59th New York not to enter the earthworks. They were to patrol the countryside from the railroad on the west to Tucker's house on the east. General Hancock had Rugg post the remainder of his troops on the left of the breastworks occupied by Murphy's brigade. Granger's gunners remounted their two 3-inch rifles in the emplacement from which they had been withdrawn earlier in the day.[134]

While Gibbon's troops had been absent, Hancock had studied the rifle pits covering the approaches to Ream's Station. The general decided that it would be wise to throw up a left "return." Working parties from Miles' division were turned to. "Soon," one of the Yanks reported, "the entrenchments were extended . . . across the Weldon and Halifax Roads, then gradually bending still farther to our rear, crossed the Dinwiddie [Stage] Road, and passing through an extensive cornfield of stunted growth, terminated at the edge of the woods not far in rear of the church, thus encompassing us on three sides."[135]

The left "return" was almost parallel with the right "return." Moreover, as the fighting developed, the troops posted there would, to their horror, discover that they were within small arms range of Confederate troops assailing the rifle pits west of the railroad. It was into these works that Gibbon's troops clambered.

About noon, Confederate troopers from Dunovant's brigade, who were covering Hill's advance, attacked the picket line manned by the 16th Pennsylvania

133 *Ibid.*, 224, 293.

134 *Ibid.*, 302, 306, 308, 311, 317, 407, 414; Billings, *History of the Tenth Massachusetts Battery*, 313.

135 Billings, *History of the Tenth Massachusetts Battery*, 312.

Cavalry on the Dinwiddie Stage Road. A sharp skirmish ensued. Gregg reinforced the 16th Pennsylvania. The Confederates fell back.

General Miles, observing the firing to his front, recalled the two regiments that he had rushed to assist the cavalry in dealing with the Confederate thrust into the area between Ream's Station and the Jerusalem Plank Road. To prevent the grey clads from again penetrating this sector and getting possession of the roads linking Ream's Station with the Plank Road, Gregg reinforced the 13th Pennsylvania Cavalry with the 4th and 8th Pennsylvania.[136]

Soon after Gregg had redeployed his horsemen, the Rebs again assailed the roadblocks west of Ream's Station manned by the 16th Pennsylvania. This time, the attackers were hard-bitten infantrymen. Hill's foot soldiers quickly brushed aside the Union cavalry. The 16th Pennsylvania retired and took position on the left of Gibbon's division.[137]

Previously, Gregg's chief surgeon, Elias J. Marsh, had established his field hospital at Emmons' house. Marsh, in making his selection, had been influenced by the shade trees, sodded ground, the ice-house, and good well—prerequisites for a field hospital. Within a short time, casualties began to arrive from the front. Surgeon Alexander N. Dougherty, General Hancock's medical director, on visiting the site liked it so well that he issued orders to set up the II Corps' field hospital alongside Marsh's. Before Dougherty's medics could do so, General Hancock vetoed the plan. Cheek's North Carolinians' thrust toward the Dinwiddie Stage Road had satisfied Hancock that the field hospitals, if allowed to remain at Emmons', might be captured. The medical personnel accordingly moved back into Oak Grove Church.[138]

General Hancock, learning that Gregg's cavalry was retiring before Confederate infantry, sent a staff officer galloping with orders for General Gibbon to reinforce Miles with one of his brigades. Since Rugg's 1st Brigade hadn't had time to take post on Murphy's left, Gibbon determined to rush it to Miles. Colonel Rugg led his men northward across the large cornfield on the double.

Prior to the arrival of Rugg's column, Miles had ridden along his front. He was disappointed to see that his right flank unit, Lynch's brigade, held such an extended front that the troops did not fill the works. The left and center were better off in regard to manpower. Colonel Broady on the left center had so many troops in relation to his front that he was able to hold one regiment, the 148th Pennsylvania,

136 OR 42, pt. 1, 251, 607.

137 *Ibid.*, 607.

138 *Ibid.*, 618.

in reserve. Consequently, when Rugg reported, Miles instructed him to post his troops behind Lynch's brigade. To protect themselves from the fire of Rebel sharpshooters who had driven in the Union cavalry, Rugg's soldiers took cover "behind an embankment on the east side of the Weldon Railroad."[139]

As soon as Confederate infantry was spotted, General Miles told Colonel Lynch to have the 140th Pennsylvania make a forced reconnaissance. The Pennsylvanians marched out the road leading by Emmons' house. After advancing three-quarters of a mile, and encountering no Johnnies, Capt. Thomas Henry called a halt and established a roadblock. Skirmishers were deployed to the left and contact established with the right flank of Miles' picket line.[140]

Miles' outposts were no more successful than Gregg's cavalry in stopping the advance of the Rebel skirmishers. About 1:00 p.m. Miles' pickets guarding the Dinwiddie Stage Road took to their heels and came tumbling over the breastworks. A number of bluecoats manning posts on the left of the picket line were engulfed by the Confederate tide. Since only a few shots had been heard, many men of Miles' division wondered what had occurred. Following the retreat of the outposts, Captain Nelson Penfield of the consolidated brigade called for 25 volunteers. These men were deployed in front of the breastworks held by the brigade and told to give "timely warning" of the approach of any Rebel battle lines.

Unknown to Captain Penfield, Colonel Broady of the 4th Brigade had taken charge of the left wing of the consolidated brigade. Broady called for Lt. George Mitchell to deploy and throw forward as skirmishers, three regiments—the 111th, 125th, and 126th New York. Leaving the protection afforded by the rifle pits, the New Yorkers advanced into the pines to their front. As they did, they drove back Confederate sharpshooters and established contact on the left with pickets from the 148th Pennsylvania, which had advanced at the same time and on the right with soldiers manning Lynch's outposts. By 2:00 p.m. Miles' troops had plugged all the gaps in their picket line.[141]

The historian of the 10th Massachusetts Battery chronicled these events:

> About noon, as we were preparing dinner, a crash of small arms broke out in front, and directly our cavalry pickets (First Maine) came dashing furiously back over the

---

139 *Ibid.*, 251, 302, 308, 312, 313.

140 *Ibid.*, 262.

141 *Ibid.*, 252, 270, 288. Company E, 148th Pennsylvania was posted as sharpshooters in a house near the picket line. When the picket line fell back, Company E was compelled to evacuate their strongpoint and retire rapidly to escape being cut off. *Ibid.*, 287.

Dinwiddie road into the line . . . riding as recklessly as if the whole Rebel army was at their heels. Nevertheless our skirmishers maintained their ground, and we sent a few shells down the road, after which affairs were quieter for a while. But we felt a crisis to be approaching. Our troops seemed to have been concentrated in a small space, and the enemy were drawing their lines closer about us. We spent a part of our leisure in anathematizing the powers that kept us here liable to be gobbled up, when the object of our coming was simply to take part in rendering the railroad still further useless, which object we understood had been accomplished. The idea generally obtained among the men that General Hancock remained of his own volition, expecting a triumph of his arms if attacked.. . .

At the right of the battery, where the road to Dinwiddie issued through the line, an opening had been left for the free passage of troops, but at the first hostile shot, a hasty barricade of logs and brush was thrown across it, and afterwards a thin line of infantry was deployed along the works.[142]

In this skirmishing, the Yanks captured two grey clads. The Southerners, upon being questioned, claimed that "all of Hampton's cavalry and part of Hill's Corps" had been sent against the II Corps. One of the butternuts admitted that he belonged to Heth's division.[143]

When he relayed this information to General Meade, Hancock wrote, "The enemy have been feeling all around me and are now cheering in my front, advancing and driving in my skirmishers." Hancock felt that the Rebels would probably send a column sweeping across the railroad to interpose between his and Warren's corps. To carry out such a movement, Hancock believed, the Confederates would be maintaining heavy pressure to his front endeavor to keep his troops pinned in the Ream's Station breastworks.[144]

* * *

Powell Hill had put his infantry columns in motion at 8:00 a.m. Screened by one of Dunovant's cavalry regiments, the foot soldiers crossed the Rowanty at Monk's Neck Bridge. A halt was called. After resting for two hours, Hill's command turned into the Dinwidddie Stage Road and headed for Ream's Station.

---

142 Billings, *History of the Tenth Massachusetts Battery*, 313-314.

143 *OR* 42, pt. 2, 483.

144 *Ibid.*, 482-483. By 12:00 a.m. signal corps personnel had succeeded in stringing a telegraph line to within one-half mile of Hancock's command post. Hereafter, throughout the day all of Hancock's messages to army headquarters were sent by telegraph. *OR* 42, pt. 1, 224.

About noon, Hill again called a stop, and, after talking with his scouts, began deploying his brigades. Brigadier General Samuel McGowan's brigade was sent into the pines south of the Stage Road to establish contact with Hampton's cavalry. Three brigades (Scales', Lane's, and Anderson's) were marshaled in the woods north of the Stage Road, with a view to attacking the northwest angle of the Ream's Station perimeter.[145]

While the brigades were forming, Brig. Gen. Alfred M. Scales sent his sharpshooters led by Maj. John D. Young forward. Young's grey clads had engaged the Union outposts by the time McGowan's sharpshooters headed by Maj. W. S. Dunlop moved out. Dunlop was to "cover and support Young while he disposed of the Federal cavalry in his front."

Dunlop's Battalion took post about 75 yards in rear of Young's line. As the Confederates worked their way cautiously ahead, Yanks were discovered in force. Their picket line overlapped Young's Battalion for as far as the eye could see. Dunlop waved his sharpshooters into position on Young's right and the two battalions advanced slowly through the pines. Letting go a yell, the Confederates charged.[146]

Just as Dunlop's and Young's sharpshooters started forward, General McGowan rushed the 1st South Carolina Rifles and the 13th South Carolina to their support.[147]

The Confederate sharpshooters clashed with Miles' pickets. Lieutenant Mitchell, sighting the oncoming grey clads, called for his New Yorkers to charge. With a shout, the men of the 111th, 125th, and 126th New York surged through the pines. At the same time, Dunlop's sharpshooters had established contact with the 148th Pennsylvania on the New Yorkers' left. The grey clads sent the Pennsylvanians fleeing back toward the rifle pits. Moments later, Lynch's pickets, unknown to the New Yorkers, took to their heels. The three New York regiments held their ground in the pines in front of the right flank of the consolidated brigade, while Confederates advanced to their right and left.

To take advantage of the confusion engendered by the retreat of the Union pickets, Brig. Gen. George T. Anderson and Alfred Scales led their cheering battle lines forward. Anderson's Georgians on the Confederate right advanced through

145 Walker, "Ream's Station," 279, 280; Charles Stedman, "Battle at Ream's Station," in *Southern Historical Society Papers*, x vols (x, x) vol. 19, 114.

146 Dunlop, *Lee's Sharpshooters*, 191-192.

147 Humphreys, *Virginia Campaign of '64 and '65*, 280; Freeman, *Lee*, vol. 3, 489; Caldwell, *The History of a Brigade of South Carolinians*, 180-181.

Brigadier General Alfred M. Scales
Library of Congress

"sparse woods." Scales' North Carolinians on the left were in a heavy growth of pine. Two regiments of Lane's brigade (At this stage of the conflict, Brig. Gen. James Conner was in command of Lane's North Carolina troops) advanced en echelon on Scales' left.

As they emerged from the timber and entered the abatis, the Rebels sighted the breastworks to their front. At first, many of the blue clads of Broady's and the consolidated brigades had to hold fire, because their retreating comrades were in the way. After what seemed ages, the last of the pickets came diving into the rifle pits. With their front no longer obstructed, the Yanks blazed away. The butternuts pointed their main thrust at the works held by the right flank of Broady's command and the left of the consolidated brigade. Although subjected to a galling fire, the butternuts came on. Before being checked and hurled back, some of the rugged North Carolinians and Georgians had penetrated to within 30 yards of the breastworks.[148]

During this attack, General Hill, who had not been feeling well, found that the heat of the day was aggravating his condition. He dismounted and lay down on the ground in front of the Union entrenchments, turning over tactical command of the troops to General Wilcox.[149]

Within the hour, Wilcox had reformed his command. While Wilcox was preparing for a new onslaught, the sharpshooters of Young's and Dunlop's Battalions took cover behind a rise, about 400 yards west of the breastworks. Major Dunlop recalled:

---

148 OR 42, pt. 1, 224, 245, 252, 287, 288; Walker, "Ream's Station," 280; Stedman, "Battle at Ream's Station," 114.

149 Walker, "Ream's Station," 280, 281.

Our line lay just back of the crest, from which we delivered our fire, and which offered us fair protection from their guns. The line of battle [Wilcox's] lay some 600 yards behind us in the wood. Here, deliberately, but without malice, planning the destruction of their enemies, the sharpshooters carefully estimated the distance between the lines, the depression of the ground where the enemy lay, the course the ball would take in its trajectory flight, and the exact point where it would cut the line of fire; then adjusting their sights accordingly, they entered upon the work in hand.

At the command the entire battalion stepped forward to the crest and delivered a volley, then dropped back to load. The enemy responded from the length of their line with musket and gun in full chorus, fairly raking the crest of the ridge with shot and shell and the deadly minie [sic].[150]

Satisfied that his sharpshooters had softened up the Union line, Wilcox told his brigade commanders to send their men forward. Once again, the Confederates in double line of battle swept forward. Covered by a strong skirmish line, Wilcox's sturdy fighters debouched from the timber. The Rebels this time aimed their blow a little farther to the right and against the rifle pits held by Broady's soldiers. Through the abatis the butternuts surged. As if the frontal fire delivered by Broady's bluecoats weren't bad enough, the Southerners found themselves exposed to an oblique fire from the rifle pits defended by the 4th New York Heavy Artillery to their left and the consolidated brigade to their right. Several of the Johnnies drove to within three yards of the breastworks before being cut down. Repulsed, the butternuts fell back into the pines flanking the Dinwiddie Stage Road.[151]

While Wilcox's attack was at its apogee, sharpshooters from McGowan's brigade posted themselves in the edge of the dense pine woods to the right of the 10th Massachusetts Battery, and in the cornfield and buildings south of the Dinwiddie Stage Road. Banging away, the snipers concentrated on the teams used to pull the limbers. Within a few minutes, every horse in two teams had been hit, some as many as five or six times. Captain Sleeper, as he was riding slowly along in rear of the guns, was shot in the arm. At first, the Captain refused to leave the field, but after about 30 minutes the pain became so acute that he had to be assisted to the hospital. Lieutenant Granger took charge of the battery.[152]

Battery historian John D. Billings recorded:

---

150 Dunlop, *Lee's Sharpshooters*, 192-193.

151 *OR* 42, pt. 1, 224, 245, 252, 278, 280, 282, 288-289.

152 *Ibid.*, 407, 414-415.

Then Private John T. Goodwin, a driver on the First piece, falls, shot through the shoulder. He calls loudly for help, and being assisted to arise, makes rapidly to the rear. Charles A. Mason, a driver belonging to the Fourth gun, is shot in the top of the head as he lies flat on his face by the side of his horses. For a time he does not move and all think him dead; but afterwards, at intervals, he utters most pitiful walls of agony. Finding life still persisting tenaciously, two of the gun's crew bring him under cover of the works out of further danger. William Foster, driver on the First piece, also receives a wound in the head, the bullet ploughing a perfect furrow from front to rear of the scalp.

Words fail to convey an adequate idea of the fortitude displayed by our horses. Standing out in bold relief above the slight earthwork, in teams of six, they were naturally a prominent target for Rebel bullets, and the peculiar dull thud of these, at short intervals, told either that another animal had fallen a victim to the enemy's fire, or, what was frequently the case, that one already hit was further wounded. Some of the horses would fall when struck by the first bullet, lie quiet awhile, and then struggle to their feet again to receive additional injuries. Frequently a ball would enter a horses' neck, with the effect only of causing him to shake his head a few times, as if pestered by a fly, after which he would stand as quietly as If nothing had happened. I remember seeing one pole-horse shot in the leg—the bone evidently fractured—and go down in a heap, then, all cumbered as he was with harness and limber, he scrambled up and stood on three legs. It was a sad sight to see a single horse left standing, with his five associates lying dead or dying around him . . . [153]

The 10th Massachusetts Battery in its turn shelled the woods, cornfield, and buildings which sheltered their tormentors.[154]

Following the repulse of Wilcox's second assault, General Miles responded to Lieutenant Granger's call for help. Skirmishers were thrown out to drive back the sharpshooters, to watch the Confederates' movements, and pick up prisoners. Several Georgians identifying themselves as members of General Anderson's brigade were disarmed and brought in."[155]

Union officers on the skirmish line reported the Rebels emplacing a battery and massing troops in the pines. Miles sent instructions for Lieutenant Dauchy of

---

153 Billings, *History of the Tenth Massachusetts Battery*, 314, 315-316.

154 *Ibid.*, 314-315; OR 42, pt. 1, 414-415.

155 OR 42, pt. 1, 252; OR 42, pt. 2, 484.

the 12th New York Battery to turn his 3-inch rifles on the woods west of the railroad. The cannoneers searched the woods with solid shot and shell.[156]

Meanwhile, word had filtered into Miles' command post that the three New York regiments still held the line of outposts in front of the consolidated brigade. A staff officer, Capt. John B. Noyes, was sent "to ascertain how far in the woods in front was the skirmish line, and whether it covered the whole front of the brigade." He soon returned and reported that the left of the consolidated brigade was unprotected by pickets, but that its right was covered. Colonel Broady thereupon told Captain Noyes to have the three New York regiments, in concert with Lynch's pickets on their right, execute a left half-wheel and pinpoint the Confederates. It was only then that the people at Miles' command post learned that there was no connection between the outposts, manned by the New Yorkers and Lynch's brigade.

When Miles investigated, he learned the withdrawal of the three New York regiments had seriously weakened the consolidated brigade. The breastworks currently held by the consolidated brigade were defended "by only a single line of men, in some places at the interval of a pace apart." To correct this situation partially, Colonel Broady rushed the 148th Pennsylvania to assist the consolidated brigade. The Pennsylvanians took position to the left and rear of the brigade.[157]

General Smyth (at 2:00 p.m.) received orders to recall his brigade and rejoin Gibbon's division behind the Ream's Station earthworks. Although his troops were shelled by McGregor's Battery, Smyth succeeded in disengaging them "in good order and without loss." The column reached Ream's Station a few minutes after Miles' troops west of the railroad had hurled back Wilcox's second assault. Marching via the Halifax Road and then through the woods, the brigade, in compliance with Gibbon's instructions, filed into position on the left of the rifle pits held by Murphy's brigade. Smyth's main line of resistance passed along the crest of a hill and through a cornfield. The brigade's left rested near Jones Hole Swamp, while the 4th Ohio Battalion was deployed and manned a picket line beyond the Stage Road. As soon as Smyth had marked out the line to be defended by his command, the troops were put to work erecting breastworks.[158]

When the Confederates made their first attack on Miles' division, General Gregg dismounted two (the 1st Maine and 1st District of Columbia) of his three regiments posted in Jones Hole Swamp. Troopers of the 1st Maine were stationed

---

156 OR 42, pt. 1, 252; Dauchy, "Battle of Ream's Station," 131.

157 OR 42, pt. 1, 289.

158 *Ibid.*, 324, 328, 332.

Major General Gershom Mott
Library of Congress

in the swamp; the 16th Pennsylvania on the Maine men's right sat their horses. The 1st District of Columbia took position behind a hastily constructed work on a hillock, somewhat advanced and to the left of the ground subsequently occupied by Smyth's foot soldiers. A squadron of the 11th Pennsylvania was advanced as vedettes in front of the works. In case the Rebels debouched from the woods southeast of Ream's Station, the pickets were to alert Gregg to the danger.[159]

* * *

Shortly before Wilcox's second attack, Capt. William W. Sanders reached Hancock's headquarters with a message General Meade had posted at 1:00 p.m. Unfolding and reading the dispatch, Hancock learned that his army commander had been notified by Warren of the thrust by Cheek's North Carolina horsemen which had broken through Gregg's cavalry screen east of Ream's Station. In view of this development, Meade had ordered Brig. Gen. Gershom Mott to rush all his available troops to his corps commander's assistance. Mott's column was to move via the Jerusalem Plank Road to the Dinwiddie Stage Road.

All information reaching Meade's headquarters seemed to indicate that the Confederates were seizing the initiative, and would either assail Hancock's men or interpose themselves between the II Corps and V Corps. Under these circumstances, Meade was satisfied that it would be impossible for the Federals to "do much more damage to the railroad." Hancock was to use his own judgment

159 *Ibid.*, 87, 607.

about withdrawing his command and resuming his former position on the left and rear of the V Corps.[160]

Before returning, Captain Sanders asked Hancock if the Halifax Road north to Globe Tavern was open. Hancock assured him that it was. When he left Hancock's command post, Sanders took that road.[161]

Strange as it seems, although the field telegraph had been in operation between army headquarters and Ream's Station since 11:45 a.m., General Meade (until 7:30 p.m.) continued to send all his messages by staff officers.[162]

At 2:45 p.m. Hancock telegraphed Meade. Since the Confederates seemed determined to prevent further destruction of the Weldon Railroad, Hancock was satisfied there was no necessity for his corps to remain at Ream's Station, and that it was important that he rejoin Warren. But with his troops "closely engaged," Hancock didn't feel he could "withdraw safely at this time." It was his opinion that his troops should be pulled out of the Ream's Station earthworks as soon as it was dark, provided they weren't driven out before.

At the moment, Hancock assured Meade, everything looked promising, except that having placed his corps in "an enclosed position," the Confederates were "liable" to push a column through the gap separating the II and V Corps. Consequently, Warren had best be on the lookout to his left and rear till such time as the II Corps had made "a practicable connection with him." Meanwhile, Hancock promised to utilize his cavalry to keep the Rebels off the Jerusalem Plank Road. A copy of this dispatch was forwarded to Warren.[163]

Hancock at 3:30 p.m., following the repulse of Wilcox's second thrust, notified Meade that so far prisoners had been taken belonging to Wilcox's division and Hampton's cavalry corps. One of the Johnnies had told his interrogators that A. P. Hill was on the field. Except for shots exchanged by opposing pickets, the fighting for the moment had died down.[164]

Ten minutes later, Hancock communicated to Meade details of Wilcox's second thrust. According to officers at the front, the grey clads had advanced

160 OR 42, pt. 2, 482. The Third division, II Army Corps, General Mott commanding, had remained in the Petersburg investment line, when Hancock had moved his other two divisions to Ream's Station. Mott's relief column was to be accompanied by one of Parke's batteries, which was camped at Williams' house.

161 OR 42, pt. 1, 224.

162 Walker, "Ream's Station," 278.

163 OR 42, pt. 2, 483.

164 Ibid., 483.

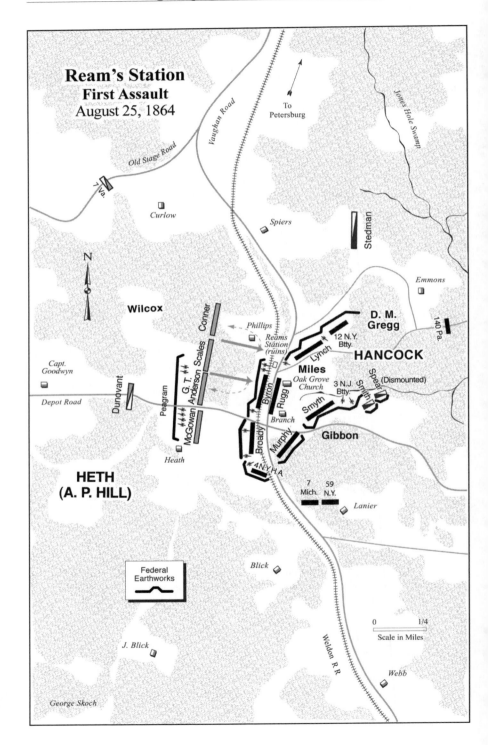

Ream's Station
First Assault
August 25, 1864

To
Petersburg

Jones Hole Swamp

Vaughan Road

Old Stage Road

7 Va.

Curlow

Spiers

Stedman

N

Emmons

Wilcox

Conner

Scales

Anderson

G. T.

Phillips

Reams Station (ruins)

Lynch

12 N.Y. Btty.

D. M. Gregg

140 Pa.

HANCOCK

Capt. Goodwyn

Dunovant

Peagram

McGowan

Miles

Oak Grove Church

Byron

Rugg

3 N.J. Btty.

Smith

Spear

(Dismounted)

Depot Road

Branch

Smyth

Murphy

Gibbon

Broaddy

Heath

4 N.Y.H.A.

7 Mich.   59 N.Y.

Lanier

HETH
(A. P. HILL)

Federal
Earthworks

Blick

0   1/4
Scale in Miles

J. Blick

Weldon R R

Webb

George Skoch

without firing a shot; prisoners had been taken within 15 paces of the breastworks.[165]

A few minutes after 4:00 p.m., Capt. Frederick Rosencrantz reached Ream's Station with a letter General Meade had drafted 75 minutes before. Meade wanted Hancock to know that he had just issued orders for Brig. Gen. Orlando B. Willcox's division of the IX Corps to march to Ream's Station. Like Mott's blue clads, Willcox's were to follow the Jerusalem Plank Road. Willcox was to be accompanied by some artillery. It was hoped at army headquarters that Hancock would give the Rebs a good thrashing.

General Meade observed that the only thing he feared was that the foe might interpose between the II Corps and Warren. Some of Warren's troops were being held in reserve to guard against this contingency. It was this apprehension that had induced Meade to send Mott and Willcox by the Plank Road instead of down the Halifax Road.[166]

But via the Plank Road, Willcox's line of march was 12 miles, whereas had he gone by the Halifax Road, which remained unblocked and open till 5:00 p.m., the IX Corps division would have had not more than five miles to travel. This would have enabled Willcox's column to reach Ream's Station by half-past four or five. By managing his movements skillfully, Willcox might have been able to fall upon the Confederates' left flank or rear.[167]

Hancock (at 4:15 p.m.) acknowledged the message he had just received from Meade. On doing so, the II Corps commander warned that he feared it would be too late when Willcox arrived for his IX Corps troops to serve any practical purpose. Nevertheless, he had determined to call up Willcox's division. Hancock in closing wrote, "I desire to know as soon as possible whether you wish me to retire from this station tonight in case we get through safe."[168]

Fifteen minutes later, Hancock telegraphed Meade that an examination of the area satisfied him that the Rebels could not turn his right without making a sweeping detour via Vaughan Road. Because of the late hour, Hancock believed this would be impossible to undertake in the time remaining before darkness blanketed the area. The right of his defense line, Hancock informed his superior, extended nearly to Jones Hole Swamp, which was impassable to troops advancing in line of battle. Hancock at the same time was "more apprehensive" about his left.

165 *Ibid.*, 484.

166 *Ibid.*, 483; Humphreys, *Virginia Campaign of '64 and '65*, 280.

167 Humphreys, *Virginia Campaign of '64 and '65*, 280.

168 OR 42, pt. 1, 225.

As it was late, however, the Southerners would have to make "vigorous use" of the hours left, if they hoped to gain an advantage in that sector.

Hancock (at 4:45 p.m.) reported to Meade that according to his scouts, the Rebs had established a line from the left of the Ream's Station perimeter, covering the railroad and the roads to Dinwiddie and Stony Creek. Hancock could hear chopping, and he reasoned that the butternuts must be strengthening their position by felling timber. His pickets, however, reported the Confederates moving artillery into position; a certain indication that another attack was about to begin.[169]

As soon as he learned that Willcox's division had been ordered down the Jerusalem Plank Road, Hancock sent one of his staff officers, Capt. John McEntee, "to conduct it up." About 5:00 p.m. Maj. John William rode up and told Hancock that Mott's "flying column," 1,700 strong, had reached the place where the Dinwiddie Stage Road branched off from the Jerusalem Plank Road.[170]

*   *   *

Chief of Staff Humphreys, upon learning that Rebel cavalry had broken through Gregg's picket line east of the Weldon Railroad, telegraphed General Mott at 12:45 p.m.: Mott was to alert the troops of his division "in the large redoubt and along the entrenchments to the Strong house" to get under arms. These men were to be ready to move in any direction.[171]

Fifty minutes later, Meade issued instructions for Mott to rush all his available troops down the Plank Road to its intersection with the Dinwiddie Stage Road. The "flying column" would be joined by one of the IX Corps batteries parked at Williams' house. As soon as the reinforcing column reached the designated intersection, the officer in charge was to communicate that fact with General Hancock.[172]

General Mott promptly placed Col. Robert McAllister in charge of the "flying column," which consisted of the 3rd Brigade and part of the 2nd Brigade of the Third division. As directed, these men were pulled out of big redoubts (Fort Davis) and rifle pits west of the Plank Road. Notifying General Humphreys of what he had done, Mott announced that he planned to redeploy men from his 1st Brigade to

---

169 *OR* 42, pt. 2, 484.

170 *OR* 42, pt. 2, 225.

171 *OR* 42, pt. 1, 487.

172 *Ibid.*, 487.

hold Fort Davis, and use the engineers to hold the entrenchments connecting with the IX Corps at the Strong house."[173]

By 2:00 p.m. McAllister had massed his column near Jones' house. After being joined by a 40-man detachment from the 3rd Pennsylvania Cavalry, McAllister put his command in motion. The troops, as directed, proceeded down the Jerusalem Plank Road to the intersection with the Dinwiddie Stage Road. On his arrival at the junction, McAllister massed his soldiers to the right and left of the Plank Road, while he sent Major William to report his position to General Hancock.

Before Major William returned, General Meade, accompanied by a large cavalcade of staff officers, rode up. Meade told McAllister "to take a good position" and deploy his command across the Plank Road. After reconnoitering the area, McAllister found ground to his liking about a mile south of the intersection. When he deployed his troops, McAllister threw a cavalry screen out toward the Blackwater.[174]

Meanwhile, Hancock had been questioning Major William. The aide told Hancock that by the time he reported back to Colonel McAllister, Willcox's division would have passed through the intersection and have turned into the Dinwiddie Stage Road. Hancock directed William to rejoin McAllister, and tell him to post his troops "well down the Plank Road" in case Confederate cavalry turned the II Corps' left. McAllister was to have his people arrest all stragglers and organize them into regiments.[175]

General Humphreys (at 12:45 p.m.) had cautioned General Parke to get his men "under arms."[176] Forty-five minutes later, General Meade, who at that time was visiting Warren's headquarters at Globe Tavern, got in touch with Parke. The IX Corps commander was informed that Mott had been directed to rush a "flying column" down the Plank Road. Mott's troops were to protect Hancock's flank and rear from the Rebel cavalry. Besides advising Parke that one of the IX Corps

---

173 *Ibid.*, 488. General Humphreys, on learning what Mott had done, decided that he had "stripped the left too much." The Chief of Staff telegraphed Mott to use his reserves to fill up the entrenchments. He was to have McAllister leave some of his men in the large redoubt, until the relieving force from the 1st Brigade arrived. Humphreys promised to send Mott some of the troops detailed to guard headquarters to hold part of his second line. Mott replied, informing Humphreys that he had pulled 250 men out of the entrenchments east of the Plank Road to hold the redoubt. With the engineers, Mott believed, he would have enough soldiers to hold the rifle pits from the redoubt to Strong's house. *Ibid.*

174 OR 42, pt. 1, 391.

175 *Ibid.*, 226.

176 OR 42, pt. 2, 494. This message was sent at the same time as the one alerting Mott to hold a strong force ready to march to Hancock's assistance.

batteries would accompany Mott, Meade told Parke to get two of his divisions—White's and Willcox's—ready to march.[177]

At 2:30 p.m. Meade telegraphed Parke to start Willcox's division down the Plank Road. Willcox's bluecoats were to take position on the Plank Road at Shay's Tavern. Upon reaching the tavern, Willcox was to contact Hancock. The Third division on taking the field would be accompanied by three batteries.[178]

Since his division was being held in reserve, Willcox encountered no trouble in getting his men ready to march. The column started promptly and passed Gurley's house at 3:30 p.m. Moving for the most part cross-country, Willcox's division, after a five-mile tramp, came out on the Plank Road. Soon after the vanguard came out on the Plank Road, Captain McEntee hailed Willcox and handed him a note signed by Hancock. Looking at the message, Willcox learned that he was to march his division "rapidly" to Ream's Station. Willcox questioned McEntee and found that he was five miles from his goal.[179]

As Willcox neared Shay's Tavern, he encountered the aide entrusted with the instructions for McAllister to employ his soldiers to arrest II Corps stragglers. The staff officer was somewhat confused and handed the message to Willcox. The IX Corps general, not seeing that the note was addressed to McAllister, deployed his leading regiment as skirmishers. Colonel William Humphrey's 2nd Brigade was formed into battle line across the Dinwiddie Stage Road. Hardly had Willcox made these dispositions, before a large number of panic-stricken bluecoats, including a number of officers, were sighted bearing down on the IX Corps straggler line. Within a few moments, the road leading westward to Ream's Station was filled with soldiers, wagons, and ambulances.[180]

*   *   *

General Miles, following the repulse of the second Rebel attack on his front, was satisfied by what he heard and the reports brought in by his scouts that the foe was shifting toward his right. So far, the Union picket line in that sector had not been disturbed. Beyond Miles' right flank, Lynch's pickets were in touch with the line of outposts held by Stedman's cavalry brigade.

177   *Ibid.*, 494.

178   *Ibid.*, 495.

179   OR 42, pt. 1, 591.

180   *Ibid.*, 226, 591.

About this time, Colonel Rugg, whose brigade earlier in the afternoon had been rushed to bolster the Union right, was redeployed. Rugg with five of his regiments (the 20th Massachusetts, 1st Minnesota, 152nd New York, 184th Pennsylvania, and 36th Wisconsin) reported to General Miles; the 19th Maine and 19th Massachusetts joined Colonel Murphy. Murphy utilized these two units to hold some "slight" rifle pits on a rise between the left of his brigade and Smyth's right.

Rugg's numerically strongest regiment (the 152nd New York) was given a special assignment by Miles. Accompanied by Miles' inspector general, Captain Marlin, the New Yorkers marched up the railroad dump. A short distance beyond the breastworks, they took position near a white house. In case the Johnnies sought to turn the Union right, Marlin was to deploy the men behind the railroad embankment and delay their advance. If, however, the next Confederate blow fell on the angle held by the consolidated brigade, the 152nd New York was to wheel to the left, and reinforced by Lynch's skirmishers, fall upon the attackers' flank and rear.[181]

So certain was Miles that the Southerners would attack the angle that he called on Lieutenant Dauchy of the 12th New York Battery to send him one of his 12-pounder guns. The Napoleon was emplaced to bear on the point where the railroad and Halifax Road passed out of the works at the northwest angle. Dauchy sent Lt. Henry D. Brower, a brave and capable artillerist, with the gun. As his comrades recalled, Brower seemed to have a premonition that he would not return. As he was riding away, he took out his watch and handed it to the carrier of the guidon, "a fine young soldier and protégé of his, and then, thinking apparently that such an act savored of weakness, replaced it in his pocket."

A little later, Captain Sleeper of the 10th Massachusetts Battery rode by. Holding his wounded arm, the captain called "gaily" as he passed, "Thirty days leave."[182]

Because of the precautions he had taken, the concentration of a strong reserve (Rugg and his four regiments) behind the consolidated brigade, the position occupied by Marlin's combat team, and Brower's Napoleon, Miles felt confident of holding his position.

General Heth had now reached the field with Cooke's and MacRae's North Carolina brigades. Mahone's command, Weisiger's and King's brigades were still on the road. With Heth came 12 of Colonel Pegram's guns. Hill still was indisposed, so

181 *Ibid.*, 252, 302, 306, 308, 313, 421.

182 Dauchy, "Battle of Ream's Station," 131-132.

Heth "assumed the arrangements for the final attack which it was resolved should be made, to turn the Confederate repulse into victory."

Like Willcox, Heth selected the northwest angle of the Ream's Station perimeter as the spot to be assailed.

After Pegram had reconnoitered the area, his cannoneers unlimbered their 12 guns. The artillerists, screened by the configuration of the terrain, manhandled their pieces across a bog to within 300 yards of the western face of the Ream's Station perimeter.

While the cannoneers were emplacing and masking their guns, in a lot covered with second growth pines, Heth redeployed his infantry. Three of McGowan's regiments (the 1st, 12th, and 14th South Carolina) were recalled from south of the Dinwiddie Stage Road. Heth's column of attack would consist of three North Carolina brigades—Lane's, Cooke's, and MacRae's. The North Carolinians were to be supported by Anderson's Georgians and the 1st, 12th, and 14th South Carolina of McGowan's brigade. McGowan's two other regiments, the 1st Rifles and 13th South Carolina, were to assist Hampton's cavalry in an assault on the left "return."

In front of Lane's brigade on the left and Cooke's in the center was the Federal abatis. MacRae's North Carolinians on the right would be called on to cross an open field. As Brig. Gen. William MacRae formed his battle line in the edge of the pines, he walked in front and told his soldiers that "he knew they would go over the works, and that he wished then to do so without firing a gun."

"All right, General, we will go there," was the reply.

A participant recalled that the men were "in high spirits, jesting and laughing, and ready to move on an instant's notice.[183]

General MacRae's sharpshooters under Lieutenant Kyle were advanced and took position alongside Dunlop's and Young's marksmen. The Rebel snipers focused their attention on the Federal batteries.[184]

By 5:00 p.m. the Confederates had completed their preparations. When General Heth gave the word, a signal gun was discharged. Within a few moments, all of Pegram's guns were in action. Although the bombardment did little physical damage to the breastworks and inflicted few casualties, it had serious repercussions among the troops of Gibbon's division posted east of the railroad. Because of the faulty location of the works in this sector, the Rebel cannoneers were able to rake the men as they crouched behind their light breastworks of rails and earth with a

---

183 Walker, "Ream's Station," 283-284, 286, 287; Stedman, "Battle at Ream's Station," 115.

184 Dauchy, "Battle of Ream's Station," 135; Dunlop, *Lee's Sharpshooters*, 195.

reverse fire. To escape the "terrific shower of shell and solid shot," Gibbon's soldiers hugged the ground and mumbled their prayers.[185]

Several Union artillerists tracked the Confederate projectiles and correctly deduced that the butternuts were employing 12 guns in an effort to soften up the Ream's Station perimeter. At the time that the shelling commenced, the gunners of the 3rd New Jersey Battery had emplaced their four pieces in a twenty-acre cornfield behind the station site. Two Confederate batteries concentrated on knocking out the New Jersey battery. Captain Woerner had his men return the Rebels' fire with what he called "good effect, silencing several of their pieces."[186]

It was reported to Hancock that the Johnnies were massing a heavy column of infantry in the pines 600 yards west of the railroad. Hancock sent word for Lieutenant Dauchy to employ three of his Napoleons in an attempt to disperse this force. The New Yorkers hammered the target area with shot and shell.[187]

Two of the four Union batteries, the 10th Massachusetts and consolidated Rhode Island unit, remained silent during the cannonade. The Rhode Islanders had to take cover, because the Confederates were able to enfilade their position.[188]

At the end of 15 minutes, Pegram's guns fell silent.

General Heth walked out in front of his line and ordered Lt. D. C. Waddell of the 11th North Carolina "to send back to the main line and bring a regimental flag." Waddell returned with the color-bearer—Thomas Minton—of the 26th South Carolina of Lane's brigade. Heth demanded the flag.

Minton refused to hand it over, saying, "General, tell me where you want the flag to go and I will take it. I won't surrender up my colors."

Heth repeated his demand, and was again refused.

Taking Minton by the arm, the general said, "Come on then, we will carry the colors together."

Heth then gave the signal to charge by waving the flag to the right and left. At this, the entire line let go a yell and started for the breastworks.

Lane's and Cooke's brigades moved off first and were "received by a heavy fire of both musketry and artillery." As the shooting increased in intensity, General MacRae, realizing that the crisis was at hand, called to his adjutant-general, Capt. Louis G. Young, "I shall wait no longer for orders . . . " Seeing that Lane's and

---

185   OR 42, pt. 1, 226, 293, 306, 308, 318, 328, 332.

186   *Ibid.*, 408, 417, 418. Two of Captain Woerner's guns were placed on a knoll near the rear line, while the other section was immediately in the rear of the church.

187   *Ibid.*, 245, 421; Dauchy, "Battle of Ream's Station," 131.

188   OR 42, pt. 1, 414, 423.

Cooke's troops were drawing the entire fire of the foe, MacRae gave the order "to advance at once."

Heretofore, MacRae's North Carolinians had received but slight attention from the Yanks. Forewarned by the loud cheers of MacRae's troops, as they emerged from the pines and advanced to the assault, the bluecoats "opened a tremendous fire of small-arms, with a converging fire of artillery" along MacRae's front.[189]

Out on the picket line in front of the consolidated brigade, the outposts spotted a powerful battle line beating its way toward them. While the pickets blazed away, several officers raced for the rifle pits to sound the alarm. Three North Carolina brigades (Lane's, Cooke's, and MacRae's) pressed on. Although shot at, the battle-harden North Carolinians held their fire. This was too much for the Union pickets; they took to their heels.[190]

The soldiers of Miles' division, as they crouched behind the breastworks, had been alerted by the scattered shots and shouts. Looking up, the bluecoats of the consolidated and Broady's brigades saw their comrades racing wildly toward them. Close behind the fleeing pickets came the Confederate battle line. Snatching up their rifle muskets, the Yanks blazed away. Undaunted, the butternuts drove through the abatis, which was thirty yards across. Lynch's left flank units and men on the right flank of the 4th New York Heavy Artillery joined in the fight and delivered an oblique fire against the flanks of the onrushing column of attack.

Here and there, the Rebel assault formation was thrown into disorder as large numbers of men were cut down and the fainthearted dropped out and slipped to the rear. General Miles and his officers called encouragement to their men. If they could just hold on a few more minutes, the onslaught would be smashed. Suddenly, three regiments (the 7th, 39th, and 52nd New York) on the left of the consolidated brigade panicked. A cheering grey clad tide poured over the breastworks. Moments later, another breakthrough occurred on the right of the consolidated brigade—as the 125th and 126th New York melted away. Troops holding the rifle pits between the points of penetration had now seen enough. It was "root hog or die" as they bolted for the rear. One of the burly North Carolinians wrested a prized trophy away from a color-sergeant—the standard of the 111th New York. General Miles at the time of the breakthrough was standing on the bank of the railroad cut. He saw a

189 George C. Underwood, *History of the Twenty-Sixth Regiment of the North Carolina Troops, in the Great War 1861–1865* (Goldsboro, NC, 1901), 86-87; Stedman, "Battle at Ream's Station," *Southern Historical Society Papers*, Volume 19, 115-116.

190 OR 42, pt. 1, 289; Caldwell, *The History of a Brigade of South Carolinians*, 181; Humphreys, *Virginia Campaign of '64 and '65*, 280-281.

North Carolina color-bearer spring over the breastworks and land in the cut almost at his feet.[191]

General Heth and his "co-color-bearer" planted the flag of the 26th North Carolina on the works. Captain G. O. Holland of the 28th North Carolina, Lane's brigade, was one of the first grey clads to reach the entrenchments. As he "stood on the works and saw them well manned on one side, and only a few Rebs on the other," he yelled, "Yanks if you know what is best for you, you had better make a blue streak towards [sic] sunset." The Federals made "the desired blue streak and Holland added greatly to his already enviable reputation for coolness and bravery."[192]

Among the first to fall when the Southerners came surging toward the works was Lieutenant Brower. The lieutenant was shot through the head while directing the fire of his Napoleon. Corporal Abram S. Liddle took charge of the piece. He pointed the gun at the oncoming grey clads and blasted them with double-charges of canister as they stormed over the works. Liddle kept his men at the Napoleon, although the supporting infantry had fled. Seeing that his detachment was about to be surrounded, the corporal bellowed for his cannoneers to limber up the piece. Before the team had drawn the gun more than a few feet, a Reb sharpshooter killed one of the wheel horses. At this, the artillerists cut the other horses loose and escaped, leaving their gun to fall into the Confederates' hands.[193]

Miles, observing that only a small force of Confederates had as yet entered the works, determined to counterattack and attempt to seal the breach. The general shouted for Colonel Rugg. The leader of the strategic reserve was nowhere in sight. Whereupon, Miles directed Rugg's brigade "to rush into the gap and commence firing." Instead of doing as Miles ordered, the soldiers of the four regiments (the 20th Massachusetts, 1st Minnesota, 184th Pennsylvania, and 36th Wisconsin) either continued to hug the ground, or if they got up they "ran to the rear."

Colonel Rugg writing after the battle defended his men. He reported that they could do nothing, as the panic-stricken soldiers of the consolidated brigade ran over them and made it impossible to shoot at the oncoming Johnnies without hitting their friends. The panic, Rugg admitted, soon spread to his men, and, except

---

191 OR 42, pt. 1, 253, 289. Recruits and substitutes in large composed the 7th, 39th, and 52nd New York. The 7th New York was entirely new, the companies being organized in New York and sent to join the army before Petersburg. According to General Hancock, some of the officers were unable to speak English. *Ibid.*, 227.

192 Underwood, *History of the Twenty-Sixth Regiment of the North Carolina*, 87; James H. Lane, "Recollections" (unpublished manuscript, North Carolina Dept. of Archives and History).

193 OR 42, pt. 1, 408, 421.

for the majority of the 20th Massachusetts and 36th Wisconsin, they fled the field. A large number of soldiers from the Massachusetts and the Wisconsin units were quickly encircled and compelled to ground arms.[194]

Captain Marlin, who was with the 152nd New York at the white house, was dismayed to see the Rebels sweeping over the works to his left. Recalling his instructions, Marlin told Capt. William S. Burt of the New York regiment to change front to the left and assail the Confederates in the flank and rear. The New Yorkers promptly carried out the desired movement, and took position to enfilade the section of the rifle pits carried by the North Carolinians. Before Captain Burt could bellow, "Fire!" the New Yorkers were terrified, when a strong Rebel force veered to the left and started sweeping along the breastworks toward their left and rear. Without having fired a single volley, the men, fearing that they would be cut off, "broke from the ranks and fled in a disgraceful manner, only two men in the regiment discharging their pieces."[195]

Disgusted by the conduct of the consolidated and Rugg's brigades, Miles rode down behind the line of the 4th Brigade which still held its ground. Miles saw Colonel Broady and shouted for him to shift his men "toward the right and hold the rifle pit." Suddenly some of the rugged North Carolinians mounted the breastworks defended by the 148th Pennsylvania. A bitter hand-to-hand struggle ensued. The bayonet, the butt stock of the rifle-musket, the knife, and the fist were used freely.[196]

After a catastrophe so sudden and terrible, it might have been expected that the "flushed and victorious" Confederates, enjoying the superiority they did in numbers, would sweep down the entrenchments to the right and left, double up the remainder of Miles' line, and then turn on and take in reverse Gibbon's line. Such a movement would have found Gibbon caught between the Rebel infantry and Hampton's cavalry. But Heth and his generals had yet "to reckon with a few indomitable spirits." Had "it been a common man, the average division commander, who ordered the First division of the Second Corps on that day, had the corps commander been one of a shade less intrepid or brilliant in his bearing, nothing but a complete rout could have ensued, owing to the altogether vicious formation of our line."

194 *Ibid.*, 226, 245, 253, 302.

195 *Ibid.*, 253, 314.

196 *Ibid.*, 253, 280, 287. The left flank of the attacking battle line extended to a point opposite the 66th New York of Broady's Brigade.

It is difficult to say just how much fight the Rebs had left at this moment. If the brigades which had rolled over the Union works at the angle were "worthy of Lee's army, flushed with success as they were, there is no other conclusion than that the personal bearing of several men" saved two divisions of the II Corps from being annihilated. Corps historian Francis A. Walker, who was captured in the fighting, recalled that on the following morning General Willcox asked him, who was the Union officer "who showed such splendid conduct in rallying and bringing forward our troops upon the right, after the line had been broken."

Walker answered proudly, "General Nelson A. Miles."[197]

Miles, observing that the Rebels had gained the angle and would be able to enfilade the rifle pits defended by the brigades to the left and right of the breakthrough, galloped for the guns of the 12th New York Battery. Hailing Lieutenant Dauchy, the general shouted for him to turn his guns on the gap in the Union lines through which the Rebels were flooding.

Up to this time, the cannoneers had been raking the Southern battle line with canister. After breaking through, the Rebs had formed a column of assault near Oak Grove Church. At a word from their officers, the column moved off, advancing up the Halifax Road, which lay to the rear of the breastworks. A second Confederate force swung to the left and swept the ground in front of the works. It was apparent to Miles and Dauchy that the foe planned to exploit their success by rolling up the right flank of the First division.

To cope with this thrust, Dauchy had his artillerists pull the left Napoleon out of the works and point it down the Halifax Road; the two other guns were sighted to command the terrain in front of, and, the exterior slope of the works to the left. As soon as the last of the bluecoated infantry had retreated out of his field of fire, Dauchy had his cannoneers blast the oncoming Johnnies with double-charges of canister. A strong Confederate force, however, beat its way through the woods to the rear of the emplacement occupied by the battery. Spotting the butternuts, Dauchy shouted for his men to "limber to the rear!" The drivers started the teams forward to hitch to the guns. In crossing the road, the right wheel horse to each limber was gunned down by Confederate sharpshooters. Two of the horses fell; the third struggled on. The cannoneers succeeded in limbering up only one of the three Napoleons. After going a short distance, the wounded wheel horse collapsed.

When the teams were being taken across the Halifax Road to limber up, Lieutenant Dauchy had stepped into the woods to secure his horse. As he turned his mount and prepared to lead off the battery, the lieutenant saw the Confederates

---

197 Walker, "Ream's Station," 289-290.

swarm over the guns. Wheeling his horse about, Dauchy touched his spurs to its flanks and galloped to safety. Discovering that the Napoleons hadn't been spiked, several butternuts manned one of the pieces and raked the fleeing Yanks.[198]

As they drove for the guns of the 12th New York Battery, the Southerners had dislodged five regiments of Lynch's brigade occupying the breastworks to the right of the breakthrough. These troops gave way before the grim North Carolinians in "considerable confusion."

Miles glancing about saw his old regiment, the 61st New York, "change direction." The New Yorkers took position with their right anchored on the earthworks and were "contesting every foot of ground gained by the enemy." Rallying a number of men from other units of Lynch's brigade, Miles formed them on the 61st New York and perpendicular to the rifle pits.

The right flank of Miles' reorganized main line of resistance extended about 100 yards in front of the fortifications. Because of the thick smoke that enveloped the area, the Johnnies failed to see this new line of battle to their left front. Miles called for the men to cease fire and prepare to charge. Letting go a shout for the Union, the bluecoats counterattacked.[199]

Only a few score of men—perhaps 200 in all—stood by Miles. With these, the general fought his way forward step by step until he and his hardcore soldiers had retaken the guns of the 12th New York Battery, recaptured a section of the breastworks, and had compelled a number of the Johnnies to take cover in the railroad cut.

Miles had transferred the fighting to the outside of the entrenchments on the Union right. If possible, Miles hoped to attack in the flank and rear the butternuts that had leaped the line at the northwest angle, or were still coming up. As fast as Miles' small party was dissipated, it was reinforced by handfuls of men personally collected by his own staff and by the appeals and exertions of General Hancock, "who, galloping to the front, exposed himself far more conspicuously than any private soldier, in his efforts to restore the fortunes of the day." Hancock's horse was shot in the neck; the beast dropped as if dead. Within a few minutes, the horse struggled to its feet, and the general remounted. Next, a ball cut his bridle rein in two. The corps flag, which always followed Hancock, was pierced by five balls, another splintered the flagstaff. Commissary of Musters Edward P. Brownson fell, mortally wounded.

---

198 OR 42, pt. 1, 226, 253, 408, 421; Dauchy, "Battle of Ream's Station," 136-137.

199 OR 42, pt. 1, 226, 246, 253, 262, 421.

At times, the troops whom Miles and Hancock were leading scarcely equaled a company. But few as they were, "their desperate push and stubborn gallantry when thus inspired not only checked the progress of the Confederates, but carried the scanty column forward until hands were laid on the Napoleon by the side of which Brower lay dead."[200]

Lieutenant Dauchy and Sgt. George Outwater reached three of the guns shortly after Miles' infantry. Dauchy and the sergeant sought to put the Napoleons back in action, but were unable to do so as they had no lanyards. The lieutenant sent Outwater to locate the rest of the cannoneers. On going to the rear to look for the gunners, Outwater was intercepted by the provost guard. Although he explained the situation to the provost people, they refused to believe the sergeant. He was not allowed to return to the front, consequently, Dauchy was unable to put his guns back in action.[201]

Meanwhile, other Confederate units had swung to the right. Supported by the 1st, 12th, and 14th South Carolina, MacRae's North Carolinians dislodged Broady's brigade and moved against the rifle pits defended by the 4th New York Heavy Artillery. After being routed from the breastworks, many of Broady's soldiers took cover behind the railroad embankment. Outflanked, they retired beyond Oak Grove Church, where the officers succeeded in halting and re-forming their units.[202]

*   *   *

The cannoneers of the 10th Massachusetts and Batteries A and B, 1st Rhode Island were unimpressed with the character of their supporting regiment—the 4th New York Heavy Artillery. During Wilcox's attacks, the historian of the 10th Massachusetts Battery chronicled, the artillerists turned infantrymen:

[They] scarcely show signs of life, much less of an active interest, as they lie crouched low in the works. Once in a while one does venture a shot, but elevates his musket over the works, pointing it skyward, as if he saw the enemy approaching from that direction. Said an ex-Confederate, who participated in the fight, "Your support didn't kill any of

---

200 Walker, "Ream's Station," 291-292.

201 OR 42, pt. 1, 421; Dauchy, "Battle of Ream's Station," 137.

202 OR 42, pt. 1, 278, 280, 282, 284, 286; Caldwell, *The History of a Brigade of South Carolinians*, 181.

our men. We never saw such queer shooting. They all pointed their guns up into the air and shot far above us."[203]

At the time of Heth's assault, one of the New Yorkers, who chanced to be looking over the works, shouted, "Look up there on the right!" One of the cannoneers of the 10th Massachusetts Battery remembered:

There, sure enough, emerging from the woods beyond the Dinwiddie [Stage] Road into the opening that stretched before the entrenchments...are charging lines of Confederates. They come at the double-quick, with flashing bayonets, and ringing out their familiar yell. On the instant we turn our muzzles to the right and give them canister. Some of our support [the 4th New York Heavy Artillery], run to the rear, many lie inert in the ditch, and a few join in repelling the enemy's assault. But even then it is a warm reception, and ere the hostile line have fairly reached the works they break, reel, and surge to the rear in confusion, seeking the woods again, and leaving the ground thickly sprinkled with their slain. We set up a shout at their discomfiture, but feel that the worst is not yet over.[204]

Upon the retreat of Broady's troops, the commander of the 4th New York Heavy Artillery called for his men to retire behind the railroad embankment. Because of the din of battle, the soldiers of the 1st Battalion, who occupied the rifle pits on the left of the regiment, did not hear the order. The cannoneers were already disenchanted with the New Yorkers' conduct. At this critical juncture, one of them recalled:

our heavy artillerymen, unable to honor the draft the situation made on their courage and manhood, started for the rear in large numbers. In our exasperation we call them cowards, with all the choice adjectives prefixed that we can summon from our vocabulary on demand, and this plan not succeeding to our satisfaction, we threaten to turn our guns upon them unless they remain. This stayed the tide, and many who had gone but a few rods came back.[205]

The retreat of the infantry left the two batteries in this sector—the 10th Massachusetts and the consolidated Rhode Island unit—in an embarrassing

---

203 Billings, *History of the Tenth Massachusetts Battery*, 317.

204 *Ibid.*, 318.

205 *Ibid.*, 319; OR 42, pt. 1, 270.

situation. At first, the cannoneers gave better than they received. Employing case-shot fused to explode in 1 1/2 seconds and then canister, the artillerists and their supporting infantry again tipped the scales against the butternuts. The Rebels recoiled and retired into a belt of pines 400 yards to the front. Whereupon, the gun captains called for their men to switch to case-shot.

Colonel Pegram had watched the repulse of the Rebel infantry that had advanced against the works south of the Dinwiddie Stage Road. Calling to his battery commanders, Pegram had them put their guns back into action.

When they did, the Southerners concentrated on the Union guns. "The air seemed filled with shrieking shells, with the flash, smoke, and crash of their explosion, and the harsh hurtling of their fragments."

A cannoneer in the 10th Massachusetts reported that it was "unquestionably the heaviest artillery fire we ever ... endured at close range, but alas! We cannot help ourselves. Fortunately for us, most of their shooting is a little too high, and damages left-rear of the line more than it does us."[206]

Simultaneously, Confederate sharpshooters posted in the woods and the cornfield to the left began to peck away. Large numbers of horses were killed. As soon as they were satisfied that their artillery had softened up the Union position, the Rebel leaders waved their men forward. Having expended their entire canister, the Rhode Islanders used solid and case-shot in their pieces. This time, the Johnnies weren't to be denied; they came pouring over the works held by Broady's troops.

When General MacRae's brigade crossed the parapet, the 10th Massachusetts Battery, which was on the Confederates' right front, opened with "canister at close quarters." MacRae shouted instructions for his North Carolinians "to take the battery!" Swinging to the right, the butternuts stormed down the works toward the four 3-inch rifles manned by the 10th Massachusetts. Charge after charge of canister was poured into the approaching grey clad column. It was like trying to sweep back the tide with a broom. The Rebels swarmed over the right piece, the cannoneers falling back to the next rifle. That gun was fired in a similar manner. So falling back from piece to piece, firing each in succession, the Massachusetts boys continued to fight until their fourth and last 3-inch rifle was overrun. The survivors took to their heels.[207]

"Our minds are instantly made up," the battery historian reported:

---

206 Billings, *History of the Tenth Massachusetts Battery*, 319-320; OR 42, pt. 1, 270, 408, 415, 423; Stedman, "Battle at Ream's Station," 117-118.

207 Billings, *History of the Tenth Massachusetts Battery*, 320-321; Dauchy, "Battle of Ream's Station," 135-136.

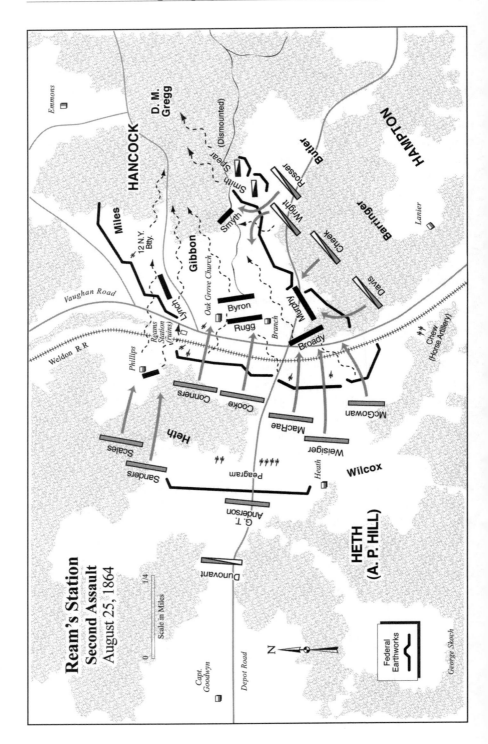

Ream's Station
Second Assault
August 25, 1864

for against the horrors of Rebel prisons on the one hand we have only to balance the chances of being shot while retreating on the other; and although the men that are falling as we pause, demonstrate most forcibly how poor those chances are, we hesitate but for an instant ere choosing the latter alternative, and take our departure, amid the hissing of bullets and the touching invitation of the "Johnnies," who tell us to "come in," or they'll shoot us. But we are not quite ready to respond to their appeal for our society, even when coupled with such a compulsory proposition, and make for the bushes in rear of,...[the consolidated New Jersey Battery], our nearest cover, where we separate, each taking the course that seemed best to him . . . [208]

When the left battalion of the 4th New York Heavy Artillery gave way, the Rebels began leaping over the breastworks. Several Rhode Islanders were yanked over the parapet as they stood to their guns. Abandoning their four Napoleons, the men of the consolidated battery broke for the rear. A detachment from Company C, 4th New York Heavy Artillery reached one of the guns ahead of the butternuts and turned it on them. The New Yorkers were able to delay but not stop the Confederates. MacRae's North Carolinians closed in, the New Yorkers sought to spike the piece, but unable to find any tools to answer the purpose, they took to their heels.

One of MacRae's North Carolinians reported:

Although entirely abandoned by its infantry support . . . [the consolidated New Jersey battery] continued a rapid fire upon the attacking column until the guns were reached. Some of the gunners even refused to surrender and were taken by sheer physical force. They were animated in their gallant conduct by the example of their commanding officer [Lieutenant Perrin]. On horse-back, he was a conspicuous target, and his voice could be distinctly heard encouraging the men. Struck with admiration by his bravery, every effort was made by General McRae [sic], Captain W. Oldham.. . . Captain Robert Bingham, and one or two others who were among the first to reach the guns to save the life of this manly opponent. Unfortunately he was struck by a ball which came from the extreme flank, as all the firing had ceased in front of him and he fell from his horse mortally wounded, not more lamented by his own men than by those who combated him. This battery, when captured, was at once turned upon the retreating columns of the enemy. It was manned by a few of McRae's [sic] sharp-shooters, all of whom were trained in artillery practice.[209]

208   Billings, *History of the Tenth Massachusetts Battery*, 321-322.

209   *OR* 42, pt. 1, 270, 408, 415, 423. The Rhode Islanders saved one limber and seven horses; Stedman, "Battle at Ream's Station," 116-117.

General Hancock in an attempt to check the surging Confederate tide called for General Gibbon's division to retake the lost guns and works. Following the breakthrough, Confederate snipers started to pepper away at Gibbon's troops, who crouched behind the breastworks to their front. To protect themselves from these marksmen, Gibbon's bluecoats vaulted the works and took cover behind the opposite side of the parapet. As the troops were bracing themselves to withstand an onslaught, Gibbon ordered Smyth to counterattack. He was to try to recover the works from which Miles' division had been dislodged.[210]

Smyth lost no time in redeploying his brigade. At the same time, he called on Colonel Murphy for assistance. Following the Rebel success, Murphy had dispatched two regiments (the 155th and 170th New York) to reoccupy the works abandoned by the 4th New York Heavy Artillery. As they pushed ahead, the New Yorkers ran into a galling fire.

Murphy, on receipt of Smyth's call, pulled the 64th New York Infantry and 8th New York Heavy Artillery out of the rifle pits. These two regiments, along with the 19th Maine and 19th Massachusetts of Rugg's brigade, joined Smyth's attacking force. Led by Gibbon and Smyth, the troops advanced on the double across the cornfield toward the works. Although the fire encountered was not as hot as that to which they had been subjected on many previous occasions, most of the bluecoats faltered before coming to grips with the Rebs. Within a matter of moments, large numbers of officers and men turned their backs to the foe.[211]

Suddenly, the soldiers of the 19th Massachusetts found themselves terribly alone. The regiments on their right and left had abandoned the charge. Lieutenant Colonel Edmund Rice therefore halted and reformed his troops behind several houses. After the men had been mustered, the regiment returned and "formed line upon the front of the works facing the enemy." Three of Smyth's regiments (the 14th Connecticut, 12th New Jersey, and an undesignated unit), however, pushed on and joined Miles' troops shortly after they had recaptured the three Napoleons of the 12th New York Battery.[212]

---

210 OR 42, pt. 1, 226, 293.

211 *Ibid.*, 293, 306, 308, 318, 324. When he filed his after-action report, General Gibbon observed, "In the attempt to obey this order, that portion of the division with me did not sustain its previous reputation, and, demoralized, partly by the shelling and musketry firing in its rear, partly by the refugees from other parts of the line, retired after a very feeble effort and under a very slight fire in great confusion, every effort of myself and staff failing to arrest the rout until the breast-work was reached." *Ibid.* 293

212 *Ibid.*, 306, 308, 324, 329, 332.

* * *

General Hampton had been listening when Pegram's artillery roared into action. No time was wasted as the cavalry leader sent aides galloping with orders for his command to get ready to advance. Prior to the receipt of this dispatch, the brigade commanders had formed their units to the left and right of the Weldon Railroad. Butler's division would advance west of the railroad and Barringer's east of the right of way. Colonel William D. Roberts' 2nd North Carolina and a squadron of the 9th Virginia screened the advance of Barringer's dismounted troopers. As the Confederates drove northward from Malone's Crossing, they crossed several fields.

About a mile beyond Malone's, Roberts' command encountered a line of "low" breastworks defended by the 7th Michigan. Putting their horses to the gallop, Roberts' troopers jumped them over the barricade, scattering the blue clad infantry. While waiting for the dismounted cavalrymen to catch up, Roberts put his men to work mopping up the area. By the time Hampton was ready to push on, Roberts' men had rounded up from 60 to 75 prisoners.

While his officers reformed their lines, Hampton called up his artillery. The cannoneers of Hart's South Carolina and McGregor's Virginia batteries unlimbered their eight guns. All the while the roar of battle to the cavalry corps' front was increasing in violence. The advance was now resumed. East of the railroad, Barringer's division entered the woods, "where an occasional shot was fired by a retiring" Yankee vedettes. A second line of rifle pits was encountered by Davis' Virginians. The 50 defenders laid down their aims almost without firing a shot. A detachment from the 13th Virginia Cavalry was given the task of escorting these Yanks to the rear.[213]

As Hampton's troopers were closing in on the Ream's Station perimeter from the south, the Rebel infantry stormed the breastworks held by Miles' division. Whereupon, Hampton withdrew his men from west of the Halifax Road. Hampton inside of a few minutes redeployed his command—Davis' brigade to the left, Cheek's in the center, and Young's to the right, Rosser's Virginians were posted in support. Dunovant's regiments remained in the saddle in case cavalry should be needed. The line being formed, the brigade commanders were instructed to keep the left flank (Davis' unit) anchored on the railroad. Advancing slowly, the right wing (Brig. Gen. Pierce B. Young's brigade) was to wheel to the right so as "to strike

---

213 *Ibid.*, 311, 943; Beale, *History of the Ninth Virginia Cavalry*, 143; Wells, *Hampton and His Cavalry*, 280; Brooks, *Butler and His Cavalry*, 304.

the rear of the enemy, who were in position behind the railroad embankment, and in a work which ran east perpendicularly to the railroad for some distance."

At a word from Hampton, the dismounted troopers took up the advance. The ground over which they moved "was very difficult," and it had been made more so by felled timber.[214]

Colonel Beale of the 9th Virginia recalled:

> We now came into woods where the bushes had been chopped off, and the trees felled, and where marching was very difficult. But we pressed on, and got through it. A gentle slope was seen to lead up from the edge of the wood to a heavy line of breastworks extending from the railroad for a quarter of a mile along the crest of the hill. The woods to our right receded from these formidable works, and a tremendous volley issued from the enemy occupying them against that part of our line, now on open ground and fully exposed. Nothing could stand against such fire. The men were ordered to lie down.[215]

Gibbon's troops, who held the rifle pits against which Hampton's dismounted cavalry drove, were placed in a quandary. To escape the fire of the Rebel infantry, they had taken cover in front of the works. Now with the approach of Hampton's battle line, they had to make an unpleasant choice. Soldiers began shifting back to the inside of the parapet.

As if the fire of the dismounted troopers, which General Gibbon described as "very feeble," weren't bad enough, the Yanks were subjected to a blistering bombardment and a galling small-arms fire from their right. The Confederates had quickly turned the captured field pieces on the bluecoats. Colonel Murphy recalled that his men to escape the Confederates' fire were compelled to cross the rifle pits as many as four times. Even so, the Federals momentarily checked Hampton's push.

Unfortunately for the Northerners, the soldiers posted in the works opposite Davis' brigade were compelled to abandon their position to escape the onrushing Confederate infantry. Seeing this, Davis waved his Virginians forward. Letting go a blood-curdling "Rebel Yell," the grey clads dashed toward the rifle pits. Two regiments from Rugg's brigade (the 19th Maine and 19th Massachusetts) and the right flank units of Smyth's command gave way first. Confederates flooded over the works. Their right flank turned, Smyth's bluecoats retired into the woods east of

214   OR 42, pt. 1, 311, 943.

215   Beale, *History of the Ninth Virginia Cavalry*, 143-144.

Oak Grove Church. Here Smyth reformed his brigade, sending the 69th and 106th Pennsylvania to establish contact with his three regiments holding the breastworks, where the three guns of the 12th New York Battery had been retaken.[216]

The breakthrough by Hampton's dismounted troopers all but isolated Murphy's brigade. For a few minutes it looked as if the entire brigade would be captured. In fighting its way out of the trap, one of Murphy's regiments, the 8th New York Heavy Artillery, engaged in a hand-to-hand struggle with some of Hampton's troopers. Before reaching the woods where they regrouped, two of Murphy's regiments, the 164th New York Infantry and 8th New York Heavy Artillery, lost their colors.[217]

Unable to leap his horse over the fortifications, Colonel Beale of the 9th Virginia rode to the left and entered the earthworks via the Halifax Road. As he was galloping forward to join his dismounted troopers inside the works, the colonel encountered Capt. Charles Robinson of Company C with several of his men escorting 200 or more prisoners to the rear.

At this time, Colonel Beale recalled:

> The firing had commenced again. Discovering how few of our men were in the works, many of the Yankees who were about surrendering, ran into a growth of sugar-cane, or sorghum, back of the line, and fired. Several heavy volleys came also from a body of woods near by. As the enemy ran back from the breastworks the right and center of our line [Cheek's and Young's brigades], which were rapidly advancing directed a steady fire upon them. The enemy had several guns [of the 3rd New Jersey] in position on the edge of the woods opposite the railroad, and these were actively engaged for several minutes with a battery [McGregor's] on our side.[218]

Several of the dismounted troopers had "such sport" with a little "Dutchman." As one of the Confederates observed:

> This fellow was as fat as a beer-barrel, not much over five feet in height, with very short legs and pudgy body, and could hardly run, in spite of his best efforts, faster than a jog-trot. Each time, as he would be flushed out of a place with his comrades, he would work his little legs as best he could, moving his arms grotesquely like a windmill, blowing like a porpoise and perspiring in streams, but quite unable to keep up with his

216 *Ibid.*, 144; OR 42, pt. 1, 294, 306, 318, 324, 329, 332, 943-944.

217 *OR* 42, pt. 1, 318.

218 Beale, *History of the Ninth Virginia Cavalry*, 144.

better conditioned companions. It was such a laughable sight that the men good-naturedly refrained from shooting him, but every time he was jumped would chaff him with jokes, and "Go it, Dutchy." Probably he was one of the "cheap substitutes" of which Grant was about that time complaining to [Secretary of War Edwin M.] Stanton as sent him by the "loyal" of the North; often becoming "too willing prisoners" he said.[219]

Elated by the easy success scored at the expense of Gibbon's division, Hampton's cheering grey clads pushed on. To their right were the light field works defended by Gregg's cavalry. Earlier in the afternoon, Captain Woerner of the 3rd New Jersey Battery had reported to Gibbon with a section of his guns. Gibbon in turn sent Woerner and his gunners to bolster Gregg. The cannoneers had thrown their two pieces into battery on the hillock defended by the 1st District of Columbia Cavalry. From this commanding elevation, the artillerists had hammered the Rebel infantry with shot and shell as it charged across the breastworks held by Miles' bluecoats. Supported by dismounted troopers of the 1st District of Columbia and about 100 infantry from various regiments, the cannoneers held their ground until Hampton's troopers hurled Gibbon's soldiers from their rifle pits.

Gregg's dismounted cavalrymen with several well-aimed volleys checked Hampton's initial effort to exploit the situation. Valuable time was lost as Confederate officers regrouped their units and wheeled them to the right. Gregg, realizing that he was badly outnumbered, ordered the knoll abandoned. Accompanied by Woerner's guns, the dismounted troopers withdrew north of a branch of Jones Hole Swamp, where they took position on the left of Gibbon's reorganized main line of resistance.[220]

Meanwhile, Colonel Lynch had assembled a striking force of about 200 men representing almost every Union regiment on the field. Learning of this, General Miles sent word for Lynch to take these men, advance across the railroad, and assail the Confederates' left. Led by Lynch, the bluecoats crossed the railroad and took position at the Camley house. Here, they were about 200 yards from, and partially to the rear of the Rebels' left. The Federals opened fire and with a shout drove forward, apparently taking the butternuts by surprise. The Rebs retired a few steps and braced themselves. Lynch's counterthrust soon bogged down, as the troops

---

219   Wells, *Hampton and His Cavalry*, 281-282.

220   OR 42, pt. 1, 227, 418, 607; Dauchy, "Battle of Ream's Station," 137.

found themselves exposed to a galling fire from both friend and foe. Moreover, the officers were for the most part strangers to the men they were leading.[221]

The stand made on the right by Miles' troops, supported by the fire of a section of the 3rd New Jersey Battery, enabled the Federals to retain control of the country road leading eastward across Jones Hole Swamp to the Jerusalem Plank Road. Undaunted by the collapse of Lynch's thrust, Miles established a picket line along the Halifax Road. When he inspected his outposts, the general heard Confederate officers and color bearers calling out their units. This led Miles to believe that the Rebels must be as disorganized by their success as the Federals were by their setback. Miles was in a combative mood; he felt certain that if reinforced he could recapture the rest of the rifle pits from which his division had been hurled. He sent one of his aides (Maj. William R. Driver) to carry this information to General Hancock.[222]

About the same time Hancock was told by General Gregg that his cavalrymen were prepared to cooperate in an effort to recover the breastworks. Before committing himself, Hancock discussed the situation with the commander of his Second division, General Gibbon. Sadly shaking his head, Gibbon stated that his troops were in no condition to participate in a counterattack. Since it was necessary to retake the lost works to protect the country road linking Ream's Station with the Jerusalem Plank Road, Hancock had but one alternative—to withdraw.[223]

It was 8:00 p.m. when Capt. Joseph S. Conrad reached Miles' command post and told the general of Hancock's decision. As soon as it was dark, Miles was to disengage his troops and march to Williams' house on the Jerusalem Plank Road. Miles' division was to cover the corps' rear as it moved eastward away from the Rebels.[224]

About dusk, the Confederates sent a strong column against Lynch's combat patrol then threatening their left. The Rebels, after a brisk struggle, compelled the bluecoats to withdraw and take cover inside the breastworks east of the railroad.

As soon as the fighting in this sector waned, Captain Woerner's gun captains reported they were out of ammunition. Woerner directed his section chiefs to limber up their pieces. The battery halted alongside the country road about one-third mile east of Oak Grove Church. Here, the teams were unhitched and sent to assist in bringing off the three Napoleons of the 12th New York Battery and such

221 OR 42, pt. 1, 253-254, 262.

222 Ibid., 227, 254.

223 Ibid., 227.

224 Ibid., 227, 254.

limbers and caissons as could be saved. Even after the teams arrived, valuable time was squandered as the officers sought to get men to manhandle the guns off the line and down into a ravine where the teams could be hitched up. Chief of Artillery A. Judson Clark was told that it would be impossible to reach the New Yorkers' fourth gun which had been abandoned at the angle. Undaunted, Clark told Lieutenant Dauchy to try to save the piece.

Dauchy started up the road which led by the church. After proceeding a short distance, he encountered Colonel Lynch. The colonel told Dauchy that the gun was outside the Union lines and couldn't be reached. In addition, Lynch continued, the infantry was "being withdrawn pursuant to orders."

Just then a column of foot soldiers came tramping up the road, Dauchy now turned his attention to getting his limbers and caissons off the field. Assisted by a detail from the 61st New York, the lieutenant was able to save three limbers. He, however, could obtain no help in drawing off the two caissons parked in the pines. As the lieutenant was about to abandon hope, Lt. Peter H. Sweeney of Miles' Provost Guard appeared with several men. Sweeney volunteered to assist in rescuing the caissons. Aided by the provost people, Dauchy was able to manhandle the heavy caissons down the country road. By the time the last caisson was wheeled off the field, all the troops of Hancock's command, except the pickets, had pulled out of the area.[225]

One of Dauchy's gunners had been wounded in the bowels, but managed to take cover behind a large tree. Calling to the lieutenant, the wounded man handed him a large sum of money, from $150 to $175 (the battery had been paid several days before), together with his watch and other valuables, with a request to send them to his family. When the last of the caissons was being withdrawn, Dauchy had the wounded gunner placed on the caisson. "But," Dauchy recalled, "the jolting along the rough road, through the woods, over stumps, and through ruts, caused him so much suffering that he begged me to lay him down by the side of the road and let him die," the lieutenant refused to listen to such a plea. The march was continued. When the battery finally halted, the cannoneer died and was "buried in a lonely field."[226]

When the Federals abandoned their Ream's Station position at dark and retreated eastward, Gibbon's shattered division took the lead. Prior to drawing off his division, Miles instructed Colonel Lynch to post a picket line covering the left and front of the brigade. Lynch gave this task to the 61st New York. The New

---

225 *Ibid.*, 262, 408-409, 421-422; Dauchy, "Battle of Ream's Station," 138-139.

226 Dauchy, "Battle of Ream's Station," 138-139.

Yorkers were deployed as skirmishers along the Halifax Road, their right resting on the rifle pits. Detachments from other regiments of the 1st Brigade were advanced and stationed on the right of the 61st New York.

At 9:00 p.m. Miles notified Lynch that the other units had cleared the area. Upon receipt of this message, Lynch recalled his men. As soon as the units had been formed and mustered, the march for the Jerusalem Plank Road was commenced.[227]

It was 7:00 p.m. when one of Hancock's aides galloped up to General Willcox's command post with an urgent message. Willcox had formed his division across the country road to Ream's Station and was halting and reorganizing the refugees from Hancock's command. The staff officer told Willcox that if he "could get up one or two brigades in time, the day might yet be saved."

Willcox called for his men to shuck their knapsacks. As soon as the units could be formed, the division moved out on the double. Willcox's panting IX Corps foot soldiers were within one and one-half miles of Ream's Station, when Colonel Morgan hailed their general. Morgan carried an order from Hancock for Willcox to take position to cover the retreat of the II Corps. Willcox was to hold his ground until Miles' division had passed, then he was to recall his soldiers and follow as a rear guard. Gregg's cavalry was to screen Willcox's bluecoats as they pulled back to the Jerusalem Plank Road. Willcox promptly posted his division to the left and the right of the road.[228]

The soldiers of the IX Corps held fast as Hancock's troops passed through their lines.[229]

Hancock kept his exhausted bluecoats on the road until they reached the fields near Williams' house. It was after midnight when the order to halt was given, and the men allowed to camp.[230]

The most humiliating day the veteran II Corps was to experience during the war was over. General Hancock had been deeply stirred by the day's events, for the first time he had felt the bitterness of defeat. He had seen his troops fail in efforts to carry Confederate entrenchments, but never before had he experienced the

227   OR 42, pt. 1, 227, 262.

228   *Ibid.*, 227, 591.

229   *Ibid.*, 591.

230   *Ibid.*, 227, 246, 254, 262, 278, 283, 290, 302, 318, 332. Teams from one of the batteries, parked near the Southall house, were sent as soon as possible to relieve the infantrymen who had drawn off the three limbers and two caissons of the 12th New York Battery, and the caissons of the 3rd New Jersey Battery, the horses from which had been appropriated to pull the New Yorkers' guns. *Ibid.*, 409.

mortification of watching his troops as they were driven from breastworks and their guns taken. In the disaster of June 22, Hancock had not been in charge, and during the indifferent behavior of the troops at Deep Bottom, the operations had been concealed from his view by dense forests. Never before had Hancock seen his men fail to respond to the utmost when he had called on them personally for a supreme effort; nor had he ever before ridden toward the foe followed by a "beggarly array of a few hundred stragglers." He could no longer hide from himself that his once mighty corps retained but the shadow of its former strength and vigor.

Riding up to Colonel Morgan, covered with dust and begrimed with ponder and smoke, Hancock placed his hand upon the staff officer's shoulder and said, "Colonel, I do not care to die, but I pray to God I may never leave this field."[231]

Colonel McAllister, whose troops were digging in a mile south of the junction at Shay's Tavern, was notified by General Hancock at 1:00 a.m. on the 26th to hold his ground until Willcox's column had turned into the Jerusalem Plank Road. He would then recall his troops and return to the Jones' house sector of the investment line.[232]

The reason behind these movements was a 7:30 p.m. message from Chief of Staff Humphreys. At that time Meade had determined to recall the II Corps and have it take "post in the vicinity of the Williams' house, or some point covering the Plank Road and looking toward Warren's left." Gregg's horsemen were to be directed to watch the countryside between Warren's left and the Jerusalem Plank Road. McAllister's foot soldiers were to be returned "to their former position in the entrenchments."

The telegrapher at army headquarters reported that the operator at the other end of the line had acknowledged receipt of the dispatch. A little before 10:30 p.m., Captain McEntee of Hancock's staff showed up at headquarters and told Humphreys that at 7:30 p.m. Hancock's telegraph station had been in the hands of the Rebels, who had undoubtedly intercepted the message. Humphreys therefore addressed a second communication, directing Hancock to withdraw his troops and have them take position near Williams' house. At the same time, Humphreys notified Hancock that Meade had ordered two more divisions, Crawford's and White's, to his assistance.[233]

Thirty minutes later, General Meade, having learned of Hancock's misfortune, addressed a message to his corps commander. Meade explained that at the time he

---

231 Walker, "Ream's Station," 294-295.

232 *OR* 42, pt. 1, 391.

233 *OR* 42, pt. 2, 485.

had spoken with McEntee, the II Corps had been holding its own, and this had caused him to defer his scheduled visit to Ream's Station. If he had had any doubt of the II Corps' ability to hold its ground, Meade observed, he would have dispatched Willcox and McAllister down the railroad. But, the general continued, his anxiety had been for Hancock's rear, or that the Southerners would penetrate the country between Warren's left and the Ream's Station perimeter. To guard against these contingencies he had rushed Willcox down the Jerusalem Plank Road, while holding Crawford and White "ready to move and attack." Furthermore, Meade was afraid that the Confederates, after failing to drive Hancock, would turn on Warren. Consequently, he hadn't wanted to commit all of his reserves. Meade assured Hancock:

> I am satisfied you and your command have done all in your power, and though you have met with a reverse, the honor and escutcheons of the old Second are as bright as ever, and will on some future occasion prove it is only when enormous odds are brought against them that they can be moved. Don't let this matter worry you because you have given me every satisfaction.

Chief of Staff Humphreys (at 11:25 p.m.) wrote Hancock. He wanted the II Corps commander to know reinforcements were en route to cover his withdrawal from Ream's Station. Should Hancock not require these troops (Crawford's and White's divisions), he was to order them back to their commands.[234]

Meanwhile, Humphreys had contacted Generals Warren and Parke. At 9:50 p.m. Humphreys notified Warren that he was to dispatch a member of his staff to communicate with Hancock and see if he required reinforcements. If so, Warren was to rush Brig. Gen. Samuel W. Crawford's division to Ream's Station. General Parke at the same time was alerted to hold Brig. Gen. Julius White's division ready to march to the aid of the II Corps. Warren and Parke were advised that Hancock had been ordered to fall back to Williams' house.[235]

At 10:15 p.m. the telegrapher at army headquarters tapped out urgent messages for Warren and Parke. Crawford and White were to put their troops into motion immediately. Crawford was to command the reinforcing column.[236]

Five minutes later, Chief of Staff Humphreys relayed additional information to Warren. Crawford, besides his own and White's division, was to take charge of

234 *Ibid.*, 486.

235 *Ibid.*, 489, 495.

236 *Ibid.*, 490, 495.

McAllister's troops currently posted near Shay's Tavern. According to the latest news from the point of danger, the Rebels had broken through Hancock's right. It was feared at headquarters that Willcox's IX Corps division might not be able to stem the tide.

Before issuing marching orders to Crawford, Warren wanted additional information. He wished to know the route to be taken by the relief column.

At 10:30 p.m. he had his answer. Humphreys expected Crawford to take the Jerusalem Plank Road, because the Weldon Railroad north of Ream's Station was in Confederate hands.[237]

Upon receipt of this message, Warren got in touch with General Crawford. Earlier in the day, Crawford's division had been ordered to change camp. While doing so, instructions were received to prepare for action. As soon as the men had been formed, mustered, and inspected, the brigade commanders assembled their units at Globe Tavern. It was there that Crawford received directions to march eastward to Temple's house. The column would then proceed to Ream's Station via the Jerusalem Plank and Dinwiddie Stage Roads.[238]

When Crawford gave the word, his division, accompanied by the 9th Battery, Massachusetts Light Artillery, moved out.

Soon after Crawford's column had taken up the march, Warren at 11:30 p.m. received another telegram from army headquarters. According to the latest information from the front, Humphreys observed, it looked as if Hancock would be able to disengage without requiring any additional reinforcements. General Meade therefore wanted Warren to halt Crawford's column. A staff officer would be sent to ascertain if Hancock desired any troops to cover his retreat. If he didn't, Crawford was to be recalled.[239]

Crawford's bluecoats had tramped about a mile, when the order to halt was received. Soon thereafter, Crawford learned that Hancock didn't require his assistance. Crawford accordingly counter marched his column, the brigades returning to their camps in the Globe Tavern area.[240]

*   *   *

237 *Ibid.*, 490.

238 OR 42, pt. 1, 505; OR 42, pt. 2, 493.

239 OR 42, pt. 2, 490-491.

240 OR 42, pt. 1, 505.

Willcox's IX Corps soldiers held their roadblock east of Jones Hole Swamp until the last of Hancock's battle weary troops had passed. Leaving Gregg's horsemen to watch the eastern approaches to Ream's Station, Willcox recalled his brigades and fell in behind the II Corps. Willcox turned his column into the Jerusalem Plank Road. Although progress was retarded by Hancock's troops, Willcox's bluecoats, by 6:30 a.m. on August 26 were back in their camp, near Parke's Aiken house headquarters.[241]

McAllister assembled his reinforced brigade on Jerusalem Plank Road, as soon as Willcox's division was out of the way. Putting his troops into motion, McAllister had them back in their old position near Jones' house at 5:00 a.m. Except for one man, who while reconnoitering had ran afoul of a Rebel patrol and had been captured, McAllister listed no casualties.[242]

Before retiring for the night, General Hancock had written Meade from Williams' house, Hancock informed his chief that his men were now massing nearby, but it would be "a long time before the stragglers are up," and he could reorganize his corps "as to be serviceable." The general described the fighting at Ream's Station as "one of the severest and most obstinate battles the corps had ever fought."

After tersely describing the action, Hancock acknowledged the loss of several guns. He attributed this to the fact that nearly all the artillery horses had been slain before the final assault. The enemy, Hancock wrote, must have "suffered heavily." So far, the disorganized condition of his command had prevented Hancock from determining his casualties. But as his men had been sheltered by breastworks, he didn't feel his losses in killed and wounded would be as severe as that of the Rebels. Even so, Hancock observed, his corps would "not be available today for any serious work."[243]

The next morning, Hancock forwarded to Meade's headquarters a more detailed account of the battle. The general was only able to "surmise" his losses, which he didn't think would exceed 1,200 to 1,500. All the soldiers he had spoken with were of the opinion that the battle was "one of the most determined and desperate fights of the war, resembling Spotsylvania in its character, though the

241 *Ibid.*, 591; OR 42, pt. 2, 533.

242 OR 42, pt. 1, 391.

243 OR 42, pt. 2, 524.

number of engaged gives it less importance." A few more troops, in Hancock's opinion, would have given the Federals "a victory of considerable importance."[244]

It was several days before the commanders of all Union units engaged at Ream's Station filed their returns. When the adjutant general totaled the casualties he found that the troops under Hancock had suffered 2,742 casualties: 130 killed, 529 wounded, and 2,073 missing. The proportion of officers lost was unusually large. In addition to the nine guns left on the field, Hancock's artillerists listed the loss of 134 horses, eight caissons, and eight limbers.[245]

*　　*　　*

General Hill decided against pursuing Hancock's shattered corps. Orders were issued for the infantry commanders to collect their commands. Hampton was directed to have his dismounted troopers occupy the abandoned rifle pits. After detailing them to roundup and disarm the hundreds of Federals wandering about the area, Hill had his infantry formations move to the west. Along toward dark, a halt was called, and the soldiers, except for the large number ticketed for outpost duty, were allowed to bivouac.[246]

At dark, General Rosser directed Capt. Emanuel Sipe of the 12th Virginia Cavalry and Captain Myers of the 35th Virginia Battalion to report to General Hampton. The cavalry leader told Sipe and Myers to relieve the infantry posted in the fortifications. Soon after the troopers moved into the earthworks, a "terrible storm of rain, thunder and lightning" began. One of the cavalrymen recalled:

> The vivid streams, not flashes, of lightning danced and glanced along the Rail Road track and over the captured guns, which still stood there, while every moment the crashing thunder just overhead pealed out as if the inky sky was being torn to splinters, and in sheets and torrents the floods of rain poured down, while through the thick blackness of the storm and night could be heard all around the shrieks and groans of the wounded and dying Federals, who, totally unable to help themselves, were gasping

244 *Ibid.,* 525-526.

245 OR 42, pt. 1, 131, 409-410. The guns abandoned on the field were: five 12-pounder Napoleons and four 3-inch Ordnance Rifles.

246 *Ibid.,* 944; Caldwell, *The History of a Brigade of South Carolinians,* 181. General Mahone reached the field with Weisiger's and King's brigades in time to assist in the mopping up operations. A soldier in the 12th Virginia noted in his diary, "Loss very slight. The expedition was altogether quite a sweep. A large number of prisoners & 16 [sic] guns were taken besides quantities of small arms &c." Sale, Diary.

out their lives in agony, without one friend to shelter them from the raging of the fierce tempest or stop the ebbing life-tide that poured from their mangled bodies, and in the morning light there lay many corpses along the ground at Ream's whose souls had gone up to the judgment-throne amid the bursting storm and thunder of that horrible night.[247]

Seven of Hampton's regiments remained at Ream's Station till the morning of the 26th. At that time Hampton, after detaching Butler's division to remove the wounded and police the battlefield, recalled his troopers. On checking with his division commanders, Hampton learned that in the previous day's fighting his corps had lost: 16 killed, 75 wounded, and 3 missing.[248]

Hill's infantry columns started for Petersburg early on the 26th. As he rode back up the Squirrel Level Road, Hill checked the reports submitted by his subordinates. On doing so, he found that his command had captured 12 stands of colors, 9 pieces of artillery, 10 caissons, 2,150 prisoners, 3,100 stands of arms, and 32 horses. All this had been accomplished at a relatively small cost—720 killed, wounded, and missing.[249]

Union signal officers late in the afternoon observed the victorious Confederates as they returned from Ream's Station. At 4:40 p.m. a squadron of cavalry and a brigade of infantry were sighted as they marched up the Squirrel Level Road. This column halted near the "lead-works." Turning his glasses to this force, the Federal observer saw that the Rebs were brandishing five of the 12 colors captured from Hancock's people. Shortly thereafter, another infantry column, which the signal corps people estimated to number at least a division (accompanied by 18 guns, several wagons, and a number of pack mules), passed up the Squirrel Level Road and disappeared into the Rebel works.[250]

Butler's division remained on picket duty for several days at Ream's Station. Only about 300 yards separated the outposts in grey from those in blue. There was no shooting, however, as both Reb and Yank "agreed to the childish proposition of 'I'll let you alone if you'll let me alone.'"[251]

---

247 Myers, *The Comanches*, 327-328.

248 OR 42, pt. 1, 944. Hampton reported that his troopers buried 143 Federals and captured 781 bluecoats, including 25 officers.

249 *Ibid.*, 940; Caldwell, *The History of a Brigade of South Carolinians*, 181.

250 OR 42, pt. 2, 523, 527.

251 Myers, *The Comanches*, 328.

A number of the butternuts watched as a Union burial party came out under a flag of truce to inter their dead. This task was done in haste; the Federals returned to their lines, leaving a few dead bluecoats for the Johnnies to lay to rest.[252]

* * *

General Gregg's Union cavalry, when the Confederates declined to pursue Hancock's troops, was able to hold its ground on the evening of August 25. It was midnight before Gregg saw fit to recall the 1st Maine and 16th Pennsylvania from their positions covering the crossings of Jones Hole Swamp.

The next morning, Gregg posted Smith's brigade at Temple's and on the Jerusalem Plank Road. Checkpoints were established on that road and the roads leading westward to Ream's Station. Stedman's brigade maintained its position on the Dinwiddie Stage Road till 10:00 a.m. Before withdrawing and rejoining Gregg, Stedman's troopers were shelled by Hart's four-gun South Carolina Battery.[253] Spear's brigade, which had retired to the Jerusalem Plank Road the previous evening was directed to report to its parent unit—Kautz's division.[254]

Although the Confederates had severely punished the II Corps, they had failed to shake the Federals' grip on the Weldon Railroad. But in the long run, the heavy casualties suffered by Hancock's people might have had important repercussions. Along with the battle of the Weldon Railroad, fought the previous week, the engagement at Ream's Station could be expected to have a depressing effect on morale in the North. With an election approaching, the peace party in the North would draw strength from the ever lengthening casualty lists. Several more successes of the Confederates'—such as Ream's Station might just cause Abraham Lincoln to lose the election.

When he wrote of the battle, Gen. A. P. Hill reported, "The sabre and the bayonet have shaken hands on the enemy's captured breastworks."[255]

Once again, as many times in the past, the North Carolina infantry brigades at Ream's Station had covered themselves with glory. General Robert E. Lee on August 29 wrote Gov. Zebulon Vance of North Carolina:

---

252 Beale, *History of the Ninth Virginia Cavalry*, 145.

253 *OR* 42, pt. 1, 525, 608.

254 *Ibid.*, 835.

255 Wells, *Hampton and His Cavalry*, 283.

I have frequently been called upon to mention the services of the North Carolina soldiers in this army, but their gallantry and conduct were never more deserving of admiration than in the engagement at Ream's Station, on the 25th instant.

The brigades of Generals Cooke, MacRae and Lane, the last under the command of General Conner, advanced through a thick abatis of felled trees, under a heavy fire of musketry and artillery, and carried the enemy's works with a steady courage that elicited the warm commendation of their corps and division commanders, and the admiration of the army.

On the same occasion the brigade of General Barringer bore a conspicuous part in the operations of the cavalry, which were no less distinguished for boldness and efficiency than those of the infantry.

If the men who remain in North Carolina share the spirit of those they have sent to the field, as I doubt not they do, her defense may be securely entrusted in their hands.[256]

Editor's Conclusion

Although some individual regiments fought well, the Confederate attack routed Hancock's II corps, which returned to its lines around Petersburg. Brig. Gen. David Gregg's Union cavalry division was the only command to leave the field intact. The battle cost Hancock 2,742 officers and men, while Confederate losses totaled about 800 (including cavalry). The end of the battle signaled the close of Grant's Fourth Offensive.

Although Hancock's men had been routed, Generals Grant and Meade were both generally pleased by the Weldon Railroad operations. Warren's seizure of the Weldon line farther north forced Lee to use wagon trains to haul vital supplies some thirty miles from the Stony Creek Depot to Petersburg. The Union success placed Grant's army closer to Lee's final supply line, the South Side Railroad.

---

256 Underwood, *History of the Twenty-Sixth Regiment of the North Carolina Troops*, 86; Stedman, "Battle at Ream's Station," 119-120.

Afterword

This volume of *The Petersburg Campaign* chronicled the first 77 days of the extensive 298-day military operation against Petersburg, beginning with Maj. Gen. Ben Butler's abortive attack against the city on June 9, 1864, and concluding the evening of August 25 with the rout of Maj. Gen. Winfield Hancock's exhausted Federal II Corps at Ream's Station.

During those two and one-half months, Gen. Ulysses S. Grant's Federals attempted to capture the city seven times. Petersburg was assaulted three times (June 9, June 15-18, and July 30). All three attacks failed. There were four attempts to starve or force Gen. Robert E. Lee's Confederates out of Petersburg by destroying the Weldon Railroad. The first, from June 22 through July 1, was a failed cavalry raid by Brig. Gens. James H. Wilson and August Kautz that put the majority of Grant's mounted arm out of commission for a month. The August 18-21 Battle of Globe Tavern ended with the Federal V Corps astride the Weldon line, but without enough men to both hold the ground and tear up the railroad. Skillful Southern counter-thrusts defeated the effort. The August 25 Battle of Ream's Station (Second Ream's Station) was the end result of a move by Hancock's II Corps to destroy the Weldon Railroad from Globe Tavern southward. Hard-hitting Confederate attacks scored a tactical victory, but left the Federals in possession of part of the railroad. Finally, there was one earlier attempt to lunge west and seize the Weldon and South Side railroads with the II Corps and VI Corps (June 22-23), but the effort ended in disaster for the Federals at the Jerusalem Plank Road.

As the following tables demonstrate, Federal losses greatly exceeded Southern casualties. After the exhausting bloodletting of the Overland Campaign, these losses crippled the morale of the Army of the Potomac and made effective operations that much more difficult.

The "Western Front" battles that would follow stretched the opposing lines west and southwest as Grant tried to sever Lee's lines of supply, including the South Side Railroad—the last Confederate railroad feeding Petersburg and Richmond. Major battles above and below the James River, including Peebles Farm, the Darbytown and New Market Roads, Boydton Plank Road, and Hatcher's Run stretched Lee's lines to the breaking point and cost both sides tens of thousands of additional casualties. Lee's desperate failed attempt to break Grant's line at Fort Stedman at the end of March 1865, followed by the disastrous loss of Five Forks on April 1 and the general assault upon the Confederate lines the next day collapsed the Army of Northern Virginia and ended the siege of Petersburg on the morning of April 3. Lee and his men tried to escape west, but surrendered at Appomattox Court House on April 9.

TABLE 1				
Union Losses June - August, 1864				
Month	Killed	Wounded	Captured or Missing	Total
June	2,013	9,935	4,621	16,569
July	915	3,808	1,644	6,367
August	876	4,151	5,969	10,996
Total	1,791	17,894	12,234	33,932

Source: John Horn, *The Petersburg Campaign*
(Combined Books, Conshohocken, Pennsylvania, 1993), 45.

TABLE 2	
Confederate Losses June - August, 1864	
Month	Total
June	6,000
July	3,000
August	5,500
Total	14,000
Source: John Horn, *The Petersburg Campaign*, 45.	

TABLE 3				
Union Strength Present for Duty Equipped				
Date	Cavalry	Artillery	Infantry	Total
June 30	14,177	9,383	86,702	110,262
July 31	8,936	9,995	62,562	81,493
August 31	6,358	7,846	45,963	60,167
Source: John Horn, *The Petersburg Campaign*, 76.				

TABLE 4				
Confederate Strength Present for Duty Equipped				
Date	Cavalry	Artillery	Infantry	Total
June 30	10,593	7,989	44,652	63,234
July 10	10,073	7,921	43,617	61,611
August 31	8,129	7,414	34,486	50,029
Source: John Horn, *The Petersburg Campaign*, 77.				

Bibliography

Manuscripts

Georgia Archives, Atlanta, GA
    Washington L. Dunn Diary
North Carolina State Archives, Raleigh, NC
    James H. Lane, "Recollections"
    Thomas Strayhorn Papers
Petersburg National Battlefield, Petersburg, VA
    William Russell Diary (typescript)
Tennessee State Library and Archives, Nashville, TN
    Bashaw, "My Experiences in the War."
Virginia State Library, Richmond, VA
    John F. Sale Diary

Official Publications

United States War Department. *The War of the Rebellion: A Compilation of the Official Records of the Union and Confederate Armies*, 128 vols. Washington, D.C.: U.S. Government Printing Office, 1880-1901.

United States Naval War Records Office. *Official Records of the Union and Confederate Navies in the War of the Rebellion*, 30 vols. Washington, D.C.: U.S. Government Printing Office, 1894-1922.

Published

Anonymous. *A Historical Sketch of the Quitman Guards, Company E, Sixteenth Mississippi Regiment, Harris' Brigade: from its Organization in Holmesville, 21st April, 1861, to the Surrender of the Army of Northern Virginia, 9th April, 1865.* New Orleans: Isaac T. Hinton, 1866.

Beale, R. L. T. *History of the Ninth Virginia Cavalry in the War Between the States.* Richmond: B. F. Johnson Publishing Company, 1899.

Beauregard, G. T. "Four Days of Battle at Petersburg." In *Battles and Leaders of the Civil War*, edited by Robert Underwood Johnson and Clarence Clough Buel, Vol. 4. New York: The Century Co., 1887.

Beauregard, G. T. "Letter of General Beauregard to General C. M. Wilcox." In *Papers of the Military Historical Society of Massachusetts*, Vol. 5. Boston: Military Historical Society of Massachusetts, 1906.

Billings, John D. *The History of the Tenth Massachusetts Battery of Light Artillery in the War of the Rebellion, 1862-1865.* Boston: The Arakelyan Press, 1909.

Boatner, Mark M. *The Civil War Dictionary.* New York: D. McKay Co., 1959.

Brainard, Mary G.G. *Campaigns of the One Hundred Forty-Sixth Regiment New York State Volunteers.* New York: G. P. Putnam's Sons, 1915.

Brooks, U. R. *Butler and His Cavalry in the War of Secession 1861-1865.* Columbia: The State Company, 1909.

Cadwell, Charles K. *The Old Sixth Regiment, Its War Record, 1861-1865.* New Haven: Tuttle, Morehouse, and Taylor, 1875.

Caldwell, J. F. J. *The History of a Brigade of South Carolinians, Known First as "Gregg's," and Subsequently as "McGowan's Brigade."* Philadelphia: King and Baird, 1866.

Colston, R. E. "Repelling the First Assault on Petersburg." In *Battles and Leaders of the Civil War*, edited by Robert Underwood Johnson and Clarence Clough Buel, Vol. 4. New York: The Century Co., 1887.

Committee of the Regiment, *History of the Thirty-Fifth Regiment Massachusetts Volunteers, 1862-1865.* Boston: Mills, Knight, & Company, 1884.

Committee of the Regiment, *History of the Thirty-Sixth Massachusetts Volunteers, 1862-1865.* Boston: Press of Rockwell and Churchill, 1884.

Craft, David, *History of the One Hundred Forty-First Regiment, Pennsylvania Volunteers 1862-1865*. Towanda, PA.: Reporter-Journal Printing Company, 1885.

Croom, Wendell D. *The War History of Company "C" (Beauregard Volunteers) Sixth Georgia Regiment, Infantry*. Fort Valley, GA.: Advertiser, 1879.

Cunningham, John L., *Three Years with the Adirondack Regiment: 118th New York Volunteer Infantry*. Norwood, MA: The Plimpton Press, 1920.

Dauchy, George K. "The Battle of Ream's Station." in *Military Essays and Recollections: Papers Read Before the Commandery of the State of Illinois, Military Order of the Loyal Legion of the United States*, Vol. 3. Chicago: Dial, 1890.

Derby, W. P. *Bearing Arms in the Twenty-Seventh Massachusetts Regiment of Volunteers Infantry during the Civil War*. Boston: Wright & Potter, 1883.

Drewry, P.H. "The Ninth of June, 1864." *Confederate Veteran*, Vol. 35 (1927).

Dunlop, W. S. *Lee's Sharpshooters; or, The Forefront of Battle*. Little Rock: Tunnah & Pittard, 1899.

Dyer, Frederick H. *A Compendium of the War of the Rebellion*, 3 vols. New York: T. Yoseloff, 1959.

Edwards, Frank, *Army Life of Frank Edwards, Confederate Veteran*. LaGrange, GA.: Printed by the Author, 1911.

Field, C. W. "Campaign of 1864–'65." In *Southern Historical Society Papers*, Vol. 14 (1886).

Freeman, Douglas Southall. *Lee's Lieutenants, A Study in Command*, 3 vols. New York: Scribner's, 1942-1944.

—————. *R. E. Lee: A Biography*, 4 vols. (New York, 1934-1935).

Hagood, Johnson. *Memoirs of the War of Secession: From the Original Manuscripts of Johnson Hagood, Brigadier General, C.S.A.* Columbia, S.C.: The State Company, 1910.

Hays, Gilbert A. and Morrow, William H. *Under the Red Patch: Story of the Sixty Third Regiment Pennsylvania Volunteers, 1861-1864*. Pittsburgh: Sixty-Third Pennsylvania Volunteers Regimental Association, 1908.

Hopkins, William P. *The Seventh Regiment Rhode Island Volunteers in the Civil War, 1862-1865*. Providence: Snow and Farnham, 1903.

Houghton, Edwin E. *The Campaigns of the Seventeenth Maine*. Portland: Short & Loring, 1866.

Humphreys, Andrew A. *The Virginia Campaign of '64 and '65*. New York: Charles Scribner's Sons, 1883.

Kautz, August V. "Operations South of the James." In *Battles and Leaders of the Civil War*, edited by Robert Underwood Johnson and Clarence Clough Buel, Vol. 4. New York: The Century Co., 1887.

Kreutzer, William. *Notes and Observations made During Four Years of Service with the Ninety-Eighth N. Y. Volunteer in the War of 1861*. Philadelphia: Giant, Faires & Rogers, 1878.

Little, Henry F.W. *The Seventh Regiment of the New Hampshire Volunteers in the War of the Rebellion.* Concord, N.H.: Ira C. Evans, 1896.

Livermore, Thomas L. "The Failure to Take Petersburg, June 15, 1864." In *Papers of the Military Historical Society of Massachusetts,* vol. 5. Boston: Military Historical Society of Massachusetts, 1906.

McCabe, William Gordon, "Defense of Petersburg." In *Southern Historical Society Papers,* Vol. 2 (1876).

Martin, W. J., "History of the 11th North Carolina Regiment," In *Southern Historical Society Papers,* Vol 23 (1895).

Mowris, J. A. *A History of the One Hundred and Seventeenth Regiment, N. Y. Volunteers, (Fourth Oneida), from the Date of Its Organization, August 1862, Till That of Its Muster Out, June 1865.* Hartford, CT.: Case, Lockwood, & Co., 1866.

Myers, Frank M. *The Comanches: A History of White's Battalion, Virginia Cavalry, Laurel Brig., Hampton Div., A.N.V., C.S.A.* Baltimore: Kelly, Piet & Co., 1871.

Peabody, Frank E. "Some Observations Concerning the Opposing Forces at Petersburg on June 15, 1864." In *Papers of the Military Historical Society of Massachusetts,* Vol. 5. Boston: Military Historical Society of Massachusetts, 1906.

Porter, Charles H. "Operations against the Weldon Railroad, August 18, 19, 21, 1864." In *Papers of the Military Historical Society of Massachusetts,* vol. 5. Boston: Military Historical Society of Massachusetts, 1906.

Powell, William H. *The Fifth Army Corps (Army of the Potomac), A Record of Operations During the Civil War in the United States of America, 1861-1865.* New York: G. P. Putnam's Sons, 1896.

Price, Isaiah. *History of the Ninety-Seventh Regiment, Pennsylvania Volunteer Infantry during the War of the Rebellion, 1861-1865, with the Biographical Sketches of Its Field and Staff Officers and a Complete Record of each Officer and Enlisted Man.* Philadelphia: B. & P. Printers, 1875.

Publication Committee of the Regimental Association. *History of the Eighteenth Regiment of Cavalry, Pennsylvania Volunteers (163rd Regiment of the Line) 1862-1865.* New York: Wynkoop Hallenbeck Crawford Company, 1909.

Roe, Alfred S. and Nutt, Charles, *History of the First Regiment of Heavy Artillery Massachusetts Volunteers, Formerly the Fourteenth Regiment of Infantry, 1861-1865.* Worcester: The Regimental Association, 1917.

Roman, Alfred. *The Military Operations of General Beauregard in the War Between the States 1861 to 1865,* 2 vols. New York: Harper and Brothers, 1883.

Roper, John L., Archibald, Henry C., and Coles, G. W. *History of the Eleventh Pennsylvania Volunteer Cavalry, together with a complete roster of the regiment and regimental officers.* Philadelphia: Franklin Printing Company, 1902.

Ropes, John C. "The Failure to Take Petersburg on June 16-18, 1864." In *Papers of the Military Historical Society of Massachusetts*, vol. 5. Boston: Military Historical Society of Massachusetts, 1906.

Rowland, Dunbar. *The Official and Statistical Register of the State of Mississippi, 1908.* Nashville: Press of the Brandon Printing Company, 1908.

Shaw, Horace H. and House, Charles. *The First Maine Heavy Artillery, 1862-1865, A History of its Part and Place in the War for the Union, With an Outline of Causes of War and its Results to Our Country. With Organization, Company, and Individual Records.* Portland: NP, 1903.

Smith, A. P., *History of the Seventy-Sixth Regiment New York Volunteers.* Cortland, N.Y.: Truair, Smith and Miles, Printers, 1867.

Smith, William F. "The Movement against Petersburg June, 1864," In *Papers of the Military Historical Society of Massachusetts*, vol. 5. Boston: Military Historical Society of Massachusetts, 1906.

Stedman, Charles "Battle at Reams' Station," in *Southern Historical Society Papers*, Vol. 19 (1897).

Survivors' Association, *History of the Corn Exchange Regiment 118th Pennsylvania Volunteers, From their First Engagement at Antietam to Appomattox.* Philadelphia: J. L. Smith, 1888.

Thompson, S. Millett. *Thirteenth Regiment of New Hampshire Volunteer Infantry in the War of the Rebellion, 1861-1865. A Diary Covering Three Years and a Day.* Boston: Riverside Press, 1888.

Underwood, George C. *History of the Twenty-Sixth Regiment of the North Carolina Troops in the Great War 1861-1865.* Goldsboro, NC: Nash Brothers, 1901.

Vautier, John D. *History of the 88th Pennsylvania Volunteers in the War for the Union, 1861-1865.* Philadelphia: J. B. Lippincott Co., 1894.

Walker, Francis A. *History of the Second Army Corps in the Army of the Potomac.* New York: Charles Scribner's Sons, 1886.

————. "Reams' Station." In *Papers of the Military Historical Society of Massachusetts*, vol. 5. Boston: Military Historical Society of Massachusetts, 1906.

Walkley, Stephen *History of the Seventh Connecticut Volunteer Infantry, Hawley's Brigade, Terry's Division, Tenth Army Corps, 1861-1865.* Southington: NP, 1905.

Wallace, Lee A. *A Guide to Virginia Military Organizations 1861-1865.* Richmond: Virginia Civil War Commission, 1964.

Warner, Ezra. *Generals in Blue: Lives of Union Commanders.* Baton Rouge: Louisiana State University Press, 1964.

Welch, Spencer Glasgow. *A Confederate Surgeon's Letters to His Wife.* New York: The Neale Publishing Company, 1911.

Wells, Edward L. *Hampton and His Cavalry in '64.* Richmond: B. F. Johnson Publishing Company, 1899.

Weygant, Charles H. *History of the One Hundred and Twenty-Fourth Regiment, N.Y.S.V.* Newburgh, N.Y.: Journal Printing House, 1877.

Woodbury, Augustus. *Major General Ambrose E. Burnside and the Ninth Army Corps.* Providence: S. S. Rider & Brother, 1867.

Index

John Matthew IV

About Edwin C. Bearss

Edwin Bearss is a world-renowned military historian, author, and tour guide known for his work on the American Civil War and World War II. Ed, a former WWII Marine severely wounded in the Pacific Theater, served as Chief Historian of the National Park Service from 1981 to 1994.

Ed is the author of dozens of articles and many books, including *The Campaign for Vicksburg* (3 vols.), *Receding Tide: Vicksburg and Gettysburg—The Campaigns That Changed the Civil War* (with J. Parker Hills), *Fields of Honor: Pivotal Battles of the Civil War*, and many more. Ed discovered and helped raise the Union warship *USS Cairo*, which is on display at Vicksburg National Military Park. His book on the subject is entitled *Hardluck Ironclad: The Sinking and Salvage of the Cairo*.

About Bryce A. Suderow

Bryce Suderow is a Civil War writer and researcher living in Washington, D.C. He received his bachelor's at Knox College and earned a master's in American history at Sonoma State University. His master's thesis, *Thunder in Arcadia Valley*, was published in 1985 (University of Missouri). Bryce has also published many articles in a number of Civil War periodicals and is recognized as one of the finest archival researchers working today. With Bryce's help, the current book on Petersburg might never have been published.